Defense economics is the study of both defense and peace issues using the tools of modern economics. It covers a range of issues, including nuclear proliferation, resource disputes, environmental externalities, ethnic conflicts, and terrorism, all of which present grave threats to peace and security. In a post-cold war world, military and political dangers are probably more numerous and more complex than ever before. In response, policy makers and researchers are increasingly applying economic techniques and insights to improve our understanding of the issues.

The economics of defense provides a comprehensive evaluation of the literature in an up-to-date, unified survey. The authors apply both microeconomic and macroeconomic methods of analysis, including static optimization, growth theory, dynamic optimization, comparative statics, game theory, and econometrics. The book includes chapters on study of arms races, alliances and burden sharing, economic warfare, the arms trade, weapon procurement policies, defense and development, defense industries, arms control agreements, disarmament, and conversion.

The authors take stock of what has been done in the field to date, and pinpoint areas needing further analysis and empirical work. This is the first book to integrate and synthesize this broad literature. It will be essential reading for students, practitioners, and researchers in the field of defense economics.

The economics of defense

CAMBRIDGE SURVEYS OF ECONOMIC LITERATURE

Editor
Professor Mark Perlman, University of Pittsburgh

The literature of economics is expanding rapidly, and many subjects have changed out of recognition within the space of a few years. Perceiving the state of knowledge in fast-developing subjects is difficult for students and time-consuming for professional economists. This series of books is intended to help with this problem. Each book gives a clear structure to and balanced overview of the topic, and is written at a level intelligible to the senior undergraduate. They will therefore be useful for teaching but will also provide a mature yet compact presentation of the subject for economists wishing to update their knowledge outside their own specialism.

The economics of defense

Todd Sandler
Iowa State University

and

Keith Hartley
University of York

CAMBRIDGE
UNIVERSITY PRESS

Published by the Press Syndicate of the University of Cambridge
The Pitt Building, Trumpington Street, Cambridge CB2 1RP
40 West 20th Street, New York, NY 10011-4211, USA
10 Stamford Road, Oakleigh, Melbourne 3166, Australia

First published 1995

Printed in Great Britain at the University Press, Cambridge

A catalogue record for this book is available from the British Library

Library of Congress cataloguing in publication data

Sandler, Todd.
The economics of defense / Todd Sandler, Keith Hartley.
    p.   cm. – (Cambridge surveys of economic literature)
Includes bibliographical references and index.
ISBN 0–521–44204–4. – ISBN 0–521–44728–3 (pbk.)
1. United States – Defenses – Economic aspects. 2. United States–Military policy.
3. Economic conversion – United States– I. Hartley, Keith. II. Series.
HC110.D4S26 1995
338.4'36233'0973 – dc20   94–26588   CIP

ISBN 0 521 44204 4 hardback
ISBN 0 521 44728 3 paperback

CE

To Jon Cauley, Thomas Sandler,
and Winifred Hartley

Contents

Preface

Defense economics involves the application of economic reasoning and methods to the study of defense-related issues. Defense economics differs from other fields of economics in at least three ways: (1) the set of agents studied (e.g., defense contractors, branches of the military); (2) the institutional arrangements of the defense establishment (e.g., procurement practices); and (3) the set of issues investigated.

As in other fields of economics, four basic economic problems are examined: allocative efficiency is germane to the study of the provision of defense within nations and among allies. Public choice considerations, which highlight the *private* motivations of elected officials and bureaucrats, underscore allocative concerns and possible waste. Whenever the income implications of defense decisions are studied within or among nations, distribution is being investigated. Because all provision decisions involve financing, distributional aspects are invariably tied to allocative concerns. Stability comes into play when examining the properties of equilibria or investigating the path of adjustment following a shock. The study of arms races is especially concerned with stability. Other defense-related stability questions involve the price trends of defense output, the stability of equilibria for allied defense spending, and the stability of existing regimes. Finally, the study of growth and defense includes a host of issues: the impact of defense spending on economic growth and development, the influence of research and development (R & D) on defense and civilian output, and the effect of defense burden sharing on growth comparisons among allies.

Interest in defense economics and the related peace science field took off during the cold war and continues to this day. A spreading conflict in any of the world's trouble spots could entangle neighbors and the major powers in a conflict of immense proportions. Peace and security confront threats from nuclear prolifertion, resource disputes, environmental externalities, ethnic conflicts, and terrorism. In many ways, the defense threats of the 1990s are more numerous and more complex than those of the last three decades. To cope with these threats, policy makers and researchers will have to apply economic methods and insights. Defense economics still has an important role to play in the post cold war era of the 1990s and the twenty-first century.

We have written this book in order to integrate the myriad contributions in the field into an up-to-date unified whole that would interest students, practitioners, researchers, and others. It is our sincere hope that this book will stimulate further research in defense economics by providing a single concise treatment, evaluation, and integration of the literature. There has been no earlier synthesis with the same broad coverage of this book. By taking stock of what has been done in the field to date, we are able to identify myriad areas needing further analysis and empirical work. Although we have made every effort to include as many articles and books as possible, space and time forced us to choose among earlier works. While we can claim to have surveyed the most important and influential pieces in defense economics, the book's extensive list of references is by no means exhaustive.

The material is presented in a manner to serve as a learning experience; hence, the survey is organized around topics and tools, and not around the contributors. We are less interested in who said what, and more interested in what insights and paradigms have come from these contributors.

We owe a great debt of gratitude to colleagues who have worked with us on a host of defense economics issues. These people include David Buck, Jon Cauley, John A.C. Conybeare, Richard Cornes, Saadet Deger, Walter Enders, Laurna Hansen, Nick Hooper, Michael Intriligator, Stephen Martin, James Murdoch, and Ron Smith. We also wish to thank Roberta Blackburn, Margaret Cafferky, and Eileen Mericle, who typed and retyped the manuscript. Their care, patience, and cheerfulness are much appreciated. We gratefully acknowledge the helpful comments of Charles Anderton, Martin McGuire, James Murdoch, and anonymous readers on earlier drafts of the chapters. Charles Anderton's comments were particularly helpful and extensive. Sincere thanks are also owed to Patrick McCartan, economics editor at Cambridge University Press, who provided encouragement throughout. His faith in us and the project was crucial. We also appreciate the efforts of the production staff at Cambridge University Press, who transformed the typescript into a book. Finally, we have been encouraged and supported by our wives (Jean and Winifred) and our children (Tristan, Adam, Lucy and Cecilia), who have borne the true cost of this venture.

Todd Sandler's research was supported, in part, by a National Science

Foundation grant, SBR–9222953. Keith Hartley's research was supported, in part, by the Economic and Social Research Council, the Leverhulme Trust and UNIDIR. Sole responsibility for the content and opinions expressed rests with the authors.

TODD SANDLER
KEITH HARTLEY

Ames, Iowa
York, England
March 1994

1   Defense economics: an introduction

Defense policy is entering a period of momentous change that necessitates the application of rigorous economic analysis if resources are to be
allocated efficiently among competing goals in both the defense and
civilian sectors. Defense economics applies the tools of economics to the
study of defense, disarmament, conversion, and peace. As such, defense
economics is a subfield of economics that tailors economic methods to a
specific set of topics, while taking account of institutional aspects that are
unique to the defense sector. Topics include, among others, the analysis
of alliance burden sharing, the effects of contract design on procurement,
the impact of defense expenditures on economic growth, and the
economic consequences of arms control treaties. In recent years, interest
in defense economics has increased greatly as documented by the large
number of books published in the last ten years, the appearance of
articles in the top general economics journals in the last few years, and
the publication of a field journal, *Defence and Peace Economics* (formerly
Defence Economics), starting in 1990. This interest is expected to grow as
nations vie for natural resources, sort out ethnic conflicts, respond to
injustices, and rethink their security needs.

Currently, defense expenditures vary among nations, but on average
about 5 percent of gross domestic product (GDP) is devoted to defense
(Hartley *et al.*, 1993, p. 17). Some Middle Eastern countries (e.g., Saudi
Arabia, Iraq) allocate about 20 percent of GDP to defense; other
countries (e.g., Japan) allocate about 1 percent of GDP to defense
(Hartley *et al.*, 1993, p. 49). The defense sector can have significant
allocative influences in nations, especially when research and development is included. In times of crisis, mobilization of forces has
tremendous present and future economic ramifications on a nation.
Given current levels of defense expenditures, an economic analysis of the
short-run and long-run choices and trade-offs posed by defense is
relevant.

With the end to the cold war, one might expect that interest in defense
economics would wane, but, in fact, the decline in superpower confronta-

tion has raised a host of dynamic issues requiring economic methods and evaluation. First, the breakup of the Soviet Union and Eastern Europe has unleashed ethnic conflicts that have erupted into war once central power was diminished. The civil war in Bosnia could spread to other countries and draw in the United States and Russia. Ex-Soviet republics (e.g., Georgia) face the prospect of civil war. Second, the possibilities of regional conflicts among lesser powers and their implications for defense expenditures in the superpowers have grown in importance. The Gulf War of 1991 underscores the potential relevancy of regional conflicts fought over resources, religion, and/or territorial interests. Third, the breakup of the Soviet Union and its satellite states has flooded the market with inexpensive military arms as these nations sought foreign exchange earnings. Some of these arms have found their way into regional conflicts. Fourth, recent treaty limits on strategic nuclear and conventional weapons have emphasized the need to spend on those defense systems that protect and deter aggression, while not undermining the stability of the face-off between the superpowers. Fifth, recent disarmament treaties have raised issues concerning verification, conversion, and the dismantling of weapons. These issues involve costs and benefits that, in turn, require an economic investigation. Apparently, peace as well as confrontation have their costs; neither is cheap.

The post cold war period poses old and new challenges. The threat of low-level conflict in the form of terrorism, guerrilla warfare, and insurrections represents an old challenge. On February 26, 1993, a terrorist bomb at the World Trade Center in New York City demonstrated that any institution is vulnerable. This vulnerability was underscored when an alleged plot to assassinate a US Senator and to blow up the United Nations Headquarters and New York City infrastructure was uncovered in the spring of 1993. Another old challenge involves burden-sharing and membership composition in military alliances. This challenge has again surfaced with the strengthening of economic coalitions, such as the European Economic Community, and the dissolution of the Soviet Union and the Warsaw Pact. A new challenge involves the development of future generations of weapons in the absence of a superpower confrontation. What, if any, are the new missions for the US military?

The downsizing of military budgets in the 1990s also brings challenges with the search for improving efficiency and better value for money. With downsized budgets, allies may have to consider the possibility for closer cooperation in terms of pooling resources; streamlined budgets may not allow nations unilaterally to meet all kinds of contingencies. Procurement of new weapons systems will also be affected. Because weapon research and development is very costly, large production runs are required to bring down per-unit cost. With smaller domestic orders, defense industries will either have to sell to allies or others to limit per-unit cost. Selling abroad poses risks because weapons may be acquired by enemies, or else may lead to instability in the world's trouble spots. Alternatively, the increasing costs of supporting a national defense industry might persuade nations to import equipment. Ironically, these risks mean that the major arms exporting nations (e.g., Russia, the United States, the United Kingdom, and France) must maintain larger military forces to offset the threat posed by their own arms sales. Military downsizing also implies that the structure of forces must be reassessed. In particular, force restructuring must confront the following issues: the manpower composition between active and reserve forces, the force composition between strategic and conventional armaments, the substitution opportunities between equipment and manpower, and the allocation among the branches of the military. Downsizing also presents fiscal consequences for growth, unemployment, the deficit, balance of payments, and the interest rate.

1.1   The nature of defense economics

To understand the nature of defense economics, one must first know the nature of economics. Economics is the study of the efficient allocation of scarce resources among alternative uses or ends. Economics also concerns the distribution of these ends as well as the growth and stability of the allocative system. As such, economics involves choice and scarcity. Without scarcity, there would be no reason to make choices of an efficient kind. The notion of opportunity costs is a crucial consideration when making choices and reflects the value of the best foregone alternative. Resources are valued in terms of opportunity costs, so that the cost of, say, a missile system is what the system's resources could have earned in their best alternative employment. When allocative decisions are being made, economic methods consist of optimizing some goal (e.g., profit, social welfare) in the face of constraints that limit the feasible or available choices. For example, a firm is limited by its technology and financial constraints; a consumer is constrained by his/her budget constraint; and an economy is limited by its production possibility frontier. In the case of cost minimization, resources are used efficiently when the marginal product (i.e., the change in output for a small change in input) per dollar spent on a resource is equated across all resources used to produce the output. An industry achieves productive efficiency when all firms are on their lowest-possible cost curves and, moreover, the marginal costs for each firm are equated. If marginal costs were not equal across firms, then it would be possible to switch resources from a high marginal cost firm to a low marginal cost firm so as to produce the same output level but at a lower cost. Since economics involves constrained optimization, the margin becomes an important consideration.

Economics often distinguishes between microeconomics and macroeconomics. Microeconomics is the analysis of economic decisions for the agents (i.e., firms, consumers, industries) that make up the economy. In contrast, macroeconomics concerns aggregate economic behavior and includes economic issues (e.g., inflation, unemployment, growth) that involve the entire economy. Both kinds of economic analyses are relevant to defense economics. A study of defense industries is a microeconomics problem, whereas an examination of the impact of defense expenditures on growth and development is a macroeconomics issue.

Classical economists viewed economic systems as needing little tinkering by government except for the provision of education, defense, a justice system, and infrastructure. In the classical paradigm, as each agent pursues his/her interests, he/she is led by an invisible hand to further the well being of everyone. The invisible hand operates when markets are competitive and private goods are being traded; however, the presence of public goods poses problems and leads to a market failure requiring government intervention. To define a pure public good, we must address the basic characteristics of publicness: nonexcludability and nonrivalry of benefits. Benefits of a good are *nonexcludable* if they are available to all once the good is provided. When exclusion cost is so prohibitive that exclusion is not practical, the good's benefits are nonexcludable and, hence, available to anyone who wants to take advantage of them. If, however, the benefits of a good can be withheld costlessly by the owner or provider, the benefits are *excludable*. Food is excludable, while the deterrence provided by a nation's military is nonexcludable to the country's citizens. A good is *nonrival* or indivisible when a *unit* of the good can be consumed by one individual (agent) without detracting, in the slightest, from the consumption opportunities still available for others from that *same* unit. If, however, the consumption of a unit of the good by one agent uses up all of the available benefits, the benefits of the good are rival. Deterrence, as provided by a strategic arsenal, yields nonrival benefits to all residents of a superpower.

A pure public good possesses benefits that are both nonexcludable and nonrival, while a pure private good possesses benefits that are excludable and rival. A nation's defense forces are often characterized as purely public, while food and clothing are classified as purely private. The removal of pollution or the achievement of a scientific breakthrough are examples of pure public goods.

Public goods are associated with market failures, because nonexcludability eliminates incentives for a user to support the provision of the good, while nonrivalry means that there is no reason to restrict users (i.e., the marginal cost for extending user's privileges is zero). Quite simply, pure public goods cannot be parceled out and sold in markets. Provision may require public supply, financed by nonvoluntary tax levies. *Public economics* studies the provision of public goods and forms an important component of defense economics, since the latter often involves public goods within and among nations. Both subfields also concern the study of *externalities*, which arise when the action of one agent influences the welfare of another and no means of compensation exists. For defense economics, the arming of one nation may impose positive or negative externalities on another nation. In the case of allies, the externality is positive or beneficial; in the case of adversaries, the externality is negative or detrimental. If the manufacture or testing of nuclear weapons release pollutants into the environment, then the defense sector creates a negative externality for the other sectors of the economy. Market failures are also associated with externalities and may require government interventions. The study of alliances (chapter 2), defense demand (chapter 3), arms races (chapter 4), procurement (chapter 5), industrial and alliance policies (chapter 9), arms trade (chapter 10), arms control (chapter 11), and nonconventional conflict (chapter 13) all involve analysis drawn, in part, from public economics.

As an area of study, defense economics encompasses aspects and topics drawn from peace science and conflict studies. Peace science is, however, broader than defense economics, because it includes all aspects of peace and conflict, including those that do not involve economic issues or methodology. As such, peace science draws from a number of separate disciplines including political science, mathematics, and sociology. Peace science is often critical of military expenditures and tends to focus on disarmament issues and the maintenance of peace (Isard, 1988). There is no ideological presumption in defense economics; that is, defense economists are *not* inclined toward military expenditures and armed confrontation. They are, instead, interested in understanding the dynamics of arms expenditures, conflict, and the associated economic aspects of the military sector. A proper understanding of these dynamics would surely assist in the promotion of means for controlling arms proliferation and conflict instability so contributing to human welfare and the future of civilization.

Our view of defense economics agrees with that of Michael Intriligator (1990, p. 3), who states that:

Defense economics is concerned with that part of the overall economy involving defense-related issues, including the level of defense spending, both in total and as a fraction of the overall economy; the impacts of defense expenditure, both domestically for output and employment and internationally for impacts on other nations; the reasons for the existence and size of the defense sector; the relation of defense spending to technical change; and the implications of defense spending and the defense sector for international stability or instability.

In his discussion, Intriligator stresses the importance of integrating strategic concerns when studying the interdependency of military spending decisions at an international level. Intriligator (1990, pp. 4–7) indicates how these strategic interactions can lead to counterintuitive results as when disarmament can create instability and the outbreak of war.

In response to Intriligator, Judith Reppy (1991, p. 269) defines the nature and scope of defense economics as that which "incorporates Intriligator examples as a subset of the domain of the field, but that pays more attention to the unique institutional features of the systems being analyzed." Reppy goes on to suggest that defense economics can be broadened still further by including nonmilitary elements in the definition of national security (e.g., protection of the environment). We agree with Reppy that unique institutional features are germane to an understanding of defense economics. Thus, for example, cost-plus contracts make more sense when one realizes that the buyer (e.g., the Department of Defense) may reserve the option to change the performance parameters of a proposed weapon system at a later stage. A cost-plus contract shifts the risks for changing the performance specifications from the supplier to the buyer (see chapter 5). We are less persuaded by Reppy's appeal for a broader definition of national security, since, if carried to an extreme, it would lose the field's well-defined identity (also see the remarks of Intriligator, 1991).

1.2   Previous literature

Defense economics has been examined since the start of the 1960s. A pioneering contribution was by Hitch and McKean (1960), which applied economic concepts of efficiency to the defense sector, and which inspired researchers to examine defense economics. This interest took off during the cold war with a theoretical literature that extended the Richardson (1960) arms race model (see, e.g., Brito, 1972; Intriligator, 1975;

Intriligator and Brito, 1976, 1978, 1984; Isard and Anderton, 1985). Empirical papers followed that tried to fit arms race models to the buildup of opposing military arsenals among the superpowers (McGuire, 1977), the Middle Eastern nations (Lebovic and Ishaq, 1987; Linden, 1991; Ward and Mintz, 1987), and Asian countries (Deger, 1986a, 1986b; and Deger and Sen, 1990b).

Since the early 1970s, other literature has attempted to analyze the impact of military spending on economic growth and development. A controversy raged whether military spending promotes or impedes economic growth following the appearance of Benoit's (1973) book, which provided evidence that military expenditures could have a growth-enhancing effect. Subsequent analyses have uncovered evidence both in support of and in opposition to Benoit's initial findings. The debate continues today.

In another area of defense economics, researchers applied principal–agent analysis and other modern tools associated with the study of incentive contracts to investigate defense procurement practices (e.g., Cummins, 1977; Tirole, 1986; McAfee and McMillan, 1986a, 1986b; Rogerson, 1990, 1991a). The revival of game theory has stimulated interest in the analysis of procurement and other topics in defense economics, including arms races, treaty formation, and terrorism.

Throughout the cold war era, economists investigated the industrial base that supplies defense procurement. This literature has been interested in the distinctive features of weapons markets and in the structure, conduct, and performance of defense industries. Moreover, this literature has analyzed the role of profits, subsidies, and competition on the industries that produce for the defense sector. Weapon development, profitability, and production profiles have been studied. The regional and national impacts of disarmaments and rearmaments have been studied with large-scale input–output models, computable general equilibrium models, and other forecasting techniques. A host of defense policies affecting individual nations and alliances have been investigated. Within nations, defense policies have concerned weapon acquisition, resource stockpiling, arms importation, promotion of domestic defense industries, the subsidization of research and development (R & D), the composition of defense budgets, and the arms trade.

Since the Vietnam War, defense economics has devoted attention to the economics of alternative systems of military recruitment: conscription versus the all-volunteer force (see, e.g., Altman, 1969; Ash, Udis, and McNown, 1983; Fisher, 1969; Greene and Newlon, 1973; Hansen and Weisbrod, 1967, and Oi, 1967). Most recently, military manpower studies have analyzed recruitment, retention, training, and other issues.

1.3 Importance of defense economics

In a recent United Nations Institute for Disarmament Research (UNIDIR) report, Hartley *et al.* (1993) indicate that the world spent approximately 950 billion US dollars on military expenditures in 1990: $800 billion in the industrialized countries (including Eastern Europe) and $150 billion in the less-developed nations. Military manpower was also impressive: just over 10 million in the industrialized countries and over 18 million in the less-developed countries. These figures do not include civilians employed directly or indirectly by the defense sector, estimated at almost 22 million. Between 750,000 and 1.5 million scientists and engineers were employed doing military research and development in 1990. Hartley *et al.* (1993, p. 18) indicate that arms imports in 1989 amounted to 45.3 billion US dollars with the less-developed countries importing $34.6 billion. Primary importers included the Middle East (26.6 percent of the total), South Asia (17.4 percent), North Atlantic Treaty Organization (NATO) Europe (14 percent), East Asia (11.8 percent), Africa (8.8 percent), Warsaw Pact (7 percent), South America (5.6 percent), and other regions (8.6 percent). Surely, these figures suggest that the defense sector is a crucial component of the world economy and is worthy of study. The defense sector contains important factors for understanding industrial policy, growth and development, employment, international trade, allocative efficiency, fiscal policy, and monetary policy.

Defense burdens are frequently measured by the proportion of GDP devoted to defense expenditures, as indicated by the ratio of military spending to GDP. In table 1.1, these burdens are depicted for the United States and its largest allies for 1987 and 1990. The table also lists estimated burdens for 1992 and 1995, based on proposed budgets. A number of features are worth emphasizing. First, these burdens are estimated to decrease for all allies, except Spain and Turkey. Such a decrease can give rise to a peace dividend provided that the resources are redirected to the civilian sector. Second, the defense sector is still expected to account for over 2 percent of GDP. These figures assume that crises in Bosnia, the Middle East, or elsewhere do not reverse these trends. Third, significant burden reductions among NATO allies may necessitate closer cooperation and coordination among allies if NATO is to meet contingencies. Fourth, the US burden will decline faster than most of its allies, thus decreasing US relative burdens.

Table 1.2 depicts the real defense expenditures for these allies in 1990, 1992 (estimated), and 1995 (estimated). The right-hand column indicates that five allies – Canada, Australia, Japan, Spain, and Turkey – are

Table 1.1 *Trends in defense spending as a percentage of GDP for Western allies*

Country	Actual 1987	Actual 1990	Estimated 1992	Estimated 1995	Estimated Percentage Change 1990–95[a]
United States	6.5	5.6	5.2	4.1[b]	−27
Germany	3.1	2.8	2.1	1.5	−46[c]
New Zealand	1.8	1.9	1.8	1.4	−26
Belgium	3.0	2.4	2.1	1.8	−26
Denmark	2.1	2.0	1.9	1.5	−26
Netherlands	3.1	2.7	2.4	2.0	−25
United Kingdom	4.6	4.0	4.0	3.4	−14
France	3.9	3.6	3.3	3.1	−14
Japan	1.0	1.0	1.0	0.9	−8
Canada	2.1	2.0	2.1	1.9	−5
Australia	2.6	2.2	2.4	2.2	−2
Spain	2.4	1.8	1.8	2.0	6
Turkey	4.2	4.9	5.3	5.3	8
Weighted average of Japan, France, Germany, and UK	3.1	2.8	2.6	2.2	−22

Notes: [a] Reported percentages have been rounded.
[b] Based on February 1993 budget estimates.
[c] This large figure is due in part to the unification of Germany which has increased GDP by more than defense expenditures.
Source: US Congressional Budget Office (1993, table 1).

expected to expand their real defense spending between 1990 and 1995. Three of these nations are still expected to have negative trends in defense burdens, because GDP is anticipated to increase at a faster pace than defense spending. In 1990, the United States spent about twice as much as the sum of its four largest allies. By 1995, the United States' relative burden is predicted to fall *vis-à-vis* the four largest allies.

In some countries, the defense sector constitutes a much greater burden. For the 1988–1990 period, the largest burdens, in terms of GDP percentages, were registered in Nicaragua (28.3 percent), Iraq (23 percent), Angola (21.5 percent), Saudi Arabia (19.8 percent), Yemen (18.5 percent), Oman (15.8 percent), Ethiopia (13.6 percent), Mongolia (11.7 percent), Cuba (11.3 percent), Jordan (11 percent), Bahrain (10.7 percent), Israel (9.2 percent), and Syria (9.2 percent) (Hartley *et al.*, 1993, table 11). In these countries, the defense sector is sure to have major

Table 1.2 *Trends in real defense expenditures for western allies (in billions of constant 1992 US dollars)*

Country	1990 (Actual)	1992 (Estimate)	1995 (Estimate)	Estimated percentage change 1990–95[a]
United States	330.5	305.2[b]	258.6[b]	−22
Germany	46.1[c]	38.2	31.2	−32
New Zealand	0.8	0.7	0.6	−19
Belgium	4.9	4.5	4.1	−18
Netherlands	7.9	7.2	6.6	−17
Denmark	2.6	2.6	2.3	−13
United Kingdom	43.8	42.9	39.7	−9
France	45.6	44.0	43.6	−4
Canada	11.7	12.0	12.2	4
Australia	6.6	7.1	7.2	10
Japan	33.4	35.2	37.0	11
Spain	10.4	10.5	12.8	22
Turkey	5.4	5.7	7.2	34
Sum of Japan France, Germany, and United Kingdom	168.9	160.3	151.5	−10

Notes: [a] Reported percentages have been rounded.
[b] Based on February 1993 budget estimates.
[c] Includes only West German expenditures for 1990.
Source: US Congressional Budget Office (1993, table 4).

impacts on the economy. Large defense budgets can contribute to budget deficits, the crowding out of investment, and high interest rates.

1.4   Methodology of defense economics

Defense economics employs the primary tools of theoretical and empirical economic analysis. Much of defense economics is a policy science, in the sense that the analysts are interested in formulating theories that enable them to determine the best government policy to bring about desired outcomes. In consequence, theories must be tested with data to ascertain whether they can predict accurately. Theories that do not perform well empirically are replaced with alternative theories that perform more accurately. The policy orientation of defense economics cannot be emphasized enough. This orientation means that data must be available to evaluate theories.

Defense economics draws from most subfields of economics, including international economics for the study of arms trade, industrial organization for the study of defense industries, public choice for the study of defense policy, public economics for the study of alliances, arms races, and defense budgeting, macroeconomics for the study of defense and growth, and labor economics for the study of military manpower. To examine strategic interactions among agents, defense economics employs game theory and microeconomic tools of uncertainty analysis. To test theories, defense economics relies on regression and time-series analysis. Advanced techniques of simultaneous equations and vector autoregression (VAR) models are also used.

1.5   Purpose of the book

The book is intended to be more than a survey of the previous literature: key concepts are presented in sufficient detail to be useful to students, researchers, and those interested in gaining an up-to-date perspective of the field. We emphasize (in our view) the most important theoretical and empirical paradigms. These paradigms are the building blocks for understanding the more esoteric contributions. By focusing our study on these key analyses, we can explain models in sufficient detail to facilitate understanding. The readers will then acquire the requisite background to pursue more advanced studies on their own.

Our book is designed for upper-level undergraduate and graduate students in economics. The book should also prove useful to researchers in defense economics as well as researchers in other fields of economics. In addition, the book contains analysis that should interest researchers in peace sciences, political science, sociology, and military sciences.

Although a limited number of books on defense economics and related topics are published yearly, our book is a novel contribution owing to the scope of its analysis. Earlier books focused on one or two key issues to the exclusion of others. Thus, for example, Denoon (1986) examined military expenditures among NATO and related allies; Isard (1988) focused on arms race models and arms control; Hartley (1991b) presented an analysis of defense policies and the military industrial sector; and Hartley and Sandler (1990) included country studies. Perhaps, the nearest competitor is Gavin Kennedy's (1983), *Defense Economics*, which is now over ten years old. Moreover, Kennedy (1983) did not analyze arms race models, military manpower, nonconventional forms of conflict, or the modern theories of procurement. Much of Kennedy's (1983) book was devoted to an analysis of NATO allies. Other potential competitors include edited books such as Schmidt (1987) and Schmidt and Blackaby (1987). More recently, Hartley and Hooper (1990) provided an annotated bibliography that summarized some 1,000 publications. Although these works contained interesting contributions, they did not survey the field, nor did they provide a pedagogic treatment. Moreover, discussion in the various chapters in the edited volumes were not integrated by the editors.

With renewed interest shown in defense economics in recent years, now seems an appropriate time to tie together the various approaches in a single work. New techniques and methodologies are compared and contrasted with earlier ones. At the outset, we indicated the many new issues raised by recent developments in world affairs (e.g., the end to the cold war); this book permits us to put these issues and others in perspective.

1.6   The plan of the book

The remainder of the book is divided into four parts. Part I concerns alliances, defense demand, and arms races, and contains three chapters. These chapters concern the determination of the level of military expenditures as a consequence of an optimizing calculation. Public good, externality, and game theory aspects are emphasized throughout the first part. Chapter 2 investigates the economic theory of alliances, as derived from the seminal study of Olson and Zeckhauser (1966). In doing so, the collective action aspects of defense are stressed as the issues of burden-sharing, allocative efficiency, and alliance membership are examined. Both the pure public good model and the joint product model for studying alliances are presented and contrasted. For the joint product model, an ally's defense activity yields multiple outputs that vary in their degree of publicness. Theoretical extensions are also presented. The theoretical analysis is then used to derive defense demand equations. Empirical tests for a variety of alliances (e.g., NATO, Warsaw Pact, Triple Alliance, Triple Entente, US–Japan Alliance, ANZUS) are reviewed.

In chapter 3, the choice-theoretic models of alliances are utilized to derive the reduced-form equations for estimating a nation's demand for military expenditures. This chapter focuses on alternative forms for these equations based on a variety of theoretical models. In the latter half of the chapter, issues concerning the empirical model are presented. Some empirical country studies are then reviewed.

Arms race models are presented in chapter 4, which opens with a simple game theory representation of arms races. Classical game forms, such as the Prisoner's Dilemma and the Chicken game, are presented and related to the study of arms races. Next, we review the basic Richardson model, complete with stability conditions. Alternative Richardson-type models are then investigated. Based on the seminal studies by Brito and Intriligator, strategic factors are included in the arms race analysis. Dynamic game representations of arms races are also presented and related to the Richardson model. Economic warfare is analyzed next. The chapter concludes with a review of selected empirical studies.

Part II contains four chapters, and involves the study of defense inputs, the defense industrial base, and growth. Chapters 5 and 6 are devoted to the two primary inputs – equipment and manpower – of the military sector. In chapter 5, the theories and policies of arms procurement are investigated. The chapter begins with a review of the traditional approaches to defense contracting, and presents the various types of contracts, including fixed-price contracts, cost-plus contracts, and incentive contracts. When analyzing alternative contractual arrangements, we focus on the importance of principal–agent analysis, whereby the principal (the buyer) cannot monitor the agent's (the producer's) actions and must instead devise an incentive scheme that motivates the agent to exert high effort. The chapter also considers the role of profit, competitive forces, decreasing cost, and cost-estimating procedures in the procurement process. Additional topics include research and development, technology transfer, performance indicators, and learning.

Chapter 6 provides a survey of the literature on military manpower, and includes an analysis of military production functions as well as the internal organization and efficiency of the Armed Forces. The manpower chapter also contains an examination of recruitment, retention, and occupational choice. Microeconomic choice-theoretic models of labor supply underlie these decisions. An analysis of conscription versus an all-volunteer force is also presented.

Chapter 7 analyzes defense expenditures and their relationship to the economy and to the military industrial base. This chapter considers budgetary aspects, the growth of the military industrial complex, the structure and conduct of the defense industries, models of firm behavior (e.g., under regulation), interest group lobbying, public choice aspects, and the opportunity cost of military expenditures.

In chapter 8, the impact of military expenditures on growth and development is investigated. We begin with a discussion of the potential benefits and costs that military spending may have on economic growth. Next, we review Benoit's (1973, 1978) provocative finding that defense spending has a net growth-enhancing effect in less-developed countries. The models and findings of subsequent studies are discussed and put in perspective. In doing so, we focus on the macroeconomic approach of Deger (1986a, 1986b), Deger and Sen (1990b), and others. This is followed by an analysis of the supply-side, production-function approach for investigating the impact of defense on growth put forward by Feder (1983) and Ram (1986). A review of the empirical studies concludes the chapter.

Part III contains four chapters and focuses on defense policies, arms trade, disarmament, and conversion. Chapter 9 presents nation-based and alliancewide defense policies including the promotion of competition, weapon stockpiling, buying at home versus abroad, strategic trade policy, and joint ventures. The nature and organization of an alliance is examined by focusing on the net transaction benefits derived by participating allies. Alliance policies include issues concerning standardization and interoperability of forces. By displaying the benefits and costs of collaborative agreements between two or more nations, this chapter also studies the performance of international projects to develop new weapons systems. Some recent collaborative arrangements are evaluated.

In chapter 10, the arms trade is investigated. First, arms trade patterns and suppliers are identified. Past trends are also reviewed. Second, the economic impact of arms trade on developed nations is presented. Third, these impacts are indicated for developing countries. Potential effects on the development of a domestic arms industry are emphasized.

Chapter 11 is on arms control and disarmament, and views disarmament as an investment process involving short-term costs in return for longer-run benefits. Thus, peace dividends from the current downturn in defense spending are anticipated to be modest in the short-term owing to adjustment costs associated with unemployment and resource reallocation. At the outset, the chapter defines disarmament and considers burdens and benefits of arms control. A host of issues are raised with respect to arms control that include substitution effects, stability considerations, verification, cheating, uncertainty, and lobby group interests. A review of significant treaties between the superpowers is also presented.

At the end of Part III, chapter 12 investigates the processes surrounding conversion. Economic impacts associated with conversion are identified. A number of alternative methodologies (e.g., input–output, large-scale forecasting models) for analyzing these processes are evaluated. Employment and multiplier effects are germane to the analysis.

Part IV includes two chapters and considers new developments and future directions. Chapter 13 investigates nonconventional forms of conflicts including terrorism, guerrilla warfare, and insurrections. A portion of the chapter is devoted to applying rational-actor models to the study of terrorism, both at the national and international levels. Game theory and other techniques are applied to answer a host of questions:

Should governments precommit to never negotiate with terrorists? Is it in a government's interest to share intelligence with another targeted government when deterrence decisions are made independently? What antiterrorist policies are most effective? Why are international agreements so difficult to formulate and enforce? What are some of the economic impacts of terrorism? Other sections of chapter 13 study theories of insurrections, revolutions, and guerrilla warfare put forward by economists and political scientists. This chapter emphasizes key contributions and their methodologies.

Chapter 14 draws conclusions and indicates directions for future research.

I   Alliances, defense demand, and arms races

2   The economic theory of alliances[*]

In a seminal article, Olson and Zeckhauser (1966) developed an economic theory of alliances by characterizing deterrence as a pure public good. If defense is purely public among allies, then a number of hypotheses can be derived. First, defense burdens are expected to be shared unevenly among allies: large, wealthy allies will shoulder the defense burdens for smaller, poorer allies. Unequal burden sharing leads to a free-rider problem where some nations rely for their defense on the provision efforts of their allies. Second, defense expenditures are predicted to be at inefficient or suboptimal levels in relation to a Pareto-optimal standard. Third, there is no need to restrict alliance size, since the addition of an ally implics positive nct marginal benefits as costs are shared among a larger number of allies, but benefits are not diminished for existing allies. Fourth, an ally's demand for defense depends on relative prices, the ally's income, the level of its allies' defense expenditures, and the perceived threat.

Olson and Zeckhauser examined the first hypothesis for the North Atlantic Treaty Organization (NATO) in 1964 and found a significant positive correlation between an ally's gross national product (GNP) and its ratio of military expenditures (ME) to GNP. Thus, the wealthier allies assumed a greater defense burden, as measured by ME/GNP, than poorer allies. Free riding accusations were leveled at these poorer allies. The Olson and Zeckhauser paper, with its suggestive test, generated a large and ever-growing literature on the economic analysis of military alliances.

During the late 1960s and 1970s, the burden-sharing hypothesis of Olson and Zeckhauser no longer seemed to apply to NATO. This was first identified by Russett (1970) and later analyzed by Beer (1972), Sandler and Cauley (1975), Sandler and Forbes (1980), Sandler (1988), Oneal (1990a, 1990b) and Palmer (1990b). Something had changed in the

[*] A slightly different version of this chapter was published as "The Economic Theory of Alliances: A Survey," *Journal of Conflict Resolution*, 37(3), September 1993, 446–483. It is republished here with the kind permission of Sage Publications, Inc.

19

motivation of the allies to assume defense burdens: smaller allies had taken on a greater portion of the defense burdens. To explain this development, researchers generalized the pure public good model to allow military expenditures to provide multiple benefits – deterrence, damage-limiting protection in wartime, and the pursuit of nation-specific interests – that vary in their degree of publicness *among* allies. Joint products are present. The joint product model generalized the pure public good model of alliances, because the former collapses to the latter when a single pure public output is present. Nevertheless, the joint product model implies profoundly different hypotheses when private and/or impure public benefits accompanied the output of deterrence. With joint products, burdens of defense are predicted to be shared more in accordance with the benefits received. Small allies that receive substantial excludable benefits may assume a large burden despite their wealth position. Moreover, defense levels may be nearer to Pareto-optimal ideals when joint products are present. Alliance membership restrictions, based on rivalry of benefits received or crowding considerations, also become relevant. Finally, an ally's demand for defense may depend on factors (e.g., the *pattern* of defense among allies) not germane to the pure public good paradigm.

The economic theory of alliances is important for a number of reasons. First, the theory has policy implications for burden sharing and alliance composition. Second, the theory has been used to derive systems of demand equations that can be used for empirical tests and forecasting. Third, the methods used in the economic theory of alliances can be fruitfully applied to the study of other supranational structures, such as environmental pacts, the United Nations, and common markets.

The body of the chapter contains six primary sections. Section 2.1 presents the pure public good model of alliances, whereas section 2.2 presents the joint product model. In section 2.3, empirical means for distinguishing between the two basic models are discussed. Theoretical extensions are analyzed in section 2.4. A review of empirical tests is contained in section 2.5, and concluding remarks are presented in section 2.6.

2.1   Pure public good model

If defense is a pure public good for the allies, then defense benefits must be nonrival and nonexcludable *among* allies. The benefits of a good are nonrival or indivisible among users when a *unit* of the good can be consumed by one agent (e.g., an ally) without detracting, in the slightest, from the consumption opportunities still available to others from that *same* unit. Deterrence, as provided by a nuclear triad, is nonrival among allies because, once the triad is deployed, its ability to deter enemy aggression is independent of the number of allies, provided that the retaliatory response is automatic. The strategic capabilities and credibility of the response determine its ability to deter aggression. If, however, the credibility of a retaliation pledge depends on the number of allies on whose behalf it is made, then nonrivalry may occur as group size expands.

For the nuclear triad, its benefits are nonexcludable whenever the defense provider cannot withhold the promised retaliation against an invader of another ally. If an enemy invasion causes collateral damage to the provider of the deterrent weapons, then the retaliatory response is likely to be executed. For example, a nuclear attack on Canada would cause widespread damage and death from fallout in the United States; hence, a US retaliation is anticipated. Canada cannot be excluded from the US nuclear deterrence. The stationing of troops of one ally on other allies' soil ensures collateral damages from an attack and increases the likelihood of alliancewide retaliation against an invasion anywhere within the alliance. Additionally, the flow of capital and business people among allies collectivizes the security of the allies, thereby increasing nonexcludability of defense benefits. Clearly, the notion of pure publicness of defense among and within allies is a theoretical ideal that is a reasonable approximation under some circumstances.

2.1.1   Mathematical representation

In the simplest representation, each of n allies is assumed to allocate national income, I, between a nondefense, private numéraire good, y, and a pure public defense good, Q. The decision maker is assumed to be some unspecified agent i whose utility[1]

$$U^i = U^i(y^i, Q, T) \qquad (2.1)$$

is representative of the nation's population. Throughout, superscripts refer to the ally. In (2.1), Q is the sum of all allies' defense allocations

$$Q = \sum_{i=1}^{n} q^i \qquad (2.2)$$

in which q^i denotes the ith ally's defense provision. Moreover, T is some threat measure and may be represented by the enemy's collective military

---

[1]   The utility function is assumed to increase in y^i and Q, and to decrease in T. Moreover, the utility function is assumed to be strictly quasiconcave in y^i and Q.

expenditures. The use of an unspecified single agent's utility function to represent the tastes for an entire nation is an abstraction that can be relaxed to include other decision makers such as the median voter (Dudley and Montmarquette, 1981; Murdoch, Sandler, and Hansen, 1991). When the decision maker's identity is altered, the resource constraint must change accordingly. If, for example, the central government is the decision maker, then government revenues, not national income, would be the relevant income variable. As a consequence, the demand function for defense is apt to include different exogenous variables, depending on the identity of the decision maker.

The notion of pure publicness is embodied in (2.2), in which alliance-wide defense is the simple sum of the allies' defense activities. This *technology of public supply aggregation* implies perfect substitutability of defense among allies, because a unit more (less) of defense in any of the allies equally enhances (detracts from) alliancewide defense. This perfect substitutability is, in large part, behind the free-rider problem, whereby an ally relies on the defense provision of others to underwrite its own security.

The resource constraint of an ally is

$$I^i = y^i + pq^i,$$ (2.3)

in which the per-unit price of y is set equal to 1 and the per-unit price of q^i is p. For each ally, a Nash equilibrium allocation is found by maximizing utility subject to the resource constraint and to the best-response level for defense in the other allies. The aggregate defense level in allies other than the ith ally equals

$$\tilde{Q}^i = \sum_{j \neq i} q^j,$$ (2.4)

and is called a *spillin* to ally i. In (2.4), the summation is from $j = 1$ to $j = n$ but excludes $j = i$. A best-response level of spillins, $\tilde{Q}^{i*}$, is attained when each ally optimizes with respect to its choice for defense, given the optimizing choices of the other allies; thus, no ally would want to adjust its allocative choices for y^i and q^i at the resulting Nash equilibrium.

The Nash problem for ally i is to solve

$$\max_{y^i, q^i} \{U^i(y^i, q^i + \tilde{Q}^{i*}, T) \mid I^i = y^i + pq^i\}.$$ (2.5)

A Nash equilibrium consists of allocations (y^i, q^i) for each ally in which (2.5) is satisfied. This requires y^is and q^is that satisfy the budget constraint and the following first-order conditions (FOCs)

$$\text{MRS}^i_{Qy} = p,$$ (2.6)

for every ally i, where MRS^i_{Qy} denotes the ith ally's marginal rate of substitution (MRS) between defense and the private good. This MRS expression indicates the ally's per-unit marginal valuation of defense in terms of the numéraire.

Suboptimality for the pure public good paradigm is established by contrasting the Nash equilibrium level of defense, Q^N, which represents the noncooperative solution, to the Pareto-optimal cooperative solution, Q^P. For the former equilibrium, the ally's decision maker is only concerned with the social welfare of his/her citizens, so that spillover benefits conferred on others, within the alliance but outside of the decision maker's borders, are ignored. The Pareto optimum would result if the allies vested a central supranational authority with the power to choose a level of alliancewide defense that maximizes social welfare for the entire alliance. The Pareto-optimal alliancewide defense level is derived by maximizing the ith ally's utility subject to the constancy of the other allies' utility level and to the alliancewide resource constraint

$$\sum_{i=1}^{n} I^i = \sum_{i=1}^{n} y^i + p \sum_{i=1}^{n} q^i. \tag{2.7}$$

The associated FOCs can be expressed as

$$\sum_{i=1}^{n} \mathrm{MRS}^i_{Qy} = p, \tag{2.8}$$

or the sum of MRSs equals the per-unit price of defense. In essence, suboptimality characterizes Nash equilibrium because each ally fails to account for the marginal benefits that its defense confers on its allies – i.e., $\sum_{j \neq i} \mathrm{MRS}^j_{Qy}$ is not included.

Because the sharing of purely public defense among allies is representative of a collective action problem, other allocative concerns can be raised by appealing to the literature on collective action (Olson, 1965; Russett and Sullivan, 1971; Sandler, 1992). As the number of allies increases, the extent of suboptimality is expected to worsen. Thus, small alliances (e.g., the Triple Entente prior to World War I) are apt to display less suboptimality than larger alliances (e.g., NATO).

A second collective action problem is the so-called *exploitation hypothesis*, whereby the large, wealthy allies shoulder the defense burdens of the smaller allies (Olson and Zeckhauser, 1966). When an ally's demand for defense is positively related to national income so that defense is a normal good, wealthier allies can be expected to contribute more defense than less wealthy allies, provided that tastes do not differ significantly among allies. The positive relationship between income and defense arises, in part, because wealth may bring forth a greater threat of invasion while providing the nation the means to protect itself. Almost all studies of defense demand found defense to be a normal good (Murdoch and Sandler, 1984). Free or easy riding is often related to the income elasticity of defense, because a positive income elasticity of defense demand is associated with a negatively sloped reaction path, in which an ally decreases its defense as perfectly substitutable spillins from allies' increase. In some cases, free riding may result if there is little need for poorer allies to provide military expenditures in excess of spillins. Consequently, unequal burden sharing based on national income levels is expected. Olson and Zeckhauser (1966) hypothesized a positive relationship between GNP and defense burdens as measured by ME/GNP. Their hypothesis was borne out for NATO during 1964, but subsequent studies found a positive, but declining, relationship for NATO (Russett, 1970; Pryor, 1968; Sandler and Forbes, 1980; Oneal, 1990b). Comparable analyses have been done for the Warsaw Pact (Russett, 1970; Starr, 1974; Reisinger, 1983).

A third collective action prediction concerns the impact of endowment asymmetry among potential members on the likelihood of group formation. Unequal endowments are conducive to group formation, because it is then more likely that at least one potential participant (ally) will get sufficient net benefits from providing the public good even if the agent must bear the entire cost (Sandler, 1992, chapter 2).

At this juncture, the simplifying assumptions that underlie the standard pure public good model are highlighted. Relaxation of these assumptions are behind the theoretical extensions presented in section 2.4. First, the resource constraint assumes constant marginal cost of defense provision both within and among allies, because p is a constant. This marginal cost is also identical among allies *so that no ally has a comparative advantage in producing defense*. Second, the threat variable is introduced as an exogenous variable; thus, the interaction between adversaries, as in an arms race, is not considered explicitly. Third, the analysis is a static equilibrium formulation. Fourth, Nash behavior is assumed so that strategic interactions that allow one ally to anticipate the reactions of the other allies are not permitted. Fifth, allied defense levels are aggregated with the use of an unweighted summation technology in equation (2.2).

2.1.2   Demand and reaction functions

We now return to the basic maximization problem of equation (2.5). This maximization problem yields three first-order conditions (FOCs) that, in principle, can be used to solve for the demands for the private good and defense good in terms of the exogenous variables[2]

$$y^i = y^i(I^i, p, \tilde{Q}, T),$$ (2.9)

$$q^i = q^i(I^i, p, \tilde{Q}, T).$$ (2.10)

In (2.10) the demand for defense expenditures in ally i depends on its national income (e.g., gross domestic product), the relative price of defense goods, the level of spillins, and the threat level. Most pure public good studies of allied defense demands are based on equations of this form.[3]

When defense is expressed as a function of spillins and other exogenous variables, the resulting demand equation is also called a reaction function. If all prices are normalized to 1 and if, furthermore, threat is left out, then the resulting reaction function could have the linearized form

$$q^i = K - \gamma^i \tilde{Q}, \qquad\qquad i = 1,\ldots,n,$$ (2.11)

in which K is the isolated purchases of the defense good (if spillins are zero) and $(1-\gamma^i)$ is the ally's marginal propensity to spend income on defense (McGuire, 1974). Since γ^i is positive, the reaction function is negatively sloped. Another way of characterizing a Nash equilibrium is to define it as the mutual satisfaction of the allies' reaction functions.

Linear reaction functions can be generated by assuming a Stone–Geary utility function

$$U^i = (Q-\beta T)^\alpha (y^i - \Theta^i)^{1-\alpha}$$ (2.12)

for each ally, in which βT is the minimal or subsistence public good level of defense (based upon threat), Θ^i is the subsistence requirement for private good consumption, and α is a positive exponent whose value is less than 1. The parameters β and α could be individualized by introducing an i index. By finding the FOCs associated with optimizing (2.12), constrained by resources, we can derive the following linear expenditure function

$$pq^i = \alpha(I^i - \Theta^i) - (1-\alpha)p\tilde{Q}^i + (1-\alpha)\beta pT.$$ (2.13)

---

[2]   If the associated 3 by 3 Hessian determinant of second-order partials of the Lagrangean function is strictly positive, then the three-equation FOCs can be solved for y^i and q^i in terms of the exogenous variables.

[3]   Examples include Conybeare and Sandler (1990), Dudley and Montmarquette (1981), Gonzales and Mehay (1990), Hansen, Murdoch, and Sandler (1990), McGuire (1982, 1990b), McGuire and Groth (1985), Murdoch and Sandler (1984, 1985, 1986, 1991), Sandler and Murdoch (1986, 1990), and Smith (1989).

Because $\alpha < 1$, the reaction function is negatively sloped in terms of spillins, $\tilde{Q}$. The linear expenditure system analysis of alliance demand has been developed in a series of important articles by Dudley and Montmarquette (1981), Hilton and Vu (1991), McGuire (1982, 1990b), McGuire and Groth (1985), and Okamura (1991).

A final implication of pure publicness concerns the *neutrality theorem*, which indicates that the Nash equilibrium provision level for any pure public good is invariant to income redistribution among an unchanged set of contributors (Bruce, 1990; Sandler, 1992, chapter 3; Sandler and Murdoch, 1990; Warr, 1983). This theorem only holds for interior solutions in which all allies provide some defense both before and after the income redistribution, which may come about because of taxes. The neutrality result is established by taking a total differential of the system of reaction functions, while holding price and threat constant. By aggregating changes across allies and then solving for the change or differential in alliancewide defense (dQ), one can show that dQ is zero when ΣdI^i is zero, so that income has been merely redistributed with no net change to total income. We refer the reader to Sandler (1992, chapter 3, appendices 1 and 2), where two alternative proofs of neutrality are given. This surprising finding hinges on the assumptions highlighted at the end of section 2.1.1. If, for example, Nash behavior is absent, or if marginal cost differs by allies, neutrality is no longer assured.

2.1.3   Graphic representation: two-ally case

We use a graphical procedure developed by Cornes and Sandler (1984, 1986) to illustrate the two-ally allocation problem. Each of two allies faces the following problem

$$\max_{y^i, q^i} \{U^i(y^i, q^i + q^j, T) \mid I^i = y^i + pq^i\}, \tag{2.14}$$

where q^j is the level of spillins for ally i. Henceforth, ally i is ally 1, and ally j is ally 2. If we substitute the budget constraint for y^1, ally 1's constrained utility is

$$\begin{aligned} U^1 &= U^1(I^1 - pq^1, q^1 + q^2, T) \\ &= U^1(q^1, q^2; I^1, p, T). \end{aligned} \tag{2.15}$$

According to (2.15), budget-constrained utility can be displayed in (q^1, q^2) space for a given income, public good price, and threat.

In figure 2.1, three budget-constrained iso-utility curves are displayed. For a given level of q^1, higher values of spillins clearly imply more preferred allocations, so that v^2v^2 is a higher level of utility than curve

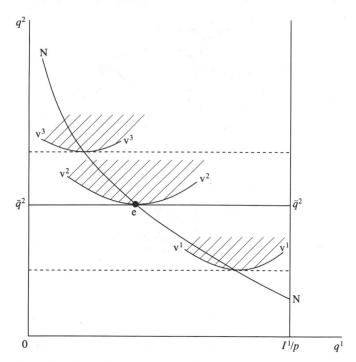

Figure 2.1 Iso-utility curves

v^1v^1. Furthermore, the set of points weakly preferred to any given allocation must be convex, because it is itself the intersection of two convex sets – the feasible set determined by the linear resource constraint and the set of allocations weakly preferred to the reference allocation. In figure 2.1, the weakly preferred sets are indicated by the cross-hatched areas on and above the iso-utility curves. The vertical line I^1/p indicates the set of allocations that would exhaust ally 1's income.

The slope of the iso-utility curves is

$$\left.\frac{dq^2}{dq^1}\right|_{U^1=\bar{U}^1} = -\frac{\partial U^1/\partial q^1}{\partial U^1/\partial q^2} = -1 + \frac{p}{\mathrm{MRS}^1_{Qy}}. \qquad (2.16)$$

When this slope is zero, the FOC for a Nash equilibrium, as in (2.6), is satisfied. In figure 2.1, at any level of spillins, say $\bar{q}^2$, the Nash condition is satisfied where the horizontal line $\bar{q}^2\bar{q}^2$ is tangent to the iso-utility curve at point e. This point of tangency represents the ally's optimal choice for defense, given the prevailing level of spillins. By varying the levels of spillins and locating the locus of tangencies, we generate the Nash reaction path, NN, for ally 1.

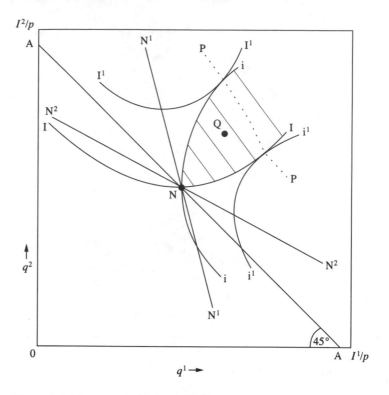

Figure 2.2 Two-person Nash equilibrium

The two-ally Nash equilibrium is depicted in figure 2.2, where two of ally 2's iso-utility curves ii and i^1i^1 are displayed along with two of ally 1's iso-utility curves II and I^1I^1. The analysis of ally 2 is analogous to that of ally 1, except that q^1 now denotes spillins and q^2 depicts the ally's defense contribution. In consequence, ally 2's iso-utility curves are translated through $90°$ so that its iso-utility curves are U-shaped with respect to the q^2 axis and has a slope equal to the reciprocal of $(-1+p/$ $MRS_{Qy}^2)$. Tangencies between the iso-utility curves and a vertical line, corresponding to a fixed level of q^1, define points on the Nash reaction path, N^2N^2, for ally 2. At the intersection of the two reaction paths, point N, both allies' Nash conditions are mutually satisfied; neither ally would want to alter unilaterally its allocative decision.

It can be shown that if all goods are normal with positive income elasticities, then the slope of ally 1's reaction path is negative with a value less than -1 (Cornes and Sandler, 1986, p. 75). Similarly, the slope of the reaction path for ally 2 is greater than 1 in value owing to the $90°$

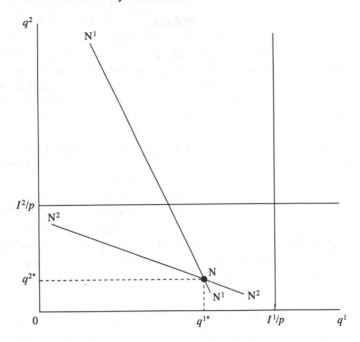

Figure 2.3 Exploitation hypothesis

translation. Under these circumstances not only is the Nash equilibrium at
N stable, but it is also unique as shown in figure 2.2. To determine the total
amount of the public good associated with the Nash equilibrium at N, we
draw line AA with a slope of -1 through point N so that this line makes a
45° angle with the two axes at their intercept. Distance OA along either
axis then measures the total contribution to alliancewide defense.

The suboptimality of the Nash equilibrium is easily shown in figure
2.2. Points in the cross-hatched region bounded by the allies' iso-utility
curves II and ii are Pareto superior to N since the utility levels of both
allies are greater – that is, the iso-utility curves through a point such as Q
are higher for both allies. The Pareto path corresponds to the dotted
curve where the allies' iso-utility curves are tangent. Along this path, the
Pareto-optimality condition $\Sigma MRS^i_{Qy} = p$ is satisfied.

The diagram is capable of extension in a number of directions. For
example, a nonlinear resource constraint can be used, provided that the
constraint defines a convex feasible region. The slope of the resource-
constrained iso-utility curve would be of the same form as (2.16), except
for the replacement of p by the ratio of marginal costs. For identical
allies, the diagram can be extended to N allies.

In figure 2.3, we represent the exploitation hypothesis where ally 1 (the well-endowed nation) provides most of alliancewide defense as compared with the efforts of ally 2 (the less well-endowed ally). The income endowments of the allies determine the relative positions of their Nash reaction paths; *ceteris paribus*, smaller income levels mean that the ally will provide a smaller level of q in response to each level of spillins if defense is a normal good. In figure 2.3, the small endowment of ally 2 implies a small feasible level of q^2 as indicated by line I^2/p. The Nash equilibrium at N has ally 1 providing q^{1*} and ally 2 providing q^{2*}. If the income of ally 1 were to increase, the Nash path N^1N^1 would shift out and a corner solution with ally 2 providing no defense is a distinct possibility.

Note further that a drop in the defense price faced by either ally would increase that ally's feasible set and shift out the Nash reaction path much the same as an income increase. Feasible sets can differ due to comparative advantage if one ally is a cheaper producer of the defense good (Boyer, 1989, 1990; Wong, 1991). If relative cost advantages were independent of the sizes of the allies, then the exploitation hypothesis need not hold.

2.2   The joint product model

Van Ypersele de Strihou (1967) pointed to defense benefits that are *private among allies*. For instance, an ally might build up its arsenal to maintain colonial control, which provides purely public benefits to the nation's population, but does *not* spill over to the nation's ally. Even if two allies have colonial interests, the stationing of troops in the colony of one ally does not afford protection to the colonial interests of another. Such colonial protection is excludable and rival among allies and, thus, is private between two allies. Other examples of interalliance private benefits include disaster relief, drug interdiction, protection of coastal resources, maintenance of domestic order, and crisis management during terrorist incidents. Van Ypersele de Strihou also indicated that defense burden sharing in an alliance is more apt to be associated with benefits received when private benefits are a significant proportion of defense benefits received by allies.

The joint product model goes a step further than van Ypersele de Strihou's extension by allowing the defense activity to produce a variety of outputs that may be purely public, purely private, or *impurely* public among allies.[4] In particular, an alliance arsenal fulfills

[4]   On joint product models, see Conybeare and Sandler (1990), Cornes and Sandler (1984, 1986), Hansen, Murdoch, and Sandler (1990), McGuire (1990b), Murdoch and Sandler (1982, 1984, 1985, 1986, 1990), Murdoch, Sandler, and Hansen (1991), Oneal and Elrod (1989), Sandler (1977, 1988), Sandler and Cauley (1975), Sandler and Forbes (1980), Sandler and Murdoch (1986, 1990), and Thies (1987). On private benefits, also see Knorr (1985), Oneal (1990a, 1990b, 1991), Russett (1970), and Oneal and Diehl (1992).

at least three general functions: (1) deterrence, (2) damage limitation or protection, and (3) private or national-specific goals. Defense outputs are impurely public among allies when their benefits are either partially rival among allies or else partially excludable by the providing nation. Partial rivalry occurs when the benefits available to other users of a good decline as the number of users or the extent of use increases. Conventional forces and arsenals yield both deterrence and damage-limiting protection, needed when deterrence fails and conflict begins. Although the deterrence benefits may be purely public, damage-limiting protection is subject to consumption rivalry in the form of force thinning as a given amount of conventional weapons is spread to defend a longer perimeter or a greater surface area. In other words, the deployment of conventional forces to limit damage does not afford equal protection to all allies. Increasing the concentration of troops along one ally's borders may increase the vulnerability of another ally's borders owing to rivalry. Since deployment decisions can exclude one or more allies, conventional armaments possess partially excludable benefits.

In general, defense activities may give forth a vector of outputs to the allies. Conventional armaments yield country-specific private benefits *and* impurely public damage limitation. Because the strength of the arsenal may deter aggression, some purely public benefits are also present. However, the relative share of private and impurely public benefits are expected to be greater with conventional armaments than with strategic nuclear weapons. The latter are not subject to thinning or spatial rivalry, provided that allies confront a common enemy.

Many factors can contribute to the mix of public and private outputs derived from military activities. First, the strategic doctrine can help determine this mix. A doctrine of flexible response, as adopted by NATO in the late 1960s, permits NATO to respond in different ways to an enemy's challenge; conventional forces or strategic forces may be used and, in the latter case, a missile exchange may be limited or complete. By allowing for a measured response in relationship to the perceived threat, this doctrine increased the importance of conventional forces as compared with the earlier doctrine of Mutual Assured Destruction (MAD) deterrence, which relied on strategic nuclear weapons. As conventional forces increase in importance, so do excludable benefits. Second, changes in military technology can alter the mix of private and public benefits. For example, the development of precision-guided munitions (smart bombs) allow some weapons, such as cruise missiles, to be used in conventional and strategic roles. Third, diplomacy can also alter the mix of benefits and costs derived from defense activities.

2.2.1   Mathematical representation

We now consider a representative ally that allocates its scarce resources between a military activity, q, and a private (nondefense) consumption activity, y. A unit of the private nondefense activity is identical by assumption to a unit of the private good; however, a unit of the military activity is assumed to yield *both* a private and a public defense output. The model can be easily extended to allow for private, impure public, and pure public benefits (Sandler, 1977; Murdoch and Sandler, 1982). Let x stand for the private defense output and z for the pure public defense output. The joint product relationships are[5]

$$x^i = f(q^i) \tag{2.17}$$

$$z^i = g(q^i), \tag{2.18}$$

where both $f(q^i)$ and $g(q^i)$ are increasing, strictly concave and twice-continuously differentiable functions. For (2.17) and (2.18), the derivatives (f' and g') measure the respective marginal productivities of the military activity in providing defense outputs. The amount of alliance-wide *public* benefit spillins, $\tilde{Z}$, provided by the other allies is a function of the aggregate military activity, $\tilde{Q}$, in the allies so that

$$\tilde{Z}^i = h(\tilde{Q}^i), \tag{2.19}$$

where $h' > 0$ and $h'' < 0$. The total level of pure public defense benefits, Z, is

$$Z = z^i + \tilde{Z}^i. \tag{2.20}$$

To simplify the analysis, we allow for fixed proportions so that

$$x^i = \sigma q^i, \tag{2.17a}$$

$$z^i = \delta q^i, \tag{2.18a}$$

$$\tilde{Z}^i = \delta \tilde{Q}^i, \tag{2.19a}$$

replace (2.17), (2.18), and (2.19), respectively. The representative ally's utility function is

$$U^i = U^i(y^i, x^i, Z, T), \tag{2.21}$$

which by (2.17a)–(2.19a) and (2.20) is

$$U^i = U^i(y^i, \sigma q^i, \delta(q^i + \tilde{Q}^i), T) \tag{2.22}$$

[5]   The $f(\cdot)$, $g(\cdot)$, and $h(\cdot)$ functions can be allowed to differ among allies to increase the generality of the model.

in activity space. A Nash equilibrium corresponds to maximizing utility in (2.22) subject to the resource constraint

$$I^i = y^i + pq^i, \tag{2.23}$$

and to $\tilde{Q}$ being set at the best-response level for the other allies.

A Nash equilibrium is, consequently, attained when the following FOCs are simultaneously satisfied

$$\sigma MRS^i_{xy} + \delta MRS^i_{Zy} = p, \qquad i = 1, \ldots, n, \tag{2.24}$$

where MRS_{xy} is the marginal rate of substitution of private defense output x for good y. A similar interpretation holds for MRS_{Zy}. The left-hand side of (2.24) is the marginal benefit derived by an ally from a unit of the general defense activity. Since each unit of q yields varying amounts of the private and public defense output, the marginal value of each must be accounted for and weighted by the respective marginal productivities, σ and δ. The right-hand side of (2.24) is the marginal cost of q. A longer series of weighted MRS expressions on the left-hand side of (2.24) would be needed if additional joint products were present.

The Nash equilibrium is still suboptimal, because the alliancewide marginal benefits that an ally's defense conveys to other allies, that is, $\sum_{j \neq i} \delta MRS^j_{Zy}$, are not included. Surprisingly, the same graphic device as displayed in figures 2.1–2.2 can be used, with some reinterpretation, to illustrate the Nash equilibrium for two allies in the presence of joint products. The slope of the iso-utility curve is now

$$\left. \frac{dq^2}{dq^1} \right|_{\bar{U}^1} = \frac{p - MRS^1_{qy}}{\delta MRS^1_{Zy}} \tag{2.25}$$

in which MRS^1_{qy} is the weighted sum on the left-hand side of (2.24). Insofar as the *simultaneous satisfaction* of the budget constraint, the joint product relations, *and* the set of allocations weakly preferred to any reference allocation consists of the intersection of convex sets, the iso-utility curves are still shaped like those in figure 2.1.

The primary difference in the graph concerns the shape of the Nash reaction path, which can have a positive slope when the joint products are complementary in the Hicksian sense (i.e., $\partial MRS_{xy} / \partial Z > 0$). This inequality means that the marginal valuation of good x is larger when there is more of good Z available. That is, the jointly produced outputs are best consumed together. As benefits derived from good Z spill in from the defense activity in its allies, a nation will want to consume more of the complement, good x, and this is only possible if the nation increases its own defense activity level. Hence, an increase in spillins no longer necessarily implies that an ally will decrease its own defense activities, provided that complementarity of joint products is sufficiently strong.[6] If a military doctrine can create a complementarity between the excludable and nonexcludable joint outputs derived from military activities, then allies may increase their own efforts in relation to those of another ally.

The joint product model has a number of implications that may differ from those of a pure public good model. If impure public defense outputs are present so that force thinning occurs, then alliance membership size restrictions must be based on these thinning considerations. Private and pure public defense outputs are not germane to the size issue, because private outputs are not shared, whereas pure public outputs do not diminish with increases in alliance size. In terms of thinning, additional allies should be admitted until the marginal benefits from reduced cost, as more allies share provision expense, match the marginal thinning costs imposed on the alliance. The latter stems from a given size arsenal and military manpower being made to protect a longer perimeter as a new ally joins. Another implication concerns the extent of suboptimality. As private and impure public benefits increase as a proportion of the jointly produced defense outputs, allies will increasingly reveal their true willingness to pay either through markets or quasi-market (clublike) arrangements. The latter could charge members for deployments of weapons and troops, not unlike what happened during the Gulf War of 1991. Yet another implication involves the likelihood of alliance formation. The existence of private nation-specific joint products provides an incentive for nations to contribute even though they are relatively small. Defense burdens are predicted to be shared more in terms of the distribution of ally-specific gains than in terms of size. A small ally, faced with domestic unrest and country-specific threats (e.g., Israel), may carry a large burden in terms of the percentage of GDP devoted to defense even in an alliance with a much larger ally (e.g., the US) (McGuire, 1982). A final implication concerns nonneutrality when income is redistributed among a set of allies. Thus, burden sharing and the distribution of welfare among allies can be influenced by taxing or other income policy (Andreoni, 1989, 1990; Cornes and Sandler, 1984; Sandler and Posnett, 1991). One such income policy could involve assigning cost shares to allies to finance the infrastructure (pipelines, satellites, early warning systems) or civil budgets of the alliance.

---

[6]   For a proof, see Cornes and Sandler (1986, pp. 118–21). This positive slope to the Nash reaction path is especially noteworthy regarding Palmer (1990a, 1990b), who tested for cooperative behavior based on there being a positive relationship between US defense burdens and those of the allied states. For complementary joint products, a positive relationship may be consistent with Nash noncooperative behavior.

2.2.2   Full income and demand functions

To devise a procedure for distinguishing between the demand function for the pure public good model and the joint product model, we introduce the notion of full income, F, which includes the sum of income and the value of spillins (Bergstrom, Blume, and Varian, 1986). With the standard pure public good model, income enters the model in the same manner as the value of spillins, since both cause a parallel outward shift of the budget constraint when displayed in (y,Q) space.

In the case of joint products, the resource constraint becomes

$$F^i \equiv I^i + p\tilde{Q}^i = y^i + pQ^i \tag{2.26}$$

when the value of spillins, $p\tilde{Q}^i$, is added to both sides of (2.23). The utility function of ally i in (2.22) can be rewritten as

$$U^i = U^i(y^i,\ Q^i,\ \tilde{Q}^i,\ T) \tag{2.27}$$

by noting that $q^i = Q^i - \tilde{Q}^i$. Maximizing (2.27) subject to (2.26) yield FOCs that can be expressed as ally i's demand for defense

$$Q^i = Q^i(F^i,\ \tilde{Q}^i,\ p,\ T), \tag{2.28}$$

where Q^i is the alliancewide defense activity level.

At a Nash equilibrium, demand level for Q by all of the allies must satisfy (2.28), and, moreover, Q^i must equal Q for all i. With joint products, an ally's demand for the defense activity is influenced in two ways by an increase in the other allies' spending on defense: indirectly through full income (because spillins are part of full income) and directly through spillins. Hence, a change in spillins affects the mix between private and pure public outputs. This follows because no ally-specific benefits are gained from $\tilde{Q}^i$.

2.3   Distinguishing between pure public and joint product models

Unless a full income approach is employed, the reduced-form equations for defense demand will not be distinguishable between the two models when general utility functions are used and there is no means for observing the δ and σ productivity parameters. These models can be easily distinguished with the use of a nested test procedure, provided that the respective defense demand equation systems are expressed in terms of full income (Sandler and Murdoch, 1990). For the pure public good model, the full-income representation of the defense demand equations derives from

$$\max_{y^i, Q^i} \{U^i(y^i, Q^i, T) \mid y^i + pQ^i = I^i + p\tilde{Q}^i\}, \tag{2.29}$$

and equals

$$Q^i = Q^i(F^i, p, T), \qquad\qquad i = 1, \ldots, n. \tag{2.30}$$

A comparison of (2.28) and (2.30) indicates that the latter is nested in the former, since only the $\tilde{Q}^i$ term is missing from (2.30). The equation system in (2.28) can be estimated using two-stage least squares (2SLS)[7] and then an F-test can be used to determine the significance of the coefficient on the $\tilde{Q}^i$ variable. If this coefficient is not significantly different from zero, then the pure public good model is more appropriate. In a test of a sample of ten NATO allies using data from 1956 to 1987, Sandler and Murdoch (1990) found the coefficient on spillins to be significantly different than zero for all sample allies, thereby supporting the joint product specification.

2.4   Theoretical extensions

For the most part,[8] theoretical extensions to the economic theory of military alliances has involved either an augmentation to the pure public good model or the joint product model. Insofar as extensions to the pure public good model can be easily applied to the joint product model, we intend to simplify the presentation by focusing on the extensions to the pure public good model.

2.4.1   Aggregating defense contributions among allies

The technology of public supply or the social composition function refers to the method used to aggregate the defense contributions among the allies. Thus far, a summation technology has been used. Imperfect substitutability is allowed by the following technology

$$Q^i = \sum_{i=1}^{n} w^i q^i, \qquad\qquad i = 1, \ldots, n, \tag{2.31}$$

where $0 \leqslant w^i \leqslant 1$ for all i. The w^i's act as weights. Adjustment of these weights can allow for a wide range of models including the case where defense is private among allies and the case where defense is perfectly

---

[7] Two-stage least squares is required, because the full income and spillin terms are correlated with the error terms in (2.28). To obtain consistent estimates, we use the exogenous variable in the equation (2.28) as instrumental variables in the 2SLS.

[8] See Conybeare (1992) for a new approach in which alliances are characterized as diversifying risk. Also see Jack's (1991) dissertation.

substitutable among allies so that the weights are 1. Once unequal weights are allowed, the defense activity is impurely public among allies.

McGuire (1990b) introduced an important generalization of this weighting scheme by defining the technology as

$$Q^i = q^i + \sum_{j \neq i} w_i^j q^j, \qquad\qquad i = 1, \ldots, n, \qquad\qquad (2.32)$$

where $w_i^j \geqslant 0$ and the summation is from $j = 1$ to $j = n$, but excludes $j = i$. On the weights, the superscript identifies the producer, while the subscript identifies the consumer. McGuire allowed for the case where w_i^j exceeds 1, so that some members have "strategic or symbolic dominance" (1990b, p. 19). With the technology in (2.32), the FOCs for Pareto optimality are as follows:

$$\text{MRS}_{Qy}^i + \sum_{j \neq i} w_j^i \text{MRS}_{Qy}^j = p, \qquad\qquad i = 1, \ldots, n. \qquad (2.33)$$

In (2.33), the indexes on w still relate superscripts to producers and subscripts to consumers, but the roles of the i and j dummies have been switched. McGuire (1990b, pp. 21–4) defined three important simplifications for spillins: (1) consumer specific spillins with $w_j^1 = w_j^2 = \ldots = w_j^n = w_j$ for $j \neq i$ and $w_j^j = 1$, (2) producer-specific spillins with $w_1^i = w_2^i = \ldots = w_n^i = w^i$ for $j \neq i$ and $w_i^i = 1$, and (3) uniform spillins with $w_j^i = w$ for all $j \neq i$. For consumer-specific spillins, the efficiency condition in (2.33) becomes

$$\text{MRS}_{Qy}^i + \sum_{j \neq i} w_j \text{MRS}_{Qy}^j = p, \qquad\qquad i = 1, \ldots, n, \qquad (2.33a)$$

while for producer-specific spillins, (2.33) becomes

$$\text{MRS}_{Qy}^i + \sum_{j \neq i} w^i \text{MRS}_{Qy}^j = p, \qquad\qquad i = 1, \ldots, n. \qquad (2.33b)$$

Finally, we get

$$\text{MRS}_{Qy}^i + \sum_{j \neq i} w \text{MRS}_{Qy}^j = p, \qquad\qquad i = 1, \ldots, n, \qquad (2.33c)$$

for uniform spillins.

The implications of these specific structures are drawn out in McGuire (1990b, pp. 23–4) and involve the determination of individual marginal prices among allies and, in consequence, the optimal assignment of burdens under ideal circumstances. McGuire also showed the influence that these spillin relationships would have on Nash equilibrium.

Based on the work of Hirshleifer (1983), an important technology for aggregating public supply is that of weakest link in which

$$Q = \min\{q^i, \ldots, q^n\}, \qquad\qquad (2.34)$$

so that the smallest provision level of the allies determines the security or defense level for the entire alliance. Weakest link may apply to the scenario where a military alliance fortifies a perimeter against a common threat. If alliancewide security depends on keeping the enemy from breaking through, as was true in World Wars I and II for conventional warfare, then the least-fortified front can be used to measure collective security. With weakest link, participants tend to match the defense contributions or efforts of the smallest contributor. Suboptimality is less of a concern, especially when allies' tastes and endowments are similar. Moreover, income redistributions among allies can be used to increase alliancewide defense levels.

A contrasting technology is best shot where

$$Q = \max\{q^1, \ldots, q^n\}, \tag{2.35}$$

so that alliancewide security solely depends on the largest individualized defense effort. An alliance that relies on the nuclear deterrence of a single ally, such as NATO in the 1950s, is expected to abide by the best-shot technology. Suboptimality is a more significant problem with best shot than with summation, since most smaller allies will attempt to free ride with best shot. There is little reason for small allies to fortify when their security depends on the single largest effort within the alliance. Equalizing income among allies will reduce defense efforts as the largest ally loses endowments. Alternative technologies can combine aspects of best shot and weakest link. In a recent article, Conybeare, Murdoch, and Sandler (1994) attempt to determine the underlying technology of four alliances: Triple Entente, Triple Alliance, NATO, and (the now defunct) Warsaw Pact. The former two alliances were instituted prior to World War I. These authors found the Triple Alliance (the aggressor) to abide by best shot and the Triple Entente (the defender) to abide by weakest link. The latter two alliances appeared to correspond to a summation technology.

2.4.2   Cost differences among allies

In Olson and Zeckhauser (1966), all allies were assumed to face the same relative price for the defense activity in terms of the numéraire. Many subsequent studies assumed no price differences among allies. When cost differences are introduced, burden sharing patterns may not adhere to the exploitation hypothesis, especially if the low-cost producers are some of the smaller allies. Olson and Zeckhauser (1967) were the first to allow for differences in the marginal cost for defense among allies. With cost differences, the lower-cost producer should, *ceteris paribus*, provide more of the defense output. If the marginal costs of defense are constant but differ between allies,[9] then Pareto-optimal conditions like (2.33) would require the prices to be indexed by the country providing defense. Similarly, prices would have to be indexed in the Nash conditions to allow for price differences among allies.

The comparative advantage theme has been developed in a series of articles that include Boyer (1989, 1990), Jack (1991), Jones (1988), and Sandler and Cauley (1975). The Boyer (1989) article is noteworthy, since it permits allies to specialize in different public goods, including defense and foreign aid, that are then traded among allies. If the traded public goods possess significant nonexcludable benefits, then difficulties in the analysis can arise. Oneal (1990a, pp. 439–40) correctly noted that the inclusion of foreign aid is unlikely to alter conclusions regarding exploitation, because defense expenditures are so much larger than foreign aid.

In a recent article, Wong (1991) applied modern trade theory to examine burden-sharing behavior between two allies that trade private goods, while facing a common enemy. Defense production can now have two influences: a terms of trade effect and an externality or spillin effect. An increase in the defense production of one ally affects the allocation of inputs between tradable private goods and a defense good. When defense production increases, the demands for factors are affected and this can, in turn, raise input prices. The relative prices of tradable goods or the terms of trade can then be altered. Scenarios can arise in which an ally's production of defense adversely changes the terms of trade faced by its allied trading partner; hence, spillins may come at a cost as terms of trade deteriorate. In such cases, there is less opportunity to free ride and defense burden sharing may be affected. The interested reader should consult Wong (1991) for a fuller discussion of myriad cases in a framework that extends the geometry displayed in figures 2.1–2.3.

2.4.3   Analyzing threat

Thus far, we have treated threat as an exogenous factor. An increase in threat is expected to shift each ally's reaction path in figure 2.2 to the right, thereby increasing the alliancewide defense levels in the new equilibrium. At the outset, we should distinguish between the role of threat in the alliance model from that in the arms race models of chapter 4. The alliance model is a static (equilibrium) analysis, whereas the arms

[9]   In fact, marginal cost is decreasing over some range of output. If marginal cost decreased without end, then a single ally should supply the defense needs of the other allies through market transactions.

race model is a dynamic analysis. Given its static nature where all decisions are made simultaneously, the alliance model is not particularly well-suited to show the *interactions* between allies and adversaries. Reactions to threat are rather artificial in the economic theory of alliances. To circumvent this difficulty, we would have to extend the model to a repeated game framework involving two or more periods of interaction.

There are a number of ways of introducing threat in the standard model, while maintaining threat's exogenous status. A security function, S, can be defined so that

$$S = S(Q, T),\tag{2.36}$$

with $\partial S/\partial Q > 0$ and $\partial S/\partial T < 0$. An increase in the ally's own defenses or those of its allies augments security, whereas an increase in the opposing alliance's arsenal reduces security (Smith, 1980a, 1989). A particularly simple expression for (2.36) is the linear form

$$S = q + \tilde{Q} - T,\tag{2.37}$$

used by Bruce (1990, p. 81). Other forms for (2.36) include those of constant elasticity of substitution (CES) and Cobb–Douglas.

If the interactions of the adversaries are taken into account, then the level of threat becomes endogenous, insofar as a Nash equilibrium can be defined in terms of the best responses of the opposing nations. Following Bruce (1990), we tailor our graphic technique to present the case of two adversaries that are denoted by superscript h for home and e for enemy. In the absence of allies, the home country faces the following problem

$$\max_{y^h, q^h}\{U^h(y^h, q^h - q^e) \mid y^h + pq^h = I^h\},\tag{2.38}$$

where q^e is threat or T, and a linear security function is assumed. By interchanging the h and e superscripts, we have the problem for the enemy country. The demand for security, S^i, is

$$q^i = S^i(I^i - pq^j, p) + q^j, \qquad\qquad i, j = \text{h,e}, \ i \neq j,\tag{2.39}$$

in the opposing nations, where $I^i - pq^j$ is now full income. These equations are derived from the FOCs associated with (2.38).

The budget-constrained utility function can be displayed in (q^h, q^e) space, as in figure 2.4. Since q^e decreases the utility of the home country, the iso-utility curves for nation h have the opposite convexity to those of figure 2.1; the convex set of weakly preferred allocations are on or below the iso-utility curve. Curve I^1I^1, which is closer to the q^h horizontal axis, represents a higher level of utility than that of curve II. The Nash

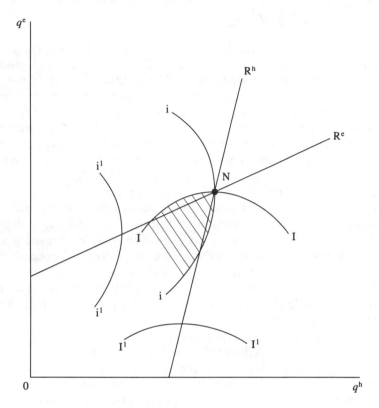

Figure 2.4 Adversarial iso-utility curves

reaction path connects the points of zero slope and is expected to be positively sloped, since

$$\partial q^h / \partial q^e = 1 - \partial S^h / \partial F^h > 0, \tag{2.40}$$

for normal goods where $F^h = I^h - pq^e$. A similar analysis holds for the iso-utility curves of the enemy, also shown in figure 2.4. The Nash equilibrium is at point N where the two reaction paths intersect. Both nations can be made better off if they were to agree to reduce defense expenditures. An increase in the defense levels of an adversary is apt to lead to the other country increasing its own defense level.

The analysis can be extended to include adversarial alliances that contain multiple allies. For this more general case, security in the home alliance becomes

$$S = q^i + \sum_{j \neq i} q^j - \sum_{k=1}^{m} q^{ek}, \tag{2.41}$$

where q^{ek} is the defense level in the kth ally of the m-member *enemy* alliance. Weights could be applied to the defense efforts to distinguish between alliances or among allies. The mathematical analysis is easily extended when allies and adversaries are present. With more than three nations, symmetry assumptions must be introduced to extend the graphic analysis (see Bruce, 1990, pp. 189–93). An interesting result is the case in which a cooperative agreement among the allies to supply more defense leads to a perverse outcome that worsens the well being of the allies and the adversary (Bruce, 1990, pp. 190–3). This follows because the increased spending of the allies over the Nash noncooperative level induces the adversary to spend more on defense, thereby leading to a scenario where more is allocated to defense all around but security stays the same. *The whole notion of suboptimality of defense provision must be reconsidered when adversaries' reactions are included.* Increased military expenditures, whether through greater cooperation among allies or unilateral actions on behalf of an ally, do not necessarily boost security when enemy defense expenditures respond positively to these increased allied expenditures.

Thus far, adversary expenditures have been introduced in a very simplistic fashion as a linear offset to the ally's own defense efforts. More complicated and realistic mappings for including enemy defense efforts exist. For instance, the incremental effect of an enemy's defense effort on ally's security may diminish as the enemy's arsenal is expanded. If enemy and allied defense efforts are made interactive in the theoretical model, then the empirical model must include enemy and allied demand equations in an interactive simultaneous-equation system that recognizes that the error terms are not independent between equations. To date, most empirical studies have treated enemy defense expenditures exogenously. Exceptions include McGuire (1982) and Hilton and Vu (1991).

2.4.4   The allocation process

The standard allocative process that underlies the economic theory of alliances is Nash. Nash is a consistent expectations equilibrium whenever each ally assumes that its counterparts use a best-response defense level and all choices are simultaneous.

McGuire and Groth (1985) have extended alliance theory to include other kinds of allocative processes. In particular, they considered a Lindahl process in which the allies are assumed to meet and exchange information concerning the level of defense, the costs of which are met by individualized cost shares. That is, the ith ally pays t^i of the total cost, pQ, of defense. Moreover, the shares must sum to one so that full costs are covered. For the pure public good model, the ith ally's problem is

$$\max_{y^i, Q^i} \{U^i(y^i, Q^i, T) \mid I^i = y^i + t^i pQ^i\}. \tag{2.42}$$

A Lindahl equilibrium is obtained when there exists a set of cost shares such that the associated FOCs are simultaneously satisfied for all allies at an identical level of alliancewide defense; hence, $Q^i = Q$ for all i. The FOCs can be used to derive a system of defense demand equations that can be tested against the Nash-based system of demand equations (Sandler and Murdoch, 1990). Alternatively, Oneal (1990b) developed an empirical test for Lindahl versus Nash behavior based on a graph from McGuire and Groth (1985, p. 921) that relates defense expenditures to wealth. For unit prices, Nash behavior implies a linear expenditure function with a negative y-intercept; Lindahl behavior implies an expenditure function out of the origin with a smaller slope.[10] Thus, Oneal (1990b) regressed ME shares on GDP shares for NATO and examined whether the slope and intercept declined with time to test for increased cooperation. Other tests for cooperative behavior were given in Oneal (1990b) and Palmer (1990a, 1990b, 1991).

McGuire and Groth (1985) also examined hybrid cases in which Nash and Lindahl behavior are combined so that one set of allies abides by Nash and another set by Lindahl. Bruce (1990) investigated leader–follower behavior, in which the leader (presumably the larger ally) moves first and the follower moves second. Leader–follower behavior may well apply to an asymmetric alliance with a large dominant ally – e.g., the US in NATO or the former Soviet Union in the Warsaw Pact. The follower is assumed to take the leader's defense level as given, so that the follower behaves as in a Nash model. In contrast, the leader takes the follower's reaction path as given and optimizes utility subject to its own budget constraint and to the follower's reaction path. In a figure like figure 2.2, an equilibrium occurs when the leader's iso-utility curve is tangent to the follower's reaction path. The slope of the follower's reaction path constitutes the leader's conjectural response for the follower and is nonzero. Since this conjecture is negative, the leader's defense level and alliancewide defense are expected to fall relative to the zero-conjectural Nash equilibrium.

---

[10]   The Lindahl result depends on the utility function being Cobb–Douglas. This and other assumptions limit the generality of the test.

2.4.5   Institutional arrangements

A Nash framework ignores the institutional issue by making alliance behavior noncooperative. Allies pool their arsenals, while making allocative decisions independently. In the standard theoretical model each ally is represented by some unspecified decision maker (Oppenheimer, 1979). Institutional structures can be investigated in at least two ways: (1) specification of a cooperative structure among allies and (2) specification of a different set of decision makers within the ally. The first can be handled by designing a supranational structure that can tax its allies or enforce decisions on its members. In a recent article, Weber and Wiesmeth (1991, pp. 191–6) considered a quasi-egalitarian equilibrium, whereby tax shares are assigned by the alliance based on individual benefits received by the allies. Sandler and Forbes (1980) and Cauley, Sandler, and Cornes (1986) indicated that the analysis of institutional structures for alliances must include transaction costs and transaction benefits associated with alternative structures. The structure with the greatest *net transactional benefits* is the best. Analyses such as Weber and Wiesmeth (1991) do not incorporate the transaction costs component and, hence, remain partial in nature.

The second means for accounting for institutional considerations is to focus on the decision maker within the alliance. For example, a public choice approach might permit defense spending levels to be determined by a referendum. If this is the case, then a median voter model may apply, so that the median voter's demand for defense determines allocations. Another possibility is a bureaucratic model in which a defense bureau decides defense levels.[11] Each alternative institutional arrangement has its own equilibrium outcome. Transaction costs considerations also concern alliance formation. Large fixed transaction costs inhibit formation and may depend on group size. Furthermore, transaction costs involve the determination of optimal alliance size. More work in this area is needed.

2.5   Tests of the theory

Since 1966, a great deal of attention has been paid to testing the economic theory of alliances. A number of issues are relevant. First, the form of the variables is important. In some studies (e.g., Murdoch and Sandler, 1984), real military expenditures (ME) is the dependent variable

[11] See Dudley and Montmarquette (1981) and Murdoch, Sandler, and Hansen (1991) on median voter models, and Gonzales and Mehay (1990) and Jones (1992) on bureaucratic models.

and GDP and spillins are the independent variables. In other studies (e.g., Russett, 1970), defense burdens (measured by defense expenditures as a proportion of GNP) and GNP are the variables. The form of the variable depends on what is being investigated and the antecedent theory. When the demand for defense or reaction function is being estimated, then ME, GDP, and spillins are usually among the relevant variables. If, however, Olson's exploitation hypothesis is examined, then a measure of defense burdens, such as ME/GNP, and a size variable (GNP) are appropriate variables. When free riding is studied using the demand for defense function, a negative and significant coefficient on the spillin variable reflects free riding. If, instead, free riding is associated with the exploitation hypothesis, then a positive and significant correlation or relationship between ME/GNP and GNP is indicative of free riding. The two tests usually, but not always, give similar conclusions. A second issue concerns the pooling of data across allies when testing relationships. In the case of demand estimates, time-series data should be used to estimate each ally's demand equation separately or within a demand system. Tests can then be performed to determine whether some or all of the equations are sufficiently similar to justify pooling. When testing for overall alliance behavior (e.g., cooperative versus noncooperative), the researcher often pools over the alliance or some cohort, such as the small allies. A third issue involves the antecedent model. For demand studies, the antecedent model is utility maximization that may include a general or specific utility function. In studies concerning exploitation, the antecedent model is Olson's collective action formulation.

Much important work has been done on the exploitation hypothesis. Olson and Zeckhauser (1966) presented a distribution-free or nonparametric correlation test to demonstrate that defense burdens were positively correlated to the NATO allies' GNP in the mid-1960s. Russett (1970) used nonparametric statistics to test the exploitation hypothesis for a number of alliances and found a significant positive correlation for the Warsaw Pact, CENTO, SEATO, and NATO. Starr (1974) also uncovered a significant positive correlation between defense burdens and GNP for the Warsaw Pact for 1967–71. Other studies of the exploitation hypothesis included Oneal (1990a, 1990b, 1992), Pryor (1968), van Ypersele de Strihou (1967), Sandler and Forbes (1980), and Murdoch and Sandler (1982).

Most empirical studies of alliances have used parametric test statistics based on either single-equation or simultaneous-equation regression estimation. Although the bulk of the studies focused on burden sharing in the NATO alliance, some have examined other alliances such as the US–Israeli alliance, the Triple Alliance, the Triple Entente, the

Australian–New Zealand–US alliance (ANZUS), and the US–Japanese alliance. In table 2.1, some representative empirical studies are listed along with the alliances that they studied. As indicated, the underlying theoretical models for these studies were either a variant of the pure public good model or the joint product model.

Many parametric tests attempted to estimate an ally's demand for defense or its military expenditures equation. Most estimates can be encompassed by the following general function,

$$ME = f(\text{INCOME, PRICE, SPILLIN, THREAT}) \qquad (2.43)$$

in which ME is military expenditures of the nation, INCOME is some GDP measure, PRICE is the relative price of defense (if available), SPILLIN is the aggregate military expenditures of the other allies, and THREAT is the military expenditures of the enemy. Insofar as the allies' demands may be influenced by similar factors, the error terms are often not expected to be independent. To account for this influence, investigators have either allowed for contemporaneous correlation between equations, or else a simultaneous-equation system. In the former case, seemingly unrelated regressions are used to derive estimates; in the later case, two-stage least squares is employed.

Table 2.1 indicates the estimation procedure under the heading "empirical model." Important conclusions or results for each of the investigations are also listed, as is the time period of estimation. A number of features are worth highlighting. First, when tested against one another, the joint product model outperformed the pure public good model (Sandler and Forbes, 1980; Sandler and Murdoch, 1990). Second, studies increasingly used simultaneous-equation estimations in recent years to account for the underlying interactions between the allies.[12] Many of the earlier single-equation estimates used lagged spillins. Third, only a few exercises built a simultaneous-equations model in which enemy demand is one of the equations (e.g., McGuire, 1982). Fourth, many studies found allies to respond positively to spillins, thus supporting the notion of complementarity between defense joint products. Fifth, threat did not always perform as hypothesized, since in a number of studies defense demands did not respond positively to threat. Sixth, some studies found that military doctrine affected the demand for

[12] Simultaneous-equation estimation is required when current values of the spillin term are on the right-hand side of the allies' demand for defense equations. Simultaneity is an issue because contemporaneous spillins are not independent of the errors in the other allies' demand equations. In particular, these spillins depend on the other allies' income, their threat level, and other exogenous factors. To account for simultaneity, researchers apply two-stage and three-stage least squares.

Author(s)	Alliance(s) studied	Theoretical model	Empirical model	Conclusion(s)	Time period
Conybeare and Sandler (1990)	Triple Alliance, Triple Entente	Joint products	Generalized least squatres	Little evidence of free riding.	1880–1914
Gonzales and Mehay (1990)	Developed Nations and Undeveloped Nations	Security function and effects of scale	Ordinary least squares	Economies of size to defense for developed countries. Some free riding on informal allies.	1982
Gonzales and Mehay (1991)	NATO	Joint products, pure public	Pooled time series, cross section	Found more support for joint-product model.	1974–84
Hansen, Murdoch, and Sandler (1990)	NATO	Joint products. Distinguishes between strategic and conventional weapons	Generalized least squares	More free riding on nuclear strategic forces than on conventional forces.	1972–85
Hilton and Vu (1991)	NATO	Pure public	Simultaneous equations. Stone–Geary utility functions and linear expenditure system	Many allies respond positively to spillins and negatively to threat.	1960–85
McGuire (1982)	US–Israeli	Pure public, impure public	Simultaneous equations. Stone–Geary utility functions and linear expenditure system	US increases aid to Israel as Arabs spend more. Israel responds positively to threat.	1960–79

Table 2.1 (*cont.*)

Author(s)	Alliance(s) studied	Theoretical model	Empirical model	Conculsion(s)	Time period
Murdoch and Sandler (1984)	NATO	Joint products	Seemingly unrelated regressions. Lagged spillins and dummy shift variable for change in doctrine	Flexible response lessening US burdens. Complementarity caused coefficients on spillins to be positive.	1961–79
Murdoch and Sandler (1985)	ANZUS	Joint products	Generalized least squares. Lagged spillins and dummy for Vietnam War	US and UK spillins matter. Dummy and income significant.	1961–79
Murdoch and Sandler (1986)	NATO and Neutral Countries	Joint products	Seemingly unrelated regressions. Lagged spillins	Sweden free rode on NATO after 1974.	1957–82
Murdoch, Sandler, and Hansen (1991)	NATO	Joint products, median voter and oligarchy choice	Two-stage least squares	Belgium, UK and the Netherlands fit median voter. France W. Germany, US and Italy fit oligarchy model.	1965–88
Okamura (1991)	US–Japanese	Pure public	Generalized indirect translog utility function. Simultaneous equations	Threat changes have a significant positive effect. Elasticities presented.	1972–85
Olson and Zeckhauser (1966)	NATO	Pure public	Nonparametric statistics. Rank correlation test	Defense burdens positively correlated with size.	1964

Table 2.1 (*cont.*)

Author(s)	Alliance(s) studied	Theoretical model	Empirical model	Conclusion(s)	Time period
Oneal (1990a)	NATO	Olson's (1965) collective action	Generalized least squares. Pooled time series, cross section	NATO provides relatively pure public outputs. Relative economic size and state of East–West tension important.	1950–84
Oneal (1990b)	NATO	McGuire–Groth (1985) graphical device	Ordinary least squares. Pooled cross section	Pursuit of private benefits. Increased cooperation by allies noted.	1950–84
Oneal (1992)	NATO	Olson's collective action	Ordinary least squares. Pooled time series, cross section	Correcting for conscription does not have much effect on exploitation hypothesis.	1974, 1981, 1987
Oneal and Elrod (1989)	NATO	Olson's collective action	Ordinary least squares. Pooled time series, cross section	NATO is a uniquely privileged group. Private benefits present. Objects to military doctrine having an effect on exploitation.	1950–84
Palmer (1990a) (1990b)	European NATO allies and neutrals	Nash model and Lindahl (bargaining)	Ordinary least squares. Pooled time series, cross section	Positive relationship between US defense burden and those of allied states. Claims support for bargaining.	1950–84
Pryor (1968)	NATO, Warsaw Pact	Olson's exploitation hypothesis	Ordinary least spares. Pooled cross section.	Exploitation hypothesis supported for NATO, but not for Warsaw Pact.	1956–62

Table 2.1 (*cont.*)

Author(s)	Alliance(s) studied	Theoretical model	Empirical model	Conculsion(s)	Time period
Russett (1970)	NATO, Warsaw Pact, SEATO, CENTO, Rio Pact, Arab League	Olson's exploitation hypothesis	Nonparametric statistics. Rank correlation test	Exploitation confirmed for SEATO, CENTO, Warsaw Pact (1965, 1967) and NATO up to 1966.	1950–67 for NATO; 1965, 1967 for Warsaw Pact, 1965 for others
Sandler and Murdoch (1990)	NATO	Joint products, full income approach, Lindahl, and Nash models	Two-stage least squares. *J* tests to distinguish between Nash and Lindahl models. Nested test to distinguish joint products and pure public	Ten sample allies abide by joint products. Nine out of ten abide by Nash. None abide by Lindahl.	1956–87
Smith (1989)	NATO (UK and France)	No antecedent model presented	Generalized least squares. Mix variables from various models based on statistical fit	Both UK and France respond positively to spillins.	1951–87
Starr (1974)	Warsaw Pact	Olson's exploitation hypothesis	Nonparametric statistics. Rank correlation test	Exploitation confirmed.	1967–71
van Ypersele de Strihou (1967)	NATO	Joint products	No true test presented	Positive relationship between defense burdens and GNP does not always hold.	1949–64

defense (Murdoch and Sandler, 1984, 1986; Sandler and Murdoch, 1986), but other studies presented opposite findings (Oneal and Elrod, 1989; Oneal and Diehl, 1992). Methods differed significantly between these researchers and may be responsible for the alternative outcomes. Seventh, free riding was not as prevalent as presupposed in the demand studies of alliances (e.g., Conybeare and Sandler, 1990); free riding was more frequently identified in the studies based upon the exploitation hypothesis. Eighth, the demand-based study that estimated separate equations for the allies supported Nash behavior over Lindahl (Sandler and Murdoch, 1990), whereas studies that used pooled data supported the Lindahl or bargaining model (Palmer, 1990a, 1990b, 1991; Oneal, 1990b).

2.6   Concluding remarks

Based on the theory of public goods, the economic study of alliances has a long tradition. As modeling advances have occurred in public good analyses, these have been subsequently incorporated in the study of alliances. Theoretical extensions have included the introduction of joint products, the endogeneity of threat, the variation of the underlying game structure, the utilization of different technologies of public supply, and the allowance of cost differences among allies. Future extensions should build more complex interactions between opposing alliances, while accounting for intra-alliance interactions. Moreover, allocative processes other than Nash, Lindahl, and leader–follower need to be examined. A repeated game structure should also be given to the alliance model so that a sequence of actions between opposing alliances and among allies is allowed. In addition, informational asymmetries within and between alliances need to be incorporated into the analysis. Alliance configurations should be studied for partitioning a set of nations. This extension involves finding the core in which no alternative grouping of allies can do better. Finally, work is needed to sort out empirical findings that appear contradictory.

3   The demand for military expenditures

In the previous chapter, the economic theory of alliances was shown to underlie the choice-theoretic demand for military expenditures. Specifically, a decision maker in each ally was depicted as allocating resources between nondefense and defense activities, while treating relative prices, national income, threat, and allied expenditures as exogenous. The current chapter further examines the demand for military expenditures based on the analysis of the economic theory of alliances. If, however, a nation has no allies, the earlier theory is easily modified to generate the nonallied nation's demand for defense.

The demand for military expenditures is an important consideration in defense economics for a number of reasons. First, this demand relationship indicates the manner in which a country allocates its resources between defense and nondefense goods (i.e., the classic guns versus butter trade-off). Second, the burden-sharing issue for allies can be addressed and tracked over time once the allies' demand equation system for military expenditures is identified. If defense burdens among allies are deemed unfair, then knowledge of this demand system would enable the analyst to predict the effect of policy changes on the pattern of burdens (see, e.g., the analysis in Sandler and Murdoch, 1986). Third, the demand relationships may be used for short-run forecasting purposes. Fourth, elasticity measures can be estimated once the demand for defense has been identified. Fifth, normative issues concerning the suboptimality of resource allocation to defense can be investigated if the demand relationships are known.

The standard analysis of the demand for military expenditures has some special features worth emphasizing. Inasmuch as the demand functions are derived from a static optimizing framework, the analysis does not allow a nation to gauge its defense expenditures in a truly interactive manner with respect to those of its rivals. Only a dynamic arms race model (see chapter 4) can permit this type of interaction, but then the within-alliance interactions involving free riding are ignored. For the demand theory, the rivals' defense expenditures serve as a *shift parameter* that influences the nation's defense levels for various values of the other exogenous variables. A second feature concerns the underlying choice-theoretic framework, since the identification of the dependent and independent variables then follows from the theoretical specification. This important insight is often missed when investigators try a host of different independent variables when ascertaining the strongest empirical relationship (Smith, 1989). Finally, the identity of the decision maker is a crucial feature, because arguments of the demand function depend on who makes the decisions.

The primary purpose of this chapter is to give an overview of the theory of demand for military expenditures. In doing so, the demand function for defense is contrasted with the demand functions for other kinds of goods (section 3.1). A secondary purpose is to indicate various forms for the demand function for military expenditures (section 3.2). A tertiary purpose is to address some empirical considerations (section 3.3). A final purpose is to review some country studies (section 3.4).

3.1   Unique features of the demand for military expenditures

Suppose that an economy has just two private goods, y_1 and y_2. To derive a demand function for these private goods, we consult the ith consumer's utility maximization problem in which levels of the goods are chosen so as to maximize utility,

$$U^i = U^i(y_1^i, y_2^i), \tag{3.1}$$

subject to a budget constraint

$$I^i = p_1 y_1^i + p_2 y_2^i, \tag{3.2}$$

where superscripts indicate the individual, I^i is the individual's income, and p_j is the per unit price of y_j for $j = 1, 2$. If the first-order conditions (FOCs) for this problem are found and then solved for the y_js, demand functions can be expressed in terms of prices and income as follows

$$y_j^i = y_j^i(p_1, p_2, I^i), \qquad\qquad j = 1, 2. \tag{3.3}$$

When a functional form for the utility function is specified, the ith agent's demand function can be solved in a less general form than that in (3.3). If the demand functions in (3.3) are aggregated over the individuals, then a market demand for a private good is derived. This market demand depends on prices and an aggregate income variable, such as mean income. At this juncture, special note needs to be taken that quantities of other goods do not enter the demand functions when only private goods are present.[1]

For public goods, provision may be private or public. When there is private provision of a public good, each individual decides his/her contribution q^i to the public good Q, while taking into account the contributions of others, $\tilde{Q}^i = \sum_{j \neq i} q^j$. Hence, the individual must choose optimizing levels for the private good y and the public good contributions to maximize

$$U^i = U^i(y^i, q^i + \tilde{Q}^i), \tag{3.4}$$

subject to

$$I^i = p_y y^i + p_q q^i \tag{3.5}$$

and $\tilde{Q}^i$ is constant, where p_y and p_q are the per unit price of good y and good q, respectively. The associated FOCs can be used to solve for the demands for y and q^i

$$y^i = y^i(p_y, p_q, I^i, \tilde{Q}^i), \tag{3.6}$$

$$q^i = q^i(p_y, p_q, I^i, \tilde{Q}^i). \tag{3.7}$$

The main feature distinguishing these demand functions from those in a private good environment is the appearance of the quantity constraint, denoting everyone elses' contributions. In chapter 2, we saw that defense contributions from others denote defense spillins from allies. The form for $\tilde{Q}$ can permit diverse ways for aggregating spillins.

For public provision of a public good, a government body or decision maker is charged with determining the demand for the public good, which is then financed with taxes. A commonly used model is the median voter model[2] in which the level of expenditures on the public good is the only choice considered by a referendum. The median voter's choice for the public good then represents the decision for the group. The public

---

[1] In more technical language, the quantities of the private goods have been optimized out of the problem. Only market data – prices and income – enter the demand functions. The presence of quantities in the indirect utility function and/or demand function would indicate the appearance of quantity constraints in addition to the budget constraint. Such quantity constraints are associated with externalities in which one agent's actions affect the utility of another agent and no mechanism for compensation exists (Cornes, 1992, chapter 7).

[2] On the median voter model, see Mueller (1989, pp. 189–95), Borcherding and Deacon (1972), and Bergstrom and Goodman (1973). Murdoch, Sandler, and Hansen (1991) have extended the median voter model to a joint product framework. Also see Dudley (1979) and Dudley and Montmarquette (1981).

good demand function follows from maximizing the median voter's utility

$$U^i = U^i(y^i, q^i + \tilde{Q}^i) \tag{3.8}$$

subject to

$$I^i = p_y y^i + \tau p_q q^i, \tag{3.9}$$

where τ is the per person tax share for the public good and $\tilde{Q}^i$ indicates public good spillins from other jurisdictions. The associated demand functions are now

$$y^i = y^i(p_y, \tau p_q, \tilde{Q}^i, I^i), \tag{3.10}$$

$$q^i = q^i(p_y, \tau p_q, \tilde{Q}^i, I^i), \tag{3.11}$$

which depends on prices, the tax rate, spillins, and *median voter's income*. If the decision maker were altered, then the relevant income variable and public good price variable would change.

Since defense is a public good, its demand function shares many of the features of public good demand that distinguish it from private good demand. Most notably, defense spillins among allies are an important right-hand side variable in the demand for military expenditures. If, however, a nation were to have no allies, then defense spillins would disappear from the demand function. The primary distinguishing feature between public good and defense demand concerns the security function,[3] which enters the nation's utility function and which indicates how various levels of the nation's defense, its allies' defense levels, and its rival's defense levels combine to determine the overall level of the nation's protection or security. A wide variety of security functions,[4]

$$S = S(q, \tilde{Q}, T), \tag{3.12}$$

can be used, where T denotes the enemy's defense expenditures.

In section 2.4.3, an additive form for $S(\cdot)$ was analyzed. Whatever form is used, the following restrictions are reasonable: $\partial S/\partial q > 0$, $\partial S/\partial \tilde{Q} > 0$, and $\partial S/\partial T < 0$, so that security increases when a nation or its allies

---

[3] On security functions, see Bruce (1990), Dudley and Montmarquette (1981), and Smith (1980a, 1987, 1989). Smith (1980a) was the first to use the terminology of security function. Also see the interesting treatment of threat and force position in Ayanian (1992). Threat is also analyzed empirically in Conybeare (1992), Conybeare, Murdoch, and Sandler (1994), Conybeare and Sandler (1990), Fritz-Aβmus and Zimmermann (1990), Gonzales and Mehay (1991), McGuire (1982), Murdoch and Sandler (1982), Okamura (1991), and Sandler and Murdoch (1990).

[4] For technical reasons, concavity restrictions may be placed on the security function so that second-order conditions are satisfied.

increase defense expenditures, while security decreases when a rival increases its defense outlays. If a rival's defense expenditure level is introduced into the model, a researcher can treat this variable as exogenous or endogenous. In the former case, the variable appears as an independent, right-hand side variable in the demand for defense; in the latter case, the rival's demand function must be included as another equation in the demand equation system. For such a system, rival defense expenditures are a determinant of the nation's defense expenditures and vice versa.

3.2   Demand for military expenditures: further theoretical considerations

3.2.1   A standard representation

Since chapter 2 presented the joint product model of alliance behavior, only the derivation of demand for military expenditures is now emphasized. A defense activity, q, is assumed to produce a nation-specific defense benefit, x, and an alliancewide defense benefit, z, in fixed proportions so that

$$x^i = \sigma q^i \tag{3.13}$$

and

$$z^i = \delta q^i \tag{3.14}$$

with σ and δ denoting positive constants. The alliancewide public benefit is deterrence, Z, where

$$Z = z^i + \tilde{Z}^i, \tag{3.15}$$

and $\tilde{Z}^i = \delta \tilde{Q}^i$. The nation's utility function is

$$U^i = U^i(y^i, \sigma q^i, \delta(q^i + \tilde{Q}^i), T) \tag{3.16}$$

in which (3.13)–(3.15) have been used to express the jointly produced defense outputs in terms of the defense activity. In (3.16), the three right-most expressions denote the security function. The demand functions are derived by choosing y^i and q^i so as to maximize utility subject to spillins and a resource constraint

$$I^i = p_y y^i + p_q q^i. \tag{3.17}$$

As before, the resulting FOCs can be used to solve for the demand for military expenditures in the following general form:

$$q^i = q^i(p_y, p_q, I^i, \tilde{Q}^i, T). \tag{3.18}$$

Frequently, the price of the private numéraire good is set equal to one, so that p_y does not appear in the demand function. If the researcher wants to account for the interactions among the allies, then a system of equations, one equation for each ally, is required (e.g., Murdoch, Sandler, and Hansen, 1991).

In practice, the researcher might assume a particular functional form for the utility function so that a specific form for the military expenditure equation can be derived – examples include McGuire (1982), Hilton and Vu (1991), and Okamura (1991). Most notably, the Stone–Geary utility function has been used to generate a linear expenditure system (Phlips, 1974). With this utility function, important restrictions of demand are automatically satisfied. The first is homogeneity in which a demand equation is homogeneous of degree zero in income and prices. As a consequence, a proportional change in all prices and income leaves demand unchanged. A second requirement is the adding-up condition in which the marginal propensities to consume for the set of goods sum to one, thereby implying that increases in income are entirely allocated to the different commodities. A third requirement is that compensated substitution effects are negative, and a fourth requirement is that the (compensated) cross-substitution effects are equal for each pair of goods, so that the resulting Jacobian matrix is symmetric.

3.2.2 Alternative representations

In section 3.1, we sketched the median voter model in which defense expenditure decisions are placed before the voters in a referendum. If the level of military expenditures is voted upon, then the choice of the median voter prevails. The demand for military expenditures now depends on median voter's income, spillins, and the tax weighted price of the defense activity.

A third variant of a choice-theoretic model of defense views government bureaucrats as making the military expenditure decision (see, especially, Gonzales and Mehay, 1990). In this variant, the bureaucrat chooses defense levels to maximize the discretionary defense budget, which is the difference between defense spending and cost, both of which depend on defense levels. This latter variable is itself a function of allied defense expenditures, rival defense expenditures, population, and cost influences. Bureaucratic models often imply that defense levels are pushed beyond the levels at which a government maximizes the social welfare of its citizens. Although this oversupply has negative normative implications in a private good world, the same implications may not hold for defense, insofar as defense is often undersupplied when social welfare is maximized as benefit spillovers conferred on other allies are ignored. Hence, bureaucratic tendencies toward oversupply can offset somewhat the undersupply bias characterizing most representations of the defense decisions at the national level (Jones, 1992; and Lee, 1990).[5] This normative conclusion holds for the overall level of defense expenditures, but may not apply to the mix of defense output – i.e., the relative amounts of strategic, conventional, and tactical weapons in a nation's arsenal. Because bureaucratic influences may be stronger for some weapon classes than for others, these influences may boost some types of weapons relative to others.

A fourth variant is a rent-seeking model in which defense lobbies pressure the government to alter its level or mix of defense outputs. The presence of lobbies might, as in the case of bureaucratic motives, push defense levels beyond those of the standard model, which ignores these pressures.

The identity of the relevant agents who make or influence defense spending decisions has an important impact on the form of the objective function and the relevant constraints. As the decision maker's identity is varied, the form of the dependent and independent variables can vary greatly among models. Thus, for example, in a median voter model the defense variable may turn out to be defense per capita (Dudley and Montmarquette, 1981) rather than real defense expenditures, as in the standard model of section 3.2.1. Moreover, the income variable is that of the median voter rather than that of national income. When the researcher has latitude to choose the form for the utility and the security function as well as the identity of the decision maker, a large number of alternative models can be manufactured. There are, consequently, a wide variety of forms for the demand functions in the literature even though the demand relationship is derived from an explicit choice-theoretic framework. As shown in chapter 2, these demand functions are also affected by the underlying strategic assumptions – e.g., Nash, leader–follower, Lindahl, or some combination of these.

In a series of papers,[6] researchers have devised empirical methods to

---

[5]   The analysis in the text ignores the oversupply that derives from *rivalrous* nations' defense spending. Enemies impose negative externalities on one another as they increase their defense expenditures, which, in turn, leads to an oversupply. These externalities can be internalized through arms control.

[6]   Conybeare, Murdoch, and Sandler (1994) devised a test for distinguishing between different aggregation functions for spillins (e.g., best shot and weakest link), while McGuire and Groth (1985) and Sandler and Murdoch (1990) put forward a test for distinguishing between Nash and Lindahl behavior. Murdoch, Sandler, and Hansen (1991) devised an empirical test for differentiating between oligarchy choice and a median voter model. Tests for the impurity of defense spillins were indicated in Dudley and Montmarquette (1981) and Goff and Tollison (1990). For other test procedures, see Murdoch and Sandler (1984, 1986), Oneal (1990a, 1990b), Oneal and Diehl (1992), Oneal and Elrod (1989) and Palmer (1990a, 1990b, 1991).

test between alternative demand formulations. Though these tests may provide an important means for determining the underlying allocation procedure, they suffer from a number of drawbacks. First, the tests may not be conclusive, since both models analyzed may be rejected or accepted. In the first instance, the test does not indicate an alternative formulation, and, in the second, the test does not discriminate between alternatives. Second, current tests distinguish between just a couple of competing formulations. Third, the tests are often not very robust, so that slight changes in assumptions can alter the outcome. Fourth, alternative demand formulations may possess the same reduced-form equations, so that test-approved empirical representations may have multiple antecedent models. Consequently, tests may be incomplete in their ability to identify the underlying theoretical model (Dasgupta and Itaya, 1992). The construction of other tests is an important area for future research.

Finally, we should mention that environmental factors may be introduced into the utility function, and, when this is done, these factors will show up as shift parameters in the demand function. A prime example is the military doctrine embraced by an alliance; for instance, the doctrine of flexible response or mutual assured destruction deterrence. In the case of NATO, a change in military doctrine may be expected to affect the mix of weapons as well as the level of defense expenditures. If, for example, weapons with greater degrees of publicness (i.e., more nonrival and nonexcludable) are stressed by a new doctrine, then the responses of allies to spillins are anticipated to change. More free riding will result for greater publicness, and less free riding for reduced publicness. Researchers (Murdoch and Sandler, 1984; Fritz-Aβmus and Zimmermann, 1990; Dudley and Montmarquette, 1981; Ayanian, 1992) have substantiated that changes in military doctrine can alter the demand for military expenditures. Another potential environmental factor is the outbreak of a war or a violent confrontation. When war starts, there should be an upward shift in national defense spending. If a ratchet or demonstration effect applies, then defense spending may not return to the pre-war levels. For most empirical estimates, a sizable drop in military expenditures took place after the war (Looney and Mehay, 1990; Murdoch and Sandler, 1985).

3.3   Empirical models

3.3.1   Single-equation approach

If a researcher is interested in a partial equilibrium analysis of a country's demand for military expenditures, then a single equation for estimating demand would be appropriate. When a country is a small participant in an alliance so that the dominant allies are unlikely to respond to the smaller participants' military expenditures, a partial equilibrium approach may have much to recommend it. In such a case, the level of both spillins from the other allies and the military expenditures of the rival can be viewed as exogenous, so that a multi-equation demand system does not have to be estimated. Thus, for example, an examination of the Australian demand for military expenditures in the ANZUS (Australia–New Zealand–United States) Alliance can treat the military expenditures or spillins from the US as well as the military expenditures of a rival (e.g., the Soviet Union prior to the end of the cold war) as exogenous. Similarly, estimates for the Swedish demand for military expenditures can treat NATO spillins and Soviet threat as exogenous.

In general functional form, the estimating equation for military expenditures (ME) is

$$ME = ME(INCOME, SPILL, THREAT, PRICES), \qquad (3.19)$$

owing to (3.18). In (3.19), INCOME denotes a measure of real national income, such as real gross domestic product (GDP); SPILL indicates the real military expenditures of the allies; THREAT is the military expenditures of the rival; and PRICES denotes the relative price of defense as compared with nondefense goods. In the standard Nash model, military expenditures consist of the level of real military expenditures and *not* per-capita military expenditures nor the share of military expenditures in GDP.

From a theoretical viewpoint, INCOME is a crucial determinant of military expenditures. As GDP rises, a nation has both more resources to protect and greater means to provide protection. Military expenditures and GDP are, thus, hypothesized to be positively related, so that defense is a normal good whose demand rises with income. For single-equation estimations, SPILL is frequently lagged by one year when time-series data are used (Fritz-Aβmus and Zimmerman, 1990; Murdoch and Sandler, 1984, 1985, 1986). SPILL may denote the sum of the military expenditures for the rest of the alliance, or a vector of military expenditure levels for the other allies. In the latter case, perfect substitutability among spillin sources no longer applies whenever the estimated coefficients associated with this vector are not equal across components. Different representations for SPILL can capture diverse technologies of publicness, such as best shot or weakest link. THREAT is often represented by the real defense spending of the enemy nation(s). If more than one enemy exists, then their defense spending must be aggregated. Lags may also be used for the rival's military expenditures under the assumption that a nation must experience the threat before responding to it. Because countries usually do not maintain indices of the price of military activity, data on price are typically not available. PRICE can be dropped from the equation without biasing results, *provided that* the price of military activities has inflated at the same general rate as that of nondefense activities. Although this is true in some countries, it has not been true for the UK where defense goods have inflated at a higher rate (Smith, 1980a). Finally, structural changes can be introduced into equation (3.19) through the use of dummy variables. If, for example, a structural change is suspected to have influenced a nation's response to SPILL, then the variable D·SPILL can be utilized where D·SPILL is SPILL multiplied by a dummy variable, equal to zero prior to the expected date of the structural change and to one on and after the date.

Because the theoretical development of defense demand is from the viewpoint of an individual nation, the appropriate estimation involves the use of time-series data for the nation, rather than cross-sectional data for a group of nations. Sometimes, sufficient time-series data are not available and the researcher may have to resort to cross-sectional data to acquire enough degrees of freedom to perform robust statistical inference. Insofar as international defense spending comparisons are required in (3.19), ME, SPILL, and THREAT must be converted into a common currency using an exchange rate. These variables must also be transformed into real terms using a (full-employment year) price deflator, such as the GDP implicit price deflator. The Stockholm International Peace Research Institute's (SIPRI) *World Armaments and Disarmament*: *SIPRI Yearbook* reports defense figures by countries, as does the International Institute for Strategic Studies' *The Military Balance*. National income must also be expressed in real terms in a common currency.

When estimating equation (3.19), the researcher must assume a specific functional form for the demand function. A frequently used representation includes the linear form

$$ME_t = \alpha + \beta_1 INCOME_t + \beta_2 SPILL_{t-1} + \beta_3 THREAT_{t-1}$$
$$+ \beta_4 PRICE_t + \varepsilon_t, \tag{3.20}$$

where subscripts on the variables indicate the time period, α denotes a constant, β_is are coefficients to be estimated, and ε is an error term. Various elasticity measures can be found for each year by multiplying the estimated β by the observed ratio of the variable to ME. Another popular specific form for the demand function is the log linear form, in which the coefficients denote the elasticities. Flexible functional forms can be used, where the researcher tests restrictions to determine the most appropriate form for the data. With time-series data, the error terms are often serially correlated, so that autocorrelation must be corrected.

3.3.2   Seemingly unrelated regressions

When a nation is a member of an alliance and demand equations are estimated for multiple allies, Zellner's (1962) iterative, seemingly un-related regression (SUR) technique may be appropriate. Strictly speaking, this technique is not a simultaneous-equation estimation procedure; instead, SUR allows the error terms to be contemporaneously correlated among equations. Given that allies' choices are surely subject to some identical random factors, error terms are apt to be correlated. Efficiency of the estimates can be improved if the data can be pooled across some allies. The following procedure can be followed: (1) estimate individual ally's demand for defense using SUR; (2) test for the equality of selected coefficients between equations when theoretical factors suggest equality; (3) pool the data across equations whose coefficients' *equality could not be rejected*; and (4) reestimate the SUR system with pooling where appropriate. Allies that face similar circumstances (e.g., the medium-sized nuclear allies in NATO, or the lowland allies) are the ones that should be examined for possible pooling. In a study of NATO, Murdoch and Sandler (1984) applied this procedure and pooled the French and the UK demand equations; they also pooled the Belgium and the Netherlands equations (see section 3.4). The same procedure was applied to the Scandinavian nations – Finland, Denmark, Norway, and Sweden – in a different study by Murdoch and Sandler (1986). Selected coefficients could not be rejected as being equal and, thus, some pooling was appropriate.

3.3.3   Simultaneous equations

A simultaneous-equation approach is appropriate for estimating the demands for military expenditures if a Nash equilibrium is assumed for the alliance and the interactions among the allies' military expenditure decisions are taken into account. For this situation, the SPILL term in equation (3.20) is correlated with the error term. Consistent estimates can be obtained from two-stage least squares (2SLS) using the exogenous variables in the system of demand equations for the allies as instrumental variables. In this system, a constant, the GDP terms for the sample of allies, THREAT, and PRICES can be used as instruments. Since a Nash equilibrium is a timeless concept, there is no reason to lag SPILL or

THREAT *when equilibrium values are assumed.*[7] Thus, lagging these variables is now dropped.

Thus far, the simultaneous-equation approach outlined permits endogeneity within the alliance, but not between opposing alliances. To allow for this latter influence, THREAT must be treated as endogenous; hence, a THREAT equation must be estimated with a set of instruments in the 2SLS procedure.[8] If contemporaneous correlation of the error terms is also allowed, then a three-stage least squares (3SLS) estimate is required. Contemporaneous correlation is often ignored for these simultaneous demand equations, owing to the need to correct for autocorrelation.

Simultaneous-equation estimation is also used when a specific utility function is assumed for the decision maker. To date, the utility function of choice is that of Stone–Geary. Following McGuire (1982), the representative decision maker's utility function is

$$U = \beta_D \ln(Q_D - \gamma_D E_D^e) + \beta_{ND} \ln(Q_{ND} - \gamma_{ND} E_D^e)$$
$$+ (1 - \beta_D - \beta_{ND}) \ln(Y - \gamma_y E_D^e), \tag{3.21}$$

where ln denotes natural logs, βs represent coefficients, Q_D is per capita defense, Q_{ND} is per capita (publicly provided) nondefense, E_D^e denotes enemy defense expenditures, γs are constant coefficients, and Y is per capita private goods. In (3.21), $\gamma_D E_D^e$ indicates the minimal subsistence per capita defense level and is proportional to enemy military expenditures, which, in turn, denotes THREAT. Subsistence levels for the nondefense public good and the private good are $\gamma_{ND} E_D^e$ and $\gamma_y E_D^e$, respectively. McGuire also included a resource constraint in which the nation's residents draw resources from foreign military aid, foreign economic aid, and domestic endowments. This cumulative revenue is then spent on defense, nondefense public goods, and private goods.

The optimization problem defines three demand functions – defense, public nondefense, and private – in terms of the exogenous variables, such as population, endowments, and prices. In addition, enemy military expenditures and foreign aid can be viewed as endogenous variables. When this is the case, these endogenous variables must also be expressed in terms of the exogenous variables. In total, five equations can be estimated using 3SLS. In an important contribution, Okamura (1991) introduced a more general (flexible-form) utility function that treated THREAT differently than McGuire (1982). To execute the McGuire model, a great deal of data is required, since many coefficients are being estimated.

---

[7] This 2SLS approach has been used for NATO by Murdoch, Sandler, and Hansen (1991) and for the Triple Alliance and the Triple Entente by Conybeare and Sandler (1990).

[8] THREAT is treated endogeneously in estimates of the Israeli–US alliance in McGuire (1982) and of NATO in Hilton and Vu (1991).

3.4   Some country studies

3.4.1   Australia

Murdoch and Sandler (1985) investigated the Australian demand for military expenditures for the 1961–79 period. Australia is a member of the ANZUS alliance; hence, US and New Zealand defense expenditures are potential sources of spillins. Inasmuch as Australia and the United Kingdom share a common heritage and are allies, spillins may also be derived from UK military expenditures. Finally, defense spillins may also come indirectly from NATO, because Australia's primary allies are members of this alliance. To determine the pattern of spillins, Murdoch and Sandler used a *vector* of spillin variables, representing the lagged (real) military expenditures from the US, the UK, and NATO (excluding the US and UK). New Zealand military expenditures were dropped since they were such a small amount and did not vary over time. The following demand for military expenditures was estimated using OLS

$$ME_t = -2.219 + 0.017 INCOME_t + 0.007 US_{t-1} + 0.252 UK_{t-1} - 0.008 NATO_{t-1} + 0.471 WAR,$$
$$\quad (-3.09)\ (2.59) \qquad\qquad (2.20) \qquad (2.37) \qquad\quad (-0.25) \qquad\quad (5.87)$$

$$(3.22)$$

where t statistics are in parentheses; $INCOME_t$ is Australia's GDP in year t; US_{t-1} is military expenditures of the US in year $t-1$; UK_{t-1} is military expenditures of the UK in year $t-1$; $NATO_{t-1}$, is the military expenditures of the other NATO allies in year $t-1$, and WAR is a dummy variable which is equal to one for the years 1965–71 and equal to zero otherwise. This last variable denotes the Vietnam War years during which Australia provided troops and material. The expenditure variables and income were deflated by a price index and converted to a common currency.

The insignificance of $NATO_{t-1}$ is noteworthy because it indicates that the direct interalliance spillins come from Australia's closest allies. Australia responds positively and significantly to its GDP as well as to spillins from the US and the UK A dollar increase in GDP implies a 0.017 dollar increase in military spending, while a dollar increase in US military expenditures induces a 0.007 dollar increase in Australian military spending. Furthermore, a dollar increase in UK military expenditures elicits about a 25 cents increase in Australian defense spending. These results indicate that Australia is not free riding on its primary allies, since it does not decrease its defense spending as its allies increase their military spending. A negative coefficient on the spillin terms is indicative of free riding; a coefficient of minus one denotes perfect substitutability between Australian defense and that of its allies.

The large difference in the coefficients on the US and UK spillin term implies that spillins are not additive. Furthermore, the positive coefficients on the spillin terms suggest a complementarity between Australian defense efforts and those of its allies. This may arise, in part, due to jointly produced private benefits that do not flow between allies. With the vast Australian territories requiring protection, thinning of protective forces is a relevant consideration that reduces the mix of public benefits and induces Australia to reveal its defense preferences through its own expenditures. Australia's isolated location makes it feasible for its allies to exclude it from their deterrent umbrella (a fear often expressed in the Australian press), since an attack on Australia would cause little damage due to fallout or otherwise to either the US or the UK

In equation (3.22), the WAR variable is quite significant. Australia's participation in the Vietnam War caused a significant short-run upward shift in its defense spending. This shift was temporary and ended once Australia withdrew its troops.

3.4.2   West Germany

Fritz-Aβmus and Zimmermann (1990) estimated a single-equation demand for defense for West Germany for the 1961–87 period. Real German military expenditures were related to German GDP, lagged French defense spending, lagged NATO defense spending,[9] lagged USSR defense spending, a dummy variable for flexible response, and a dummy for the composition of the government. The latter dummy was used to distinguish between rule by the Social Democratic Party and rule by the Liberal and Conservative parties, which were both aligned with more traditional interests. The political dummy (POL) was set equal to 1 for 1960–70 and 1984–7 and 0 for 1971–83. The estimated equation is given in table 3.1 along with the definition of each variable (see footnote (a) of the table). Surprisingly, the coefficient on GDP was negative, but insignificant. In most studies, GDP is a positive and significant influence on defense spending. West Germany responded positively and significantly to lagged French defense; hence, these forces were not viewed as substitutable for West German forces. This response, however, changed after 1974 as shown by the negative and significant coefficient on D·FSPILL. In contrast, West Germany responded negatively and significantly to NATO spillins, thus indicating a small degree of free riding. Any free riding was curtailed greatly after the doctrine of flexible

---

[9]   NATO spillins included the sum of defense spending in the US, UK, Italy, Belgium, Denmark, the Netherlands, and Norway.

Table 3.1 *Selected single-equation estimates of countries' demand for defense spending.*

Fritz-Aβmus and Zimmerman (1990): West Germany 1961–87[a]

$ME_t = 10.8504 - 0.0064INCOME_t + 0.5778FSPILL_{t-1} - 0.5117D·FSPILL_{t-1}$
    (6.8021) (−1.3136)   (2.6518)   (−3.0147)

$- 0.0958NATOSPILL_{t-1} + 0.0495D·NATOSPILL_{t-1} + 0.2115SOVME_{t-1} + 0.9056POL$
   (−7.438)   (2.6498)   (6.7826)   (1.2075)

Looney and Mehay (1990): United States 1965–85[b]

$ME_t = -68.046 + 0.935ME_{t-1} + 5,227.27NATODEV + 0.361SOVME_t + 17,282VIET$
           (14.22)   (7.62)   (5.21)   (3.78)

$- 247,085UCPI + 261.36DEVFED - 91.91DEFICIT_{t-1}$
   (−7.66)   (5.50)   (−2.74)

Murdoch and Sandler (1984): Selected NATO Countries 1961–79[c]

US

$ME_t = 67.322 + 0.035INCOME_t - 0.236SPILL_{t-1} - 0.472D·SPILL_{t-1}$
   (3.78)   (2.14)   (−0.38)   (−0.376)

UK

$ME_t = 8.63 + 0.015INCOME_t - 0.012SPILL_{t-1} + 0.003D·SPILL_{t-1}$
   (16.6) (8.77)   (−2.87)   (2.26)

France

$ME_t = 9.192 + 0.015INCOME_t - 0.012SPILL_{t-1} + 0.003D·SPILL_{t-1}$
   (16.48) (8.77)   (−2.87)   (2.26)

Belgium

$ME_t = 0.220 + 0.017INCOME_t + 0.002SPILL_{t-1} + 0.002D·SPILL_{t-1}$
   (1.76) (12.75)   (2.53)   (6.22)

Netherlands

$ME_t = 0.763 + 0.017INCOME_t + 0.002SPILL_{t-1} + 0.002D·SPILL_{t-1}$
   (6.06) (12.75)   (2.53)   (6.22)

Denmark

$ME_t = 0.119 + 0.007INCOME_t + 0.003SPILL_{t-1} + 0.0009D·SPILL_{t-1}$
   (1.45) (4.40)   (3.67)   (4.67)

Norway

$ME_t = -0.029 + 0.024INCOME_t + 0.002SPILL_{t-1} + 0.0002D·SPILL_{t-1}$
  (−0.68) (12.99)   (4.23)   (1.17)

W.Germany

$ME_t = 6.79 + 0.007INCOME_t + 0.023SPILL_{t-1} + 0.017D·SPILL_{t-1}$
   (4.00) (2.02)   (1.59)   (3.57)

Italy

$ME_t = 1.515 + 0.025INCOME_t - 0.005SPILL_{t-1} - 0.005D·SPILL_{t-1}$
   (2.58) (9.23)   (−1.04)   (−3.00)

Murdoch and Sandler (1990): Sweden 1953–85[d]

$LME_t = 4.300 + 0.770LINCOME_t - 3.165LPOP_t + 0.331LNORSPILL_{t-1}$
   (2.61)   (3.15)   (−2.70)   (4.16)

Table 3.1 (*cont.*)

$$-0.102D \cdot \text{LNORSPILL}_{t-1} - 0.005 \text{LSOVME}_{t-1} - 0.058 \text{FISC}$$
$$(-2.08) \qquad\qquad (-0.12) \qquad\qquad (-2.69)$$

Smith (1989): Britain and France 1951–87[e]
Britain
$$\Delta\text{SHARE}_t = -1.25 + 0.20\Delta\text{USSHARE}_t - 0.14(\text{SHARE}_{t-1} - \text{SOVSHARE}_{t-1}) - 0.49\text{RD} + 1.18\text{KD}$$
$$(-3.57)\ (6.67) \qquad\qquad (-3.5) \qquad\qquad\qquad\qquad (-4.45)\ (5.9)$$

France
$$\Delta\text{SHARE}_t = -1.56 + 0.37\Delta\text{USSHARE}_t - 0.17(\text{SHARE}_{t-1} - \text{SOVSHARE}_{t-1})$$
$$(-2.36)\ (7.40) \qquad\qquad (-2.43)$$

Notes: [a] OLS estimates, where ME_t is German military expenditures in 1980 prices; INCOME_t is German GDP in constant 1980 prices; FSPILL_{t-1} is lagged French military expenditures in 1980 prices; $D \cdot \text{FSPILL}_{t-1}$ includes a multiplicative dummy shift of $D = 1$ for 1974–87 and 0 otherwise; NATOSPILL_{t-1} is lagged spillins in 1980 prices from the US, UK, Italy, Belgium, Denmark, Netherlands, and Norway; $D \cdot \text{NATOSPILL}_{t-1}$ includes a multiplicative dummy shift of $D = 1$ for 1974–87 and 0 otherwise; SOVME_{t-1} is lagged Soviet military expenditures in 1980 prices; and POL is a dummy variable for the government in power and equals 1 for 1960–70 and 1964–67 and 0 for 1971–83.
[b] Generalized least squares (GLS) corrected for autocorrelation. The t ratio for the constant was not reported. ME_t is real US military expenditures; ME_{t-1} is real lagged US military expenditures; NATODEV is the deviation from trend in NATO spillins net of US defense spending; SOVME_{t-1} is lagged Soviet military expenditures; VIET is a dummy variable for the Vietnam War equal to 1 for 1967–72 and 0 otherwise; UCPI is unanticipated US inflation; DEVFED is the deviation from trend in federal revenue; and DEFICIT_{t-1} is the lagged federal deficit.
[c] SUR estimates with pooling over Belgium and the Netherlands and over Britain and France. ME_t is the country's real military expenditures in 1975 prices; INCOME_t is the nation's current GDP in 1975 prices; SPILL_{t-1} is the aggregate lagged real military expenditures for the other NATO countries in the sample; D is a dummy variable equal to 1 for 1974–9 and 0 otherwise; and $D \cdot \text{SPILL}_{t-1}$ is lagged spillins multiplied by D.
[d] OLS estimates in log-linear form. LME_t is the log of Swedish real expenditures in 1980 prices; LINCOME_t is the log of Swedish GDP in 1980 prices; LPOP_t is the log of Swedish population; LNORSPILL_{t-1} is the log of the lagged Norwegian military expenditures in 1980 prices; D is a dummy equal to 1 for 1974–85 and 0 otherwise; $D \cdot \text{LNORSPILL}_{t-1}$ is D times the Norwegian spillin term; LSOVME_{t-1} is the log of the lagged Soviet military expenditures in 1980 prices; and FISC is a dummy for Swedish fiscal restraint and equals 1 for 1983–5 and 0 otherwise.
[e] GLS estimates corrected for autocorrelation. ΔSHARE_t is the change of the respective country's defense share $(\text{ME}_t/\text{GDP}_t)$ of GDP; SHARE_{t-1} is the respective country's lagged defense share $(\text{ME}_{t-1}/\text{GDP}_{t-1})$; SOVSHARE_{t-1} is the lagged Soviet defense spending share of GDP; $\Delta\text{USSHARE}_t$ is the change in the US defense share of GDP; RD is a dummy for British defense reviews in 1967, 1968, and 1969 and equals 1 in these years and 0 otherwise; and KD is a dummy for the Korean War that equals 1 in 1952 and 0 otherwise.

response took hold in 1974, as shown by the $D \cdot \text{NATOSPILL}$ term. Apparently, the doctrine's emphasis on conventional forces induced West Germany to strengthen its forces *vis-à-vis* those of NATO. West Germany also displayed a significant and positive response to Soviet defense spending or threat. The political variable had no effect.

3.4.3   Sweden

Murdoch and Sandler (1990) presented a single-equation estimation of Swedish defense demand for 1953–85. As an armed neutral nation, Sweden aims to be self-reliant on its own defense expenditures. The single-equation demand representation can be used to test this self reliance by estimating SPILL coefficients and searching for negative and significant values, which would indicate a degree of free riding. A host of different specifications for SPILL were tested to determine which of Sweden's potential allies' military expenditures might substitute for Swedish defense. NATO spillins were used, as were spillins from Sweden's neighbors – Norway and Denmark. The estimated demand equation included Swedish GDP, population, and lagged Soviet defense spending as additional independent variables. A dummy variable, equal to 0 for 1953–73 and to 1 for 1974–85, was used to test the impact of the doctrine of flexible response. This dummy was multiplied by the Norwegian spillin term, so that a change in the slope coefficient was attributed to this doctrine. Other forms for this dummy variable were tried. A second dummy (FISC) was used to capture any effect on military expenditures from the policy of fiscal restraint; this dummy equaled 0 for 1953–82 and 1 for 1983–5. For the various statistical representations, a log-linear demand equation was estimated. A series of statistical tests were applied to determine the best representation.

In table 3.1, the best model and its estimated coefficients are given. Swedish defense responded positively and significantly to GDP; hence, defense was a normal good. The only significant source for spillins was Norway. Until the doctrine of flexible response took effect, Sweden increased its defense expenditures as Norway augmented its expenditures, indicating no free riding prior to 1974. A small degree of free riding, however, took place *after* the start of 1974 as shown by the negative and significant coefficient on the D·NORSPILL term. Apparently, Norwegian fortification of its northern border with the USSR afforded some protection to Sweden. A Soviet attack initiated from the Kola peninsula was believed to pass through Norwegian territory prior to reaching Sweden. Swedish defense did not, however, respond significantly to the Soviet threat. Additionally, population was a negative influence on Swedish defense demand. This may be due to greater nondefense needs required to support a larger population. The fiscal response dummy indicated a negative and significant cutback in defense.

3.4.4   The United Kingdom and France

Single-equation estimates for British defense demand were presented by Smith (1980a, 1987, 1989, 1990b), while estimates for French defense demand were also given by Smith (1989). For British estimates, we focus on those in Smith (1989), which were loosely based on the choice-theoretic model indicated earlier. Unlike most other demand studies, Smith (1989) was able to put together separate price indices for defense and civilian goods. These were used to deflate expenditure series. The use of separate price indices is an important step forward (also see Smith (1980a) for further details). In Smith (1989), the analysis was focused on determining the best statistical fit even though an antecedent theoretical model might not exist. Smith's estimates for Britain are listed in table 3.1, where SHARE denotes the ME/GDP ratio. In addition, RD is a dummy for British defense reviews undertaken in 1967, 1968, and 1969, and KD is a dummy for the Korean War. Changes in British defense burdens, as measured by its defense share of GDP, responded positively and significantly to changes in US burdens and to the Korean War. Threat was captured by the difference between lagged UK defense burdens and Soviet defense burdens. An expected negative and significant response was found for this threat proxy. When British shares grew relative to that of the Soviet Union, less defense burdens were needed in the ensuing period. The defense review had a negative impact.

In table 3.1, Smith's (1989) estimates for French defense demand for 1951–87 are indicated. The form of this equation is similar to that of Britain except for the absence of dummy variables. Changes in French defense burdens responded positively to changes in US burdens, thus implying the absence of free riding. The threat proxy again performed as expected. By examining the estimates for Britain and France, we discover that the two countries responded similarly to threat and spillins. This similarity agrees with the Murdoch and Sandler (1984) findings, discussed below, which allowed the defense equations for Britain and France to be pooled, since the coefficients were not significantly different from one another.

3.4.5   The United States

Looney and Mehay (1990) presented generalized least squares (GLS) estimates, corrected for autocorrelation, for the US for 1965–85. As in Smith (1989), Looney and Mehay (1990) were more interested in the statistical fit and did not relate their final estimates to an explicit theoretical model. Their best estimate is given in table 3.1. Real military expenditures were positively related to these expenditures in the previous period. This finding means that bureaucratic influences were present (see chapter 4). Deviations from NATO defense trends, Soviet military expenditures, the Vietnam War, and deviations from federal revenue trends exerted positive influences on US military expenditures. Inflation and budget deficits had a negative influence on US defense spending.

Looney and Mehay's (1990) estimates did not contain an income or price term; hence, their expenditures equation did not include two standard variables associated with demand. It is probably best not to characterize their estimates as those of demand.

3.4.6 NATO Allies

Murdoch and Sandler (1984) applied SUR to estimate a demand equation system for the US, the UK, France, Belgium, the Netherlands, Denmark, Norway, West Germany, and Italy. These estimates covered the 1961–79 period. For each of the sample allies, the following equation was estimated:

$$ME_{it} = \alpha_i + \beta_{it}INCOME_{it} + \beta_{2i}SPILL_{i,t-1} + \beta_{3i}D\text{·}SPILL_{i,t-1} + \varepsilon_{it},$$

$$(3.23)$$

where subscript i denotes the nation, and subscripts t and $t-1$ indicate the time period. D·SPILL is SPILL multiplied by a dummy variable, equal to zero before 1974 and one after 1974. This latter variable was intended to test for structural shifts following the institution of the doctrine of flexible response. In table 3.1, the defense estimates are given for the nine sample allies, after pooling data for Britain and France and for the Netherlands and Belgium.

The study found the following results: (1) income was a positive and significant determinant of defense demand; (2) free riding was primarily associated with Italy and the nuclear allies (the US, the UK, and France); (3) a structural shift in defense demand was attributed to the doctrine of flexible response; (4) the French and British equations had virtually identical coefficients and could be pooled; and (5) the Dutch and Belgian equations had virtually identical coefficients and could be pooled. The first result implies that nations augmented their defense spending as their income rose. An increase in income implies that a nation has more to lose from an invasion and, hence, a positive response is to be expected. The second result is consistent with the notion of substitutable *and* complementary joint products. The nuclear allies, which supplied purely public deterrence, were more apt to free ride on the outputs of others. As a flanking nation, Italy, was also in a position to free ride. The remaining allies in the sample apparently viewed their defense activities as complementary to those of the other allies, so that they increased their defense expenditures in response to an increase in the defense spending of their allies. The third result indicates that, after the doctrine of flexible response took effect, most allies responded more positively to spillins, thus indicating enhanced complementarity of strategic and conventional weapons systems. The fourth and fifth results imply that allies in similar circumstances behaved in a like manner.

In a subsequent study for NATO allies, Sandler and Murdoch (1990) presented 2SLS estimates, corrected for autocorrelation, for 1956–87. These estimates contained a threat variable and were in log-linear form. Their results (not shown) found that spillin coefficients were positive, defense was a normal good, and threat stimulated defense spending.

3.4.7 Japan

Using a simultaneous-equation framework, Okamura (1991) analyzed the US–Japanese alliance for 1972–85. He built a two-equation demand system based on the homogeneous indirect-translog utility function, which is a generalization of the Stone–Geary utility function. Soviet threat was included in both the US and Japanese equations as an exogenous variable. Both Japan and the US responded positively and significantly to the Soviet threat, but Japan displayed a greater sensitivity. The income elasticities were positive for both allies, while the military price elasticity was negative for the US, but positive for Japan (Okamura, 1991, p. 205).

As a nice innovation, Okamura (1991) empirically estimated the Nash reaction paths for Japan and the US, respectively, as follows

$$JME = 190.2432 - 0.919177USME \qquad (3.24)$$

$$USME = 200.1664 - 0.956155JME, \qquad (3.25)$$

where JME is Japanese real military spending and USME is US real military spending. These reaction paths can be characterized as follows: First, both reaction paths are negatively sloped, indicating free riding. Second, the resulting equilibrium is stable and unique, since both slope coefficients are less than one in absolute value. Third, this equilibrium occurs at the intersection of the two paths, where US defense spending is $150.79 billion and Japanese defense spending is $51.64 billion. Fourth, reaction paths are linear.

Okamura's (1991) study is an excellent representation of how the economic theory of defense demand can be applied in practice. Other worthwhile examples include McGuire (1982) and Hilton and Vu (1991).

3.5   Concluding remarks

To date, the theory of public goods and joint products has served as the theoretical underpinning for the derivation of the demand for military expenditures. Although results have varied among studies, some common findings have emerged. In particular, defense is a normal good with a positive income elasticity of demand. When defense outputs are purely public, free-riding behavior characterizes an ally's demand for defense. Defense outputs may be complementary, and, hence, free riding may be attenuated in the case of private nation-specific joint products. Finally, rival defense expenditures (threat) tend to raise a nation's demand for defense.

The estimation of the demand for defense may be extended in a number of directions. Dynamic interactions of an arms race nature need to be built into the standard public good model of defense demands. More complex security functions should be used and estimated. In addition, the extent of free riding by nations outside of the established alliances should be investigated. Interalliance free riding should also be investigated, especially since some nations may be members of more than one alliance. Finally, public choice elements should be included to a greater extent than is done thus far.

4   Arms races

When thinking about the application of mathematics and statistical analyses to the study of international relations and defense economics, one surely must consider the analysis of arms races put forward by Lewis F. Richardson (1960). Portions of Richardson's analysis were first published in 1939 in the *Journal of the Royal Statistical Society* and *Nature*, but did not generate much notice until the posthumous publication of his *Arms and Insecurity* in 1960. Works by Anatol Rapoport (1957), Thomas Schelling (1966), and Kenneth Boulding (1962) focused on Richardson's model and generated significant interest in the mathematical representation of an arms race. Since the 1960s, a vast literature has been written on theoretical, conceptual, and statistical aspects of the Richardson arms race model.

The purpose of this chapter is to give an overview of the analysis of arms races, and to elucidate the Richardson formulation as well as more recent representations. Although we refer to over seventy-five references, we do not attempt to provide a comprehensive survey of the literature. Recent useful surveys include Anderton (1989), Intriligator (1982), Intriligator and Brito (1989a), Isard and Anderton (1985, 1988), Isard (1988), and Moll and Luebbert (1980). The works by Isard and Anderton are especially comprehensive and up to date.

When two or more nations or alliances with conflicting goals engage in a competitive increase in their armaments and military manpower, an arms race is taking place (see, e.g., Anderton, 1990b). Arms races are often characterized as an action–reaction process in which one nation increases its military arsenal in response to increases in a potential adversary's arsenal. The process is especially worrisome if no stable equilibrium exists, so that an ever-increasing amount of resources is allocated to arming, or the armament configuration induces one or more nations to initiate war. During the cold war, the analysis of arms races was of understandable importance; sizable portions of gross domestic product (GDP) were allocated to the arms race in both the United States and the Soviet Union. The buildup included both nuclear strategic weapons and conventional armaments.

In the post cold war era, the study of arms races is still of importance. First, an understanding of arms races allows us to gain a better perspective on history. Second, arms races still exist on a regional basis even though the United States and the Commonwealth of Independent States (CIS) are not currently in confrontation. These regional races have been associated with the outbreak of the Gulf War in 1991 and numerous wars in the Middle East since Israeli statehood. India and Pakistan may have also been engaged in an arms race.[1] Third, arms race phenomena may occur within a country's border – e.g., between rival street gangs in an urban center or between a government and paramilitary terrorist groups (e.g., the Shining Path in Peru). Arms races may also take place between an organized crime network and law enforcement agencies (Anderton, 1990b). Fourth, the study of arms races is important for promoting the process of arms control. Because arms reduction could lead to instability, policy makers must learn what types of arms control maintain a stable equilibrium (Anderton, 1992, 1993; Intriligator, 1975; Intriligator and Brito, 1984, 1989a).

The body of the chapter contains eight sections. Section 4.1 presents a simple game representation in normal form for analyzing arms races. In section 4.2, the basic Richardson model is examined. Alternative Richardson-type models are investigated in section 4.3 and include emulative arms races, bureaucratic models, and political models. Strategic factors are included in section 4.4. Differential game representations are presented in section 4.5, while supply-side considerations are discussed in section 4.6. Selected empirical analyses are briefly reviewed in section 4.7. Concluding remarks are given in section 4.8.

4.1   Simple game representations

A simple representation of the arms race dilemma consists of a game in which each of two nations has two strategies or choices: (1) to limit its arms or (2) to escalate its arms acquisition.[2] Although this representation is admittedly simplistic, it nevertheless serves to highlight some of the factors at work. The representation also allows us to introduce some key definitions, germane to the more complex analyses.

---

[1]   See Ward and Mintz (1987) on the Middle East arms race and Deger and Sen (1990b) on the alleged race between Pakistan and India. Deger and Sen (1990b) did not find econometric evidence of a Richardson-type arms race for the subcontinent.

[2]   On these matrix game representations, see Boulding (1962), Brams (1985), Brams and Kilgour (1988), Majeski (1984), Schelling (1980), Shubik (1987), and Wagner (1983).

nation 2

	limit	escalate
limit	4, 4	–16, 8
escalate	8, –16	* –12, –12

nation 1

Figure 4.1 Arms race Prisoner's Dilemma

In figure 4.1, a game scenario for two adversarial nations is depicted. The matrix indicates hypothetical payoffs for four strategy combinations: (1) both nations limit arms, (2) nation 1 limits arms, while nation 2 escalates arms acquisition, (3) nation 2 limits arms, while nation 1 escalates arms acquisition, and (4) both nations escalate arms acquisition. The matrix displays the game in normal or strategic form and depicts the players, their strategies, and payoffs. In the matrix, the rows indicate the two strategies of nation 1, while the columns depict the two strategies of nation 2. The first number in each cell indicates the payoff to nation 1, while the second number denotes the payoff to nation 2. The matrix shows that each nation is best off when it escalates and its counterpart limits arms. The next-to-worst outcome for each nation takes place when both engage in the arms race, and the next-to-best outcome occurs when both countries limit their arms. The worst outcome occurs when the nation limits its arms, but its adversary escalates. This follows because the arms-reducing nation's decline in relative strength may induce the other nation to attack or extract extortion.

The pattern of payoffs in figure 4.1 is an example of the Prisoner's Dilemma game, which is much used in the study of international relations.[3] If given the choice between mutual arms limitation and mutual arms escalation, the payoffs in figure 4.1 clearly suggest that mutual limitation is in everyone's interests – i.e., this strategic combination Pareto dominates the arms escalation scenario. The dilemma results because as each nation pursues its self-interest, the payoff pattern of the Prisoner's Dilemma leads both nations to escalate their arms acquisition. To explain this outcome, we must first introduce the concept of a *dominant strategy*. A strategy is dominant if it gives a greater payoff to the player regardless of the other player's actions. In figure 4.1, arms

[3] On the Prisoner's Dilemma, see Brams (1985), Majeski (1984), Sandler (1992, chapter 2), Schelling (1980), and Shubik (1987).

escalation is dominant for nation 1, since its payoffs (of 8 and −12) in the escalate row exceed the *corresponding* payoffs (of 4 and −16) in the limit row. For column player, arms escalation is also dominant, as the payoffs in this column exceed the corresponding payoffs in the limit arms column. When a game contains more than two strategy choices, a strategy is dominant when the resulting payoffs in that row (column) is greater than or equal to *all* corresponding payoffs in all other rows (columns). As the rival nations play their dominant strategy in figure 4.1, both escalate their arms acquisition and end up in an arms race in the cell marked with an asterisk. Paradoxically, each spends more on defense, but may end up with no more security, because the rival also spends more. The negative payoffs in the matrix reflect the fact that a positive opportunity cost in terms of less civilian goods is paid with no resulting benefits.[4]

The escalate-escalate cell is also a *Nash equilibrium*, which corresponds to a strategy combination from which neither player would *unilaterally* want to alter its strategic choice if given the opportunity. In figure 4.1, neither nation would want unilaterally to change its strategy of escalation in the cell marked with an asterisk: Nation 1 or 2 would lose four if it unilaterally disarmed, because payoffs would change from −12 to −16. A Nash equilibrium is also characterized as the optimizing choice with respect to the best response of the other player(s). For the Prisoner's Dilemma of figure 4.1, each nation's optimizing response is to escalate when the other nation escalates.

To identify the pattern of payoffs associated with a Prisoner's Dilemma, we ordinally rank the payoffs in figure 4.1 from best to worst. The best payoff (of 8) is assigned a rank of 4, the next best payoff (of 4) a 3, and so on. These ranks are given in the corresponding matrix of figure 4.2. When a matrix indicates this ordinal payoff pattern, it is a Prisoner's Dilemma. Many patterns exist; in fact, 2 by 2 games admit seventy-eight distinct ordinal patterns. Another game form, relevant to international relations, is that of Chicken and differs from the Prisoner's Dilemma by switching the placement of the ordinal ranks of 1 and 2. In figure 4.3, a Chicken game is depicted for two nations in a confrontation in which each country can either back down or attack. As the ordinal payoffs show, mutual attack leads to the worst outcome for each nation. A nation is best off when it attacks and the other backs down. The next best scenario is for each to back down. There is no dominant strategy in the Chicken game, since 4 > 3 but 1 < 2; there are, however, two Nash

---

[4]   Wolfson (1985) and Wolfson and Farrell (1989) refer to this scenario as economic warfare. See section 4.6.

nation 2

	limit	escalate
limit	3, 3	1, 4
escalate	4, 1	* 2, 2

(nation 1 — row player)

Figure 4.2 Arms race Prisoner's Dilemma (ordinal)

nation 2

	back down	attack
back down	3, 3	* 2, 4
attack	* 4, 2	1, 1

(nation 1 — row player)

Figure 4.3   Chicken game

equilibria as indicated by the asterisks.[5] The Chicken game is especially apropos for crisis situations but is not typically relevant to the arming choice.

The stability of the Prisoner's Dilemma representation of the arms race may be especially troublesome when the game is played repeatedly with a *known* end point. Suppose that two nations know that they must confront one another over a ten-year period. Each adversary solves the game backwards by starting at the start of the tenth period and choosing its best strategy in that period. In this last period, the game matrix is that of figure 4.1 or 4.2 and, consequently, the dominant strategy is to escalate arms; hence, both nations escalate. In the ninth period, the best strategy is again to escalate arms, given that the nations will escalate their arms acquisition in the last period. And so it goes, so that the arms race is carried on for all periods. If, however, the end of the game is unknown or the game is played indefinitely, then disarming may be a

---

[5]   These are the pure-strategy Nash equilibria in which a single strategy is chosen. If, however, a random or mixed strategy is permitted in which the players choose their strategies probabilistically, then another Nash equilibrium exists.

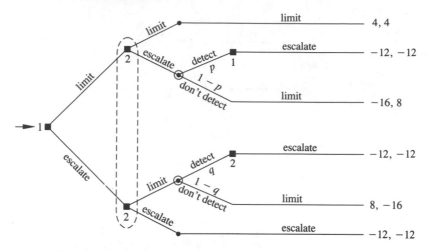

Figure 4.4   Game tree: arms race and detection

Nash equilibrium if nations value the future sufficiently (see, e.g., Majeski, 1984; Sandler, 1992, pp. 79–89).

Many additional considerations may be added to the basic Prisoner's Dilemma. An interesting example is due to R. Harrison Wagner (1983), who introduced incomplete information by allowing for the possibility that a nation's escalation may go undetected by its counterpart. During much of the nuclear era, a nation might have been able to increase its stockpile of missiles without being caught. Moreover, Germany succeeded in secret rearmament during the 1930s. In figure 4.4, the game is depicted in *extensive form* by the game tree.[6] Nation 1 moves first and can either limit or escalate its arms holdings. Arms can be limited by destroying weapons or else not replacing depreciated weapons. Next, nation 2 must decide whether to limit or escalate, but without knowing for certain the earlier actions of nation 1; hence, the dotted line around the two nodes for nation 2 indicates that it does not know what action of nation 1 preceded nation 2's choice. We then assume that nation 1 (or 2) can detect its counterpart's escalation with probability p (or q). That is, nation 2's escalation may go undetected $1-p$ portion of the time. If an escalation is undetected, the disarming nation will continue to limit its arms; but, if detected, the nation will change its disarmament decision and escalate arms acquisition.

In figure 4.5, we display the associated game in normal form. The four

[6]   The exposition of the game relies on Wagner (1983) and Ordeshook (1986). On other game representations of arms races, see Bueno de Mesquita and Lalman (1988), Lambelet (1973), and Wallace (1974).

nation 2

	limit	escalate
nation 1 limit	4, 4	$4p - 16, -20p + 8$
nation 1 escalate	$-20q + 8, 4q - 16$	$-12, -12$

Figure 4.5 Normal form for detection game

cells correspond to the four *initial* strategic choice combinations. If both nations limit their arms, the top branch of figure 4.4 applies and payoffs are 4 to each nation. If, for example, nation 1 escalates, then nation 2 may first limit arms and then detect with probability q, or else not detect with probability $1 - q$ for an expected payoff of $-12q - 16(1 - q) = 4q - 16$ in the left-hand bottom cell. The other payoffs are computed from the game tree in a similar fashion.

The game in figure 4.5 can have two Nash equilibria depending upon the detection probabilities. If, for instance, we have $4 > -20q + 8$ and $4 > -20p + 8$, then neither nation would unilaterally want to move away from an agreement to mutually limit arms in the top left-hand box. When both detection probabilities are each greater than 0.20, the disarmament agreement is an equilibrium. *Thus, verification can help support disarmament.* With less than perfect verification, joint escalation is also a Nash equilibrium with $-12 > 4p - 16$ and $-12 > 4q - 16$, or equivalently, verification probabilities are less than one. With perfect verification, the only Nash equilibrium is disarmament. Moreover, if verification is impossible, so that $p = q = 0$, then the game in figure 4.5 degenerates to the Prisoner's Dilemma of figure 4.1. In fact, for verification probabilities less than 0.20, the game has the payoff configuration of a Prisoner's Dilemma with mutual escalation as the unique Nash equilibrium.

Many variations on this theme are possible. For example, detection may also be germane to the limitation decision, so that a nation may mistakenly think that its counterpart is escalating when it is not. Other variations concern additional players and/or additional stages to the game. The probabilities of detection may be made endogenous and learning could be introduced. The latter could be based on a Bayesian updating process, whereby actions taken in a preceding period serve as a signal by which the uninformed nation reassesses its prior probability distribution.

As a final game example, we illustrate a generic two-stage *Conflict game* introduced by Brams and Kilgour (1988). This game is notable because it is able to embrace as special cases a host of simple game structures including the Prisoner's Dilemma and Chicken. In addition, it can be generalized to an infinite number of stages with the use of discount factors. In the first stage, two nations – A and B – must each decide whether to cooperate (C) or not cooperate ($\overline{C}$). Cooperation may denote limiting arms, while not cooperate may indicate escalating arms acquisition. In the second stage, each nation that chose C in the initial stage must now decide whether to retaliate (R) or not retaliate ($\overline{R}$) if its adversary had chosen $\overline{C}$ in the initial stage. If, however, both nations failed to cooperate in the first stage, then this noncooperation continues, retaliation is unnecessary to heighten the ongoing conflict. This two-stage game determines the potential influence of the threat of subsequent retaliation on the initial choice of cooperation. If retaliation is sufficiently costly, then a nation may be deterred from not cooperating initially.

After cooperating initially, each nation has two strategies in the second stage: (1) tit-for-tat, denoted by CR, or (2) unconditional cooperation, indicated by $C\overline{R}$. For tit-for-tat, the nation's second-stage choice matches its opponent's first-stage choice; hence, the nation retaliates if the opponent failed to cooperate initially, while the nation cooperates if the opponent cooperated initially. In total, each nation has three strategies for the two-stage game: $\overline{C}$, CR, and $C\overline{R}$. There are nine strategy combinations as depicted in the 3 by 3 game matrix of figure 4.6. In each cell, r_i is the payoff to nation A and c_j is the payoff to nation B. Six distinct payoff combinations are possible: a trap (TR) or arms race; B retaliates (BR); A retaliates (AR); A wins (AW); B wins (BW), and the status quo (SQ). Status quo occurs when both players cooperate in the first round, since no retaliation would come in the second stage. The nine cells are labeled accordingly in figure 4.6.

We follow Brams and Kilgour (1988, p. 191) and assume that
(1) winning is preferred to the status quo so that $r_4 > r_3$ and $c_4 > c_3$;
(2) the status quo is preferred to the other player winning, so that $r_3 > r_2$ and $c_3 > c_2$; and
(3) the status quo is preferred to any of the three noncooperative outcomes, so that $r_3 > \max\{r_A, r_B, r_T\}$ and $c_3 > \max\{c_A, c_B, c_T\}$.

Given these assumptions, the asterisks denote the four possible Nash equilibria of figure 4.6, depending upon the values assigned to the r_2, r_A, r_B, r_T and the corresponding c_js. The tit-for-tat combination and its implied cooperation to limit arms is the sole Nash equilibrium provided that either

		nation B		
		$\bar{C}$	CR	$C\bar{R}$
nation A	$\bar{C}$	* TR $\qquad$ r_T, c_T	BR $\qquad$ r_B, c_B	* AW $\qquad$ r_4, c_2
	CR	AR $\qquad$ r_A, c_A	* SQ $\qquad$ r_3, c_3	SQ $\qquad$ r_3, c_3
	$C\bar{R}$	* BW $\qquad$ r_2, c_4	SQ $\qquad$ r_3, c_3	SQ $\qquad$ r_3, c_3

Figure 4.6 Conflict game

$$r_A > \max\{r_2, r_T\} \text{ and } c_2 < \max\{c_B, c_T\}$$

or

$$c_B > \max\{c_2, c_T\} \text{ and } r_2 < \max\{r_A, r_T\}.$$

These conditions imply that one nation places a high value on retaliating, while the other places a low value on losing. In this case, cooperation is maintained because each nation believes that its opponent is committed to retaliating and that the consequences of retaliation are very undesirable. As Brams and Kilgour (1988, p. 194) point out, the CR combination may result even for other payoff patterns if the nations can credibly precommit to retaliation. Automatic retaliatory responses, as embodied by the "Doomsday Machine" from *Dr Strangelove* that launches all missiles as soon as an attack is sensed, is a precommitment mechanism. The reader should identify the other inequalities that must hold for TR, AW, and BW to be Nash equilibria.[7]

The Conflict Game is analogous to Chicken if both nations prefer losing to the outbreak of war. If, moreover, the tit-for-tat strategy is removed for both nations, then the analogy is precise whenever $c_2 > c_T$ and $r_2 > r_T$. On the other hand, a Prisoner's Dilemma results when the

---

[7] BW is an equilibrium if and only if $r_2 \geqslant \max\{r_A, r_T\}$; AW is an equilibrium if and only if $c_2 \geqslant \max\{c_B, c_T\}$; and TR is an equilibrium if and only if $r_1 \geqslant \max\{r_A, r_2\}$ and $c_T \geqslant \max\{c_B, c_2\}$.

players prefer the war outcome to losing – i.e., $c_T > c_2$ and $r_T > r_2$ – and tit-for-tat is not an option.

For most examples, we have assumed complete information on the part of rivals, so that each knows the payoffs of its counterpart and can identify likely strategies. Dixit and Nalebuff (1991, pp. 107–13) examined conflict-type games when players may have misperceptions in which a cooperative action may be misinterpreted as noncooperative. If such misperceptions are allowed, then tit-for-tat may compound errors and lead to undesirable outcomes. According to Dixit and Nalebuff (1991, p. 111), "[w]hen misperceptions are possible, in the long run tit-for-tat will spend half the time cooperating and half of it defecting." Thus, tit-for-tat may have drawbacks under some scenarios.

Kuenne (1989) has presented a contrasting analysis of mature-rivalry conflict, where a repeated interaction "restrains conflict through the fostering of mind-sets, institutions, and conditions that enhance cooperation." Nations, locked in perpetual confrontation, will learn one another's mind sets and this leads to reduced uncertainty that, in turn, lessens conflict. The superpowers at the end of the cold war may be a case in point. To properly model this situation, we would need a repeated game with learning.

Space does not permit us to examine the various extensions to these simple game representations or experimental findings. Significant extensions include the study of n-players Prisoner's Dilemmas (Boulding, 1962; Schelling, 1980; Ordeshook, 1986), alternative multi-stage games (Majeski, 1984), and uncertainty (Brams and Kilgour, 1988; Brams, Davis, and Straffin, 1979). The simple game representation has provided important insights. First, it has demonstrated that a nation's independent or noncooperative pursuit of its self interest may give rise to an arms race dilemma at which both opponents are worse off than had they limited arms. Second, this suboptimal equilibrium may be resilient; even repeated interactions may give the same outcome. Third, the simple game structure has demonstrated the importance of arms-limitation verification. Fourth, the threat of retaliation, if credible and automatic, can alter the payoffs for a repeated game scenario, so that the nations begin to limit their armaments. Fifth, the game framework can accommodate further complexities including asymmetric information, n-nations, signaling and learning.

4.2   The Richardson model

Many of the current theories of arms races are related in some manner to the seminal study by Lewis F. Richardson (1960). Even though the original Richardson model is a mechanical exercise wherein the identity of the optimizers or agents is not clearly identified, the model can be derived from a host of explicit optimization models.[8] Our discussion focuses on a two-nation Richardson model where the opponents are labeled as nations A and B. For the basic Richardson model, each nation is treated as a single unified actor; the exact identity of the decision maker is not addressed. Additionally, M_i, i = A, B, denotes the stock of military weapons in nation i and can represent the stock of missiles. In some representations, M_i is used to indicate the nation's military expenditures. An overhead dot denotes a time derivative, so that $\dot{M}_i = dM_i/dt$ or the change in the military weapon stock (or expenditures) over time.

The Richardson model for two nations consists of two differential equations

$$\dot{M}_A = kM_B - \alpha M_A + g, \qquad (k, \alpha > 0) \qquad (4.1)$$

$$\dot{M}_B = \ell M_A - \beta M_B + h, \qquad (\ell, \beta > 0) \qquad (4.2)$$

where g and h can be positive or negative. In equation (4.1), the change in the military stock in nation A over time is positively related to its adversary's military weapon stock and negatively related to its own stockpile. If g is positive, then the change in a country's military stockpile is also positively related to g, known as a *grievance factor*, which indicates that a nation may augment its armament even though the other nation poses no threat. Grievance may arise from a past defeat (Germany after World War I, or Iraq after the Gulf War) or else from territorial or religious disputes. In (4.1), the first right-hand side term depicts the arms race or *reaction component* where k is the reaction coefficient. This term represents nation A's change in its weapons stock in reaction to the level of nation B's stockpile. The second right-hand side expression depicts the *fatigue factor* in which nation A diminishes its rate of armament expansion in proportion to its existing forces. This expression reflects economic considerations or constraints that limit the nation's ability to redirect resources from civilian uses. Moreover, the fatigue term may also reflect the depreciation of the existing weapons stock as resources must be allocated to maintain current stockpiles. The interpretation of (4.2) for nation B is analogous.

A *steady-state* equilibrium is found by assuming that the weapons stocks do not change in the opposing nations, so that $\dot{M}_A = \dot{M}_B = 0$. By replacing these latter terms with 0 in (4.1)–(4.2), we can solve for the

[8] See, especially, Abelson (1963), Isard and Anderton (1988), Caspary (1967), Intriligator (1975), Intriligator and Brito (1976, 1989a), and Simaan and Cruz (1973, 1975).

steady-state equilibrium levels of military stocks, denoted by M_A^o and M_B^o:

$$M_A^o = (kh + \beta g)/(\alpha\beta - k\ell), \tag{4.3}$$

$$M_B^o = (\ell h + \alpha h)/(\alpha\beta - k\ell). \tag{4.4}$$

The denominators are positive if $\alpha\beta > k\ell$ or the product of the fatigue coefficients is greater than the product of the reaction coefficients. The condition for equilibrium stability is also dependent on the product $\alpha\beta$ exceeding that of $k\ell$ (Richardson, 1960, 23–8; Wolfson, 1968, 1990).[9] Roughly speaking, stability results when fatigue influences eventually overwhelm the reaction influences. If, on the other hand, $k\ell$ exceeds $\alpha\beta$, then the equilibrium is unstable. When the two products are equal, the reaction paths are parallel straight lines, and either no equilibrium exists or else every point is an equilibrium on the reaction paths if they are coincident.

To depict the Richardson model geometrically, we now assume specific parameters. In particular, we have

$$M_B - 2M_A + 2 = 0 \tag{4.5}$$

$$M_A - 2M_B + 2 = 0 \tag{4.6}$$

for the steady-state equations when $\dot{M}_A = \dot{M}_B = 0$ and $\alpha = 2$, $\beta = 2$, $\ell = 1$, $k = 1$, $g = 2$, and $h = 2$. These equations can be expressed as

$$M_i = 0.5M_j + 1 \qquad i, j = A, B; \qquad i \neq j. \tag{4.7}$$

The equilibrium occurs at $M_A^o = M_B^o = 2$, as can be seen from equations (4.3)–(4.4). Furthermore, this equilibrium is stable, since $\alpha\beta = 4 > 1 = k\ell$. We illustrate this stable Richardson model in the phase diagram of figure 4.7, where M_B is measured on the vertical axis and M_A on the horizontal axis. The steady-state path for nation B (i.e., $\dot{M}_B = 0$ line) in equation (4.7) has y-intercept at $M_B = 1$ and slope of 0.5; the steady-

---

[9]   For stability, we investigate the steady-state equation system

$$-\alpha M_A + kM_B + g = 0$$
$$\ell M_A - \beta M_B + h = 0,$$

whose coefficient matrix is $A = \begin{bmatrix} -\alpha & k \\ \ell & -\beta \end{bmatrix}$,

which is a Metzler matrix, since its nondiagonal elements are nonnegative. The eigenvalues of the system are the solution to the roots of the characteristic equation $[\lambda I - A] = 0$, where I is the identity matrix. This equation implies that

$$\lambda^2 + (\alpha + \beta)\lambda + (\alpha\beta - k\ell) = 0,$$

where λ is the eigenvalue. By the Routh sign test, stability results if all coefficients are positive so that both roots are negative which, in turn, requires $(\alpha\beta - k\ell) > 0$.

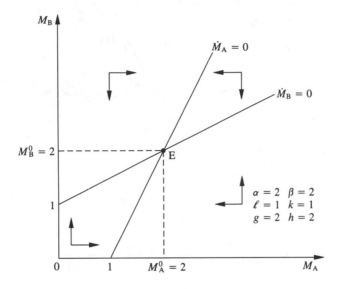

Figure 4.7 Stable Richardson model

state path for nation A (i.e., $\dot{M}_A = 0$ line) has x-intercept at $M_A = 1$ and slope of 2. The equilibrium at point E is at (2, 2).

We next construct the phase dynamics that tells us the movement of trajectories from points away from point E. To determine the behavior of M_A, we determine when $\dot{M}_A > 0$ by setting equation (4.5) to be greater than zero. This tells us that M_A increases (decreases) to the left (right) of the $\dot{M}_A = 0$ line, since $\dot{M}_A > 0$ (< 0) when $M_A < (>) 0.5M_B + 1$. Hence, we put horizontal arrows pointing rightwards (leftwards) to the left (right) of the steady-state line $\dot{M}_A = 0$. A similar exercise determines the behavior of M_B above and below the steady-state path $\dot{M}_B = 0$. The phase diagram indicates that the equilibrium is stable in figure 4.7, because weapons stock combinations away from E are funneled towards point E.

To illustrate an unstable Richardson model, we change the parameters, so that $\alpha = 1$, $\beta = 1$, $\ell = 2$, $k = 2$, $g = -2$, and $h = -2$. These parameters are associated with an unstable equilibrium, because $\alpha\beta = 1 < 4 = k\ell$. In figure 4.8, the steady-state lines are displayed along with the unstable equilibrium at point E. The phase indicators imply that trajectories that get between the steady-state lines above point E are deflected towards a never-ending arms race, while trajectories that get between these lines below point E are deflected towards the origin.

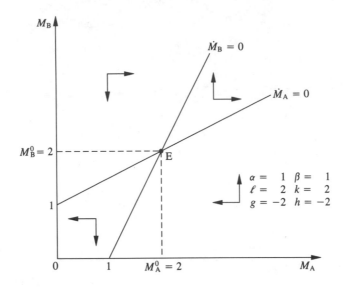

Figure 4.8 Unstable Richardson model

For empirical analyses, the Richardson equations are often given in discrete form

$$\Delta M_A = k M_B(t) - \alpha M_A(t) + g \qquad (4.8)$$

$$\Delta M_B = \ell M_A(t) - \beta M_B(t) + h \qquad (4.9)$$

in which t denotes the time period and $\Delta M_i = M_i(t) - M_i(t - 1)$, $i = A, B$, is the annual difference in military stocks in country i. Another variant of the discrete form is

$$\Delta M_A = k M_B(t - 1) - \alpha M_A(t) + g \qquad (4.10)$$

$$\Delta M_B = \ell M_A(t - 1) - \beta M_B(t) + h \qquad (4.11)$$

in which the change in M_i is related to its enemy's lagged stock value (McGuire, 1977). Of course, many other variants are possible.

The Richardson model consists of a linear dynamic system. Non-linearities would change the dynamics and analysis considerably (Wolfson, 1968, 1990). As mentioned at the outset, the Richardson model does not have much to say about who is making the decision or what is being optimized. Recent optimization-based models can be made to generate, under special assumptions, the Richardson system (see sections 4.4 and 4.5). Economic constraints are implicit to the model insofar as the fatigue terms may serve to limit uncontrolled arms races. A clear drawback of the model is the absence of any kind of strategic considerations in terms of the targeting decisions (see section 4.4). Hypothetical scenarios of missile exchanges would enable decision makers to judge the stability associated with opposing weapon stockpiles. In addition, the model does not really tell when an arms race might lead to the outbreak of war. The model does not allow the coefficients to change with time or experience; hence, parameters are static. Furthermore, alliance interactions are not modeled explicitly. The extensions to the Richardson analysis attempt to examine these issues.

4.3   Alternative Richardson models

The variants of the Richardson model are, indeed, large in number; hence, space limitations require that we be rather selective. We, therefore, choose some representative models to highlight the following themes: emulation, rivalry, submissiveness, secrecy, bureaucracy, and politics.

Murray Wolfson (1968) introduced a variant of the Richardson model in which the opponents attempt to emulate one another's military stock or military expenditures (see also Isard and Anderton, 1988). In the emulative model, military expenditure is a natural choice for the arms variable. A standard representation for this model is

$$\dot{M}_A = k(M_B - M_A) - \alpha M_A + g, \tag{4.12}$$

$$\dot{M}_B = k(M_A - M_B) - \beta M_B + h, \tag{4.13}$$

which can be rewritten as

$$\dot{M}_A = kM_B - (\alpha + k)M_A + g, \tag{4.14}$$

$$\dot{M}_B = \ell M_A - (\beta + \ell)M_B + h. \tag{4.15}$$

In equations (4.12)–(4.13), the change in military armaments is based on the *difference* between a nation's own activity and that of its opponent, a fatigue term, and a grievance term. When rewritten as (4.14)–(4.15), we see that the emulation assumption serves as an additional drag or fatigue factor, in terms of $-kM_A$ in (4.14) [or $-\ell M_B$ in (4.15)], to the arms race. Reactive factors give rise to fatigue, since reaction is based on achieving parity not dominance. This check to the arms race is highlighted by computing the new requirement for stability

$$(\alpha + k)(\beta + \ell) > k\ell. \tag{4.16}$$

For positive coefficients, as assumed, *this stability condition always holds*. Thus, Wolfson (1968) indicated that the emulation model is inconsistent with an unchecked arms race. Although this is true, the equilibrium levels of military expenditures (stocks) may be very high and may take many years to achieve, over which time an arms race is in progress.

With the cold war period in mind, Wolfson (1968, 1990) formulated a *rivalry* model that characterized the United States (nation A) as resisting the Soviet Union's (nation B's) success in the arms race. This success is measured by the difference between the two nation's stock of armaments in the preceding period. In contrast, the Soviet Union is depicted as wanting to dominate the United States, so that the Soviet Union reacts to *a multiple of its own success*. The Wolfson (1968) model is indicated in discrete form

$$M_A(t) = k[M_B(t-1) - M_A(t-1)] + \alpha M_A(t-1)$$
$$+ k'M_B(t-1) \tag{4.17}$$

$$M_B(t) = \ell[M_B(t-1) - M_A(t-1)] + \ell'M_B(t-1)$$
$$+ \beta M_B(t-1). \tag{4.18}$$

Wolfson's rivalry model differs from the emulative model in a number of ways. First, the rivalry model does not have grievance factors. Second, and most important, stability is no longer assured (Wolfson, 1990, 225–6). Low levels of reactive coefficients are more apt to be stable than high levels. *Ceteris paribus*, the closer are the propensities of the two countries to react to Soviet success, the more likely is the arms race to be stable. Third, the opponents are not treated symmetrically: The Soviet Union is characterized as trying to outdo the United States, while the United States is seen as attempting to keep up with the Soviet Union. Wolfson claimed that his model provides a more accurate picture of the arms race during the cold war than alternatives such as the emulative model, since the dynamics of the rivalry model appear more realistic. This may be true, but the claim can be best substantiated by empirical estimation, which Wolfson (1968, 1990) did not attempt. In an interesting empirical study, Zinnes and Gillespie (1973) comes to a different characterization of the cold war rivals – the Warsaw Pact tended to be submissive, while the NATO alliance was reactive and nonsubmissive.

Wolfson (1968, 1990) also analyzed a nonlinear representation of his rivalry model where the reaction coefficients are allowed to vary (see also Lucier, 1979; Wallace and Wilson, 1978). In particular, the values of the reaction coefficients, k and ℓ, might depend on the relative values of M_A and M_B. In the case of the United States, it may have a zero reaction once its armaments exceed those of the Warsaw Pact. Wolfson allowed for discrete shifts in the values of these coefficients and simulated some numerical solutions.

Yet another variant of the Richardson model is the submissiveness model (Isard and Anderton, 1988, p. 22; Zinnes and Gillespie, 1973). In this variant, the difference between the military expenditure levels in the two rival countries serves, in part, as a weighting factor on the reaction coefficients. For nation A, the differential equation is

$$\dot{M}_A = [1 - \phi(M_B - M_A)] \cdot k M_B - \alpha M_A + g. \tag{4.19}$$

An analogous equation holds for nation B. The last two terms in (4.19) denote the fatigue and grievance terms, respectively. When nation A has the disadvantage, so that $M_B > M_A$, the standard reaction term $k M_B$ is weighted by the negative term in brackets. If, however, nation A has the advantage, then it is more aggressive than in the standard model, which, in turn, applies when $M_A = M_B$, so that $\phi(M_B - M_A) = 0$. This model highlights asymmetries and how these asymmetries can promote stability.

As mentioned earlier, the Richardson models may be formulated in terms of military expenditures or military stocks. Often, these alternative representations are implicitly assumed to be interchangeable. Brito (1972) and Ward (1984), among others, are careful to distinguish between expenditures and stock terms. In general, a change in military stocks, S, can be related to military expenditures by

$$\dot{S}_A = M_A - \delta S_A, \tag{4.20}$$

where S_A denotes the current military stock in nation A, and δS_A indicates the depreciation of the stock in that period.[10] Hence, stocks grow by the difference between current expenditures and depreciation.

Other variants of the basic Richardson model include using military expenditures or stocks in ratio form (e.g., Rattinger, 1975; Wallace and Wilson, 1978; Zinnes and Gillespie, 1973), or employing alternative lag structures for the variables (e.g., Gillespie, Zinnes, and Rubison, 1978; Majeski, 1985; Majeski and Jones, 1981; and McGuire, 1977). The use of the ratio form permits alternative representations for threat and is closely related to the rivalry model when fatigue and grievance factors are absent (Isard and Anderton, 1988, p. 23). An alteration to the lag structure can be associated with vastly different dynamics and stability.

Thus far, the variants analyzed share the same mechanistic setup as the Richardson model, since economic constraints, the identity of the agent, strategic considerations, and the agents' objective are not *explicitly* identified. The alternative models considered in the remainder of this

---

[10] In equation (4.20), the price of military expenditures has been normalized to equal 1. For nonnormalized prices, we replace M_A with M_A/p where p is the per unit price of military goods. On stock adjustment models, see Caspary (1967), Moll and Luebbert (1980), Rattinger (1975), and Smoker (1965).

section and in sections 4.4–4.6 account for one or more of these considerations.

In an important contribution, McGuire (1965) introduced the utility maximization assumption, the economic constraint, and the strategic aspect. With a static resource allocation framework, McGuire characterized a nation as maximizing its citizens' social welfare, W, subject to a linear resource constraint. The exact identity of the nation's decision maker was not indicated; hence, it could be the executive branch or some other body. Social welfare in nation A depends on its security and civilian consumption. Security, in turn, is a function of $\bar{M}_A$ and $\bar{M}_B$, where

$\bar{M}_A$ = is the minimal (assured) number of A's missiles from its stockpile, M_A, that survives an attack by nation B; and

$\bar{M}_B$ = is the maximal (assured) number of B's missiles from its stockpile, M_B, that is destroyed during an attack by A.

In each case, "assured" refers to an acceptable probability level. $\bar{M}_A$ denotes nation A's deterrence potential, since surviving forces can be used in a retaliatory strike. $\bar{M}_B$ represents nation B's retaliatory strength and, hence, B's deterrence. Both of these factors are themselves a function of missile stocks as well as other strategic factors. Hence, social welfare in nation A equals

$$W_A = W_A[\bar{M}_A(M_A, M_B), \bar{M}_B(M_A, M_B), Y_A], \qquad (4.21)$$

where Y_A indicates civilian output.

When social welfare is maximized subject to the resource constraint, marginal cost of M_A must equal the sum of two marginal benefits derived from M_A. The first marginal benefit stems from the increase in A's deterrence, and the second from the decrease in the retaliatory threat from abroad. The static nature of McGuire's (1965) allocation model is an obvious drawback,[11] but his model is nevertheless of crucial importance for arms race modeling, since it indicates that strategic considerations of deterrence and retaliatory threat must be included.

Another class of arms race models are *bureaucratic*, insofar as bureaucratic influences in a nation's military establishment are viewed as making defense budget decisions. In general, bureaucrats are characterized as basing these decisions on the following factors: the size of the previous year's military expenditure, $M_i(t - 1)$; the level of perceived

---

[11] Other parts of McGuire's (1965) analysis were dynamic and extended Richardson's analysis to uncertain situations, where secrecy and intelligence played a role (Isard and Anderton, 1988, pp. 44–6). Secrecy can worsen an arms race if a risk-averse opponent reacts to uncertainty by increasing missile stockpiles.

tension or threat posed by the rival; and grievances. Models may include some or all of these factors. Rattinger (1975), for instance, distinguished between the desired defense budget in nation A, m_A, and the actual defense budget, M_A. Bureaucratic influences were said to make desired military expenditures in the current period (year t) proportional to the military expenditures in the previous period

$$m_A = KM_A(t - 1), \qquad (4.22)$$

where K is constant. Relationships, such as (4.22), form the basis of most bureaucratic models in which decision makers are attempting to increase the size of the budget that they manage, based on earlier budgets. Equation (4.22) can be used to predict defense levels, but, strictly speaking, it does not denote an arms race, because there is no interaction between rivals.

This rivalry factor can be introduced by making some measure of the *change* in nation A's military expenditures dependent on the military expenditures in B. Rattinger (1975) proposed the following alternative

$$m_A(t) - M_A(t) = K'[M_B(t - 1) - m_B(t - 1)] + g, \qquad (4.23)$$

and a similar expression for nation B. In (4.23), the difference between desired and actual defense spending in the current period is proportional to the difference between the rival's actual and desired defense spending in the preceding period. The additive constant is a grievance factor. Many variants for (4.23) exist. If the term in brackets vanished or if $K' = 0$, then (4.23) degenerates to the bureaucratic model in (4.22).

Sometimes the bureaucratic model is represented as a stock adjustment model (Boulding, 1962; Intriligator and Brito, 1989a; McGuire 1977), so that we have

$$\dot{M}_A = K(m_A - M_A) \qquad (4.24)$$

$$\dot{M}_B = K(m_B - M_B) \qquad (4.25)$$

for the continuous case. Desired stocks are a linear function of the rival's expenditures

$$m_A = kM_B + g' \qquad (4.26)$$

$$m_B = \ell M_B + h'. \qquad (4.27)$$

If the latter two equations are substituted into (4.24) and (4.25), respectively, for the desired expenditures, then the Richardson model results. This means that the Richardson model is entirely consistent with bureaucratic behavior.

Stoll (1982) presented a bureaucratic model in which the change in nation A's military expenditures is proportional to the previous year's budget

$$\Delta M_A = K'' M_A(t - 1). \tag{4.28}$$

This equation implies the following time path for M_A:

$$M_A(t) = (1 + g_A)^t M_A(0) \tag{4.29}$$

where g_A is the growth rate of A's military expenditures and $M_A(0)$ is the initial expenditure level. A similar equation holds for nation B. Equation (4.29) can be expressed as

$$\Delta M_A = (1 + g_A)^{t-1} g_A M_A(0). \tag{4.30}$$

Stoll made the interesting observation that we can find constants where

$$M_A(0) = s M_B(0) \tag{4.31}$$

and

$$g_A = r + g_B, \tag{4.32}$$

which when substituted into (4.29) implies that ΔM_A is related to *both* countries' growth rate in military expenditures even though the true model only depends on the nation's own expenditures level. This has significant implications for econometric estimation: multi-collinearity will exist between the rivals' defense expenditure levels even when bureaucratic influences are independent of threat.

Yet another class of models bases defense expenditure decisions on political or public choice factors (also see chapter 5). Important contributions include Cusack and Ward (1981), Hartley and Russett (1992), Lucier (1979), Luterbacher (1975), Ostrom (1977), and Rattinger (1975). Hartley and Russett (1992), for example, used US data to show that changes in public opinion have a lagged effect on policy making. An increase (decrease) in the public's support for defense spending is predicted to be followed by an increase (decrease) in defense budgets. Ostrom (1977) developed two models to depict the arms race and its relationship to organization politics. More complicated models have tried to show the relationship among multiple agents (e.g., defense contractors, the public, and the Congress) in the procurement and budgetary process.

A distinction is sometimes made between arms-building and arms-using models (Anderton, 1990a; Moll and Luebbert, 1980; Taylor, 1974). The former includes the Richardson model and its myriad offshoots, while the latter is based on the Lanchester (1916) model of warfare, which depicts a dynamic process of engagement. In a Lanchester (1916) model, the reduction in forces in, say, nation A is based on the rate of fire and effectiveness of its opponent's arsenal. During engagement, missile or weapon stocks, M, are depleted as follows

$$\dot{M}_A = -\beta M_B \tag{4.33}$$

$$\dot{M}_B = -\alpha M_A, \tag{4.34}$$

where M_B denote the weapon stock in B that is directed against A, and β indicates the "hitting power'" of these missiles in terms of losses in A. A similar interpretation holds for (4.34) and country B. The Lanchester model is akin to models by Intriligator, Brito, and others[12] that include strategic factors in the Richardson framework (see section 4.4), since these strategic models often include an arms-using analysis as a hypothetical device to assess security. How weapons might be drawn down during hypothetical military engagements influences the kinds and quantity of weapons accumulated. Anderton (1990a, 1993) have explicitly used the Lanchester framework to derive an attack/defend model to analyze arms races. His interesting analysis identified arms race stability and instability, and was applied to the study of disarmament. Insofar as the Lanchester formulation is typically utilized to explain conventional wars, weapon attrition owing to the firing decision is not included. Tanks and bombers can be used over and over again. If, however, the Lanchester model were applied to a nuclear missile exchange, then attrition due to firing would have to be included.

The Lanchester model can be used in a number of ways; for example, Anderton (1993) extended the model to include armament attrition and resupply during war. In doing so, he demonstrated the importance of rivals' *relative* economic supply potential. Balanced arms reductions may give imbalanced outcomes if the opponents have vastly different re-supply abilities. These supply-side factors are especially important when wars are protracted.

4.4   Strategic factors

Strategic elements were combined with the Richardson model in a series of influential papers written by Dagobert Brito and Michael Intriligator during the 1970s and 1980s (see, e.g., Intriligator, 1975, 1982; Intriligator and Brito, 1989a, 1989b; Wolfson, 1992). This analysis not only

---

[12]   Other strategic models include Anderton (1986, 1990b), Anderton and Fogarty (1990), Brito and Intriligator (1974, 1977), Fischer (1984), Intriligator and Brito (1976, 1978, 1984, 1987), Intriligator (1975), Mayer (1986), and Wolfson (1992).

conceptualized the arms race interaction during the cold war era, but it also provided policy conclusions concerning arms escalation, proliferation of nuclear weapons, arms control, and the outbreak of war.

We shall focus on the basic model, used to represent two superpowers who confront one another with missile stockpiles (Intriligator, 1975). Each nation is interested in ascertaining the levels of its missile stockpile that, given the rival's stockpile, would deter an attack. Deterrence requires that a second-strike retaliatory attack can inflict unacceptable casualties on the attacker. Moreover, each nation wants to know the levels of its missile stockpile that would allow it to attack with impunity, where retaliation-induced casualties are acceptable. Following Intriligator (1975), the notation for this model is:

$M_i(t)$ = stock of missiles at time t in nation i, i = A, B;

$\dot{M}_i(t)$ = change in stock of missiles at time t in nation i;

$C_i(t)$ = civilian casualties at time t in nation i;

$\dot{C}_i(t)$ = change in civilian casualties at time t in nation i;

$\alpha(t)$ = rate of fire in nation A at time t;

$\beta(t)$ = rate of fire in nation B at time t;

$\alpha'(t)$ = counterforce proportion in nation A (i.e., proportion of A's missiles aimed at rival's missiles);

$\beta'(t)$ = counterforce proportion in nation B;

f_A = the number of B's missiles destroyed by one of A's missiles;

f_B = the number of A's missiles destroyed by one of B's missiles;

v_A = the number of B's casualties caused by one of A's missiles;

v_B = the number of A's casualties caused by one of B's missiles;

M_A^o = $M_A(0)$; and

M_B^o = $M_B(0)$.

The Intriligator model is made up of four equations: two for the rivals' change in missile stocks and two for the rivals' change in casualties. Missiles change according to

$$\dot{M}_A = -\alpha M_A - \beta' \beta M_B f_B, \tag{4.35}$$

$$\dot{M}_B = -\beta M_B - \alpha' \alpha M_A f_A. \tag{4.36}$$

In (4.35), A's stock of missiles drops by $-\alpha M_A$ owing to A's firing decision and by $-\beta' \beta M_B f_B$ owing to B's counterforce attack consisting of $\beta' \beta M_B$ missiles. An analogous interpretation holds for the change in

B's stock of missiles. Initially, each nation starts with no casualties. Casualties would then change according to

$$\dot{C}_A = (1 - \beta')\beta M_B v_B, \tag{4.37}$$

$$\dot{C}_B = (1 - \alpha')\alpha M_A v_A. \tag{4.38}$$

In (4.37), casualties in A are proportional to the number of B's missiles fired (βM_B), the proportion of these missiles aimed at A's population $(1 - \beta')$, and the effectiveness of B's missiles in causing casualties in A (v_B). Missiles directed at A's population are termed *countervalue*, while missiles fired at A's missiles are *counterforce*. Countervalue missiles fired from B inflict $(1 - \beta')\beta M_B v_B$ casualties in A. A similar interpretation holds for B's casualties, given in (4.38).

Strategic elements are introduced by examining deterrence and attack scenarios. An attacker must recognize that surviving missiles in a targeted country will be used against the aggressor on a second strike. Deterrence is based on second-strike countervalue capabilities, while the attack decision is dependent on first-strike capabilities.

If two opponents want to deter, then each must possess sufficient missile stockpiles to absorb an all-out first-strike and still respond with a second strike that leaves unacceptable devastation. Suppose that nation A initiates war. It would choose a maximum rate of fire, $\alpha = \bar{\alpha}$, aimed at B's missiles so that $\alpha' = 1$. This strategy gives the maximum crippling blow. Further suppose that this first strike lasts t_A minutes during which time the targeted nation cannot respond so that $\beta = 0$. By inserting these parameter values into equations (4.35)–(4.36) and integrating from $t = 0$ to $t = t_A$, we find that nation A would be left with

$$M_A(t_A) = M_A^o \exp(-\bar{\alpha} t_A) \tag{4.39}$$

missiles, and nation B would have

$$M_B(t_A) = M_B^o - f_A[1 - \exp(-\bar{\alpha} t_A)]M_A^o \tag{4.40}$$

remaining missiles. In (4.40), the term $[1 - \exp(-\bar{\alpha} t_A)]M_A^o$ denotes the number of missiles fired by A.

During the retaliatory phase, nation B desires to punish nation A as severely as possible; hence, it would fire at the maximum rate, $\beta = \bar{\beta}$ and would target B's population, so that $\beta' = 0$. If the retaliatory phase goes from $t = t_A$ to $t = t_A + t_B$, then during this phase we set $\alpha = 0$. With these parameters plugged into (4.35)–(4.38), integration of the resulting equations gives the number of casualties in A as

$$C_A(t_A + t_B) = v_B\{M_B^o - f_A[1 - \exp(-\bar{\alpha} t_A)]M_A^o\}[1 - \exp(-\bar{\beta} t_B)]$$

$$\tag{4.41}$$

by the end of the retaliatory strike. An analogous analysis would apply if the role of the attacker and retaliator were switched.

We first determine the number of missiles in each country that would deter its opponent. To simplify the analysis without losing conceptual content, we assume that the firing interval is sufficiently long that the $\exp(\cdot)$ term can be replaced with zero in equations (4.39)–(4.41) (Wolfson, 1985). If nation B believes that $\bar{C}_A$ represents an unacceptable number of casualties for nation A, then nation B needs sufficient missiles to cause this level of deaths after absorbing a first-strike counterforce attack. We thus set $C_A = \bar{C}_A$, $M_A = M_A^o$, and $M_B = M_B^o$, and solve for M_B in equation (4.41). This gives

$$M_B = f_A M_A + \bar{C}_A / v_B \qquad (4.42)$$

as the "B deters" relationship. In (4.42), f_A, $\bar{C}_A$ and v_B are treated as constants. Roughly speaking, nation B needs sufficient missiles to absorb a first strike (with losses equal to $f_A M_A$), and still possess sufficient missiles to inflict $\bar{C}_A$ casualties, where $1/v_B$ converts casualties into missile requirements. Equation (4.42) is analogous to a linear Richardson equation that relates M_B and M_A at a steady state. Missile stockpiles in B that are greater than or equal to the right-hand side of (4.42) will deter an attack. Using an analogous derivation, nation A can deter an attack by B if nation A's missile stockpile satisfies

$$M_A = f_B M_B + \bar{C}_B / v_A. \qquad (4.43)$$

The system of equations in (4.42) and (4.43) is consistent with a stable equilibrium when $f_A f_B < 1$ (see section 4.2). Intriligator (1975, p. 345) referred to f_A and f_B being less than one as the "hardness" condition, because more than one missile is required to destroy an enemy missile. The hardness condition is sufficient for stability. If the time intervals were reintroduced, then these intervals would also influence the stability condition.[13] As compared with the Richardson condition, the stability condition takes a simpler form since neither (4.42) nor (4.43) contains a fatigue factor owing to the relatively short time level that a nuclear missile exchange would require.

We next turn to the scenario in which a nation contemplates the initiation of an attack. Conceptually, this requires the aggressor to have enough missiles to deliver a counterforce blow that leaves its foe with too few missiles to cause many casualties during a retaliatory strike. We denote the maximum acceptable casualty level for B by $\hat{C}_B$. To determine

---

[13] The stability condition then becomes
$$f_A f_B[1 - \exp(-\bar{\alpha} t_A)][1 - \exp(-\bar{\beta} t_B)] < 1.$$

the level of B missiles needed for an attack, we substitute $\hat{C}_B$ into the left-hand side of (4.41) as before,[14] and solve for M_B to yield

$$M_B = M_A/f_B - (\hat{C}_B/f_B v_A),\tag{4.44}$$

which is a Richardson steady-state equation. By a similar derivation, nation A will attack when its missile stockpile is

$$M_A = M_B/f_A - (\hat{C}_A/f_A v_B).\tag{4.45}$$

The simultaneous satisfaction of equations (4.44) and (4.45) gives an unstable equilibrium, since the product of the slopes of these equations must exceed one if the hardness condition is satisfied. Equations (4.42) and (4.45) have the same slope if graphed in (M_A, M_B) space; hence, the B deters line is parallel to the A attacks line. Similarly, equations (4.43) and (4.44) have the same slope in (M_A, M_B) space, so that the A deters line is parallel to the B attacks line. In each case, the intercept of the deter line is greater than the corresponding parallel attack line, because $\bar{C}_i > \hat{C}_i$ for $i =$ A, B.

4.4.1 Graphical presentation

Based on Intriligator's (1975) analysis, we present a diagrammatic depiction of the linear equation system of (4.42)–(4.45) in figure 4.9, where M_A is measured on the horizontal axis and M_B on the vertical axis. For example, the B deters line indicates the level of B missiles just sufficient to cause unacceptable second-strike losses to A for each level of A's missiles. The arrow indicates that levels of M_B above the B deters line are more than sufficient to deter A. A similar interpretation holds for the A deters line. In contrast, the B attacks line depicts the levels of B's missiles, for various M_A levels, that are adequate to destroy A's missile stockpile on a first strike, so that A's response causes acceptable casualties in the view of B's decision makers. The arrow indicates that M_B levels above this line are more than sufficient to permit B to attack.

Following Intriligator (1975), nine regions are distinguished. In region 4, both sides have sufficient stockpiles to forestall war; this is a region of stability and peace, known as the cone of mutual deterrence. In region 6, nation A has sufficient missiles to deter B, but insufficient to attack, while nation B has neither enough to attack nor deter A. Region 7 reverses these roles with B having the advantage. Intriligator called region 5 *jittery deterrence*, since neither side can deter nor attack the other. Equilibrium E is stable, and equilibrium E' is unstable. Upward

---

[14] We again set $M_A^\circ = M_A$, $M_B^\circ = M_B$ and ignore the exp$(\cdot)$ terms.

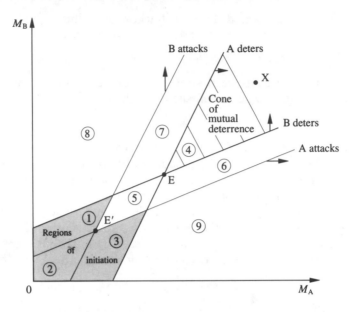

Figure 4.9 Cone of mutual deterence

spiralling arms races can occur between the parallel reaction paths in regions 5–7. In region 8, B has a decided power advantage, since it can both attack and deter A, but the latter can do neither. The power advantage is reversed in region 9. These regions can be peaceful, provided that the powerful nation possesses peaceful intentions. Potential concerns are associated with regions 1–3, which Intriligator called the *regions of war initiation*. In region 2, both nations can attack, but neither can deter. A *preemptive strike* by either side would end its fear of a surprise attack. In region 3, nation A has the means to attack, but not to deter, while nation B has inadequate missiles to attack or deter. According to Intriligator (1975, p. 350): "The result is that A is forced to initiate, since it has enough missiles for a first strike but not enough for a second strike. Only by preempting can A eliminate the fear of an attack by B which A is unable to deter." Roles are reversed in region 1.

A host of comparative static changes can be represented with the Intriligator graph (see Anderton, 1990a; Brito and Intriligator, 1974; Intriligator, 1975; Intriligator and Brito, 1989a). If, for example, $\bar{C}_B$ decreases so that nation A perceives that the minimal casualty level necessary to deter B has fallen, then the A deters line shifts leftwards in a parallel fashion and the cone of mutual deterrence increases in area. A similar effect occurs when v_A increases, implying that A's countervalue efficiency increases – each of A's missiles causes more casualties. A change in v_A would also shift the B attack line. Changes in either f_A or f_B would affect the slope of the two lines and, in consequence, would change the configuration of the regions. Stability may also be affected.

In a series of articles, researchers have used the Intriligator–Brito analysis to investigate other considerations. For example, Anderton and Fogarty (1990) generalized the analysis to include alternative assumptions about weapon effectiveness. This analysis also introduced two additional parallel lines for the case in which one side has sufficient missiles to disarm its opponent. Anderton and Fogarty examined three types of damage that result from an attack: ancillary (relating to weapon production and storage), civilian casualties, and consequential (occurring subsequent to the attack).

Wolfson (1992) extended the Intriligator–Brito analysis to question whether cones of deterrence exist when conflict involves more than three nations.[15] Wolfson demonstrated that a sufficient condition for a stable cone in the n-nation case is that $f_i \leqslant 1/(n - 1)$ for all i, where f_i is the effectiveness of i's counterforce missiles. Wolfson's finding indicates that missiles must become progressively less accurate as n increases if a stable cone is to exist. The proliferation of nuclear nations also brings into question the influence that coalition or alliance formation may have on stability (Brito and Intriligator, 1977).

Anderton (1992, pp. 79–81) has raised concerns about the pessimism of the Intriligator–Brito analysis. In particular, he questioned whether war would in reality be initiated in region 2 by a nation that is significantly outgunned. While a preemptive attack by a weak nation would cause great casualties in the more powerful rival, this would provide little comfort, since the (outgunned) initiator would suffer greatly from the nation that it attacks. A shift out of the attack lines gives a more optimistic scenario. Anderton's analysis seems to point to the need for additional constraints when identifying the zone of war initiation.

4.4.2   Policy implications

An important policy implication concerns arms control (also see chapter 11). Suppose that each nation has accumulated missile stockpiles corresponding to point X in figure 4.9. Mutual disarmament implies a movement from point X towards the origin as both nations decrease their stockpiles. If disarmament takes arms levels into region

---

[15] On n-nation arms races, also see Schrodt (1978).

1, 2, or 3, then a risk of warfare may result. According to Intriligator (1975, p. 351):

The process of disarmament can lead to highly explosive combinations of missile stocks, which could lead to war outbreak. Even if the process of disarming does not lead to war, the disarmed state itself is explosive, since, from it, either country could acquire a minimal stock of missiles which would enable it to attack the other with impunity.

Thus, large weapon stockpiles may have a stabilizing or deterring effect. Major disarmament ventures may be best if combined with policies that augment the size of the cone of mutual deterrence. Policies that, for example, reduce the minimal acceptable casualty level may be supportive for disarmament programs. A host of influences, including the effectiveness coefficients, the rates of fire, and the time intervals for firing, have an impact on the cone of mutual deterrence and need to be considered when initiating arms control or arms escalation, or adopting new weapons technology if stability is to be preserved (see Intriligator and Brito, 1984).

4.5   Normative analysis: optimal control and differential games

With the exception of the analysis of McGuire (1965) and Boulding (1962), the objectives of the two rivals are not explicit in the analysis. Thus, the arms race models tend to focus on the reactions to one another's weapons stockpiles, without indicating what drives these actions. In this section,[16] we briefly review more normative analyses that depict a nation's decision makers as maximizing their citizens' social welfare subject to a resource constraint and a dynamic stock adjustment constraint. The analysis is normative in the sense that a value judgment must be made when deciding what objective *should be* optimized. Normative papers are usually interested in establishing the existence and stability of an equilibrium. Typically, Richardson-type reaction paths are shown to follow from the analysis.

Brito (1972) presented an optimal control analysis in which each of two rival nations optimally allocates resources between civilian consumption, Y_i, and arms expenditure, Z_i. The social welfare, U_i, in each nation depends on civilian consumption and the level of security, D_i, which, in

---

[16] Since this section relies on some mathematically sophisticated concepts involving optimal control and differential games, some readers may want to skip to the next section.

turn, depends on the stocks of weapons in the rival nations. Social welfare equals

$$U_i = U_i[Y_i, D_i(M_i, M_j)], \qquad i = A, B, \qquad (4.46)$$

in which security increases with own weapon stocks and decreases with rival stocks. The marginal changes in security are assumed diminishing (i.e., $\partial^2 D_i/\partial^2 M_i \leqslant 0$) and the cross partials are assumed nonnegative ($\partial^2 D_i/\partial M_i \partial M_j \geqslant 0$). Furthermore, social welfare is assumed to increase in civilian consumption and security. At an equilibrium capital–labor ratio, the decision maker, in say A, is depicted as choosing civilian and military expenditure levels to

$$\text{maximize } \int_0^\infty e^{-rt} U_A[Y_A, D_A(M_A, M_B)]dt \qquad (4.47)$$

subject to:

$$\dot{M}_A = Z_A - \delta_A M_A \qquad (4.48)$$

$$I_A = Z_A + Y_A. \qquad (4.49)$$

The objective in (4.47) is the discounted value of social welfare, where r is the discount rate and t is time. Equation (4.48) is the equation of motion, which indicates that weapons stocks change according to the difference between new weapon acquisition and the depreciated stock, where δ_A is the rate of depreciation. In (4.49), national income, I_A, is divided between civilian and military expenditures.

If the optimal control problem in (4.47)–(4.49) is optimized subject to a given level of $\bar{M}_B$, then the resulting first-order conditions and the transversality condition[17] can be used to derive the reaction path

$$\dot{M}_A = F_A(M_A, \bar{M}_B), \qquad (4.50)$$

for nation A. An analogous path

$$\dot{M}_B = F_B(\bar{M}_A, M_B), \qquad (4.51)$$

would apply to B's equivalent optimal control problem solved with respect to a given level of M_A. When these reaction paths are linearized, Richardson reaction paths result. Based on some additional assumptions

---

[17] If H denotes the current value Hamiltonian, then the following first-order conditions must be satisfied

$$\dot{p}_A = -(\partial H/\partial M_A) + (r + \delta)$$
$$\partial U_A/\partial C_A = 0, \qquad \partial U_A/\partial Z_A = 0,$$

the equation of motion and (4.49). The co-state variable attached to (4.48) is p_A. The transversality condition is

$$\lim_{t \to \infty} e^{-rt} p_i(t) M_i(t) = 0.$$

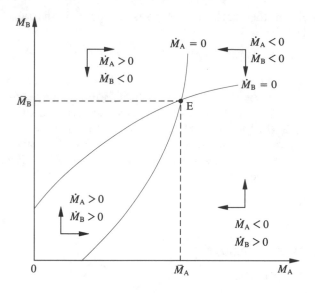

Figure 4.10 Stable phase diagram

(e.g., $\delta_A > 0$), Brito (1972, p. 364) established that equilibrium levels of armaments – i.e., $F_A(\bar{M}_A, \bar{M}_B) = F_B(\bar{M}_A, \bar{M}_B) = 0$ – exist and can be stable. A stable configuration is displayed in the phase diagram in figure 4.10. Except for the nonlinearity of the steady-state reaction paths, this figure is interpreted in an identical fashion as figure 4.7. Of course, unstable configurations may also exist.

Brito (1972) also derived a stable equilibrium for the case in which nation A acts like a Stackelberg leader and its counterpart is a follower. In this case, the follower maximizes its control problem, as before, taking $\bar{M}_A$ as given. Then the leader optimizes its control problem using the follower's reaction path as its constraint.

Simaan and Cruz (1973, 1975) extended the analysis of Brito (1972) to a differential game perspective in which competitive and interactive aspects of the rival's optimization problem are more fully taken into account.[18] For nation i, the objective functional is

$$J_i(Z_i, Z_j) = \int_0^T e^{-rt} U_i[Z_i, D_i(M_i, M_j)]dt, \quad i, j = A, B, i \neq j, \tag{4.52}$$

---

[18] Other noteworthy differential game analyses include Gillespie *et al.* (1977) and Intriligator and Brito (1989a).

where civilian expenditure has been dropped from the problem for simplicity. Also, the time horizon is not infinite, since a finite end point occurs at T. As T goes to infinity, the implications for an infinite time horizon can be found. The relevant constraint includes an equation of motion

$$\dot{M}_i = Z_i - \delta_i M_i, \qquad\qquad i = A, B, \qquad\qquad (4.53)$$

and resource constraints,

$$Z_i \leqslant I_i(t), \qquad\qquad i = A, B. \qquad\qquad (4.54)$$

A *closed-loop* solution requires us to determine the optimizing levels of M_A and M_B in which

$$Z_i = Z_i[t, M_A(t), M_B(t)], \qquad\qquad i = A, B, \qquad\qquad (4.55)$$

so that the dependence between the control variable, Z_i, and the state variables are accounted for at each moment of time.

For a closed-form solution, each agent must predetermine at $t = 0$ how its military expenditures should evolve with respect to *both* nations' military stocks for all time periods. Simaan and Cruz (1975) derived reaction paths based on the closed-loop Nash equilibrium, at which neither nation wants unilaterally to alter its military expenditures. Thus, the following conditions are fulfilled

$$J_A\{Z_A^*(\cdot), Z_B^*(\cdot)\} \geqslant J_A\{Z_A(\cdot), Z_B^*(\cdot)\}, \qquad\qquad (4.56)$$

$$J_B\{Z_A^*(\cdot), Z_B^*(\cdot)\} \geqslant J_B\{Z_A^*(\cdot), Z_B(\cdot)\}, \qquad\qquad (4.57)$$

where asterisks denote the best response levels and the Js correspond to equation (4.52). Finding the first-order condition is similar to Brito's (1972) problem except that both nations' equations of motion serve as constraints when optimizing each $J_i(\cdot)$.

Simaan and Cruz (1975) showed that, for the infinite horizon problem, a quadratic social welfare function would give rise to linear Richardson reaction paths. A quadratic objective is consistent with the desire to limit the arms gap with a rival, while minimizing military expenditures. Gillespie *et al.* (1977) derived a similar result for a zero-sum game, where $U_A + U_B = 0$. Thus, specialized forms for a differential game can serve as a foundation for the Richardson model.

4.6   Toward a supply-based theory

In the Intriligator–Brito analysis, the economic constraint is not explicit. This is evident when examining the four Richardson-type reaction curves, germane to their analysis. None of these curves contains a fatigue term. Murray Wolfson and associates[19] have extended the Intriligator–Brito analysis to include economic constraints. We should, however, point out that the Intriligator–Brito analysis is logically sound to ignore resource constraints, since their hypothetical exercise refers to a nuclear exchange that transpires in a matter of one hour, during which time the economic constraints are not really relevant. Moreover, Intriligator and Brito are concerned with the use of an existing stock of missiles.

In the Wolfson (1985) analysis of economic warfare, missile stocks are meant to refer to all types of armaments, not just missile stockpiles. Economic warfare occurs when armament buildup in one nation forces another to lose productive capacity when it reallocates further amounts of gross national product to augment its own military stockpile and manpower pool. Economic warfare results when a nation must erode its capital stock to provide sufficient military arms to deter an opponent. Capital stocks are eroded when gross investment is less than the level necessary to replace depreciated stocks. At full employment, a trade-off between military and civilian goods is necessary; hence, military buildups during this period will have an economic cost even though the capital stock is not depleted. Surely, the superpowers, and the ex-Soviet Union in particular, experienced a high opportunity cost as resources were channeled to arms during the cold war period. These costs were behind the cold war defeat of the ex-Soviet Union.

A brief introduction to Wolfson's model of economic warfare is provided in figure 4.11. In the bottom right-hand quadrant, the four reaction paths of the Intriligator (1975) model are reproduced. The shaded areas refer to the cone of mutual deterrence and the region of war initiation. The production possibility frontier for nation B (denoted by PPF_B) is displayed in the top right-hand diagram, while the investment relationship for B is given in the top left-hand diagram. The PPF indicates the full employment trade-off between civilian and military goods for a fixed capital and labor stock. Gross investment (G Inv) in B equals the average (marginal) propensity to save (s) times the civilian sector's real output (Y_B). In the bottom left-hand diagram, Wolfson (1985) depicted a relationship between B's net investment and A's military expenditures. Net investment is less than gross investment by the

---

[19] Relevant papers include Wolfson (1985, 1992), Wolfson and Farrell (1989), Wolfson, Puri, and Martelli (1992), and papers cited in these works. The reader is encouraged to see Intriligator and Brito's (1985) response to Wolfson (1985). For a somewhat different but related approach that stresses intergenerational externalities, see Johns, Pecchenino, and Schreft (1993). This latter paper indicates that costs of arms races are imposed on current and future generations.

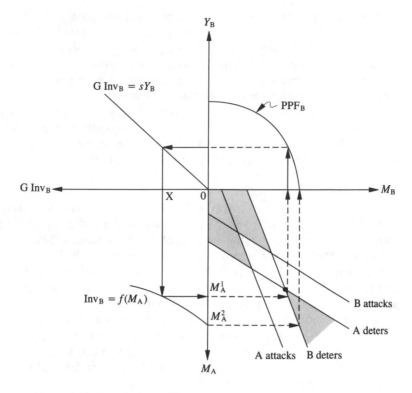

Figure 4.11 Economic warfare

amount of depreciation; hence, the horizontal axis needs to be rescaled to reflect depreciation. If, for example, depreciation equals X in figure 4.11 along the G $\mathrm{Inv_B}$ axis, then this defines the zero level of net investment in the lower left-hand diagram. Negative levels of net investment occur to the right and positive levels to the left of X. The graph in the bottom quadrant relates net investment in B to military expenditures in A. A negative relationship results, because an increase in M_A necessitates an increase in M_B if B is to deter A and this means less allocation to B's civilian sector and to investment.

In figure 4.11, nation B maintains its capital stock unchanged at X, since gross investment just equals X when M_A^1 is spent in A. If, however, nation A spends M_A^2, then net investment is negative in B and this would result in a shift inward of $\mathrm{PPF_B}$ (not shown) as nation B increases its military expenditures to a level on the B deters line sufficient to deter nation A.

Although Wolfson's approach is insightful and important, the geometrical apparatus is somewhat cumbersome and does not really lend itself to a true dynamic representation. Moreover, the graphs for nation A, including its PPF, are not explicitly displayed. A mathematical growth representation might be the best means for displaying the important concept of economic warfare. The introduction of supply-side elements to the arms race analysis is an important innovation.

Wolfson (1985) also related the notion of economic warfare to the technologies employed by the rivals to produce their mix of military outputs. Wolfson distinguished two types of technologies: high technology (H) and low technology (L). He went on to relate the production of military security to the combination of these technologies used. Some nations may have a comparative advantage in one technology rather than another. If the two rivals differ in terms of their comparative advantage, then a nation will be more successful in winning economic warfare if it could direct the arms race to the weapons favoring the technology that it is best in producing. If, for example, the United States had a comparative advantage in high-tech systems, such as the strategic defense initiative (SDI), and the ex-Soviet Union had a comparative advantage in low-tech systems. The United States would cause the ex-Soviet Union relatively greater economic hardships by redirecting the arms race to this high-tech weaponry. This *may* have been a deciding factor to ending the cold war. A nation would also be at an advantage if its rival used the same (similar) technological mix as it did, but the rival was less well endowed in the factors.

4.7   Empirical analyses

An extensive empirical literature has applied the theory of arms races to the analysis of historical and contemporary arms races. Representative articles include Byers and Peel (1989), Cusack and Ward (1981), Linden (1991) Majeski and Jones (1981), McGuire (1977), Rattinger (1975), Taylor (1974), Wallace (1979), and Ward and Mintz (1987). To date, the empirical results can be best described as disappointing. In most empirical analyses, the Richardson reaction paths do not give statistically significant or robust results when tested with real world data. This may be due to many factors. First, and foremost, the Richardson equations may not be an adequate representation for arms races. Second, nations may not be engaged in arms races. Third, the use of time-series data may be associated with autocorrelation problems that must be corrected. Fourth, the error terms in the system of dynamic arms race equations may not be independent; simultaneity may be a real concern that needs to be addressed. Despite this concern, ordinary least squares (OLS) regressions have been used most frequently. Fifth, data might be unreliable, especially when currency is not convertible (Hartley, 1991b). Bias may, thus, be introduced. Sixth, the proper proxies need to be determined for the military variables (see especially McGuire, 1977). Seventh, the proper lagged structure for the estimates must be ascertained. Eighth, causality must be established.

Since space does not permit a discussion of the myriad contributions to the empirical literature, we focus on a few representative articles and their approaches. McGuire (1977) used historical data for the 1960–73 period to investigate the alleged nuclear missile arms race between the United States and the Soviet Union. Only strategic weapons were considered. McGuire's analysis is noteworthy because it grappled with many of the problems mentioned above. For example, McGuire used four alternative measures to proxy military stocks in the rival nations. These included: (1) the number of inventory vehicles with bombers and missiles counted equally, (2) the number of warheads with single and multiple-warhead missiles counted equally, (3) inventory megatonnage, and (4) an index of destructive power with smaller weapons weighted more heavily than larger weapons. This last index equals $\Sigma(\text{Yields})^{2/3}$.

McGuire used the following discrete representation for the Richardson model

$$\Delta A_t = a - bV(A_t) + cV(R_t), \tag{4.58}$$

$$\Delta R_t = d - cV(R_t) + fV(A_t), \tag{4.59}$$

where A_t and R_t denote strategic missile stocks in period t in the United States and the Soviet Union, respectively. The Δ term indicates annual differences in stocks (e.g., $A_t - A_{t-1}$), while $V(\cdot)$ stands for the annual average [e.g., $(A_t + A_{t-1})/2$]. McGuire investigated a number of military proxies with different lag and lead structures when the data were fitted to equations (4.58) and (4.59).

McGuire found that the index of strategic strength proxy gave the most realistic results and a stable equilibrium. Alternative proxies were associated with either unstable equilibriums or else intuitively unacceptable signs on the variables (McGuire, 1977, p. 332). Moreover, a one-period lag was judged superior to instantaneous or anticipatory reactions. The best empirical results had the following steady-state reaction paths

$$\Delta A_t = 0 = 695 - 0.368V(A_t) + 0.030V(R_{t-1}) \tag{4.60}$$

$$\Delta R_t = 0 = 201 - 0.139V(R_t) + 0.370V(A_{t-1}). \tag{4.61}$$

Cusack and Ward (1981) employed variants of the Richardson and bureaucratic models to investigate arms race dynamics in the United

States, the Soviet Union, and the People's Republic of China. In general, these authors related a country's change in military expenditures (ΔME) to changes in the ME of its rival, a defense burden measure, tension with rivals, and a war dummy. In all three countries, the Richardson model performed poorly from a statistical viewpoint. For the United States, some success was noted for the bureaucratic model where key independent variables included the electoral cycle, changes in aggregate demand, the change in previous year's military stocks and the war dummy. Rattinger (1975) also tested the bureaucratic model for twelve European countries and seven Warsaw Pact allies with some success. For NATO, Rattinger (1975) discovered that the smallest military powers behaved most in keeping with the bureaucratic model.

In a novel study, Majeski and Jones (1981) used different distributed lag structures for a nation's past ME and its rival's past ME. First, these authors employed ARIMA techniques to estimate the lag structure for twelve different rivalry dyads during either the 1949–75 or 1948–74 period. They next calculated the cross-correlation between the residual series for each of the dyads. Finally, they used Granger-causality tests on these cross-correlations to ascertain whether there had been causality between the time series. For seven dyads – the US–USSR, India–Pakistan, Argentina–Brazil, Argentina–Chile, Argentina–Peru, Brazil–Chile, and Chile–Peru – no causal relationship existed in either direction, which suggested the absence of arms race interactions. For the superpowers, the best-fitting model was purely autoregressive, which is consistent with a bureaucratic influence. The Arab–Israel dyad was associated with two-way contemporaneous causality. The four remaining dyads – NATO–Warsaw Pact, Greece–Turkey, Iran–Iraq, and Brazil–Peru – displayed one-way causality between the rival ME series. Recent studies by Byers and Peel (1989) and Linden (1991) applied more sophisticated time-series modeling and causality tests to the superpowers and the Middle East, respectively.

4.8   Concluding remarks

This chapter has covered much ground. After over fifty years of effort, it is fair to say that there is a rich array of arms race models to choose from. The most recent models have included strategic concerns in an interesting fashion and have begun to account for economic constraints. These models have been conceptually helpful for understanding the behavior of the superpowers during the cold war. In a number of studies, the roles of intelligence and verification were shown to promote stability. Additionally, sufficiently large stockpiles may further peace through deterrence, whereas disarmament *may* be destabilizing if it brings stockpiles into the region of war initiation. Unilateral disarmament may also be destabilizing.

Despite the many extensions and clarifications to the Richardson model, many further improvements are needed. Economic constraints need to be introduced in a fashion with a more explicit dynamic structure. Without this advance, the true consequences of economic warfare will not be known. Another extension requires that more interesting information structures be used, including asymmetric information, two-sided uncertainty, and learning. The analysis of multi-polar systems could also be advanced further. This last goal may prove especially important for the post cold war period in which France, Britain, the United States, China, the Commonwealth of Independent States (CIS), and others have acquired sizable nuclear arsenals. Additionally, arms race theorizing needs to focus on tailoring the theory to regional dyads. Strategic thinking, as applied by Intriligator, Brito, and others to the cold-war missile confrontation, must be extended to analyze these regional confrontations. New models of simulated warfare and their consequences must be formulated. Civil war in Bosnia underscores the need to understand small-scale arms races and their instability, in which the role of third parties, such as the United Nations, are considered. Finally, the theories of alliances and arms races should be married. In doing so, alliance considerations should be added to the arms race model rather than the other way around, so that the synthesis is dynamic. The Richardson model is really one attempt at specifying a general theory of military expenditures.

Although the theoretical models have achieved a great deal of success, the empirical implementation of the theory needs more development. If the theory cannot be used for forecasting purposes, it will not, in our estimations, have much lasting value. The application of advanced time-series techniques to the study of arms race empirics is viewed as a fruitful avenue of empirical research.

The three chapters in Part I have a number of common themes. Much of the work on allies, defense demand, and arms races has stressed the notion of constrained maximization. Although alternative equilibrium concepts have been employed, Nash equilibrium is the most common. All three chapters have been concerned with resource allocation, equilibrium stability, empirical results, and comparative statics.

II   Defense inputs, industrial base, and growth

5   Procurement: theories, evidence, and policies

The procurement of defense equipment is big business. Expenditure on major weapons procurement in 1992 accounted for between 17 percent and 22 percent of total military expenditure for European NATO nations and for the USA, respectively (SIPRI, 1993). These share figures are based on major weapons procurement only, so under-stating real procurement expenditure. In the UK, for example, in the early 1990s expenditure on equipment accounted for about 40 percent of defense spending.

Critics of defense equipment procurement policies point to the high costs of weapons, cost escalation, delays in delivery, deficiencies in performance, poor reliability, and cancellations of costly projects. Contractors are further criticized with allegations of excessive profits, waste, fraud, and inefficiency (Austin and Larkey, 1992; McNaugher, 1990). Such criticisms immediately raise a methodological problem: What are the criteria for assessing procurement policy and defense contracting? Is it assumed that the ideal contract type is one of a perfect project which encounters no technical, cost or time problems? Or are comparisons being made with actual previous project experience within a country or in other countries?

This chapter reviews the literature on the various types of defense contracts and competitive procurement. Decisions to buy defense equipment are reflected in the award of a contract whereby a supplier provides a product or service of a specified quality over some time period in return for an agreed payment. This description simplifies the problems reflected in the transaction costs of acquiring information about products and suppliers, organizing competitions, bargaining with contractors, and then writing, monitoring, and enforcing contracts. Contracting requires the government as a buyer or principal to specify its requirements to a contractor or agent, and to ensure that the agent pursues the goals of the principal. Contracts which cannot specify all the details of a buyer's requirements provide the contractor with opportunities for discretionary behavior (e.g., pursuing managerial preferences). Similarly, writing, monitoring, and enforcing contracts requires outputs to be specified in measurable form. However, the incentives and penalties incorporated into the contract will affect the behavior of agents: individuals and groups can play any games and the results might be unexpected and undesirable. The chapter starts by reviewing the traditional approach to defense contracting; it then considers the literature on cost-estimating relationships and various types of contracts including the more recent theoretical developments. Throughout the survey, there will be a focus on the features of the market within which contracting takes place, the behavior of agents, including contractors, and their response to different contractual incentives and regulatory constraints. Competitive procurement policies are then evaluated. The opportunities for competition are assessed and consideration is given to its benefits and costs.

5.1   Market features

At one level, defense equipment markets are like any other market: they bring together buyers and sellers (Hooper and Buck, 1991). National defense ministries and their armed forces as well as overseas governments demand defense equipment. On the supply side, defense industries both nationally and overseas, provide equipment. And the demand and supply sides are brought together through a legally binding contract whereby the buyer agrees to pay a certain price for a specified product delivered on time. In some instances, the government as the buyer might impose regulatory requirements on the contractor (e.g. profit controls). Figure 5.1 illustrates the market situation with an example from the UK.

Defense equipment markets, however, have some distinguishing features concerning the role of governments, cost trends, technical progress, cost curves, and regulation (Peck and Scherer, 1962):

(i)   Governments are central to understanding defense equipment markets. Where it is a monopsonist, a government determines technical progress through its choice of equipment and it can choose whether to import or buy from its domestic industry. As the sole or major buyer (e.g. combat aircraft, missiles, submarines, tanks, warships), it can determine the size of its domestic defense industry, its structure, entry and exit, prices, exports, profits, efficiency, and ownership. In this context, the view has been expressed that defense ministry purchasing should be used as an instrument of national industrial policy, awarding contracts to support "key" technologies and to back "the winners" (an interventionist industrial policy). Supporters of free markets (e.g.,

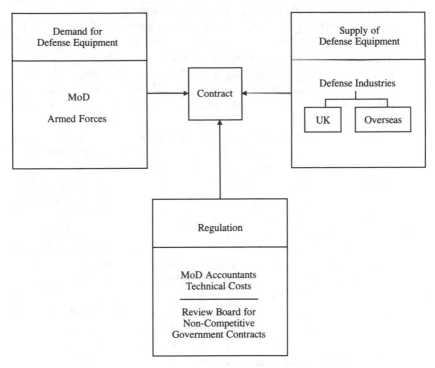

Figure 5.1 UK defense equpment markets

Austrian economists) are critical, stressing that the future is
uncertain and that there are unintended secondary effects, so that
today's winners might be tomorrow's losers; and that governments
have no competence as entrepreneurs. Interestingly, public choice
analysis also predicts that governments can fail in their efforts to
improve economic performance. Furthermore, using defense procurement as an instrument of industrial policy raises fundamental
questions about the objectives of defense policy. Is defense
procurement aimed at the efficient purchasing of equipment for
national defense or the pursuit of wider economic and social
objectives, including protection of the national defense industrial
base (Faltas, 1986; Taylor and Hayward, 1989; see also chapter 7)?

(ii)   Defense equipment, especially high technology equipment, is costly
and the trends are toward rising costs in real terms. The American
B2 stealth bomber was estimated to cost $35 billion for fifteen
aircraft and the US F-22 advanced tactical fighter aircraft is likely
to cost some $130 million per copy (1991–2 prices). Similarly, new

equipment is much costlier than the previous generations which it replaces (although the new equipment is more productive). Typically, the real unit production costs of defense equipment (aircraft, helicopters, missiles, warships, submarines) increase by about 10 percent per annum, implying a doubling in cost every 7.25 years (Pugh, 1993). Since defense budgets usually fail to match such cost increases, there are inevitable downward pressures on the size and formation of armed forces with an associated need to reshape the defense industries which supply the forces (e.g., the long-run trend towards a one-ship navy and a one-aircraft air force). Not surprisingly, faced with such pressures, efforts are made to introduce new procurement policies, such as competition policy, which might at least postpone some of the adjustment effects (Pugh, 1993).

(iii)   Technical progress has been a distinctive feature of defense equipment markets. Major technical advances resulting in new products (e.g. jet engines, missiles, electronics, helicopters, etc.), have created new markets requiring firms to offer new development and production facilities with a greater emphasis on research and development (R & D). Since 1945, the long-run trend has been towards a smaller number of larger firms, reflected in mergers and exits from the defense sector. As a result, the high technology sectors (e.g. aerospace, avionics) usually consist of one or a relatively few large national suppliers either publicly or privately owned (monopoly or oligopoly). Such markets are a major departure from the economists' model of perfect competition. The cuts in defense spending in the USA, UK, and elsewhere in the EU during the 1990s are likely to reinforce the trend towards exits from the industry and restructuring around an even smaller number of large defense contractors. As a result, EU states will only be able to maintain competition by opening up their national markets to foreign suppliers.

(iv)   A number of defense industries, particularly the high technology sectors, are characterized by decreasing costs: hence, if the aim is to exploit scale economies, a national market will only support one firm (monopoly). In such sectors, quantity is a major determinant of unit costs and hence competitiveness. Long production runs mean that high fixed R & D costs can be spread over a larger volume and, in addition, there are scale and learning economies in production (Bittleston, 1990; see also section 5.4).

(v)   Defense markets and industries are government regulated. Governments can determine whether their national markets should be open or closed, they can insist upon monitoring costs, and there is often state regulation of profits on defense contracts (usually noncompetitive contracts). Typically, the aim of profit controls is to ensure that defense contractors do not make either excessive profits or excessive losses on defense business; and the prevention of excessive losses is designed to retain a domestic defense industrial base. As a result, profits on defense work might not provide the standard signaling mechanism for entry or exit. Moreover, profit-conscious firms are likely to adapt to regulatory constraints. For example, where profits are controlled, firms are likely to increase expenditures on unregulated items which give satisfaction to their managers (e.g., luxury offices, company cars, hoarding valuable scientists and engineers: Hartley and Tisdell, 1981).

5.2   Demand: procurement policy

Procurement policy represents the demand side of the defense equipment market. It involves a set of related choices, with defense contracts as one element in the choice set:

(i)   The choice of equipment required for the armed forces with implications for technical progress. This involves choosing between competing demands from each of the armed forces for a larger share of a limited defense budget. In principle, such choices need to be made in relation to the nation's security requirements, regardless of the traditional monopoly property rights of each of the services. For example, why not allow the army with its land-based missiles to compete with the air force and its manned combat aircraft for a nation's air defense (similarly aircraft versus warships)? In reality, such decisions are often made on the principle of Buggin's Turn. Last year, the navy obtained its new aircraft carrier; this year it is the turn of the air force to receive its new fighter aircraft; next year, the army can have a new tank!

(ii)   The choice of contractor. A contractor has to be selected either by direct negotiation with a preferred supplier or by competition based on price and nonprice criteria, with the market restricted to domestic firms or open to foreign suppliers. Public choice analysis predicts that domestic firms will oppose opening the national market to foreign suppliers: they will lobby vote-sensitive governments claiming that relying on foreigners will impair national security and will mean the loss of jobs, technology, and valuable foreign exchange (depending on whether the exchange rate is viewed as a policy objective or a policy instrument). Economists can critically appraise such arguments pointing to the costs of national independence (protection); showing that there are alternative and often more efficient methods of achieving jobs, technology, and other policy objectives; and raising questions as to whether the aims of defense procurement policy are to protect the nation's citizens or its domestic defense industries [who is maximizing what for the benefit of whom? (Hartley, 1991a, b)].

(iii) The choice of contract. A contract has to be selected from the extremes of firm or fixed-price contracts, a cost-plus contract, or some intermediate target cost-incentive sharing arrangement. With a firm price contract, the firm receives the contract price, no more and no less. Fixed-price contracts allow for variations of price based on an agreed price index reflecting inflation in labor and materials inputs. Where a prime contractor receives a fixed-price contract (with agreed price variations), it has every incentive to negotiate *firm* prices with its suppliers, so that the prime contractor appropriates all the financial benefits of price variations. An alternative solution would be to award competitively determined firm price contracts, leaving contractors to make their own judgments about future inflation, incorporating such estimates in their tender bid. Of course, another solution is to award a cost-plus contract in which the contractor recoups all its costs incurred on the project plus an agreed profit rate based on costs or with a fixed fee. Such contracts are used for development work where there might be considerable uncertainty. Not surprisingly, these "blank cheque" contracts lead to inefficiency, labor hoarding, cost escalation and "gold-plating" (Scherer, 1964; Kennedy, 1983). A comparison of firm price and cost-plus contracts identifies two policy issues. First, how should the risks of the program be distributed between the state (buyer) and the contractor? Second, what are the implications of different contractual arrangements for firm behavior and efficiency, and for efficiently meeting the buyer's requirements. Of course, it is not always possible for the buyer (defense ministry) to specify in advance all its detailed requirements: hence, it might prefer a contract which allows it some discretion to modify its requirements. But, once the contract has been awarded, any contract modifications have to be negotiated with the monopoly contractor.

(iv) The incentives to choose. Ultimately, efficient solutions depend upon the set of incentives and penalties incorporated into the employment contracts of procurement staff in the armed forces and defense ministries. Often individuals and groups in the armed

forces and defense ministries have every incentive to spend: there
are no inducements to economize if all the savings by, say, the navy
are used to buy more tanks for the army, or they eventually benefit
the national Treasury.

(v) How are choices made? Within any procurement organization,
     equipment choices will often be made by a committee. Clearly, the
     size of committee, its objectives, the composition of its membership,
     the conditions of entry and exit, the background of the chairman
     and the voting arrangements are central to determining actual
     procurement choices.

Consideration of the choices and organizational arrangements outlined
above are usually ignored or neglected by economists. This is not
surprising since economists have often regarded governments as a "black
box" which always pursues the "will of the people". Such an approach
ignores the insights provided by public choice analysis which applies the
neo-classical concepts of exchange and self interest to the political
market place of voters, parties, governments, bureaucracies, and interest
groups; and also ignores the fact that in defense the "will of the people"
is not always apparent [so providing governments and defense ministries
with opportunities for discretionary behavior (Buchanan, 1986)]. Public
choice analysis provides two predictions of relevance to defense contracting and procurement policy. First, government policies tend to favor
producers more than consumers. Second, budget-maximizing bureaucracies will be inefficient: their budgets will be too large as they
exaggerate the demand for their services and underestimate the costs of
their preferred activities [e.g., exaggerating the threat; resulting in cost
escalation on equipment projects (Hartley, 1991b, chapter 5; Dunleavy,
1991; Mayer, 1991)].

In evaluating procurement policy, economists have traditionally
applied their standard economic models of free trade and competition,
including the opportunities for competitive bidding at various stages in a
project's life cycle. Here, many of the pioneering contributions in the
microeconomics of defense emerged in the 1960s and were made by
American economists, with the Rand Corporation in the forefront. The
classic text by Hitch and McKean devoted a short section to defense
contracting (Hitch and McKean, 1960, pp. 223–33).

5.3   Competition, firm behavior, bargaining, and contract types

One of the early definitive economic texts in this field is *The Weapons
Acquisition Process: Economic Incentives* (Scherer, 1964). This provides a
benchmark and sets the scene for assessing the subsequent theoretical,

empirical, and policy developments in defense contracting. The book starts by outlining four features of the weapons acquisition process. First, development work is characterized by uncertainty and risk often resulting in the shifting of financial risks from contractors to government usually through cost-reimbursement contracts. Second, once a project starts, the contractor acquires specialized information and physical assets which restricts the government's ability to shop around and bring in an alternative contractor. The result is a bilateral monopoly bargaining situation. Third, these features of the weapons acquisition process mean that a conventional market system is not possible: hence, the reliance on a nonmarket, quasi-administrative buyer–seller relationship. Fourth, in the absence of market forces, successful weapons acquisition requires governments to intervene either through controls on contractors or through incentive mechanisms to reward good performance and penalize poor performance. Of course, to be effective, contractors have to believe that incentive and penalty arrangements will be enforced by the government's procurement agency. Incentives can be either *competitive* or *contractual*.

Competitive bidding for production contracts has been achieved via break-out and second sourcing. By the early 1960s, US evidence appeared to show that competitive break-outs[1] resulted in price reductions of 20 percent compared with prices negotiated noncompetitively (Scherer, 1964, p. 106). However, break-out and competitive bidding involves costs in preparing manufacturing information and specifications, in maintaining quality, and in disputes about transferring private property rights (proprietary data). Problems also arise where the original contractor possesses immobile specialized facilities. Price competition can also be achieved through second sourcing where one or more firms are selected to produce a weapon system (or subsystem) concurrently with the original contractor. Second sourcing was used extensively during World War II and the Korean War (often for reasons other than competition). A subsequent example of second sourcing involved the US Navy's Sidewinder program. Sharing the production work between Philco (the original contractor) and General Electric (second source) on the basis of each firm's success in reducing costs resulted in the price per unit falling to one seventh of its initial price [although the price reductions also reflected learning curve effects based on a 76 percent progress curve (Scherer, 1964, pp. 118–19)]. But, as with

[1]   Break-outs can involve no competition with government buying parts directly from subcontractors; or subcontractors can enter into competitive bidding; or the complete production contract can be subject to competitive bidding.

break-out competition, second sourcing is not costless. Also, where learning economies are important, the original producer may have a decisive cost advantage over a new entrant. Or, where economies of scale are substantial, and the production order will support only one firm of optimal scale, it is inefficient to share an order between two firms (Scherer, 1964, p. 127). In addition to competition, contractual incentives can be used to monitor and police contractors.

Agreement on a defense contract for development and/or production work, will reflect the preferences of the government's procurement agency and the contractor. Governments will aim to maximize contractor efficiency incentives, minimize the risk of excessive profits paid to contractors and minimize contract outlays. With fixed-price contracts, there are conflicts between contractor efficiency incentives and the risk of excessive profits; whereas cost reimbursement contracts minimize the risk of excessive profits but at the price of removing contractor efficiency incentives and also of requiring stringent accounting and reporting requirements. Incentive contracts offer a compromise solution between the various competing goals of contractor efficiency, profitability, and contract outlays. However, governments must reach an agreement with a contractor on the type of contract to be written for a procurement decision. Here, contractors will pursue conflicting objectives concerned with profit maximization and minimizing the risk of contract failure and losses (Scherer, 1964, chapter 6). The various objectives and preferences of the buyer and the contractor have to be reconciled in a bargaining situation.

In negotiating a contract, the final outcome will reflect the bargaining power of the two parties, as well as their bargaining strategies and tactics. Clearly, contractors have every incentive to negotiate favourable cost and price targets: on cost-sharing arrangements, they will seek to shift the risks of cost overruns to the government; and where the government demands a maximum price liability, the contractor will seek the highest possible maximum price. A contractor's knowledge of costs gives them a major advantage over the buyer in the bargaining process. Demands by the government for access to a contractor's accounting data will always be resisted and even where granted, accounting information is historical and does not indicate the extent of contractor inefficiency. However, the government is not powerless. It can use competition from either national or foreign firms to check on a contractor's price bid. But even where contracts are based on "keen" competitive prices, there might be some "incompleteness" in the contract, enabling contractors to make cost-quality trade-offs (Scherer, 1964, chapter 8).

5.4   Cost-estimating relationships

Industry and defense procurement agencies use various methods to estimate the development and production costs for large equipment projects (e.g., aircraft, helicopters, tanks, warships). Such estimates are used in the initial planning phase for new equipment projects (e.g., for use in a defense ministry's long-term costings); or as a basis for a firm's bid for a new project; and as a check by defense procurement agencies on the cost estimates submitted by firms. For example, defense ministry cost estimates have been used to identify the cost savings which have resulted from competition although some of the claimed savings could reflect poor estimating!

Typically, early estimates of the development and production costs for an advanced technology defense project are unreliable. American and British studies show that projects usually increased in real cost by some 40–70 percent from their earliest estimates to completion (MoD, 1988; Pugh, 1993; Perry et al., 1971). Such cost escalation results from modifications and changes in requirements, technical uncertainties making it difficult to define the work to be done and contractor optimism reflected in low bids (Martin et al., 1992). Also, governments often believe that costs will be lowest when a contract is awarded to the firm whose initial estimate or bid is lowest. However, it is possible that low estimates in themselves create conditions that contribute to cost escalation; and there is some limited support for this hypothesis (Large, 1974). In the circumstances, it needs to be recognized that early cost estimates are notoriously unreliable: a situation which requires either better estimating techniques and/or alternative procurement policies (e.g. competitive fixed-price contracts for development work). Here, though, some analysts have recommended caution. It has been suggested that no single procurement method or acquisition strategy can possibly serve for all situations. Whilst incremental development or prototyping are appropriate in some situations, neither should be recommended as universal practice (Martin et al.,1992, p. 72).

The methods used to estimate costs include:
(i)   Engineering estimates
(ii)   Comparative methods
(iii) Parametric methods
(iv)   Learning curves

5.4.1   Engineering estimates and comparative methods

Engineering estimates are based on the estimated costs of all the materials, equipment, components, labor, and overheads involved in the project (Fox, 1974; Sissons, 1986). Comparative methods are based on historical comparisons of similar projects (e.g., combat aircraft; transport aircraft). For example, on UK combat aircraft development work, graphs of the relationship between technical man hours per pound of empty weight and the date of start show a positive and increasing trend over time: hence the launch costs for a 1970 combat aircraft were some fifteen times greater than that of a 1930s combat aircraft (Boot, 1990, p. 213). Rules of thumb are also used. For example, on UK guided weapons a typical ratio of development cost to unit production cost might be 1,000:1; for combat aircraft with an existing engine, the corresponding ratio might be 100:1; and for warships the ratio is under 1:1 [based on 1,000 guided weapons; 100 aircraft, respectively (Pugh, 1986, p. 346)]. Similarly, rules of thumb might be used to estimate life-cycle costs comprising acquisition and ownership costs (i.e., R & D, production, operating, maintenance, and disposal costs). UK evidence suggests that on warships, development and procurement account for 25 percent of life cycle costs whilst for combat aircraft the corresponding share might be 13 percent [based on six ships in a class over twenty-five years; 250 aircraft produced over twenty-five years (Pugh, 1986, p. 124)]. But, of course, rules of thumb and extrapolation based on past relationships might need to be adjusted to allow for variations in the complexity of new programs compared with "typical" projects.

5.4.2   Parametric methods

Methodologies also exist for forecasting future R & D project costs. These are often based on the cost profiles of historical R & D project data which map the relationship between the cumulative proportion of both project costs and project time. Typically, project R& D costs are front loaded, rising steeply toward the midpoint of the system development project, then falling steeply with production beginning about half way through the program. Cavin (1991) has formulated an optimal control model of new weapon system development which is broadly consistent with the empirical data.

Parametric methods are based on multiple regression analysis and have been widely used, particularly for estimating the development and production costs of aerospace equipment. Much of the published work in this field has emerged from the US Rand Corporation. Typically, log-linear equations are used in which engineering and manufacturing hours are estimated as a function of aircraft weight, speed, and the number of aircraft produced (Elstub, 1969). A Rand study based on a limited post-1960 sample of US military aircraft found that the most accurate cost-estimating relationships (as exponential equations) were based on empty weight and speed. Incorporating additional variables for program structure and airframe construction characteristics (e.g., wing type, number of black boxes, contractor experience) did not improve the overall fit of the equations (Hess and Romanoff, 1987). However, it was recognized that the Rand equations might not be applicable for estimating the costs of future aircraft. Changes in airframe materials (e.g., composites), design concepts (e.g., stealth), systems integration, and manufacturing techniques are likely to affect the reliability of conventional cost-estimating relationships (Hess and Romanoff, 1987).

Similar models have also been developed for estimating the cost of changes in US Navy ship-building programs. These statistical models show that man hours per ship depend on such variables as the number of workers, the average daily hours worked, the experience and skill level of the labor force, the ship construction sequence, the labor input applied to other programs, and delays in ship delivery. In its log-linear form, the model explained 94 percent to 99 percent of the variations in man hours per ship, with learning curves of 78–88 percent for two programs (Hammond and Graham, 1983).

5.4.3   Learning curves

Learning curves apply to production programs, and are widely used by governments and industry for cost-estimating and contract negotiations. They reflect the fact that productivity increases with experience (hence they have been called experience curves) and they provide a basis for estimating manufacturing costs. Learning curves are usually expressed:

$$y = aX^{-b}, \tag{5.1}$$

where y = number of man hours per unit produced,
X = cumulative output of a given type of equipment,
a = man hours required for the first unit,
b = slope of the learning curve usually defined in
relation to a doubling of cumulative output.

Although originally estimated for the aircraft industry and widely used throughout the world's aerospace industries, learning curves also apply to a range of defense equipment and to civil products such as electrical appliances, machine tools, petroleum refining, and steel industries. An 80 percent learning curve, which is often used in aircraft manufacture, indicates that direct labor inputs decline by 20 percent for each doubling of the cumulative output of a given aircraft (Asher, 1956; Hartley, 1969).

Table 5.1 *Labor learning curves*

Equipment	Percentage slope (%)
Aircraft	78–90
Aero-engines	85–94
Helicopters	80–93
Missiles	90–95
Avionics (radar)	80–90
Electronics	92–96
Main battle tanks	80–92
Warships	75–80

A distinction can be made between unit and cumulative average learning curves with the unit curve referring to the man hours required for the nth unit (marginal), whilst the cumulative average refers to the average time required to produce a total of n units. Both unit and cumulative average curves can have 80 percent slopes and, after an initial output has been produced, they become parallel in their log-linear form (Sissons, 1986, p. 89).

Examples of labor learning curves based on European experience for a variety of defense equipment are shown in table 5.1. The slopes of the curves range between 75 percent and 96 percent, with a median slope of 85 percent to 90 percent. There is evidence of a limit to learning, especially for warships, where the limit occurs between four and twelve units. Even where learning is continuous, it is often assumed that the curve tends to flatten out with greater output. However, learning curves are not unit cost curves. The effect of labor learning on unit production costs will depend on the share of labor costs in total production costs. On aircraft, for example, labor can represent 30–50 percent of total costs; for helicopters, the labor share can be 30 percent; and for missiles, electronics and tanks, the labor share can vary between 27 percent and 33 percent (Hartley and Cox, 1992).

Inevitably, using learning curves as a cost-estimating technique encounters difficulties. Both the a and b parameters have to be estimated (i.e., man hours for unit 1 and the slope of the curve: see table 5.1) and questions arise as to whether learning continues indefinitely and whether the b parameter remains constant. Moreover, the introduction of modifications and breaks in production can affect learning (e.g., leading to jagged effects). More generally, problems arise because the underlying determinants and causes of learning have not been explained satisfactorily. Instead, there are various hypotheses about operator and management learning, the impact of machine-intensive operations compared with assembly work, and the effects of labor turnover and payment systems (Large *et al.*, 1974; Hartley, 1969; Sissons, 1986).

5.4.4   Some gaps in the costing literature

The general area of cost-estimating relationships is deficient in the industrial economics domain. There is a lack of good quality industrial economics case studies of cost conditions in defense industries. Here, there is a need for evidence on the shape of long-run average cost curves, minimum efficient scale, the relative position of long-run cost curves between different nations (opportunities for trade) and the relationship between scale and learning curves (see chapter 7).

Nor is it possible to ignore the tremendous differences in the scale of output between the USA and EU member states with implications for unit costs. Efficient production will become an even more important policy issue as nations reduce their defense spending and "stretch-out" production programs so as to maintain a domestic defense industrial base. In the USA some attention has been given to the cost implications of stretching-out production and whether defense plants are "too large." Evidence exists on the minimum and maximum economic annual production rates for American combat aircraft, missiles, and land equipment (e.g., the minimum economic rate for F-15 aircraft is 120 units per annum; for the Apache helicopter 72 units per annum; for the M-1 tank 720 units per annum). Decreasing basic production rates of US modern weapons systems by 50 percent could increase real unit costs by from 7 percent to over 50 percent; whilst a 50 percent increase in output would reduce unit costs by 3–18 percent (CBO 1987; see chapter 7).

As nations reduce their defense spending and search for efficiency savings, they are increasingly likely to examine the cost implications of the current scale of their domestic defense plants and the extent of excess capacity. There is a widely held view in the defense community that weapons production occurs in plants which are too large relative to the outputs actually produced. US evidence suggests that inefficient production is in fact occurring: data identifying a particular weapons system as having large amounts of excess capacity and/or steeply declining short-run average cost curves can be interpreted as implying that production is occurring in an inefficiently large plant. Thus, existing outputs could be produced more cheaply in smaller-scale plants (Rogerson, 1991a and b).

Various explanations have been offered for this situation. One possibility is that the US military and Congress persistently overestimate the rate at which procurement will occur, so building production lines which are too big. An alternative explanation suggests that the organization of the decision-making process itself creates incentives for rational actors to strategically choose too high a scale (Rogerson, 1991b; see also section 5.6).

5.5   The new economics of defense procurement and contracting

Since the pioneering work of Scherer (1964), there have been a variety of theoretical developments which have been incorporated into the literature on defense contracting:-

(i)   The buyer–seller relationship is treated in a principal–agent framework with the defense ministry as the principal (buyer and regulator) and the prime contractor as the agent [supplier and regulated firm (McAfee and McMillan, 1986a; Laffont and Tirole, 1993)].

(ii)   Transaction costs and contract theory. Specifying, negotiating, agreeing, and monitoring contracts involves transaction costs; transactions are characterized by bounded rationality (limited information) and opportunism (incentives to hoard valuable information); and, inevitably, many contracts are incompletely specified (Williamson, 1986).

(iii) There are information asymmetries between the buyer and contractor in situations of uncertainty and where procurement is characterized by adverse selection, moral hazard and risk sharing between purchaser and supplier (Cummins, 1977). Adverse selection means that the government does not know the firm's expected costs and moral hazard arises where the government cannot observe the selected contractor's efforts to minimize costs (e.g., firms which pay only a small share of any cost overruns have a diminished economic incentive to minimize costs).

(iv)   Game theory has been used to analyze strategic behavior and interaction by both the purchaser and the contractors (Laffont, 1986; Shubik, 1983).

(v)   It has been recognized that defense contractors might not be profit maximizers, especially in imperfect and regulated markets (Williamson, 1986).

(vi)   Efficient outcomes do not require large numbers of firms in an industry (as in the perfectly competitive model). Instead, contestability (the threat of rivalry) rather than industry structure determines performance (Baumol, 1982).

(vii) Public choice analysis and economic models of regulation provide
       new insights into procurement policy (Cowen and Lee, 1992;
       Leitzel, 1992; Lichtenberg, 1989).

The following sections will survey the major theoretical developments,
their implications for understanding the problems of defense contracting
and their contributions to policy formulation. Issues associated with
regulation are reviewed later in this chapter (see also Hartley and
Hooper, 1990, pp. 440–99).

5.6   Game theory and procurement

In chapters 2–4, games figured prominently in the analysis at various
points. A game involves two or more agents (players) whose interactions
determine their payoffs or outcomes. A noncooperative game is characterized by the players, their strategies, and the outcomes associated
with various strategy combinations. In chapter 2, for example, allies
decided their defense levels, based on the aggregate defense levels
(spillins) of the other allies and based on economic factors. Higher levels
of spillins provided an ally with free-riding opportunities that would, in
turn, make it reduce its own defense provision. A Nash equilibrium was
depicted as the simultaneous determination of defense levels and was
used to derive demand curves (chapters 2–3). Strategic interactions other
than Nash (e.g., leader–follower) were also discussed. In chapter 4, the
agents included two or more adversaries whose choices of defense level
were interdependent. Both static and dynamic game representations were
presented. Arms races resulted when the arming of one adversary
induced the other nation to follow suit.

When defense procurement is analyzed, three potential agents are
relevant; namely, the government (e.g., the Congress in the United
States); the military (DoD, MoD); and the firm. The military is
frequently referred to as the contractor, and the firm is the producer or
supplier. To facilitate analysis, the researcher often suppresses one of
these three agents and focuses on the other two. Some formulations
emphasize the interactions between the Congress and the military
(Rogerson, 1990, 1991a), others concern the interactions between the
Congress and the firm (Cummins, 1977; McAfee and McMillan, 1986a,
1986b) and still others involve the interaction between the military and
the firm (Tirole, 1986). These game analyses emphasize either the
sequential nature of the game, or the information structure, or both. For
sequential aspects, the game is typically depicted as a two-period game in
which in the first period one player decides a choice variable, based on
his/her anticipation of the other player's optimizing choice in the second

period. The game is solved backwards by first depicting the optimizing choice in the second period and then using this choice as a constraint on the optimizing choice in the first period. In so doing, the agents are made to anticipate their counterpart's reaction to their own behavior.

Information is relevant to the procurement problem when one player is informed and the other is not about, say, a random variable. This situation is termed asymmetric information and is germane to principal–agent problems in which the agent knows its own effort but the principal, while able to observe an outcome, cannot observe effort. Suppose that *ex post* cost, c_i, is made up of three components: (1) the agent's expected cost of the project, c_i^*, *(2) an additive random variable, ψ,* and (3) cost reducing effort, e_i. Thus, we have

$$c_i = c_i^* + \psi - e_i. \tag{5.2}$$

Suppose further that the contractor (the principal) can monitor *ex post* cost, but its three components' values are *only* known to the agent. Thus, high *ex post* cost may result from low effort to reduce cost or a bad draw of the random factor, or both. The principal is unable to determine whether nature or the agent is the cause behind cost overruns. To motivate the agent, the principal must design an incentive scheme or contract where expending high effort is a dominant strategy (i.e., it rewards the agent with higher payoffs regardless of the state of nature).

McAfee and McMillan (1986a, 1986b) examined bidding for contracts in a principal–agent framework where n potential agents bid for a defense procurement contract. If the agents are risk averse and the principal is risk neutral, then the optimal (linear) incentive compatible contract is *never* cost plus and is usually an incentive contract with risks shared (McAfee and McMillan, 1986a). For an incentive contract, the agent receives a fixed-price (i.e., its bid price) and a proportion of the cost overrun (i.e., the difference between the actual cost and the bid cost). As this proportion falls, the agent is motivated to keep costs down after getting the contract, since more of the cost overrun falls on its shoulders. But the agent is also expected to raise its bid during the competitive round as too low a bid puts greater cost on the agent as the sharing proportion falls. Additionally, a fall in the recoverable proportion of cost overruns means greater risks for the agent, who will require greater compensations. An optimal contract fixes the risk-sharing proportion so as to equate the marginal benefit from greater cost-reduction effort by the agent with the marginal cost from reduced-bidding competition and larger compensation for risk sharing.

The problem is solved in three steps. First, the agent's choice of effort is ascertained for a given sharing proportion and bid so as to maximize the firm's expected utility of profit, with expectation taken over period t. Second, the agent's optimal bid for each sharing proportion is determined in which effort choices are constrained by the first step. Third, the principal chooses the sharing proportion to minimize its expected cost, while constrained by the agent's optimizing bid and effort choices derived in the first two steps. This is a noncooperative game, because the strategic interactions of the two players – the military (contractor) and the firm (the agent) – are taken into account. The principal moves first and fixes the parameter of the contract, then the agent acts to decide its bid and, if successful, its effort choice. Since the game is solved backwards, the solution is found in reverse order.

In two interesting contributions, William Rogerson (1990, 1991b) presented two sequential game representations of the procurement process. In one representation, the military first chooses the quality or sophistication of a weapon system, and then the Congress chooses an output level, taking the military choice of quality as given. Asymmetric goals characterize the players: the military is concerned with maximizing the military value of a proposed weapons system, while the Congress is interested in maximizing the net (of cost) military value of a proposed weapons system. Rogerson (1990) showed that the organizational setting for military procurement decision making leads to a greater than first-best level for quality. The resulting level for quantity may be too great or too little and depends, among other things, on whether quality and quantity are substitutable.

For purposes of illustration, we focus on Rogerson's (1991a) game analysis of weapons procurement when plant scale and output levels are decided. The game again consists of two players: the military and the Congress. Rogerson demonstrated that the plant scale and output are too high in equilibrium. Furthermore, output is produced in too large a plant, which, in turn, raises per-unit cost. The military is better informed about technical design decisions concerning production facilities than is the Congress and, hence, the latter delegates the scale of plant decision to the military. After scale is decided, the Congress determines the output decision. By choosing a larger than first-best scale decision, the military is able to induce the Congress to pick a larger than first-best output level. This follows because an augmented scale reduces marginal cost and this, in turn, increases the attractiveness of higher production runs.

The first-best problem corresponds to

$$\max_{x,s} [V(x) - C(x, s)], \tag{5.3}$$

where x is output, s is plant scale, $V(\cdot)$ is the military value function of the weapons, and $C(\cdot)$ is the cost function. $V(\cdot)$ is assumed to be an increasing, strictly concave function, and $C(\cdot)$ is assumed to be a strictly convex function. The latter increases in output. A unique first-best solution (x^*, s^*) is assumed to exist and is strictly preferred to $(0, 0)$. For a given output level, a second-best scale minimizes cost and corresponds to

$$\min_s C(x,s). \tag{5.4}$$

We denote the unique second-best scale for each $x > 0$ as $\phi(x)$.

The long run cost is

$$L(x) = \begin{array}{ll} 0, & x = 0 \\ C(x, \phi(x)), & x > 0. \end{array} \tag{5.5}$$

Given s, a second-best output level follows from

$$\max_x [V(x) - C(x, s)], \tag{5.6}$$

where the difference between military value and procurement cost denotes the net social surplus perceived by the Congress from the weapons. The second-best level of output, associated with equation (5.6), is indicated by $\Omega(s)$. Rogerson (1991a) also assumed that there is a capacity level to scale, $\bar{s}$, such that negative net social surpluses result for $s > \bar{s}$. If, that is, plant scale is made sufficiently large, the cost is prohibitive by exceeding the resulting military value at all output levels. Hence, a zero output level is then optimal. Clearly, even the most zealous military does not want to push scale beyond $\bar{s}$, since no procurement results. At $s < \bar{s}$, a positive surplus is assumed, so that we have

$$V(\Omega(s)) - C(\Omega(s), s) \gtreqless 0 <=> s \lesseqgtr \bar{s}. \tag{5.7}$$

We indicate an interior second-best output level at $\bar{s}$ as $\bar{x} = \Omega(\bar{s})$. Finally, we assume

$$C_{xs}(x, s) < 0, \tag{5.8}$$

which implies that marginal cost of ouput falls with scale. This assumption is sufficient to imply that $\phi'(x) > 0$, or that a larger scale is optimally chosen for a larger ouput level. (The sign of $\phi'(x)$ follows from differentiating the first-order conditions associated with equation (5.4) so that $\phi'(x) = -C_{xs}/C_{ss}$.)

We are now prepared to investigate the equilibrium for this sequential game. The military moves first and decides scale so as to maximize $V(x)$. That is, the military is only concerned with military benefits associated with a weapons system where more weapons is preferred to less ($V'(x) >$

0). The Congress then decides the choice of output so as to maximize the net social surplus, *conditional* on the military's choice of scale. Following Rogerson (1991a) the Congress only pays for the production facilities if procurement is nonzero.

Working backwards, we first allow the Congress to choose a second-best output level, given s, to maximize net social surplus as depicted in (5.6). The Congress will choose a positive output provided that the net social surplus is nonzero, or that $s \leq \bar{s}$; hence, we have the Congress's choice of x for each s – denoted by $\Theta(s)$ – as

$$\Theta(s) = \begin{cases} \Omega(s) & s < \bar{s} \\ \{0, \bar{x}\}, & s = \bar{s} \\ 0, & s > \bar{s}. \end{cases} \tag{5.9}$$

The military then chooses an s so as to maximize:

$$\max_s V(\Theta(s)), \tag{5.10}$$

where the dependency of the military choice on the anticipated behavior of the Congress is acknowledged. An equilibrium weapons program satisfies

$$\max_{x,s} V(x) \tag{5.11}$$
$$\text{subject to } x \in \Theta(s).$$

Both player's choices must be mutually consistent at an equilibrium, so that $x^e = \Theta(s^e)$ and $s^e = \phi(x^e)$, where superscript e denotes equilibrium value.

Obviously, the military wants to choose scale to maximize x since V increases with x. This is accomplished by choosing $s = \bar{s}$. For each s, an interior maximum for $x > 0$ must satisfy the first-order condition associated with equation (5.6)

$$V'(x) - C_x(x, s) = 0. \tag{5.12}$$

This equation implicitly defines $\Omega(s)$. By the implicit function rule, we have

$$\frac{dx}{ds} = \frac{C_{xs}(x, s)}{V''(x) - C_{xx}(x, s)} > 0. \tag{5.13}$$

The inequality follows from $C_{xs} < 0$ and the concavity of the objective function. The derivative in (5.13) corresponds to $\Omega'(s)$ and indicates that larger scale increases the Congress's optimizing choice of output up to $\bar{s}$, at which point the net social surplus disappears. In fact, the unique (second-best) equilibrium program occurs at $(\bar{x}, \bar{s})$. The military exploits

its first-mover advantage by choosing $\bar{s}$ and, in doing so, extracts all of the social surplus which is driven to zero at $\bar{x}$.

It is easy to show that the equilibrium leads to greater than first-best scale and output – i.e., $\bar{x} > x^*$ and $\bar{s} > s^*$. When, for example, the first-best condition

$$V'(x) - C_x(x, s) = 0, \tag{5.14}$$

is evaluated at $(\bar{x}, \bar{s})$, we have

$$V'(\bar{x}) - C_x(\bar{x}, \bar{s}) < 0, \tag{5.15}$$

since $V'(\bar{x}) = 0$ and $C_x > 0$. Owing to the concavity of the objective, we have gone too far in choosing $\bar{x}$, so that a smaller level is needed to satisfy (5.14). A similar demonstration can show that $\bar{s} > s^*$.

The Rogerson game analysis allows us to understand better that the manner in which procurement decisions are organized may lead to strategic interactions that do not further society's interest. This is an important insight, since it can be used to design more optimal procurement structures. For example, Rogerson (1990, 1991a) investigated the beneficial effects of fixing a budget prior to the sequential game. With sufficient foresight, this budget setting process could result in a first-best outcome. When player's interests are not concerned with the same objective functions, strategic interactions become a crucial consideration. The introduction of additional constraints, such as an incentive compatible mechanism, can lead to a better outcome. Game theory is a particularly appropriate tool for analyzing procurement.

5.7   The impact of market features on contracting

At the policy level, governments have used various strategies to ensure that private firms fulfill defense contracts at reasonable cost, in a timely manner and with suitable quality. These strategies have included (Burnett and Kovacic, 1989; Laffont and Tirole, 1993; Rob, 1986):
(i)   Incentive contracts;
(ii)   Various regulatory arrangements relating to the disclosure of costs and the control of profits;
(iii)   The use of competition at various stages in a project's life cycle.

The new economics of defense contracting starts from the distinctive features of the defense market:
a)   In the domestic market, the buying side is dominated by a single large customer. The customer can be lobbied but it can be, and has been, a producer in the industry; it also has taxation, regulatory, and coercive powers. Furthermore, the buyer operates in a political

market place where procurement choices can be influenced by lobbying and by vote considerations (Lichtenberg, 1989).

b) The use of costly, rapidly changing, high technology means that procurement is dominated by uncertainty about buyer requirements, cost, and performance requirements.

c) The market is characterized by information gaps and asymmetries. Differences in the information available to the buyer and sellers accentuates uncertainty. Contractors have a comparative advantage over the knowledge of the technological possibilities and cost conditions, but buyers have some advantage through their monopsony powers and ability to change their requirements frequently. Not surprisingly, pre- and post-contractor opportunism and strategic behavior occur on both sides of the buyer-seller relationship (e.g., the buyer can threaten to cancel a project or buy from abroad; or the buyer can use any cost information gained from post-costing to drive a "hard bargain" on future contracts; or it can threaten renegotiation of profits).

d) Contractual relationships are often long-term extending over many years and embracing design, development, production, and in-service support. Long-term contracts agreed under uncertainty cannot be specified completely. Such contracts are inevitably *incomplete* because:

   (i)   It is impossible to anticipate all future contingencies. In bidding, firms will specify multiple parameters reflecting various contingencies (i.e., the terms on which it will accept the contract).

   (ii)   The appropriate response to uncertainty is not apparent at the start of the contract.

   (iii) It is costly to write complex contingent contracts where there is bounded rationality, so preventing identification of all contingencies and the specification of desired actions for each contingency.

   (iv)   Some long-term transactions require the supplier to invest in specific human and physical capital which is contract specific. At the same time, the buyer cannot turn to alternative suppliers without incurring additional set-up costs. *Ex post*, once specific investments have occurred, the parties will be in a bilateral monopoly; and the absence of *ex post* competition increases the possibility of opportunism (i.e., one party capturing all the gains). In principle, then, a long-term contract has *ex post* to guarantee the parties a fair return *ex ante* to encourage specific investments (Baron, 1988; Tirole, 1986 and 1988; Williamson, 1986).

With long-term contracts, the problem is to find the optimal trade-off between flexibility and the prevention of opportunism. The problem is accentuated because long-term relationships tend to promote collusion between buyer and contractor personnel (e.g. defense ministry officials become friendly with the firms they have dealt with repeatedly: Tirole, 1988, p. 27).

e) Long-term contracts involving development and production work provide contractors with incentives to bid low to obtain the development contract and aim to obtain monopoly rents on the resulting production work. However, over the development and production program as a whole, it is likely that the contractor will earn only a normal return: hence, efforts to introduce separate competitions at both the development and production stages might encourage exits or a change in the relative prices of development and production work (Kovacic, 1991). In this context, a model has been developed where it is assumed that the initial contract is awarded competitively and that the winner will become a monopolist subject to profit regulation. On this basis, the model shows that both expected contractor profit and government expenditure can be reduced by raising the profit policy mark-up. The result arises because not only do firms "buy-into" the initial contract, but also differential subsidization induced by the profit policy (higher-cost producers receive larger absolute mark-ups) promotes more aggressive competition (Bower and Osband, 1991; Rogerson, 1989).

f) For high technology projects, the supply side is characterized by monopoly or oligopoly. Also, most contractors are multi-product firms with a variety of military and civil products. The fact that, at any one time, a firm has a number of defense contracts creates product cost measurement problems and further possibilities for opportunistic behavior by the buyer and seller.

g) The industry is regulated with regulations on cost estimating, accountancy practices, and the profitability of noncompetitive work. Regulations also determine how future contingencies and disagreements between the buyer and the regulated firm will be resolved. Defense ministries often fear that firms will be dishonest in negotiating fixed-prices and will exploit opportunities for shirking in meeting quality specifications: hence, governments have adopted elaborate regulatory requirements including equality of information, truth in negotiations laws, post costing, and renegotiation of excessive profits. Similarly, incentives for firms to shirk on quality are policed by including warranties in contracts and by maintaining inspection teams at the contractors' plants (Baron, 1988; Laffont and Tirole, 1986).

These distinctive features of defense markets have determined contractual relationships (i.e., the terms of exchange between buyer and seller). Contracting for standard items is relatively simple (e.g. batteries, cars, office furniture). The real problems arise with the need to negotiate long-term contracts under uncertainty where the contractual relationship is complicated by asymmetrical information, adverse selection, moral hazard, risk sharing, and monitoring (Baron and Besanko, 1987). Fixed-price, cost reimbursement and incentive contracts are the policy instruments available to "solve" these procurement problems.

5.7.1   Fixed-price contracts

Fixed-price contracts are usually adopted under competition or sole source purchasing where there are few technological and economic uncertainties. But governments might be reluctant to sign fixed-price contracts where there are information asymmetries. Governments might be ignorant about a firm's cost conditions so that they are unable to dispute *ex ante* cost estimates. In the circumstances, firms can earn informational rents. Laffont and Tirole (1986) have considered some of the conditions for optimal incentive contracts when the contractor's costs can be observed, concluding that the optimal contract moves toward a fixed-price contract as demand increases.

Underlying fixed-price and other incentive contracts is the assumption that firms are profit-maximizers. However, in imperfect (and regulated) markets, the pursuit of other objectives, such as the maximization of sales, growth or utility, or even satisficing, means that firm behavior will depart from that implied by the profit-maximizing model (Cummins, 1977; Demong and Strayer, 1981). For example, long-run sales maximization may be served by hiring additional R & D staff on defense contracts with the aim of increasing the firm's advantage in future competitions or even to improve its position in civil markets (Cummins, 1977). In these circumstances, the pursuit of aims other than maximum profits needs to be recognized when formulating incentives and regulatory arrangements for defense contracts (Hartley, 1991b, p. 88). Similarly, on the buying side, it is often assumed that procurement and regulatory agencies are acting in the public interest, maximizing social welfare or minimizing program costs (Laffont, 1986). Instead, they might be maximizing budgets, or satisficing or seeking a quiet life, all of which will affect contractor behavior. For example, procurement staff might "satisfice" in contract negotiations if they lack performance incentives in their employment contracts and if they can rely on regulation, post-costing, and renegotiation of "excessive" profits.

5.7.2   Cost-plus contracts

Cost-plus contracts avoid excessive profits but there is the potential for cost *maximization*. With cost-plus contracts, the government acts as an insurer providing full insurance to the firm by bearing all the risks (Kovacic, 1991). Here, it has been suggested that if the firm is risk averse and the government buyer is risk neutral (due to the size of the financial assets it commands and the ability to pool risks), cost-plus contracts represent an optimal risk-sharing arrangement – but they are inefficient (Samuelson, 1983). In contrast, fixed-price contracts will include a risk premium for meeting cost uncertainties (i.e., a risk premium which is charged to the government by the winning firm). But in terms of risk sharing, it has been suggested that fixed-price contracts are suboptimal, although they offer efficiency advantages (Samuelson, 1983). The implications for contractor profitability of these limiting cases can be shown

$$\Pi_a = \Pi_t + s(C_t - C_a), \tag{5.16}$$

where Π_a = actual contractor profitability,

$\quad\;\; \Pi_t$ = target profit allowed by the government,

$\quad\;\; s$ = sharing ratio, namely, the rate at which any difference between target or estimated cost and actual costs will be shared between the firm and the government. On fixed-price contracts, $s = 1$; on cost–plus contracts, $s = 0$; and on incentive contracts s varies between 0 and 1,

$\quad\;\; C_t$ = target or estimated costs,

$\quad\;\; C_a$ = actual costs.

The extremes of fixed-price and cost–plus contracts show the trade-offs between risk sharing (insurance) and efficiency. The problem for procurement agencies is to formulate an incentive contract which specifies an optimal insurance arrangement between the contractor and the government, which contains desirable risk-sharing features and which provides incentives for efficient performance (Cummins, 1977; Peeters, 1993; Samuelson, 1983).

5.7.3   Incentive contracts

Incentive contracts can be viewed as a compromise between the extremes of fixed-price and cost-plus (Cannes, 1975; McCall, 1970; Moore, 1967).

All too often, defense ministries make an all or nothing choice: cost-plus or fixed price. In fact, McAfee and McMillan argue that the optimal contract is never cost-plus, may be fixed-price, but is usually an incentive contract (McAfee and McMillan, 1986). Using various simulations, they show that, compared with fixed-price contracts, incentive contracts result in cost savings ranging from under 1 to 35 percent, with a median saving of some 3 percent (McAfee and McMillan, 1986, p. 333). However, this result is based on a number of highly restrictive assumptions about the buyer having perfect information on a firm's *ex post* costs, that accounting costs approximate opportunity costs, that principal and agent do not incur transaction costs in the bidding process, and that bidders differ only in their expected costs. Relaxing such assumptions could easily lead to increased costs which could more than absorb the typical estimated 3 percent saving from incentive contracts (McAfee and McMillan, 1986, p. 335, footnote 16; Laffont, 1986).

With incentive contracts, there will be bargaining between buyer and seller about the target cost, the target profit, the sharing ratio, and the government's maximum price liability. For US defense contracts between 1978 and 1984, sharing rates varied between 15 percent and 25 percent, although there were examples of 50 percent sharing.[2] Of course, with incentive contracts, firms will aim to negotiate a high cost target, a favorable (to the firm) sharing arrangement, and a high maximum price liability (De Mayo, 1983). To control such behavior, proposals have been made for budget-based schemes. Under these proposals, the incentive fee depends on actual costs and on a cost estimate which the firm selects at the start of the project (i.e., the firm selects a budget in the form of a target cost) and the incentive fee is proportional to the budget variance. Analysis suggests that budget-based schemes create desirable reporting and performance incentives. As a result, the government receives information that is useful for its budget-planning process since the contracting firm has an incentive to submit true, realistic, and unbiased cost estimates (Reichelstein, 1992).

In a model of incentive contracting developed by Cummins (1977), it is argued that the popular public policy focus on the percentage profit fee and the magnitude of cost overruns on the contract is misplaced simply because these factors provide no useful information on the efficiency of the incentive contracting mechanism, nor the extent to which actual project costs are being controlled. Instead, attention should be directed

---

[2]   One rule for estimating the sharing ratio is: $s = A/(1 + A)$
where s = sharing ratio and A = overheads (Peeters and Veld, 1989).

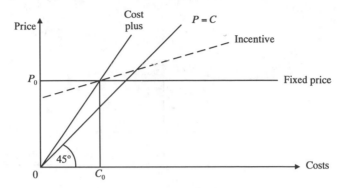

Figure 5.2 Contract types

at learning more about the contractor's attitudes toward risk and moral hazard (Cummins, 1977). However, procurement agencies might find it both difficult and costly to learn about such subjective factors amongst a firm's managers.

The relationship between fixed-price, cost-plus, and incentive contracts is shown in figure 5.2. In the figure, price is based on estimated costs (C_0) plus a target profit, Π_t [where $P_0 = C_0 + \Pi_t$ (Poussard, 1983)]. Fixed-price contracts are represented by a horizontal price line, cost-plus by a positive slope with profits as a mark-up on the 45° line, and incentive contracts are intermediate between the two, the slope of the line reflecting the sharing ratio.

Further insights into the efficiency properties of different contract types is shown in figure 5.3. This brings together the role of pressure (e.g. competition or regulation), the sharing ratio for the firm, a firm's effort and its implications for efficiency (or the lack of it). In this model, high pressure (P_1), together with a high sharing ratio (s_1 = fixed-price contract), has favorable effects on a firm's effort (E_1) – and high effort levels promote efficiency resulting in output Q_1 being produced on the lowest attainable average cost curve (AC_0).

Shubik offers a fitting conclusion: "It is easy to produce a general impossibility theorem to show that no simple rule will be universally optimal for the multi-faceted needs of large-scale procurement" (Shubik, 1983, p. 24). Auctions, for example, are efficient for selling many commodities but not for the procurement of large systems. Fixed-price contracts (sealed bids) seem attractive but there are risk-sharing problems, whilst cost-plus offers simplicity, risk sharing but poor incentives (Shubik, 1983).

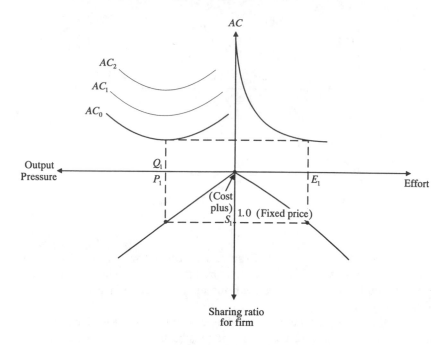

Figure 5.3 Pressure, sharing, effort, and efficiency

5.8   Regulation

Defense contracting is dominated by the desire of government procurement agencies to negotiate contracts based on "fair and reasonable"
prices (Kahn, 1993). Procurement agencies have the task of designing
contracts which provide efficiency incentives without offering contractors
excessive profits at the taxpayers' expense. Competition is one possible
policing mechanism. Where competition is possible, contract prices can
be determined by market forces with competitive pressures stimulating
efficiency and profits "policed" through entry and exit. But in
noncompetitive situations, prices and profits have to be negotiated. For
noncompetitive fixed-price contracts, "fair and reasonable" prices are
based on estimated costs plus a government-determined profit margin
(Sissons, 1986). Such contracts assume that contractors are profit
maximizers and that procurement agencies can estimate efficient costs.
However, if the procurement agency's cost estimates are unreliable, it
might agree "too high" a fixed-price which allows the contractor to earn
"excessive" profits (i.e., exceeding the profit rate allowed by the
government's profit formula: see section 5.4). Such "excessive profits"

result from estimating errors and reflect information asymmetries between the buyer and contractor. Predictably, governments have responded to the situation by introducing various regulatory arrangements concerned with equality of information, post-costing, and renegotiation of profits, usually administered through a regulatory agency (e.g. UK Review Board for Non-Competitive Government Contracts: Hartley, 1991b; Sissons, 1986). A procurement agency's cost-estimating staff and its accountants, together with a clearly specified set of rules about allowable costs and overhead rates, are a central part of the process of negotiating and checking on "fair and reasonable" prices (Sissons, 1986). Accountants are also central to policing cost-plus contracts whereby contractors recover all actual allowable costs incurred on the work (Turnip, 1989).

Regulatory rules about allowable costs, prices, and profitability can affect firm behavior. Contractors in imperfect and regulated markets subject to, say, profit controls, have every incentive to pursue nonprofit objectives such as managerial preferences for staff, luxury offices, and a quiet life (Williamson, 1965). Similarly, with cost-based pricing, defense firms have an incentive to shift more of their costs (e.g. from commercial business) to well-funded sole source procurements instead of to more competitive procurements. This can be achieved if the firm increases the amount of overhead allocated to a contract by increasing the amount of direct labor used on the contract. As a result, a contractor is likely to deliberately select too much in-house production (to maximize direct labor costs) for its products where income is cost sensitive (i.e., income depends on costs) and too much subcontracting for its products where revenue is not cost sensitive (Rogerson, 1992b). Elsewhere, it has been suggested that US defense contractors with cost-reimbursement contracts have an incentive to inflate pension costs (Thomas and Tung, 1992). These results are a development of the general point that, depending on how costs are allocated, a firm operating in regulated and unregulated markets may have an incentive to distort its output and/or input decisions so as to shift overheads to the regulated sector (Brennan, 1990).

Regulation is not costless. It involves policing, monitoring, reporting, checking and controlling functions which can result in substantial, but often ignored, transaction costs. Of course, regulation appears attractive to politicians who can use it to demonstrate that they are safeguarding the "public interest." One study has examined the hypothesis that the US weapons acquisition process is overregulated with adverse effects on the timeliness and costs of developing weapons. The study estimated that regulatory control costs probably accounted for 5–10 percent of total program costs. There was, though, no evidence that regulatory activity had affected the performance or quality of the final product (either favourably or adversely). However, there was some limited evidence of delays, with acquisition times increasing at the rate of 15 percent per decade, although this could be due to other factors (Smith *et al.*, 1988).

Continued criticism of weapons acquisition programs creates greater pressure for elected politicians and audit and procurement agencies to expand regulatory arrangements, thereby demonstrating that they are actively involved in protecting the "public interest." However, it is possible that attempts by governments to micromanage procurement (i.e., monitor and control in detail) can have unexpected and undesirable consequences for the efficiency of procurement. Paradoxically, government efforts to ensure accountability and to protect the taxpayer can result in inefficiency and project failures – and hence demands for even more regulations and control to "solve the problem"! Extreme micromanagement can destroy creativity and initiative and can lead to a focus on monitoring inputs rather than outputs (e.g., number of hours in the office). Indeed, an obsession with zero fraud and zero waste in procurement is likely to ignore the fact that the marginal costs of reaching zero targets can be prohibitive (Austin and Larkey, 1992). Furthermore, it is possible that the rising costs of regulation will have adverse effects on the willingness of firms to do business with the government. Typically, in the USA, all aspects of government contracting are governed by laws and regulation, usually introduced in response to some scandal, fraud, or abuse [e.g., false statements and claims, labor charges, bribes, collusive bidding (Failing, 1989; Weisman, 1987)]. The result of regulatory costs could be reduced entry and increased exit, making it even more difficult to maintain rivalry for defense contracts (Kovacic, 1992). In the circumstances, critics of US weapons acquisition programs have suggested that reforms need to focus on market-type incentives rather than increased government regulation (i.e., incentives and regulations do not go together: Gansler, 1989a and b; Baron, 1988).

More fundamental questions have been raised about efforts to reduce waste in the military and the usefulness of inefficient procurement. A public choice analysis shows the politics and pitfalls of reducing waste in the military. If waste in the form of excessive prices, expensive, gold-plated equipment, and operationally questionable weapons is so obvious, why hasn't it been eliminated? Special interest groups in the form of the military-industrial complex are the major source of waste and the primary obstacle to reforms which would reduce waste. Lee (1991), however, questions whether it is desirable to reduce the political power of the military-industrial complex: the result might be an *increase in the general level of inefficiency in the economy* as the composition of government spending becomes more distorted toward other civilian special-interest programs. Similarly, a public choice and rent-seeking analysis of procurement has shown that inefficient procurement is useful and that there is optimal inefficiency in the procurement of public goods (Cowen and Lee, 1992). The approach uses two kinds of agents, namely, politicians and special interest groups. Politicians can award contracts to special interest groups. In turn, special interests in the form of defense contractors earn rents which can be used to induce politicians to procure weapons systems. In the absence of political rents, politicians have no motivation to incur the costs of setting a procurement agenda: hence inefficient procurement can be an optimal second-best means of encouraging public goods production (Cowen and Lee, 1992).

The role of profits in noncompetitive contracts is also a source of controversy (Baron, 1988; Greer and Liao, 1984; Pownall, 1986). On negotiated contracts, procurement agencies usually calculate contractor profitability on the basis of factors such as performance risk (e.g., technical risk; management), contract risk (e.g., type of contract), facilities capital (for land, buildings, equipment), and working capital, with the appropriate profit rates applied to either cost or capital (Hartley, 1992). Typically, the policy debate focuses on the regulation of profits. Such an approach fails to recognize that, from an economic perspective, profit consists of different conceptual components each performing a distinct economic function in the procurement process. On this basis, Rogerson has divided profit into two components. First, as reimbursement for some economic costs of production which are not recognized as costs in US government accounting regulations. Second, as economic profit in the form of an excess over the necessary economic costs of undertaking the contract. Rogerson argues that rather than focusing on regulation, profit policy should provide appropriate incentives for promoting innovation (Rogerson, 1992).

Given the regulatory constraints, questions arise as to whether the profitability of defense contractors differs from that of other firms. Lichtenberg has tested the hypothesis that US defense contractors are more profitable than other firms, mainly because of their ability to shift costs from commercial to defense business. Using econometric analysis for the period 1983–89, Lichtenberg found strong support for the hypothesis that US defense contractors are substantially more profitable than other segments (Lichtenberg, 1992). Similarly, a study for the period 1970–1989, found that the top US defense firms outperformed the market by a huge margin (Trevino and Higgs, 1992). For the UK, econometric analysis has been used to estimate the determinants of profitability for the UK aerospace industry (Hartley and Watt, 1981). There are, however, serious problems in undertaking empirical work on the profitability of defense contracts and contractors. A satisfactory model of profitability is required which allows for all other relevant influences (including uncertainty and risk, market contestability, and the role of regulation), and for the heterogeneity of the civil business of defense contractors. Data problems abound, particularly the absence of published data on the profitability of individual defense contracts (competitive and noncompetitive, etc.) and on the profitability of a defense contractor's civil business. Opportunities also exist for applying economic models of regulatory capture. On this basis, procurement policy and regulatory arrangements might be consistent with the actions of an industry-captured regulator, who manages competition and regulates profitability among defense contractors for the benefit of the industry (Leitzel, 1992). For example, government cost estimators and accountants have discretion in accepting cost estimates and allowable costs (e.g., allowing a favorable price index and adjustment for inflation in fixed-price contracts); they can agree to offer profit rates at the top end of the permissible range; they can accept project modifications which benefit contractors; and they might accept jobs in the regulated industry.

5.9   Competition, contracts, and performance

Critics have often argued that defense contractors are inefficient and that inefficiency reflects the market environment of single source procurement: hence the suggestion that the introduction of competition should generate substantial price reductions (Burnett and Kovacic, 1989; Gansler, 1989a; Leitzel, 1992; McNaugher, 1990; Udis, 1992). Expressed more formally, it has been stated that "Competition solves ... the moral hazard problem by solving the adverse selection problem ...", and that bidding decreases the rents received by the winning firm (Laffont, 1986, p. 25).

Some proposals for reforming weapons acquisition, particularly in the USA, have been based on a preference for market-type incentives rather than increased government regulation. It is, though, admitted that there are no "right answers" nor any single change which would dramatically transform the US weapons acquisition process (Gansler, 1989b, p. 9). Instead, a package of policy measures have been suggested such as improving the quality of acquisition personnel, streamlining the acquisition organization and procedures, expanding the use of commercial products, and a greater use of commercial style competition. With this approach, competition is seen as only one element in the model for improving the weapons acquisition process (i.e., other variables cannot be ignored). Interestingly, Gansler estimates that competition would produce net savings of 20 percent and such savings could be obtained from about 50 percent of US production programs (Gansler, 1989b, p. 14; McNaugher, 1990). In the UK, competition was expected to produce savings of 10 percent on the equipment budget (HCP 189, 1991, p. 3). Admittedly, such US and UK estimates of the impact of competition are "ball park" figures with no indication of the basis of the estimates; but such estimates do raise three questions. First, what is the evidence on the economic impacts of competition; second, how reliable is the evidence; and, third, why might the estimated savings differ between the USA and the UK?

This section reviews the economics literature on the impact of competitive procurement, including the effects on R & D, scale economies, and performance indicators such as cost escalation, delays, and profitability. Some of these issues raise methodological problems: should performance on actual projects be compared with some perfect, ideal project never encountering problems or with the typical average project? This survey of evidence should also be placed into the context of current policy developments. The prospect of substantial cuts in future defense spending will mean a different defense market environment. The future is likely to be characterized by fewer new projects and smaller production orders. This is likely to create two conflicting pressures. First, pressure to move away from competition and instead, to provide support for "key" firms which are believed to be "essential components" of a nation's defense industrial base. Second, the continuous search for "better value for money" will create pressures to "open-up" defense equipment markets to foreign competition (e.g. EU Single Market; also chapters 7 and 9). The result of a changing market environment is likely to be further modifications in weapons acquisition policies.

5.9.1   Defining competition

Defense markets do not resemble the economist's perfectly competitive model. Often, they are characterized by a single buyer, one or a few large suppliers, nonprofit-maximizing firms, uncertainty, imperfect information, and barriers to entry and exit (Gansler, 1989a; Hartley, 1991b). However, this interpretation ignores second-best considerations, the role of contestability and the contribution of Austrian economics. It also takes a limited view of a market since the number of actual and potential suppliers in a national market can be increased by "opening-up" the market to allow foreign firms from the rest of the world to bid for national defense contracts.

The standard economic case for competition in defense equipment markets is that it "spurs efficiency, alters attitudes and lowers prices" (Bittleston, 1990, p. 62). What is interesting is the way in which attitudes toward competition have changed over time. In the early 1970s, for example, a US view was that competition was less desirable than single source procurement because (Fox, 1974, p. 256):

(i)   Competition requires more time and effort (e.g. in evaluating proposals).
(ii) Competition increases the chances of disputes and protests from contractors.
(iii) Competition disrupts long-established relationships between the government and contractors.
(iv) Competition requires government to evaluate the capabilities of rival firms.

But already in the early 1970s, US policy was changing. Under the Packard Initiatives of 1970, policy aimed to restore competition to weapons acquisition: the aim was to extend competition between prime contractors throughout the development stage, so avoiding developer monopoly when awarding initial production contracts (Dews, *et al.*, 1979; Udis, 1992). There followed the Competition in Contracting Act of 1984 (CICA), which required the US Department of Defense (DoD) to use "full and open competition" through competitive purchasing. Next came the Defense Authorization Act of 1986 which prevented the DoD from beginning full-scale development for major systems until Congress received an acquisition strategy. This strategy required that competitive alternative sources be available for major systems and subsystems from the start of full-scale development to the end of production: hence dual sourcing and second sourcing for production work. Finally, the DoD Appropriations Act of 1987 required the use of competitive prototypes in developing major weapons systems. As a result of these Acts, competition became the primary acquisition strategy throughout the procurement life cycle. Exceptions are allowed under limited circumstances, such as a DoD finding that competition will increase total program costs without commensurate, offsetting benefits (Burnett and Kovacic, 1989; Gansler, 1989a). Similar trends toward more competitive procurement were also occurring in the UK during the 1980s [although without legislative sanction (Hartley, 1991, 1992; HCP 189, 1991)].

Applying the principles of competition to a project's life cycle suggests the classification system shown in table 5.2. Traditionally, weapons were acquired on a single source basis, after a competition based on design

Table 5.2 *Competition*

Competition possible at	Type of competition	Risks – uncertainty
1 Design stage	Non-price	Maximum
2 Development stage – prototype	Non-price; budget limit	Great to prototype stage

3 Production stage
   all production work
   (winner takes all)
   batches (dual sourcing)
	
	Price
	Price
		
		Little – none

4 In-service support, repairs, servicing, mid-life up-dates	Price	Some – none
5 Disposal	Price	None to great (nuclear)

and development proposals. The winning firm would be awarded a contract for both full development and all production work. As a result, the winning firm established a monopoly position with potentially adverse implications for innovation, efficiency, prices, and profits. However, as table 5.2 shows, there is considerable potential for introducing and extending competition at various stages in the project's life cycle. Competition can, of course, be limited to domestic suppliers or extended to firms from the rest of the world (hence the need to define the geographical extent of the market). Typically, at the design stage, nonprice competition dominates as procurement agencies consider design proposals from a variety of bidders. Inevitably, at this stage, the risks and uncertainty associated with the project are at a maximum. The development stage could be characterized by competitive prototyping. This could be between two rival firms or two teams comprising groups of firms which agree to share risks and to share the work [the winning team members might later compete against each other for production contracts (Anton and Yao, 1990; Burnett and Kovacic, 1989; Gansler, 1989a; Leitzel, 1992)]. With competitive prototyping, there are trade-offs in the form of additional development costs but potential benefits through improved equipment performance, reduced risk of project failure, and reduced production costs (Gansler, 1989a; Burnett and Kovacic, 1989). At the production stage, competition can be introduced in various forms. The total production contract can be subject to competition with the winner receiving the total order (winner takes all competition); or an alternative supplier can be created so that two firms will be able to bid for batches of production work; or a "storing" option might be possible whereby a second producer is created but not used [i.e., maintaining the threat of rivalry (Anton and Yao, 1987; Smith, 1983; Burnett and Kovacic, 1989; Leitzel, 1992)]. Once again, such policies involve benefits and costs. There are benefits through improved incentives to reduce costs and increase quality. Here, the assumption is that the intensity of competition affects unit prices through reduced profit margins and/or reduced costs (reductions in fixed or variable costs and shifts in the slope of the learning curve). Policy costs arise in the form of additional set-up costs, the costs of transferring technology, and a failure to exploit learning economies (Leitzel, 1992). In some cases, competition might not be worthwhile (e.g. small production contracts, high set-up costs, major learning economies). Such costs and benefits of competition now need to be analyzed in more detail, particularly issues concerned with R & D, technology transfer, and scale and learning economies.

5.9.2   Research and development

What are the likely impacts of competition policy on R & D and innovation? A starting point in answering this question is to consider equipment procurement as a multi-stage process embracing design, development, initial production, and full production (see table 5.2). With sole source procurement, competing firms will bid "vigorously" (bid low) for the development contract and plan to earn monopoly profits on the resulting contracts for production and spares (*ex ante* competition; *ex post* monopoly). Whether the winning firm earns monopoly profits over the program as a whole will depend on the extent of competition at the time of the initial contract award. Competition at the initial award stage will tend to lead to a winning bid which results in normal profits in the long run. If, however, at the initial competition stage, bidders expect a second source, they are likely to bid less aggressively for the initial production contract: hence defense ministries pay higher prices for initial production but this might be exactly offset by savings on second source reprocurement. Thus, if the initial contract award for development and production is competitive, then competition at the production stage (e.g. dual and second sourcing) is unlikely to lead to significant improvements in weapons procurement (Riardon and Sappington, 1989; Leitzel, 1992). But, as Leitzel asks: is the initial contract award held in a competitive environment? (Leitzel, 1992, p. 46).

Can competition have an adverse effect on innovation? Rogerson has argued that profits (prizes) on production contracts represent a reward for earlier innovative activity by defense contractors. In such circumstances, rent-seeking firms will spend their own money in an effort to win the production contract (e.g. innovation through privately funded R & D; or lobbying, etc.). It follows that competitive procurement policies, such as dual or second sourcing, which reduce the economic profit on production contracts may reduce innovation (Rogerson, 1989).

5.9.3   Technology transfer

Competition at the production stage requires technology transfer and this might be costly. The creation of an alternative producer requires the transfer of technology from the initial developer. This can involve costs through legal disputes about intellectual property rights, as well as costs in actually ensuring that a second source fully understands the initial developer's drawings, designs, and specifications (e.g., the original supplier has incentives to hoard valuable information and to conceal knowledge from the second supplier). Experience with voluntary, commercially motivated technology transfer, as reflected in international coproduction programs, suggests that it is feasible to transfer production technology at a reasonably modest cost (Hall and Johnson, 1967, p. vii).

Technology transfer also involves indirect costs. US experience with the CICA of 1984 is illuminating. Originally, the DoD interpreted the CICA 1984 competition laws as requiring all bidders to offer to relinquish proprietary technical data rights as part of their proposals. Private developers submitting proposals which restricted the government's data rights were often eliminated from the competition (prime contractors bidding for DoD contracts often imposed similar requirements on innovative subcontractors). Not surprisingly, such requirements affected entry and exit. Firms with commercial markets which might be adversely affected by government data rights requirements, are likely to exit from the initial bidding if the value of their commercial operations is high relative to the expected profitability of defense contracts. Predictably, the CICA was modified in 1988: contractors relying on privately developed products which they offer to DoD are not to be disadvantaged in the competitive process. This modification aimed to provide private industry with an incentive to invest in risky new technology (Brunette, 1989).

5.9.4   Economies of scale and learning

Competition at the production stage appears attractive. It can take the form of dual sourcing which involves simultaneous production from two suppliers: production is split between the two firms, with the majority of

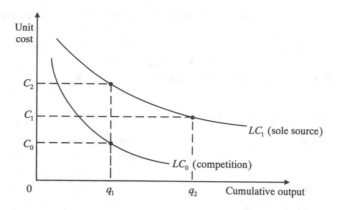

Figure 5.4 Sole source versus competition

production awarded to the lower-cost producer in the previous award. Alternatively, with second sourcing, a second supplier is created (via technology transfer) and all future production contracts are awarded to one of the two firms in a "one-off" competition (Burnett, 1987; Leitzel, 1992). At first sight, though, competitive procurement for production work involves costs. If the original developer has undertaken initial production work, it will have acquired production (learning) experience which should be reflected in a unit cost advantage over a new entrant; and the advantage to the incumbent will be increased by the size of the set-up costs needed to create a second supplier (Anton and Yao, 1987; Gansler, 1989a; Leitzel, 1992). However, it is argued that introducing competition at the production stage will limit sole source monopoly profits and provide incentives to remove X-inefficiency in the incumbent firm. In this case, the new entrant's costs provide information on the incumbent's costs and a means of limiting the incumbent's rents. Indeed, it has been suggested that it may be optimal to replace the incumbent, even when the entrant has higher production costs (Demski, *et al.*, 1987).

The learning curve provides an analytical framework for evaluating the relative merits of single source versus competitive procurement in production, as shown in figure 5.4 (Gansler, 1989a). Assume that prices are based on unit costs and that the aim is to buy quantity $0q_2$ in two equal batches of $0q_1$. The original developer is asked to produce the initial output $0q_1$, after which the production work is subject to competition. The original developer will produce $0q_1$ at a unit cost of C_2 and $0q_2$ (the sole source solution) at a unit cost of C_1 on LC_1 (figure 5.4). If LC_1 is X-efficient, then the incumbent will win any competition by offering to supply $q_2 - q_1 \, (= 0q_1)$ at a unit cost substantially below C_2

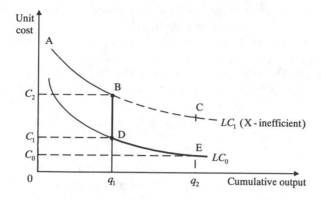

Figure 5.5 Adaptive response

(reflecting marginal rather than average costs), compared with a new entrant's unit costs of C_2 for the second production batch ($0q_1$). But, if the original developer is not X-efficient, then a second supplier might have lower unit costs reflected in a lower and steeper learning curve, LC_0. Thus, the new entrant offers $0q_1$ (second batch) at a unit cost of C_0 and the savings from competition are $C_1 - C_0$, and not $C_2 - C_0$ (i.e., the sole source producer would have been at C_1 on LC_1).

Figure 5.4 can be modified to allow the sole source producer to respond to the threat of entry. An example is shown in figure 5.5. Contestability might shift the sole source cost curve from ABC (LC_1 without rivalry, as in figure 5.4) to ABDE with rivalry as in figure 5.5: this would maintain the incumbent's unit cost advantage over the new entrant (the incumbent would offer a unit cost below C_1 for $q_2 - q_1$). Of course, the framework outlined in figures 5.4 and 5.5 is no more than a starting point and it raises a set of questions:

(i)   What assumptions should be made about the sole source learning curve under competition? Will the sole source supplier offer lower unit costs than the new entrant due to the removal of X-inefficiency and the advantages of production experience?
(ii)   What would happen to unit costs in the absence of competition (the counterfactual)?
(iii)   Is it reasonable to assume that defense production is a decreasing cost activity: what about the possibility that for some activities, and some scales of production, unit costs might rise?
(iv)   What are the pricing assumptions – will competition reduce profit margins as well as unit costs?

(v)   What is the likely impact of other influences (e.g., expectations about future cuts in defense spending)?

(vi)   What are the costs of competition compared with monitoring, policing, and auditing a sole source producer?

Evidence on the savings due to competition has focused on the production stage. Researchers have estimated savings by using learning curves and assuming that prices reflect contractor costs (see figures 5.4 and 5.5). A survey of the US empirical literature estimated average savings due to competition ranging from 11 percent to 53 percent, with a median saving of 33 percent. However, one study found that dual sourcing was more expensive than sole sourcing. Moreover, once allowance is made for start-up costs, it is not always obvious that savings were realized. Interestingly, the second source won most of the competitions (Anton and Yao, 1990). But, after reviewing the literature, Anton and Yao have concluded that the empirical studies on competitive savings are flawed: "There is no question that the difficulties of measuring, much less forecasting, are immense, yet the magnitude of the problem is no excuse for models based on weak theory" (Anton and Yao, 1990, p. 77).

5.9.5   Performance indicators

Evidence is available on various performance indicators concerned with fixed-price contracts, cost escalation, and profitability. American experience with total package procurement introduced in the 1960s is illuminating. Under total package procurement, firms committed themselves to a single fixed-price contract for the development and production phases of the acquisition cycle. The "classic" examples of this approach were the Lockheed C-5A transport aircraft and the Grumman F-14 fighter aircraft. Both firms seriously underestimated their costs and incurred massive overruns and severe losses. Lockheed, for example, massively miscalculated the costs of building a technologically complex new transport aircraft which considerably exceeded the state of the art. As a result of huge cost overruns, Lockheed was driven to the verge of bankruptcy, from which it was rescued by a DoD unilateral price increase and Congressional loan guarantees. This experience highlights the problems of fixed-price contracts where projects involve substantial technological uncertainties. Such contracts are likely to involve defense ministries and contractors in costly disputes over the proper interpretation of the contract and its requirements. And, in the last resort, fixed-price contracts are difficult to enforce if the result is likely to be the exit of a major firm (Kovacic, 1991; Udis, 1992; Fox, 1974).

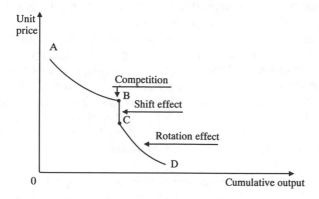

Figure 5.6 Price reduction curves

Contract and contractor performance can also be assessed in terms of cost control, delivery schedules and equipment performance. A US study has estimated the impact of the 1970s Packard Initiatives, including the increased use of hardware competition. A comparison of competitive with noncompetitive programs supported the claimed advantages of competition. Competitive programs had slightly better performance and schedule ratios and substantially less cost growth (e.g., an average cost growth ratio of 1.16 compared with 1.53 for projects with little or no competition: Dews *et al.*, 1979, p. 28). It must be emphasized, though, that these results were based on a relatively small sample and might reflect the influence of "other factors". Similarly, a comparison of the 1970s and 1960s programs is a further means of assessing the impact of the 1970s Packard Initiatives in the USA. By almost every measure of systems performance, program schedule, and cost escalation, the comparison favored the 1970s experience [e.g., average cost growth of 1.44 in the 1960s compared with 1.34 in the 1970s (Dews *et al.*, 1979, p. 57)].

Profitability is a further indicator of contractor performance and questions arise about the impact of competition on profitability. Under what circumstances does competition lead to reductions in production costs, to profit reductions, or to both? Consider the price reduction curve shown in figure 5.6 (based on a learning curve). The introduction of competition is predicted to result in lower prices due to two factors: first, a shift effect and, second, a rotation effect reflecting a steeper price reduction curve.

In examining prices and profitability, Greer and Liao have suggested that when business slackens and excess capacity emerges, prices tend to fall and profit margins weaken (Greer and Liao, 1986). Their empirical results suggest that when industry capacity utilization is below the 80 percent normal level, introducing competition into major systems acquisition results in price savings. With capacity utilization below 80 percent, the industry is "hungry." Incorporating a role for capacity utilization might explain why dual sourcing results in added net costs as often as it has produced the desired net savings. Dual-source procurement seems to lead to net savings when industry capacity utilization averaged less than 80 percent: hence it is argued that introducing dual sourcing when capacity use is above 80 percent is unwise (Greer and Liao, 1986, p. 1268).

There are relatively few empirical studies of the impact of the UK's competitive procurement policy. Claims have been made of improved efficiency by defense contractors reflected in price savings varying from 10 percent to 70 percent, better export performance and a wider supplier base (Hartley, 1991b; HCP 189, 1991). Elsewhere, there have been studies of the impact of competition on the structure of the UK defense market showing reduced concentration and increased competition (Smith, 1990; Willett, 1993). Concern has also been expressed about the impact of competition on exits from the industry, on the costs of bidding, delays in reaching decisions, and on the reluctance of firms to invest in private venture R & D with implications for innovation (Bittleston, 1990).

5.10   Conclusion: the results of competition

Although it has legislative support, US competition policy has to be implemented by procurement officials who have discretion in determining how to apply competition; and when exceptions are allowed (Burnett and Kovacic, 1989). The possibility arises of anti-competitive behavior by the buyer (rather than the supplier). Indeed, public choice analysis suggests that various interest groups in the military–industrial–political complex who are likely to lose from the policy will oppose it. Contractors prefer "cosy" relationships with the defense ministry, and procurement agencies prefer the simplicity of avoiding competition and continuing to work with known firms.

It also needs to be recognized that policy makers' simplified economic models of competition are limited and can produce unexpected and undesirable results. Some examples can be given:

(i)   Estimates suggest that second sourcing designed to promote competition might lead to higher overall program costs of 40 percent compared with the cost of sole sourcing (Burnett, 1989; Mayer, 1991).

(ii)   Contract winners expect lower future profits, so that they invest less in R & D compared with sole sourcing. Also, the prospect of reduced future profitability causes every bidder to bid less aggressively in the initial procurement phase compared with sole source acquisition (Brunette, 1989).

(iii) Teaming arrangements can lead to anti-competitive behavior [e.g., collusion, exchange of price data, cartels (Burnett and Kovacic, 1989)].

(iv)   There are potential conflicts between competition policy and regulatory policy. Regulation assumes the absence of rivalry and it can impede competition policy. With rivalry and contractors assuming a greater financial risk, they need greater financial rewards for successful performance.

(v)   It has been argued that US DoD procurement practice is consistent with the actions of an industry-captured regulator, who manages the competition among defense contractors for the benefit of the entire industry. The stylized facts of source selection, contract management, and gold plated weapons can be explained by a regulatory capture model of the DoD (Leitzel, 1992).

The examples given above show that economic models of competition will be implemented by agents in the political market place. Recent developments in game theory, strategic behavior, transaction costs, contestability, and Austrian economics have led to substantial modifications in some of the more simplified interpretations of economic models of competition.

6   Military manpower

The armed forces are a major employer, but military manpower and the human resource dimension of defense economics is a neglected field (Withers, 1991). Admittedly, there have been extensive economic studies of conscription versus an all-volunteer force, but there remain considerable opportunities for applying the analytical tools of labor economics to military manpower. Issues on the demand side embrace recruitment, factor substitution, and retention whilst supply-side factors include demography, relative pay in the civil sector, training, and skill acquisition. Military manpower operates in an administered or internal labor market dominated by hierarchies, rules, and contractual commitments.

Over various periods of history, nations have manned their armed forces using different combinations of voluntary and compulsory service or conscription. During major wars, manpower in the armed forces is increased by an extensive system of conscription; and, since 1945, nations in NATO and the former Warsaw Pact retained large standing forces mostly through peace-time conscription. Partly as a result of conscription, where military manpower is a "free good," the armed forces have established an internal labor market which was independent of relative scarcities in the civil economy.

Compared with the civil sector, military employment or service has some distinctive features. First, all individuals in the armed forces are subject to a set of legally enforceable rules known as military discipline, breaches of which can involve punishment such as demotion, imprisonment, or expulsion from the forces (during wars, the ultimate sanction might be a firing squad). As a result, individuals cannot voluntarily withdraw their labor (cf. strikes in the civil sector). Second, conscripts have to accept pay, conditions, and a duration of employment determined by the state. Similarly, volunteers usually sign a contract for a specified number of years. Whilst premature voluntary release is possible, it can be costly. Such contractual commitments create lags in adjusting the size of the armed forces to new equilibrium values (e.g., due

156

to emergencies, wars, or disarmament). Third, the distinctive feature of military service is that part of the job involves individuals voluntarily or compulsorily accepting a contractual commitment under which they could sacrifice their lives (i.e., they can be killed). This is an extreme form of the nonmonetary disadvantages of military service and might be expected to be a determinant of military pay for volunteer forces.

This chapter starts by examining military manpower as part of the military production function. It then considers the labor market for military manpower dealing with the demand and supply sides of the market, embracing recruitment, retention, pay, and training, and the choice between conscription and an all-volunteer force. A final section deals with internal organizational issues.

Various policy issues will be considered such as the impact of changes in the relative prices of service personnel and defense equipment on the employment of service personnel; the problems and costs of recruiting an all-volunteer force where the armed services are a major recruiter of young people; and the opportunities for substitution between military manpower and equipment, between reserves and regulars, between men and women, and between armed forces personnel and civilians. Once again, it will be seen that US studies dominate the theoretical, empirical, and policy literature on military manpower. Two issues have been preeminent. First, studies of conscription versus an all-volunteer force. Second, the 1990s concern with downsizing and its implications for military manpower.

6.1   The military production function

The military production function specifies the relationship between factor inputs and output. The inputs of technology, capital, and labor take the form of defense equipment, bases, facilities (infrastructure), together with the military and civilian manpower needed to provide defense forces. The macro-level production function can be viewed as the aggregation of a set of micro-level production functions. At the micro-level, defense can be regarded as an industry which uses resources of land, manpower, capital, and entrepreneurship in the form of military commanders. This industry comprises a large number of military units (bases) or firms, each of different size, each producing different products (air, land, and sea forces), with all contributing to defense output. In principle, this is the same optimization problem faced by private firms in competitive markets aiming to use their factor inputs to maximize profits.

Defense, however, differs from private competitive markets in that there is an absence of market prices for the output of defense, there are no rival suppliers of defense in a national market, and profitability cannot be used as a performance indicator. Indeed, within the military production function, commanders often regarded manpower as a resource which, compared with defense equipment, was inexhaustible, inexpensive, and readily available. This traditional view of military manpower had a major impact on strategic thinking in which the *use* rather than the *preservation* of manpower was the purpose of strategy. Since 1945, the increasing emphasis on technology and nuclear weapons has meant a subordinate role for military manpower. More recently, though, strategists have recognized that the claimed performance capabilities of modern defense equipment depends on human resource inputs for their operation, repair, and maintenance. Furthermore, the human resource dimension is being recognized in the form of leadership, creativity, initiative, and courage (cf. entrepreneurship), all of which can be important determinants of the outcome of a conflict (e.g., the Falklands conflict). Thus, manpower has ceased to be a plentiful, cheap, replenishable, and short lead-time resource. Instead, whilst the numerical size of armed forces in Western nations has declined, the resources required to recruit, train, and maintain modern military forces have continued to consume substantial proportions of the defense budget. Military manpower costs comprise recruitment, salaries, allowances, retention, retirement and death benefits, training, housing, feeding, clothing, and other fringe benefits [e.g., sports facilities (Downes, 1991)].

Increasing manpower costs suggests incentives and opportunities for factor substitution. Changing relative factor prices provides incentives to substitute between labor and capital. Ridge and Smith (1991) have estimated the elasticity of substitution between capital and service personnel for the UK. They used a simultaneous demand–supply model, starting with a constant elasticity of substitution (CES) production function. Labor supply is a function of the civilian wage, the working population of the relevant age, together with shift factors such as conscription and wars. The resulting basic estimating equation was

$$S = a_0 + a_1 M + a_2 W_c + a_3 Z + a_4 N \tag{6.1}$$

where S = log of service personnel,
$\quad\quad M$ = log of real military expenditure,
$\quad\quad W_c$ = log of real civilian wages,
$\quad\quad Z$ = other factors such as the unemployment rate, and dummy variables (1,0) for conscription and the Falklands conflict,
$\quad\quad N$ = log of population (15–19 year olds).

The equation was estimated for the UK using annual data for 1952–1987. After estimating a variety of functional forms, the preferred equation incorporated a dynamic element allowing for a lagged adjustment to the desired level of service personnel. Most variables were significant with the expected signs: negative for civilian wages and positive for military expenditure and conscription. However, the population variable was not statistically significant; and the Falklands dummy although significant had a negative coefficient, so that there was no support for the view that recruitment becomes easier in times of conflict. The elasticity of substitution is estimated to be unity: hence over time, the share of service personnel costs in the defense budget will remain constant, with increases in factor cost being exactly offset by reductions in numbers. Furthermore, the supply elasticity of service personnel with respect to the military wage was estimated to be low (0.2), with a 10 percent increase in service pay relative to civilian pay leading to a 2 percent increase in military personnel (Ridge and Smith, 1991). However, the results are qualified by data problems, particularly the lack of data on military wages and the price of military physical capital (a methodology for measuring military-physical capital has been developed by Hildebrandt, 1990). There is also scope for a more disaggregated approach allowing for different types of service personnel (e.g., officers, etc.) and for differential regional responses in labor supply (Bellany, 1978, 1983). Finally, the approach assumes the military to be a cost minimizer when it is more realistic to assume X-inefficiency, discretionary behavior, and organizational slack. Departures from cost-minimizing behavior are likely to reduce the incentives for factor substitution.

Within the military production function, major problems arise in measuring output. Typically, at the macro-level, reference is made to peace, protection, security, and defending national interests. Alternatively, reference might be made to the size of a nation's armed forces reflected in the numbers of service personnel and their equipment (e.g., aircraft, ships, tanks): these are measures of intermediate, and not final, output in the form of protecting and saving human lives. Here, a human capital approach would view defense output in terms of providing safety and hence securing life-time earnings. With this approach, the value of avoiding the premature death of an individual through the protection provided by defense is measured by the discounted present value of the individual's future output (Jones-Lee, 1990a). The human capital approach can also be applied to estimating the real costs of war. Applying this approach to the Vietnam War suggests that human capital costs added almost 15 percent to US budgeted costs during the period 1961–71 (Eden, 1972; Kiker and Birkeli, 1972). There is also some support for the hypothesis of an inverse link between casualties and the civilian earnings potential of servicemen, which suggests a regressive implicit tax (Leigh and Berney, 1971).

An alternative approach to measuring defense output focuses on people's aversion to the prospect of death and injury *per se*. This approach values safety in terms of each individual's "willingness to pay" for reductions in their own and other people's risk of death and injury as reflected in different levels of defense expenditure. For example, defense expenditure can be viewed as reducing the risk of being subject to nuclear attack, which if it occurred would cause loss of life on a catastrophic scale. Using different assumptions about the value of a statistical life, the probability of a nuclear attack, and the number of deaths avoided by preventing a nuclear attack, it is possible to assess whether a country is spending too much or too little on defense. Such exercises are, of course, highly speculative and need to be subject to sensitivity analysis (Jones-Lee, 1990a,b; McClelland, 1990).

6.2   The labor market

Military manpower is usually obtained from a nation's labor market. Exceptions occur where nations hire mercenaries from overseas or allow foreigners to serve in their armed forces (e.g., French Foreign Legion). Nevertheless, the labor market for military manpower comprises a single buyer and large numbers of individuals supplying labor services either voluntarily or under compulsion (draft). The buyer has a demand for military manpower reflected in recruitment and retention policies to achieve the desired number of service personnel. Labor supply will vary with wages and will be further affected by training which will create human capital. The interaction of demand and supply will result in a market rate of pay and nonmonetary compensation. Each of these aspects – namely, demand, supply, and pay – will be reviewed separately, followed by the general issue of conscription versus an all-volunteer force.

6.2.1   The demand for military manpower

As a major buyer of labor, a defense department and its armed forces might be analyzed as a monopsony, particularly for skills which are only of value to the military [e.g., tank gunners, para-troopers, submariners, missile operatives (Quester and Nakaoda, 1983)]. Economic theory suggests that as a buyer of military manpower, a defense department will have a labor demand function in which employment will be determined by output (e.g. the threat), relative wages, relative factor prices and the opportunities for factor substitution (Ridge and Smith, 1991). The demand for labor will differ between the services, with armies being labor intensive, whilst air forces and navies are capital-intensive forces. Efforts have been made to model the employment behavior of the armed forces and the defense ministry using economic models of bureaucracy. Such models suggest that utility-maximizing bureaucrats are likely to prefer expenditure, organizational slack, and possibly certain types of inputs. For example, faced with defense cuts, the capital-intensive air force will seek to protect its new equipment program, whilst the Army as the labor-intensive service might aim to protect its manpower through labor hoarding. Empirical work in this area has estimated standard employment functions for the UK armed forces and the Ministry of Defense. The results for the period 1952–78 showed that UK defense expenditure had a significant and positive effect on employment in each of the services and that labor adjustment was extremely slow, particularly in the Army. To some extent, this labor adjustment could reflect the use of long-term contracts for recruitment and retention, although a seven-year adjustment period for Army manpower might also provide support for labor hoarding by the manpower-intensive service (Hartley and Lynk, 1983a). A study by Withers (1977) found that armed forces recruitment in Great Britain between 1966 and 1973 was influenced by economic factors in the form of wages and unemployment, as well as by other influences such as patriotism and attitudes to the military.

A number of US studies have dealt with issues of recruitment, retention, marketing, and reserve forces. It has been found that enlistment into the US forces has been affected by the impact of the business cycle on unemployment, by regional variations in unemployment rates, by civilian earnings, by military pay and benefits, and by the recruitment effort (Brown, 1985; Dale and Gilroy, 1985; Epps, 1973). An econometric model of cost-efficient military recruiting has been developed by Lovell et al. (1991). The model assumes that the US Army Recruiting Command has the task of minimizing the cost of recruiting the required number and quality of recruits, given monetary incentive prices and the recruiting environment. The recruiting environment includes the number of recruiters, the size of the eligible population and unemployment rates. A model is developed which is a modification of a conventional flexible cost function which allows for departures from cost minimization and which provides measures of the magnitude, the direction, and the cost of any inefficiencies. The explanatory power of the model is very high; it estimates that an 18 percent cost saving could be achieved over two quarters by reducing the reliance on bonuses; and that efficient recruiting technology is characterized by constant returns to scale. Constant returns means that a 10 percent cutback in manpower requirements will generate a 10 percent decline in monetary incentive requirements. The authors conclude that their model can be used to project cost-efficient responses to the expected cutbacks in recruiting targets during the 1990s (Lovell *et al.*, 1991).

6.2.2   Retention

Recruitment is not the only method of obtaining military manpower. Retention or reenlistment is an alternative method of achieving service manpower targets. Each involves benefits and costs and hence trade-offs. Retaining experienced personnel leads to savings on recruitment, wastage, and training costs which are required for new entrants; but there are additional costs associated with retention which need to be included in any analysis (e.g., bonuses, pensions, educational benefits, fringe benefits, etc.). In effect, recruiting and retention provide inputs of inexperienced and experienced personnel, respectively. The task of each of the services is to select the optimal mix of inexperienced and experienced personnel, namely, that combination which minimizes the cost of achieving their missions. A cost-effectiveness study of reenlistment in the US Navy found that where experienced and inexperienced men are substitutes, raising the reenlistment rate can be cost-increasing (inefficient) with the Navy buying "too much" high quality, experienced manpower. This result arises from the Navy substituting fewer but costlier experienced men for a greater number of cheaper, inexperienced men: such substitutions were found to be cost-increasing. The study concluded that the Navy should adopt selective reenlistment incentives rather than raising the general reenlistment rate (Fisher and Morton, 1967). There is also evidence based on comparisons of the cost streams for retention and replacement which shows that retention rather than replacement leads to substantial financial savings for the armed forces and results in improved military effectiveness (Binkin and Kyriako-poulos, 1979).

6.2.3   Reserves

Reserve forces are an alternative method of achieving military manpower targets. Unfortunately, there is a lack of published cost-effectiveness studies comparing reserve and regular forces. Certainly, reserves are substantially cheaper than regular forces, but little is known publicly about the relative effectiveness of reserve forces and the length of time needed for reserve units to reach combat-ready status. The fact that a number of nations such as Israel, Sweden, Switzerland, and the USA use reserve forces in a variety of roles, including flying modern combat aircraft, suggests that reserves are potential substitutes for regular forces.

There have been a number of novel economic studies of reserve forces which have considered recruitment, labor turnover, and reserve participation as moonlighting. Although some of these studies are of labor supply, they will be considered here because there is relatively little analytical and empirical work on reserve forces. Buddin (1993) reports the results of a national experiment with a new US Army recruiting program which recruits individuals for joint active/reserve tours. The "2+2+4" recruiting program expands eligibility for the Army's post-service educational benefits to include recruits entering two-year active duty tours in selected non-combat occupations provided they agree to serve another two years in the Selected Reserve and about four years in the Individual Ready Reserve. Under the scheme, the education benefits are tied to individual participation in the reserves. The study found that the 2+2+4 program expanded the market for high quality male recruits by some 3 percent, so making a useful contribution to meeting future US reserve manning requirements (Buddin, 1993).

The decision by civilians to join the military reserves can be regarded as equivalent to the decision by civilians to moonlight (i.e., hold a second job). On this basis, it is assumed that participation in the reserves and moonlighting are influenced by similar economic factors. An alternative view challenges the moonlighting hypothesis and stresses instead the unique institutional features of the military, namely, training, fringe benefits, and camaraderie which are not duplicated in moonlighting jobs. Mehay (1991) has used a choice-based model to examine whether individuals view the military and civilian sectors as competing alternatives in the secondary labor market. A multi-nomial logit model is developed where individuals in full-time work choose between moonlighting, participation in the reserves, or holding one primary job. The estimated model includes variables for weekly hours of work and rates of pay on the primary job, other family income, education, personal family features, and regional differences. The occupational choice equations estimated by the logistic model are of the following general forms

$$\ln{(Pr/Pf)} = g\,(E, D, G) \tag{6.2a}$$
$$\ln{(Pm/Pf)} = h\,(E, D, G) \tag{6.2b}$$

where Pr, Pm, and Pf refer to the probability of participating in the reserves, of moonlighting or of holding only one full-time primary job, respectively. The vector E includes moonlighting variables, D is a vector

of personal characteristics, and *G* is a vector of labor market characteristics. The empirical results show that the decision to participate in the
reserves is not equivalent to the decision to moonlight. However, the
results confirm that reserve force participation is a labor force decision
strongly influenced by individual and family income status and local
employment conditions (Mehay, 1991). A further study has investigated
turnover amongst US Army reservists, concluding that gender differences
are important in explaining retention in the reserves. The retention of
male reservists was explained by a wide range of factors similar to the
determinants for full-time job turnover. In contrast, only a few factors
(e.g., retirement benefits) exerted a significant influence on the retention
of women reservists (Thomas and Kocher, 1993).

6.2.4   Labor supply

Labor supply curves for military manpower have been estimated for
countries such as Australia, Canada, the UK, and the USA, particularly
in the context of debates about the budget costs of replacing conscription
with an all volunteer force (Ash *et al.*, 1983; Bellany, 1978, 1983;
Lightman, 1975; Withers, 1972). Typically, empirical work on military
personnel supply models has focused on the role of military–civilian
earnings differentials and the unemployment rate, as well as other
influences such as tastes and preferences for the military, regional
differences, the role of the draft in stimulating volunteers, the number of
recruiters, and advertising expenditure (Horne, 1985; Dertouzos, 1985;
DeBoer and Brorsen, 1989). Individuals are assumed to choose between
military and civilian occupations and there is a military reservation wage
at which the individual is indifferent between the two occupations. The
result is an estimating equation of the following form (Ash *et al.*, 1983)

$$\text{A/P} = f(Wc/Wm, U, \Pi, T) \tag{6.3}$$

where *A*   = applications to enlist,
       P   = population of 18–19 year old males,
       Wc = median civilian pay for 18–19 year old males,
       Wm = average military pay of enlisted men, including quarters,
              subsistence allowances and tax advantages,
       U   = unemployment rate of 18–19 year old males
       Π   = the probability of not being inducted into the armed forces,
       T   = a time-trend for changing tastes with respect to military
              service, based on the period 1967–1976.

When the equation was estimated for US forces, it suggested a pay elasticity of 0.86 for all male enlistment in 1976. Also, during the period 1967–79, there was evidence of a weak change in tastes away from military service and no evidence was obtained of any significant effect of unemployment on recruitment (Ash *et al.*, 1983).

Much of the labor supply literature has focused on the estimated elasticities for relative pay and unemployment. Some of this literature suggests that high-quality enlistments are elastic with respect to relative pay and unitary elastic with respect to unemployment. However, such studies have taken the high-quality enlistment goal as a predetermined variable with implications for model misspecification and biased (over-estimated) elasticities. Work by Berner and Daula (1993) presents new insights into military labor supply and the linkages between institutional incentives and the effectiveness of recruiting resources. In an important methodological breakthrough, they show that the institutional environment in which US Army recruiting takes place requires a switching simultaneous equation specification of the aggregate labor supply process. They also show that the procedures for allocating recruiting goals for high-quality soldiers results in these goals being endogenous to the supply process. Failure to control for these statistical issues will bias empirical estimates of the labor supply function and result in flawed analyses of related resource allocation issues. Their empirical results provide estimated elasticities for relative pay, unemployment, recruiters, national advertising, bonus benefit, and educational benefit. Interestingly, compared with previous studies, their estimated elasticities for relative pay and unemployment are 0.480 and 0.485, respectively (Berner and Daula, 1993).

6.2.5 Training and civilian benefits

The military is a major provider of on-the-job training. As an investment in creating human capital, training involves present costs which are incurred in the expectation of future benefits. Questions arise about the magnitude of the costs and benefits of military training, who bears the costs and who receives the benefits? Here, the distinguishing feature of human capital is that the property rights in training investments are vested in the individual worker, so that human capital and workers cannot be separated. This has implications for the distribution of training costs between individuals and firms and requires a distinction between general (transferable) and specific (nontransferable) training. Becker (1964) recognized the implications of this distinction for military training. The military provides some forms of training which are extremely useful in the civilian sector (general or transferable skills), such as driving, computer skills, vehicle repair and maintenance, and pilot training. Indeed emphasis is sometimes given to the social benefits of military training (Binkin and Kyriakopoulos, 1979). Other forms of military training are only of minor use to the civilian economy (specific or nontransferable skills), such as missile operators, tank gunners, and parachutists. Such training is specific because it raises productivity in the military but not elsewhere.

In providing and paying for training, the military seeks a return on its training investments. For an all volunteer force, this is achieved though employment contracts which require a minimum period of service and by offering attractive inducements for reenlistment (i.e., serving a second term). Pilot training, for example, is both lengthy and costly but provides a transferable skill. UK evidence shows that pilot training for the RAF takes three years at an average cost of over £5.5m ($9.7m, 1991–2 prices) with a requirement for at least five years productive service after training before any release from the service (HCP 53, 1981; for US data, see Smith, 1991). However, Becker (1964) recognized that reenlistment rates are inversely related to the amount of civilian-type skills provided by the military. At the end of their contract, personnel with transferable civilian skills leave the military because they can receive higher wages in the civilian economy; but they are attracted to the military in the first instance because of its willingness to pay for their training costs. As a result, for transferable skills, the military has easy access to students and trainees, and heavy losses of graduates and skilled labor (Becker, 1964).

A number of studies have attempted to measure the civilian benefits of military training and experience. Various US studies have compared the civilian earnings and employment experience of Korean War and Vietnam War veterans, of different racial and ethnic groups with and without military service, and of military and civilian personnel (Browning et al., 1973; see also Hartley and Hooper, 1990, references 722–735). Often, studies have compared the earnings of military veterans with the earnings of a control group of individuals identical to veterans but never having served in the military. These studies aim to estimate whether military veterans earn more than their nonveteran counterparts: if so, the veteran premium in earnings is due to the superiority of military training and experience. However, such studies have not analyzed different military occupations which may provide varying degrees of general and specific training. A basic model used as a starting point for exploring these issues is (Goldberg and Warner, 1987)

$$\log Y_t = b_0 + b_1 c + b_2 c^2 + b_3 m + b_4 m^2 + b_5 mc \qquad (6.4)$$

where Y = earnings (natural logs),
        m = years of military experience,
        c = years of civilian experience.

When this equation was estimated for nine US military occupations, it was found that for all nine groups, military experience increased potential civilian earnings. Significantly, for four categories, military and civilian experience had approximately equal impacts on potential civilian earnings. The four occupational groups were medical, electrical-mechanical equipment repair, other technical, and electronics equipment repair – all corresponding to transferable or general human capital. For the remaining five occupations, military experience increased civilian earnings but not at the same rate as civilian experience: these five groups embraced infantry-combat occupations which provide specific human capital (Goldberg and Warner, 1987).

Efforts have been made to estimate separately the contribution to civilian earnings of military training and military experience. Here, there are two contrary views. One view asserts that military service enhances civilian earnings via military-induced productivity growth (training) and favorable signals from veteran status. An alternative view is that military service lowers productivity and sends unfavorable signals, which is why Vietnam veterans can expect lower returns than Korean War veterans (unfavorable signals include the military mind; military discipline; conformity to, and dependence on, routine and orders). The separate contributions of military experience and military training have been estimated using the following model (Bryant and Wilhite, 1990)

$$CEP = f(ME, MT, X),\tag{6.5}$$

where CEP = civilian earnings potential,
      ME = military experience (length of service),
      MT = military training,
      X = vector of social, economic, and demographic variables affecting wages.

It is predicted that where the military provides general training, the result will be higher civilian wages, but that military-provided specific training will have little value in private markets. When the above equation was estimated for US forces, it was found that military training exerted a positive influence on civilian wages, but length of time in the military reduced wages earned during the early years of civilian work. The branch of service also matters, with veterans from the US Army, Marines, or Navy at a relative disadvantage compared with Air Force veterans (especially Army and Marines: Bryant and Wilhite, 1990).

6.3   Military pay

For an all volunteer force, military pay determines recruitment, retention, and the capital–labor mix. As a starting point, military pay will be determined by market forces and relative scarcities reflected in manning problems, the need for comparability with earnings in the civilian sector and the need to reflect some of the special features of the military job. Typically, the military salary comprises pay, allowances, and benefits-in-kind (e.g., housing, medical support, training, education for dependents, and recreation activities). On this basis it might be assumed that the military employer aims to adjust wages such that when combined with the market value of net military benefits, total military compensation matches civilian-equivalent earnings. Since individual recruits to the military have different preferences for various combinations of wages and benefits, the task of the military employer is to select a total compensation package which minimizes the cost of achieving military manpower targets. The task is made more difficult where it is impossible or costly to discriminate between different types of individuals with varying preferences for wages and benefits.

Melese, Blandin, and Fanchon (1992) have developed a simple framework for analyzing the economics of military compensation. Their model distinguishes between basic military pay and various benefits, namely, in-kind benefits (e.g., health care, training), supplementary or lump-sum income payments (e.g. cash bonuses, incentive payments), and price savings or subsidies (e.g., price savings for buying from military shops, favorable prices for recreational activities). In meeting their recruiting targets, the armed forces have to select an efficient wage–benefit package, recognizing that excessive benefits may inflate labor costs. The central elements of the model are outlined in figure 6.1.

Assume that the labor market in which the military operates to recruit and retain personnel is composed of two types of individuals: Type I and Type II. Type I individuals prefer less in-kind benefits than the military provides, whilst Type IIs generally choose more than the military offers. The two types have different utility functions (U_I, U_{II}) representing their preferences between market-provided goods and services (Y) and military-provided goods and services or "in-kind" benefits (X). The initial civilian budget constraint is shown by I_1, with Type Is selecting combination A and Type II's choosing combination B. The level of "in-kind" benefits provided by the military is assumed to be the same for both types of individuals, equal to X^*: it is assumed that these benefits cannot be exchanged. As a result, Type Is working for the military are forced to consume more X than they would choose in a private market

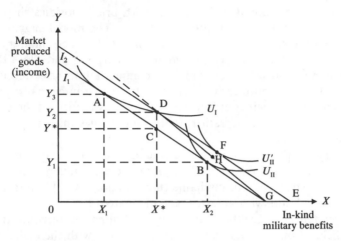

Figure 6.1 Economics of military compensation

setting; whilst in private markets, Type IIs consume a greater level of X than that provided by the military.

Now let I_2 represent the military income required to compete with the income of I_1 paid by the equivalent occupation in the private sector. Point C in figure 6.1 represents Type I's initial military-constrained choices (a corner solution), which would yield a lower utility than in the private civilian occupation A. Thus, to attract or retain Type Is, a military employer has to provide additional benefits to enable point D to be reached (utility level U_I). Point D can be reached by offering either additional income (e.g., incentive and special pay) or price subsidies. Raising income to Y_2 (on the kinked budget line Y_2 D E) would leave Type Is indifferent between the military (point D) and the private sector (point A). Alternatively, the same objective can be achieved by reducing the price of Y (e.g. via military discounts on gas prices and meals). Whilst the effective budget constraint (B C Y^*) in figure 6.1 is binding for Type Is, this is not the case for Type IIs: hence Type IIs are able to obtain the same utility in the military as they achieve in the civil sector. As a result, without any supplementary income payments or price subsidies, Type IIs are willing to join or stay in the military.

Consider the situation where it is difficult or costly to discriminate between Type Is and Type IIs. Assume also that there are not enough Type IIs to meet the military's requirements. In this case, the supplementary income payments and/or price subsidies offered to attract Type I's guarantee that Type IIs will be better off in the military than they would be in the private sector. With supplementary income, Type

IIs would move from B to F whereas with price subsidies they would move from B to H (with F preferred to H). The model suggests three policy recommendations. First, discriminate between military skills (occupations) which have close civilian counterparts and those that do not. Second, convert some military compensation now received in nonmonetary form into cash payments. Third, guarantee that people are paid according to their contribution with some awareness of their civilian compensation prospects, rather than simply guessing at their needs (Melese *et al.*, 1992).

Military work is more onerous, uncertain, and more hazardous compared with employment in the civilian sector. Military personnel are subject to a strict code of discipline (they cannot resign) requiring them to work long hours without extra pay; there are the dangers of death and injury on active service; there are poor conditions and discomfort whilst in the field or on a ship; and the costs associated with the high mobility needed by the military. These nonmonetary disadvantages of military work have been described as the X-factor which requires compensating wage differentials (Cmnd 4079, 1969). Quit rates have been used as a proxy for the disutility of a job and hence as a basis for estimating compensating wage differentials in the military. A US study of comparable jobs in the Air Force and Navy estimated that the Navy would have to pay a median wage premium of about 12 percent to achieve the same reenlistment rates as the Air Force [the estimated premium ranged from 4 percent to 24 percent for single white males (Solnick *et al.*, 1991)].

The military pay system operates in a distinctive internal labor market. Unlike the civil sector where scarcity determines pay, military pay is based on rank and seniority. There is a danger that military pay will be especially attractive to personnel with less valuable skills while it fails to satisfy those with more valuable skills (i.e., the Forces pay some of their personnel more than they need to and others less than they ought to): as a result, they lose people they need to keep and keep people they can afford to lose (Binkin and Kyriakopoulos, 1981). A further distinctive feature of the military's internal labor market is that entry occurs only at the bottom of the institution's hierarchy and promotion from within means a commitment to recruit at young entry points rather than allowing recruitment at all ages. In other words, a future chief of the air force will be drawn from an intake of 18–21 year olds, one of whom will eventually become the air force chief. In contrast, in the civil sector, the company president might be provided from within or recruited directly from outside the company, with entry or recruitment at varying ages. Critics have suggested that "military pay and benefits have little relevance to occupational requirements and corresponding training costs, and even less resemblance to civilian rates for workers possessing similar skills. By compensating their members across the board and regardless of occupational area, on the basis of longevity, the armed forces inadvertently overpay some and short-change others" (Binkin and Kyriakopoulos, 1981, pp. 78–9).

6.3.1   Contractorization

Some of the problems created by the traditional military manning system might be solved through contractorization. This involves market testing and the possibility of private contractors undertaking "in-house" activities traditionally performed by the armed forces. Examples include catering, cleaning, transport, training, the repair and maintenance of vehicles and equipment, and the management of facilities. Cost savings from market testing and contracting-out defense support functions average 25 percent. At the same time, contracting-out has contributed to substantial manpower savings in both the armed forces and in the numbers of civilians employed by the defense ministry. But the policy is not without its problems. Efforts are needed to ensure that there is genuine competition and rivalry for contracts, so avoiding private cartels and collusive tendering. Competitions also need to be extended to embrace different levels of service rather than restricting rivalry to a single, buyer-determined specification. And, inevitably, the armed forces will resist contractorization by stressing its adverse impact on their operational capabilities (Hartley, 1993b; Hitch and McKean, 1960, p. 228).

6.4   The draft or an all-volunteer force

Nations can obtain their military manpower by conscription (the draft), or by relying upon voluntary enlistments, or by a mix of both methods. The historical developments are interesting. In Europe, the eighteenth-century soldier was "a poor creature, the liveried servant of his king, sometimes – in Russia and Prussia – an actual serf delivered into the states' service by his feudal master. The volunteer was almost the rarest, if the best of soldiers. Because so many of his comrades-in-arms were unwilling warriors, the penalties for desertion were draconian and the code of discipline ferocious" (Keegan, 1989, p. 19). In contrast, the nineteenth-century European soldier was a willing, often an enthusiastic soldier: he was usually a conscript but one who accepted his term of service "as a just subtraction from his years of liberty ..." (Keegan, 1989,

p. 19). Universal conscription became connected with liberty and the ideal of "every citizen a soldier and every soldier a citizen": hence the slogan of "no conscription without representation" (Keegan, 1989, p. 22).

Alternative military manpower systems involve benefits and costs. The benefits of conscription include guaranteed short-term employment for young people and investment in human capital, especially for disadvantaged groups; the bringing together of men from diverse regions and backgrounds and hence the contribution to creating "good citizenship"; the draft is a reliable method of obtaining military manpower, especially in wartime; and there is the view that the draft resembles "coercive" jury service and is one of the essential features of democracies (i.e., jurors are conscripted). But the draft is not costless. Compulsory service means that individuals have no choice; below market wages are paid, so that an implicit tax is paid by conscripts; the men of draft age are subject to uncertainty over when and how long they might serve with implications for human capital investment, together with marriage and family-planning decisions. Since the draft results in relatively cheap labor, the military responds by hoarding labor, using it wastefully, adopting "too low" capital–labor ratios and generally adopting highly labor-intensive production methods. The draft also imposes high administrative costs on the public sector (e.g., costs of registration, selection, exemption, etc.) and results in higher training costs compared with an all-volunteer force (AVF). In other words, the draft involves allocative costs and distributive effects (Fisher, 1969; Hansen and Weisbrod, 1967; Oi, 1967).

Conscription or national service was abolished in the UK in 1960 with an AVF achieved by 1963, and in the USA an AVF was introduced in 1973. In the period 1967–73, US economists contributed to the debate about the relative merits of the draft versus an AVF. This debate in the USA occurred against the background of the Vietnam War with its heavy draft demands, criticisms of the selection procedure (e.g., criteria for exemptions, rejections, etc.), and a concern about discrimination against low income, low education, and under-privileged members of society. In other words, worries in the USA reflected the fact that the draft was not universal and hence the tax which it imposed was selective and discriminatory. Criticisms were also made against the combat effectiveness of US military manpower in the Vietnam War. In the circumstances, economists were persuaded that a voluntary military is preferable to the draft (Fisher, 1969; Hansen and Weisbrod, 1967; Leigh and Berney, 1971).

The debate about conscription versus an AVF is a good example of applied economics embracing theory, analysis, statistical-econometric estimation, and policy evaluation. In evaluating the draft, economists used the free market voluntary system as a standard of comparison. The supporters of an AVF argued that the draft led to excessive purchases of enlisted men. The abolition of conscription raises the relative costs of military manpower providing incentives to substitute relatively cheaper for more expensive inputs. As a result, an AVF will involve substitution effects between capital (equipment) and labor, between service personnel and civilians, and between skilled and unskilled military manpower. Furthermore, an AVF is expected to be associated with greater motivation and hence increased productivity, and with more reenlistments leading to reduced turnover and lower training costs (Fisher, 1969; Gates, 1970; Oi, 1967).

During the 1960s and 1970s, various estimates were made of the budgetary implications of introducing an AVF, particularly for the USA. In principle, estimates are required of demand functions, military manpower supply, and market-clearing wages. Often, though, the estimates specified the manpower requirements of the armed forces and then estimated a labor supply curve from which it was possible to derive the wage rate needed to achieve the target size of military manpower. In estimating labor supply curves, it was assumed that individuals had a choice of two occupations, namely, military or civilian, with the need for equalizing differentials. For example, for 1960–70 it was estimated that even in peace time, a pay premium of over 60 percent of average civilian earnings would be needed to attract AVF officers in the USA [i.e., higher pay is necessary for an AVF (Altman and Barro, 1971)]. Predictably, all the estimates showed that to achieve a US military force of 2.65 million men in the early 1970s would involve higher budgetary payroll costs, with the figures varying from $4 billion to $8.3 billion per annum (Altman and Fechter, 1967; Fisher, 1969; Oi, 1967). However, the reliability of these estimates depended on the stability of the estimated labor supply curves [i.e., the estimated supply curve was based on a mixed draft and voluntary systems which was used to forecast the budgetary payroll implications of an AVF (Oi, 1967)]. Moreover, once standard demand functions are included in the analysis, the size of the AVF is likely to be smaller, with corresponding improvements in social welfare. An example is shown in figure 6.2 where a conscript force of N_c could be obtained at a wage of W_c compared with wage of W_2 if the same size of force were recruited on a voluntary basis: the difference $W_2 W_c \times 0 N_c$ shows the budgetary payroll costs of an AVF of size N_c. Also, a force of size N_c involves a welfare loss of ABC, compared with the market-determined and welfare-maximizing AVF of N^*. However, further complications can arise. With an AVF, a potentially important

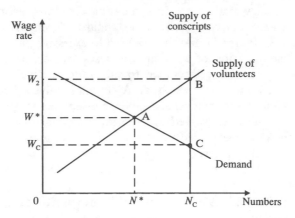

Figure 6.2 The draft versus AVF

welfare cost might result from the monopsonistic behavior of the defense establishment as a buyer of military personnel (Borcherding, 1971). Further studies have estimated the cost of an AVF for Australia and Belgium. For Australia, Withers (1972) estimated the cost of an all volunteer army using an enlistment function in which enlistments were dependent on the present value of expected military and civilian incomes. He concluded that a voluntary enlistment system would require only "... a moderate increase in defense spending" (Withers, 1972, p. 337). A study of the draft versus an AVF for Belgium estimated that the social cost of the draft was at least twice its budgetary cost, and that a switch to an AVF implied a more capital-intensive army and required a substantial (23 percent) increase in the nominal defense budget. It was also estimated that draftees in Belgium paid implicit taxes much above the observed average income tax rates (Kerstens and Meyermans, 1993).

Conscription also has implications for debates about burden sharing in NATO. Various estimates can be made of the budgetary savings of conscription based on different assumptions about average civilian wages and average military pay. On this basis, it has been estimated that for the European members of NATO the average budgetary savings from conscription averaged some 6 percent of national military expenditures in 1987 (Oneal, 1992; also chapter 2).

Since the introduction of the AVF in the USA, there have been two broad sets of concerns. First, by the early 1980s, doubts were expressed about the quality of recruits for the American AVF, the racial balance of ground forces, shortages of skilled military personnel, and the recruiting problems likely to result from the predicted demographic trough of young people in the 1990s (Bowman *et al.*, 1986; Binkin, 1984; Sabrosky, 1982). Second, with the end of the cold war, the central focus for the 1990s is on the downsizing of armed forces. Some nations with conscript forces are shifting toward volunteer systems. Cuts in defense budgets will lead to a greater search for substitutions between equipment (including technology) and military personnel, between military personnel and civilians, between regulars and reserves, and between older and younger service personnel.

6.5   Internal organization, incentives, and efficiency

In private firms, incentives to operate efficiently and to substitute relatively cheaper for more expensive factor inputs are provided by the profit motive and competition. Such incentives are absent in the military "firm." Instead, the military sector is a good example of a command economy, operating in a world without markets. In such a world, individuals and groups of military personnel are unlikely to minimize costs unless there are strong pressures for them to do so. Opportunism, bounded rationality, uncertainty, and information asymmetries provide the circumstances for "shirking" and X-inefficient outcomes (Thompson and Wright, 1988). The noncompetitive environment for military units (e.g., noncompeting army, navy, and air force bases) and the nature of employment contracts for military personnel do not provide strong incentives for individuals and groups to minimize costs. In this situation, efficiency improvements might be achieved by modifying the institutional framework within which the military operates.

Proposals have been made to simulate markets within the military sector. A classic example was the Lerner proposal which suggested that the whole military establishment be organized in a network of markets with decentralized decision making. Military commanders would be given fixed budgets which would be used to bid for various types of materiel (from supply commands) and men (from training commands), so resulting in a set of market-clearing prices (Hitch and McKean, 1960, p. 222). A less ambitious proposal would expand decentralized decision-making with delegated budget authority. Here, the idea is that at various levels in the military hierarchy, officers would be given a fixed budget and output targets and encouraged to seek lower-cost solutions for achieving their targets. However, problems arise if employment contracts for military personnel do not provide incentives and rewards for good performance and penalties for poor performance. In addition, the opportunities for economizing can be heavily constrained if budget holders have only limited discretion for changing their expenditure choices. Even more problems arise in specifying appropriate output targets or performance indicators. It follows that if it is difficult to create a market economy within the military sector, an alternative possibility is to transfer military activities to private contractors (Bailey, 1967; Hitch and McKean, 1960; see also section 6.3.1 above).

6.6   Conclusion

Military manpower as a subset of labor economics involves an extensive range of theoretical, empirical, and policy issues. Amongst this rich research agenda, three areas are worth stressing. First, in a world of uncertainty and the need for insurance policies, analysis is needed of the costs and benefits of reserve forces. These forces are relatively cheap and they provide the basis for regenerating armed forces in an emergency and conflict. Second, the military sector is a major training industry. Little is known about the benefits and costs of such training from the viewpoint of the military, individuals and the community (Benoit 1973).

Third, employment contracts create the micro-economic foundation of behavior and efficiency in the military "firm." Proposals to improve efficiency in the military are likely to fail if they ignore the underlying behavior of individuals and groups as determined by their employment contracts. People can play any games and incentive schemes are unlikely to be successful if all the benefits of any savings accrue to the national Treasury. In other words, the armed forces are not profit-conscious firms: typically, their employment contracts are divorced from profit and efficiency incentives, so that costs are unlikely to be minimized. A possible solution might be to change the military employment contract to include a performance-related pay component.

7   Defense and the industrial base

This chapter focuses on the supply side of the market for defense equipment. In an era of expensive equipment, rising weapons costs, and increasingly constrained defense budgets, nations cannot avoid questioning the efficiency and competitiveness of their defense industries. What are the benefits and costs of a defense industrial base (DIB)? Critics point to monopoly-oligopoly and the absence of competition for contracts, the gold plating of equipment, cost overruns, delays in delivery, cancellations, excessive profits, poor labor productivity, labor hoarding, and a failure to export. In addition, the defense industries in Europe are criticized for excessive and wasteful duplication of costly research and development (R & D) and for relatively short production runs as each state supports its national champions. It is generally believed that Europe's defense industries are inefficient and uncompetitive, especially in relation to the USA and that the situation can be improved through greater European collaboration (see chapter 9).

Some developing countries have also created a DIB (e.g., Brazil, China, India, South Korea, Malaysia). To such countries, a DIB provides a means of acquiring new technology and acting as a growth point for industrialization, as well as contributing to import saving and possibly earning "valuable" overseas currency through exports (see Arms Trade, chapter 10). Critics question the "sacrifices" incurred in creating a DIB in developing countries which are characterized by poverty, starvation, illiteracy, ill-health, and homelessness.

The policy debate about efficiency, competitiveness, and the benefits and costs of a domestic DIB has generated an extensive list of questions for which there are few reliable answers. There is a general lack of detailed and authoritative economic studies of the world's defense industries and their performance. This is an important part of defense micro-economics. A nation's DIB and the efficiency with which it supplies equipment are major inputs into "national protection". Moreover, the prospects of cuts in defense spending will affect the size, structure and composition (i.e., mix of air, land and sea equipment suppliers) of a nation's DIB (see also chapters 11 and 12).

The chapter presents a survey of the available literature and data on defense industries. It seeks to identify what is known and what we need to know (i.e., a research agenda) for an informed policy debate about the DIB. It starts by placing equipment expenditure in the budgeting framework. There follows a discussion of the concept of the DIB, its benefits and costs and criteria are presented for assessing its efficiency.

7.1   Defense budgets and equipment spending

Defense budgets can be viewed as either reflecting society's preferences for defense or showing the outcome of the political bargaining process between various interest groups in the military–industrial complex (see chapters 2–4). Either way, defense budgets show how expenditure is allocated between equipment, personnel, infrastructure, and other inputs required to produce the output of defense. Examples for NATO countries are shown in table 7.1 where it can be seen that personnel and other operating expenditures dominate defense budgets. The variations in the personnel shares reflect the fact that the UK and the USA rely on all-volunteer forces with the remaining NATO countries using different mixes of volunteers and conscripts (see chapter 6). The equipment share figures shown in table 7.1 are also misleading indicators of spending on a nation's DIB. They do not show the distribution of equipment spending between home and overseas purchases; they do not reflect the extent to which other operating expenditures involve purchases from defense industries; nor do they distinguish between expenditure on R & D and production.

Defense budgets can be presented in a variety of ways, depending on such factors as the needs of the ministry of defense or defense department, government, public accountability, secrecy, and constitutional requirements. One approach to budgeting focuses on *inputs*, showing annual expenditure by the defense ministry and armed forces on service personnel, resources, and civilians together with outlays on research and production by each of the services. However, input budgets are limited as a means of assessing the efficiency of resource allocation decisions in defense. They do not show any output other than the vague heading of "defense"; it is not possible to relate inputs to outputs nor do they show the opportunities for substitution between different defense forces and the implications for output. Input budgets are also limited by focusing on the use of resources for a one-year budgeting period and for showing only money outlays rather than real resource costs. In other

Table 7.1 *NATO defense budgets*

Country	Percentage share of defense budget allocated to							
	Equipment (%)		Personnel (%)		Infrastructure (%)		Other operating costs (%)	
	Average 1985–89	1992	Average 1985–89	1992	Average 1985–89	1992	Average 1985–89	1992
Belgium	12.1	8.6	63.4	65.0	4.0	3.6	20.4	22.9
Canada	19.7	17.6	46.2	49.9	2.8	2.4	31.2	30.0
Denmark	14.0	16.7	56.6	57.8	3.4	4.2	25.8	21.3
Germany	19.6	9.3	48.9	57.8	5.9	5.0	25.5	28.0
Greece	18.2	21.5	60.5	65.8	2.2	0.9	18.4	11.8
Italy	19.7	13.8	57.8	67.1	2.6	2.5	19.8	16.6
Luxembourg	3.5	4.5	76.9	73.6	7.3	12.3	11.9	9.5
Netherlands	19.8	16.9	52.8	54.0	5.2	6.8	22.0	22.4
Norway	21.7	23.6	43.9	44.0	8.2	9.4	26.0	23.0
Portugal	7.6	6.4	67.7	79.2	3.7	3.2	19.8	11.2
Spain	na	16.6	na	64.3	na	0.8	na	18.3
Turkey	18.2	25.4	37.1	46.5	5.4	3.3	38.4	24.7
UK	24.8	17.6	38.6	44.1	3.9	5.4	32.5	32.9
USA	25.6	22.1	37.0	37.0	1.8	1.4	35.5	39.4

Note: R & D expenditures are included in equipment expenditures.
Source: NATO, 1993.

words, input budgets do not convey the sort of information which is needed to assess efficiency, namely, the products or outputs of the armed forces and their costs of production (ideally marginal costs).

Hitch and McKean (1960) provided a pioneering contribution in this field. They explained that the efficient use of military (and other public sector) resources is a special problem because of the absence of incentive mechanisms, like those in the private sector, which lead to greater efficiency. In the private sector, the profit motive and competition provide efficiency incentives. On this basis, it has to be asked whether defense budgets convey the sort of information about performance that is automatically generated by private firms operating in competitive markets.

Criticism of input budgets for defense (and other government departments) led to the development of an alternative approach, namely, *program* or *output* budgeting. With its emphasis on objectives, outputs, and total program costs over a period of years, it is in complete contrast to input budgets. Program budgeting or a planning, programming budgeting system (PPBS) provides information for assessing the efficiency with which defense ministries use resources. It requires answers to four questions:

(i)   What are the objectives of the defense ministry or defense department and is it possible to formulate a set of programs which can be related to these objectives? Examples of programs include nuclear strategic forces, nuclear tactical forces, conventional forces, special forces, and reserve forces.

(ii)   What are the current and expected life-cycle resource costs of each program? For example, for nuclear strategic forces, information is needed on the life-cycle costs of providing and operating the necessary equipment (e.g., aircraft, submarines, missiles, rockets, and bombs), together with the service manpower and associated infrastructure (military bases, communications systems, etc.).

(iii)   What are the results or outputs of each program? Here, difficulties arise because of the nature of output in the form of peace, protection, security, and deterrence. Moreover, whilst simulation methods, war games, and exercises can be used to estimate outcomes (e.g., combat performance and effectiveness), the opportunities for actually verifying output only arise in real world conflict situations (World War II, the Gulf Conflict). Published data usually show only measures of intermediate, rather than final, output. Examples include the numbers of combat aircraft, warships, tanks, and service personnel without any information on the average age of equipment and its operational availability and on the training and productivity of military manpower.

(iv)   Are there alternative methods of achieving each program and what are the costs and outputs of each alternative (i.e., the use of cost-effectiveness studies)? For example, air defense can be provided by manned combat aircraft or ground-based missiles; an anti-submarine capability can be provided by warships or by submarines or by land-based maritime patrol aircraft; and nuclear strategic forces can be provided by bomber aircraft, by land-based rockets, or by submarine-based missiles.

Program budgeting had its origins in the US Rand Corporation and was pioneered by the US Department of Defense as part of a management revolution introduced by Secretary Robert McNamara and implemented by Charles Hitch in 1961 (Enke, 1967). It provided a framework for applying cost–benefit or cost–effectiveness analysis in which individual and alternative force structures such as a bomber squadron or a warship (program elements) were properly costed with costs then related to the benefits, outputs, or effectiveness of each force structure. In this way, program budgeting draws attention to important trade-offs in defense choices.

The shift to program budgeting reflected the revolution in military technology since the end of World War II. "The great technical complexity of modern day weapons, their lengthy period of development, their tremendous combat power and enormous cost have placed an extraordinary premium on sound choices of major weapon systems" (Hitch, 1965, p. 23). There was also a need to take a defense and national security perspective rather than a single service perspective in selecting new, costly equipment. Traditionally, each of the armed forces had pursued its own priorities and missions, often to the detriment of joint missions, seeking a larger share of the defense budget for its new weapons systems and protecting the overall size of its own forces sometimes at the cost of combat readiness.

Program budgeting is not without its limitations. It should be seen as an information system for planning and evaluation; but it does not remove the need for individuals to make decisions. Also, the costs presented by program budgets do not always represent X-efficient solutions; nor does the system necessarily provide incentives for personnel in defense departments and the armed forces to provide valuable information and to use it (McKean, 1967). Some of these limitations have led to new defense budgeting initiatives. The UK, for example, has moved from program budgeting to management-based defense budgets (the New Management Strategy). This is designed to improve internal efficiency through creating clearly defined budget holders with specific defense tasks (e.g., submarines, air defense) and delegated budget responsibility within each task. However, problems arise where the budget holders have little choice over most of their inputs and expenditures, and where their employment contracts provide no incentives to improve efficiency.

Program budgeting and especially cost-effectiveness studies had major implications for equipment choices and hence for a nation's DIB. It focused attention on the life-cycle costs of new weapons systems, namely, the development, production, and in-service operating costs. In turn, this created pressures for defense departments to improve the accuracy of their cost-estimating techniques and to move away from cost-plus contracts where contractors have an incentive to offer "optimistic" estimates in the early bidding (see chapter 5). Certainly new weapons systems are costly to develop and procure. For example, the new US F-22 combat aircraft was estimated to cost some $87 billion for development and production giving a unit cost of almost $134 million for the procurement of 648 aircraft [1992 prices (CRS 1994; CBO 1993)]. Interestingly, the bulk of the costs come after the aircraft has been procured (e.g., maintenance and operational costs, including fuel and mid-life updates). Such cost figures and facts have led to two developments affecting defense industries. First, a greater interest and emphasis by defense departments in reducing the life-cycle costs of new weapon systems (e.g. via procurement contracts providing incentives related to reliability and maintainability). Second, a greater willingness by defense departments to consider alternative weapons systems available for buying off-the-shelf (imports or using civil equipment). The rising real costs of modern equipment means that it is increasingly costly to support a national DIB. What are the costs and benefits of a DIB? As a starting point, a definition is needed.

7.2   Defining the DIB

In some countries, a DIB is a central part of national defense policy. Emphasis is given to the need to maintain a "strong" indigenous DIB. However, the concept of the DIB has been the victim of various definitions, meaning different things to different people. Consider the following examples:

(i)   The DIB comprises the wide range of firms which supply the defense department and the armed forces with the equipment which they require (Taylor and Hayward, 1989, p. 1).

(ii)   The DIB consists of those industrial assets which provide key elements of military power and national security: such assets demand special attention by government (Taylor and Hayward, 1989, p. 1).

(iii) The DIB embraces industrial sectors that unequivocally manufacture military goods (e.g., artillery, missiles, submarines) as well as sectors which produce civil goods. Designation as a defense industry depends upon the destination of the bulk of the industry's output: should most of it be earmarked for defense markets, the industry is classified as a defense industry (Todd, 1988, pp. 14–15).

(iv)   The DIB refers to "those sectors of a country's economy that can be called upon to generate goods, services and technology for ultimate consumption by the state's armed forces." A DIB has to fulfill two requirements: it must provide the "normal peacetime material requirements of the country's military; and it must be rapidly expansible to meet the increased demands of wartime or emergency situations" (Haglund, 1989, pp. 1–2).

(v)   For the USA, the DIB comprises prime contractors, subcontractors, and parts suppliers operating publicly and/or privately owned facilities supplying air, land, and sea systems. In addition to ensuring that the USA is self sufficient, the defense industry is required to expand rapidly in times of national emergency [surge capability (Gansler, 1989a, chapter 8)].

(vi) A further US definition of the DIB applies the following rules:
   a) select the top n industries ranked by Department of Defense dollar purchases; and
   b) add to the list other industries considered vital to defense production (Ratner and Thomas, 1990).

Inevitably, these various definitions have been criticized for being too broad, too vague, too arbitrary and subjective, and for omitting some important firms and sectors. Sometimes, the different definitions reflect the nature and purpose of studies of the DIB. Nor is any effort made to distinguish between industrial capabilities in R & D, in production and for in-service support, and to identify those industrial capabilities which are defense specific. For example, at one extreme, some defense industries supply lethal equipment which can destroy, threaten, or deter (e.g., combat aircraft, warships, tanks, missiles); whilst at the other extreme are products bought by the armed forces but which are also produced on a large scale for the civilian population [e.g., computers, food, motor cars (Taylor and Hayward, 1989, p. 2)].

Data problems abound. For researchers, difficulties arise in obtaining accurate and reliable data on the size of the world's defense industries. For example, data on employment, the skill composition of the labor force, and especially on the employment of qualified scientists and engineers in defense R & D work, are difficult to obtain (UN, 1993; Buck et al., 1993). These difficulties reflect secrecy and the problems of defining the extent and composition of the DIB. Defense research work is particularly shrouded in secrecy, so that published employment data are conspicuous by their absence. Nor can total employment be estimated without identifying all firms in the DIB, including the network of suppliers involved in subcontracting and the suppliers of materials, parts, and components (i.e., the supply chain). Some suppliers might not be aware that they are involved in defense production. For example, ball bearing manufacturers are unlikely to know whether their products are used in motor cars or main battle tanks. Even at the prime contractor level, it is difficult to obtain published data showing the proportion of the firm's labor force involved in defense work. Often major defense contractors are large conglomerates with a range of military and civil products [e.g., General Electric, British Aerospace, McDonnell Douglas (Wulf, 1993)]. Elsewhere, firms might be involved in dual-use technologies (OTA, 1989; SPSG, 1991). In addition to the firms directly and indirectly involved in defense work, there are induced multiplier effects reflecting the spending of defense workers in their local economies (Bolton 1966; Braddon *et al*, 1992).

It is also misleading to refer to the DIB as a single, homogeneous entity. In many nations with a DIB, the supply side of the defense market consists of varying numbers of small to large-sized firms, either publicly or privately owned, with different degrees of specialization. Indeed, it is misleading to refer to a single defense market and industry. There are, in fact, a set of related markets for air, land, and sea systems supplied by firms, some of which specialize in one sector or in a subsector (e.g., components) with different degrees of dependence on defense sales. For example, the aerospace industry in Britain, France, Germany, and the USA has aircraft, helicopter, and guided weapons sectors and comprises firms supplying equipment, electronics, and engines to final assemblers which might be building both military and civil aircraft (Hartley, 1993a). The efficiency with which a firm supplies equipment determines its unit costs and the quantity which can be bought from increasingly restricted defense budgets. On this basis, defense industries are a major element in national defense. However, their efficiency cannot be assessed independently of procurement policy since governments have created an administered and regulated market which departs substantially from the economists' competitive model (see chapter 5). This raises the wider issue of whether governments should intervene to support their DIB.

A free market view would leave the size and structure of the DIB to be determined by market forces, including foreign competition (Taylor and Hayward, 1989, chapter 7). However, defense departments and the armed forces might wish to retain key national assets. Examples include capabilities in nuclear and communications systems and in critical technologies regarded as essential for maintaining the long-term qualitative superiority of a nation's weapon systems (e.g., sensitive radars, target recognition, fiber optics). These arguments for state intervention to support a DIB raise two related issues. First, what characteristics should the DIB have in order to meet a nation's strategic objectives? Is an R & D capability vital; if so, is this capability required for all major weapons systems? Or, are certain basic inputs necessary, such as strategic metals, essential ingredients, and some types of skilled labor (which?); or, is a production capability for either components or whole system assembly sufficient; or, is it only necessary to have a capability for operation, maintenance, and conversion? Questions then arise as to whether these various capabilities can be separated and at what cost. Second, are there alternative and lower-cost methods of achieving the strategic objectives of the DIB through, say, inventories and strategic stockpiles, long-term contracts, licensed production, subsidies to civil industry, and membership of a military alliance. Answers to such questions are a necessary input into a more general evaluation of the benefits and costs of a DIB and whether a nation's DIB is too large. Moreover, the rising costs of modern weapons and the prospect of a continuing squeeze on defense budgets mean that such issues can no longer be ignored. If governments are willing to pay for a DIB, what do they believe they are buying and how much are they willing to pay?

7.3   The benefits and costs of a DIB

Various benefits have been suggested, some of which might differ between advanced and developing countries. Often these benefits are not explained carefully, nor are they evaluated critically. Economists need to ask who gains and who loses from maintaining a national DIB: which agents in the political market will argue for the status quo and what sort of arguments will they use? The benefits from a DIB include the following:

(i)   **National independence, security of supply (self sufficiency) and responsiveness in emergencies and war**. This is often presented as a major benefit from a national DIB. It frees a nation from dependence on potentially unreliable foreign suppliers of essential defense equipment, particularly during a crisis or conflict. It also enables a nation to modify its equipment quickly during a conflict. Sometimes, though, these "potentially unreliable" foreign suppliers might be allied members of a military alliance (e.g., UK, USA), where common sourcing would promote standardization and interoperability of equipment in the alliance. Moreover, whilst governments might value national independence and the self sufficiency offered by a DIB, such an insurance policy can be costly (Hawes, 1989; Kolodziej, 1987; Taylor and Hayward, 1989).

(ii) **The need to maintain a capability which a nation believes will be required in the future**. It is claimed that importing high technology defense equipment means the loss of a capability and recreating this technology for future weapons systems development could be both costly and time consuming. But this argument ignores uncertainty and the nature of technical progress. Revolutionary rather than evolutionary technical progress could render obsolescent today's successful design teams: success today does not guarantee future success. Moreover, in the future, it might still be cheaper to buy from abroad.

(iii) **Foreign supply leaves the buyer vulnerable to monopoly price**

increases. It is argued that once a nation is locked into a foreign supplier, perhaps as a result of a low price for the initial equipment, the supplier is then able to charge monopoly prices for spares and support, so that life-cycle costs are higher than the domestic alternative. But life-cycle costings should be undertaken for both home and overseas purchases and a nation can equally well become dependent on a small-scale inefficient domestic monopoly providing unsuitable equipment.

(iv)   **Foreign supply provides unsuitable equipment not tailored to a nation's requirements**. It does not follow that a national DIB will always provide suitable equipment at an affordable price within the required time scale. All nations can point to examples where their national DIB has failed to deliver equipment on time, within budget, and which meets the operational requirement, with cancellations not unknown (Gansler, 1980, 1989a,b; Haglund, 1989; Peck and Scherer, 1962). And, where a nation has special needs, it has to ask how much extra is it willing to pay for weapons designed specifically to its requirements.

(v)   **Leverage**. A DIB may enable a country to be a more informed buyer and improve its bargaining power when considering buying from abroad. The strength of the leverage will depend on the potential cost of domestic development. However, this argument does not necessarily justify maintaining a large DIB with high technology capabilities in air, land and sea systems. For instance, a small core of state or privately owned R & D establishments could provide sufficient knowledge for a country to be an informed buyer. Also, where a nation is a substantial buyer it could exert leverage by threatening to buy from rival foreign suppliers in the world market. Even small nations could increase their buying power by combining to form a multi-national purchasing consortium [e.g. the four-nation European consortium which purchased the F-16 aircraft (Dorfer, 1983; Hartley, 1983)].

(vi)   **A DIB provides national economic benefits**. These take the form of jobs, technology, support for the balance of payments, and a contribution to the national exchequer (e.g., tax revenue, avoiding unemployment payments). For the UK, some estimates suggest that when comparing British and foreign equipment a premium of 25 percent to 40 percent should be applied to the overseas purchase price to allow for some of these wider national economic benefits [balance of payments, exchequer impacts (HCP 22–I, 1982, p. xlvi)]. However, the use of such shadow prices depends on whether a nation's exchange rate is overvalued and, if so, any premium needs to be applied universally to all industries and not solely to the DIB. In addition, a proper cost–benefit analysis of a nation's DIB would need to incorporate the whole range of benefits listed above and not solely the economic benefits: such studies are conspicuous by their absence. The point also has to be made that other forms of public expenditure provide a flow of benefits (e.g., health and training from expenditure on health and education) as well as such indirect economic effects in terms of jobs, the balance of payments, government finance, and technology. Thus, if these wider economic benefits are to be counted, the issue is whether the net benefit from these indirect economic effects due to the DIB is large or small relative to the average net benefit that would arise from the possible alternatives (Acost, 1989; Gansler, 1989a; Hartley, Hussain, and Smith, 1987; Kolodziej, 1987; Taylor and Hayward, 1989).

(vii) **The DIB in developing countries**. Some of the benefits outlined above apply to the case for creating a DIB in developing countries, although they will differ in importance and relevance. For example, the desire to reduce dependence on arms imports and excessive reliance upon one foreign nation (e.g., USA) can be an important factor in the decision to create and develop a domestic defense industry. This was the case for example, in Taiwan and South Korea (Nolan, 1986). Similarly, developing countries might view a DIB as an important contributor to saving and/or earning valuable foreign currency. Also, a number of developing countries regard the defense industry as a leading sector providing spin-off benefits to the rest of the economy. On this view, military R & D is seen as beneficial for the development of key high-technology sectors which it is believed through various spin-offs will eventually improve the international competitiveness of the economy (Molas-Gallart, 1992). The question remains, though, whether the defense industry is more or less useful than other industries as a driving force for technological modernization and a source of economic and infrastructural spin-offs in developing countries (see also chapter 8).

A feature of the debate about the DIB is the general lack of quantitative evidence on its benefits and costs. The arguments are qualitative in which various benefits are described, sometimes too vaguely, without any indication of policy-makers' willingness to pay (a feature which applies to many policy areas and not solely to defense). Often, though, some insights emerge when defense departments consider and review their major procurement choices. For example, the alternatives to buying from the DIB include a direct import purchasing off-the-shelf (with or without an offset agreement, see chapter 9) or licensed production of foreign equipment. During such project appraisals, any costs of supporting the DIB will be revealed and are likely to be reflected in higher prices or longer delivery time scales or in inferior equipment. Simple notions of comparative advantage suggest that nations will have different comparative advantages and are likely to gain from specialization and international trade: hence self sufficiency is costly. For example, the costs of supporting the UK DIB by buying British were expressed by the Secretary of State in 1986 "there is practically nothing you cannot buy cheaper from the United States of America because they have huge production runs, huge resources, huge research programs funded by the taxpayer ..." (HCP 518, 1986, p. xli; see also chapter 9). There is some evidence from EU countries suggesting that by opening up their national defense markets to foreign competition, EU nations might obtain average price savings of about 25 percent on defense equipment purchases (Hartley and Cox, 1992; Hartley, 1985). Further insights into the efficiency of defense industries can be obtained from industry studies.

7.4   The supply side: defense industries

There are a variety of studies of defense industries, although most are general, using qualitative methods and descriptive statistics. There is a need for much more theoretical and quantitative empirical work, applying the new industrial economics [e.g. game theory (see chapter 5)] and estimating models of profitability, productivity, cost curves, employment, and export performance. Useful contributions to knowledge about defense industries might also be made by comparative industry studies and by case studies of firms and major projects. Certainly, there is no lack of an appropriate analytical framework. The structure–conduct–performance paradigm of industrial economics provides an obvious starting point for analyzing defense industries. This model suggests that industrial performance depends on structural features reflected in the number and size distribution of firms and in entry conditions. Structural features are measured by concentration ratios, entry barriers, and scale economies. Industrial performance is reflected in technical efficiency, the relationship between prices and marginal cost, product variety, innovation, and profitability. A simple model used widely by industrial economists, but less so for the study of defense industries, is shown below (Tirole, 1990)

$$\Pi = f(CR, EB, Z), \tag{7.1}$$

where Π = industry or firm profitability,
  CR = a concentration ratio,
  EB = a measure of entry barriers
    (e.g., minimum efficient scale),
  Z = other relevant influences.

New developments have modified or replaced the traditional structure–performance approach. These include transaction costs, contestable markets, game theory, principal–agent theory, and Austrian economics (see chapter 5; Laffont and Tirole, 1993; Tirole, 1990). For example, the principle of contestable markets stresses the importance of the *threat* of entry and rivalry: a contestable market need not be populated by a large number of firms (as in perfect competition) and it is contestability rather than structure which determines performance (Baumol *et al.*, 1982). On this basis, governments can make their domestic monopoly defense industries contestable by threatening or actually opening up their national markets to competition from a few foreign firms.

In surveying this part of the literature, it has to be stressed that there is a general lack of an adequate, comprehensive, in-depth and up-to-date data base on the world's defense industries. The studies which are available are dated, often presenting only a general and limited overview and usually restricted to the major arms-producing nations. Consider some of the information which is needed:

(i)   Each nation's spending on its domestic defense producers as a share of its total spending on defense equipment. This is one possible indicator of protectionism.

(ii) The proportion of defense orders which are awarded on a competitive basis. This is an indicator of market competitiveness.

(iii) The number and size distribution of firms in defense industries (a measure of concentration).

(iv) The distribution of defense contracts by industry sector, firms, and regions, and the relative importance of defense business for industries, firms, and regions. This would indicate the industrial and regional dependence on defense spending and hence their vulnerability to cuts in defense budgets.

(v)   Performance indicators for both defense and civil industries and firms so enabling comparisons between the military and civil sectors (e.g., profitability, exports, labor productivity).

Once again, some of the pioneering work on defense industries, learning curves, cost conditions, and project case studies has been published by American economists (see Hartley and Hooper, 1990, references 500–660). A classic text in the field using a structure-performance approach is Peck and Scherers' *The Weapons Acquisition*

Process (1962). This study analyzed the nonmarket characteristics of weapons acquisition, the structure and dynamics of the weapons industry, and the execution of weapons programs. American weapons makers are assessed up to the early 1960s in terms of the impact of technical change on the size, product mix, and geographical location of the industry, the concentration of prime contract awards among a few relatively large firms, and the relatively minor role of small businesses. The impact of technical progress on the changing importance of various factors of production is assessed, particularly the growing importance of R & D resources. On economies and diseconomies of scale, the book arrives at an inconclusive position: "they may or may not exist ..." (Peck and Scherer, 1962, p. 188), a result which reflects the fact that throughout the weapons industry up to the early 1960s, the use of cost-reimbursement contracts made economies of scale less decisive than in commercial operations. There is a chapter on entry and exit from the weapons industry, and further chapters on the conduct and performance of weapons programs. Interestingly, Peck and Scherer adopted a case study-project history approach reflecting the fact that "statistical information about the weapons industry is fragmentary, and in any case the weapons acquisition process is not one that lends itself to statistical analysis" (Peck and Scherer, 1962, p. 12).

Since 1962, there have been further studies of the US defense industry, some of which have used a structure–conduct–performance paradigm (Fox, 1974; Gansler, 1980, 1989a), whilst others have been concerned about the military-industrial complex (Adams and Adams, 1972; Galbraith, 1972; Melman, 1971). The US defense industry is dominated by large defense contractors, with relatively high concentration ratios in specialized markets (e.g., fighter aircraft, helicopters, transport and tanker aircraft, aero-engines, nuclear submarines). Worries about monopoly power and the effect on performance have led some analysts to propose that the US government needs an industrial strategy to create "effective competition" in the defense industry. Suggestions have been made that from the US government's viewpoint, there should be two or three strong competitors in each major segment of the industry (Gansler, 1989a, p. 284). Although such a proposal appears attractive, it might be increasingly costly if, in the 1990s, nations continue to reduce their defense spending; contestability might then require a greater willingness to open up the US market to foreign firms (see also chapter 5).

Elsewhere, outside the USA, there have been a number of studies of defense industries in other nations of the world. The Stockholm International Peace Research Institute (SIPRI) publishes annual reviews of world arms production, including statistical data on the 100 largest

Table 7.2 *Top twenty defense companies, 1991*

Company	Country	Industry	Total sales ($US million)	Arms sales as percentage of total sales (%)	Total employment
McDonnell Douglas	USA	Ac, El, Mi	18,448	55	109,123
General Dynamics	USA	Ac, El, Mi, Mv, Sh	9,548	80	80,600
British Aerospace	UK	Ac, A, El, Mi, Sa/o	18,687	40	123,200
General Motors	USA	Ac, Eng, El, Mi	123,056	6	756,000
Lockheed	USA	Ac	9,809	70	71,300
General Electric	USA	Eng	60,236	10	28,400
Northrop	USA	Ac	5,694	90	36,200
Raytheon	USA	El, Mi	9,274	55	71,600
Boeing	USA	Ac, El, Mi	29,314	17	159,100
Thompson SA	France	El, Mi	12,634	38	105,000
Martin Marietta	USA	Mi	6,080	75	60,500
Rockwell International	USA	Ac, El, Mi	11,927	34	87,000
United Technologies	USA	Ac, El, Mi	20,840	19	185,100
GEC	UK	El	16,693	24	104,995
Daimler Benz	Germany	Ac, Eng, El, Mi	57,252	7	379,252
DCN	France	Sh	3,715	100	30,000
Aerospatiale	France	Ac, Mi	8,614	40	43,287
Litton Industries	USA	El, Sh	5,219	60	52,300
IRI	Italy	Ac, Eng, El, Sh	54,794	5	368,267
Grumman	USA	Ac, El	4,038	72	23,600

Notes: (i) Companies are ranked by arms sales: OECD and developing countries only.
  (ii) A = artillery; Ac = aircraft; El = electronics; Eng = engines; Mi = missiles;
     Mv = motor vehicles; Sa/o = small arms/ordnance; Sh = shipbuilding.
Source: SIPRI (1993).

arms-producing companies in the OECD and the Third World (SIPRI, 1993). A further SIPRI study provided an empirical account of the size of the world arms industry, its current problems, and the different industrial strategies being pursued in the USA, the former USSR, Western Europe, Poland, Czechoslovakia, Turkey, China, Japan, Australia, and third tier countries (Wulf, 1993). In the early 1990s, employment in the arms industry world wide fell below 15 million, with over 80 percent of world employment concentrated in the former Soviet

Table 7.3 *A country and industrial analysis*

	Number of companies in the largest 100 arms producers (1991)				
Country	Aerospace industry	Electronics industry	Shipbuilding	Land equipment	Total number
USA	16	23	3	5	47
UK	5	5	2	1	13
France	4	4	1	2	11
Germany	1	1	2	4	8
Total number	26	33	8	12	79

Notes: (i) Largest arms producers are for the OECD and developing countries in 1991. (ii) Some of the industrial classifications are approximate since a number of companies are involved in a range of defense industries (e.g., aerospace and electronics). (iii) Land equipment comprises artillery, military vehicles, small arms, and ordnance.
Source: SIPRI (1993).

Union, China, and the USA; a further 3 million to 4 million job losses world wide are forecast for the period 1993–8 (Wulf, 1993). The top twenty largest arms producing companies in the OECD in 1991 are shown in table 7.2. The top twenty is dominated by US companies, by firms in the aerospace industry, and by large conglomerates with both military and civil business. Relatively few of the top twenty are heavily dependent on defense sales (with defense accounting for 90 percent or more of sales). Indeed, within the top 100 in 1991, only six companies were totally dependent on defense sales (i.e., 100 percent dependent: DCN and Matra, France; Newport News and Science Applications, USA; VSEL and Devenport Management, UK). Moreover, only three developing countries (India, Israel and South Africa) had a combined total of six arms producers in the top 100 arms producers in 1991.

Table 7.3 provides a country and industrial breakdown of the top 100 arms producing companies in 1991. The USA accounted for almost 50 percent of the top 100 arms companies, with the UK, France, and Germany accounting for a further 32 percent of the total. For these four nations, the electronics and aerospace industries provided most of their largest arms producers.

Typically, in industrialized nations, defense industries are dominated by a small number of large companies, with domestic markets characterized by monopoly or oligopoly. The long-run trend has been toward a smaller number of larger defense companies reflected in mergers, or prime contractors becoming subcontractors, or by exits from the industry: such trends are likely to continue with disarmament and falling defense budgets (see chapters 11 and 12). An overview of the world's defense industries is provided by Todd (1988). This book shows how national defense industries are protected sectors, with governments using their monopsony power to determine technical progress, rivalry for contracts, profitability, location, ownership, and the imposition of constraints on arms exports. As a result, industries such as aerospace, electronics, ordnance, and shipbuilding, together with local communities can become dependent upon defense contracts. Such industries are more appropriately analyzed using public choice models. This approach explains procurement choices in terms of the role of powerful producer groups (defense contractors) lobbying governments to support their national DIB.

In addition to US studies, there are some limited studies of defense industries in Western Europe and in various European countries as well as studies of specific European defense-intensive industries such as aircraft and shipbuilding (Creasey and May, 1988; Drown et al., 1990; Faltas, 1986; Fontanel, 1989; Hayward 1989; Kolodziej, 1987; Molas-Gallart, 1992; Walker and Gummett, 1993; Willett, 1993). For Europe, there is a lack of good analytical and empirical industry and market studies similar to Peck and Scherer (1962) in the USA. Elsewhere, there are studies of defense industries in nations such as India, Israel, Japan, South America, South Korea, and Taiwan (Brauer, 1991; Chinworth, 1992; Hartley and Sandler, 1990; Nolan, 1986; Ward et al., 1991). Japan is an interesting example of re-entry into the defense market through the development and application of dual-use technologies (e.g., micro-electronics), the increasing acceptance of commercial product specifications for use in the defense sector and the widespread integration of defense and civilian production within single manufacturing plants (Edgar and Haglund, 1993).

In the early 1990s, the DIB of the former Soviet Union was the world's largest, employing almost 6 million people. From the 1930s, the state central planning and nonmarket resource allocation system had given the highest priority to the defense industries. It had three distinctive features. First, the separation of research and design organizations from production facilities (e.g., aircraft, missiles, land equipment), with the former often located around Moscow and the production plants widely dispersed throughout the country. Second, was the standardization of defense equipment throughout the former Warsaw Pact nations, so enabling the former Soviet Union to obtain the scale economies associated with long production runs of each type of equipment. Third, unlike the defense industries in NATO, competition was restricted to the research and design agencies (production being undertaken separately) and to two competing agencies for each type of equipment [e.g., Mikoyan and Sukhoi for combat aircraft (Cooper, 1993)].

7.5   Cost conditions: scale and learning

Cost conditions resulting from the presence or absence of scale and learning economies are a major determinant of industry structure: they affect the size of firms and concentration ratios. There are at least five characteristics of cost conditions which affect defense industries and the economics of equipment procurement (see also chapter 5):

(i)   **The importance of development costs.** Development forms a total fixed cost. Where such costs are substantial, as in the case of complex, high technology weapons (e.g. combat aircraft), they represent a significant entry cost. High development costs also raise the costs of small production runs: hence, in such conditions, independence and self sufficiency for a small domestic market is costly.

(ii)   **Cost and time overruns.** Underestimation of development time and cost is common and affects all types of weapons. It often arises because the weapons which are eventually produced differ substantially from those originally planned (Large, 1974).

(iii)   **Cost trends.** Defense equipment is costly and, in real terms, the trends in the unit production costs of successive generations of equipment are upwards. Inevitably, defense budgets have not kept pace with the cost escalation in new equipment. The result has affected the numerical strength of the armed forces and the size and structure of the industries supplying defense equipment. For example, since 1945, in nations such as the USA and the UK there has been a long-run decline in the number of combat aircraft in the air force and in the number of firms in the aerospace industry.

(iv)   **Economies of scale and learning.** Although there is a substantial amount of evidence on scale economies, much of it is from the 1960s and 1970s, there is little which relates directly to defense industries. In contrast, there is a substantial literature on learning economies (chapter 5: section 5.4). Here, difficulties arise in ensuring that learning economies are not included in estimates of scale economies. Furthermore, it is possible that large defense firms might gain economies of scope (Smith, 1990). Nonetheless, the general findings on scale economies provide useful indicators of which defense industries are likely to be characterized by substantial economies of scale. The industries for which there are large economies of scale for development and production include aircraft, motor vehicles, other vehicles, office machinery, together with mechanical, electrical, and instrument engineering. Evidence from these industries suggests that for large-scale, high technology defense projects, the unit cost savings of moving from one-third minimum efficient scale (MES) to minimum efficient scale could be in the range of 15–20 percent (Pratten, 1988; Rogerson, 1991b).

(v)   **The cost penalties of stretching-out programs**. Because of budget limitations, it is not unknown for procurement programs to be stretched-out over a longer period, so slowing down production: a response which is increasingly likely with falling defense budgets. A US study of air and land systems estimated that a 50 percent reduction in annual production rates compared with the basic rate would increase real unit costs by a median figure of a little over 20 percent (CBO, 1987).

As a result of the importance of spreading costly R & D over a larger output, together with economies of scale and learning, defense industries are usually characterized as decreasing cost activities. This is reflected in the industry's structure, namely, the number and size of firms and concentration ratios. Domestic monopolies, duopolies, or oligopolies are typical for the suppliers of major air, land, and sea equipment. Inevitably, nations with a small domestic defense market have to make a choice between firm size and competition: larger firms obtaining scale economies do so at the price of monopoly.

An indication of the optimum size of firm in defense industries can be obtained by examining the size of the major defense firms surviving in the EU, the USA, and elsewhere (the survivor method). However, it is recognized that in defense industries, firm size is determined by government policy and its willingness to pay for an independent DIB. Nonetheless, the evidence shows that large US firms dominate the top 100 arms producers in the OECD and the Third World (table 7.2 and SIPRI, 1993). The size of US defense firms reflects their scale of output which in turn affects unit costs. Comparisons with European nations are striking. For combat aircraft, US output for its national forces (i.e., excluding exports) can be up to eight times the typical output for the French and UK air forces and for some equipments, the US annual production rates were equivalent to the total output in France and the UK (e.g., F-16; Blackhawk helicopter; M1 tank). Clearly, scale of output is a major determinant of firm size and unit costs and there are major differences between the USA and Europe (Hartley, 1983, 1993a).

7.6   Industrial performance

The structure-performance approach of industrial economics identifies some of the major determinants of efficiency in a nation's DIB. Two related factors are important. First, the extent of competition (contestability); and, second, the scale of output which determines the impact of scale and learning economies on unit costs, firm size, and concentration ratios. The resulting performance of defense industries will be reflected in indicators such as labor productivity, unit prices, competitiveness, R & D, spin-off, and profitability.

Evidence on labor productivity and the employment behavior of defense firms has involved comparative industry case studies and estimation of various employment functions. Industry studies of the US, UK, and EU aerospace industries have sought to explain higher American labor productivity in terms of its greater scale of output and more competitive market structure (Hartley, 1993a). It has also been hypothesized that defense firms follow a labor retention policy and that such labor hoarding is financed by cost-based contracts (e.g., retaining valuable scientists in anticipation of the next competition). Other empirical studies have compared the employment behavior of defense and civil firms and have tested whether major defense cuts have resulted in a shake-out of labor from weapons-intensive industries (Arditti and Peck, 1964; Hartley and Corcoran, 1975). The general form of the estimated employment model is as follows

$$L_t = L(Q, t, L_{t-1}, DV) \tag{7.2}$$

where L_t = current employment,
    Q = output,
    t = a time-trend representing the capital stock and technology,
    L_{t-1} = a lagged dependent variable,
    DV = a dummy variable (1, 0) for shocks such as the announcement of major defense reviews.

When estimated in log-linear form, the coefficient on output shows the elasticity of employment with respect to variations in output. Comparisons of such elasticities for defense and civil firms indicates the extent of any labor retention and hoarding behavior by arms producers. UK evidence, for example, shows that British defense firms do not respond to changes in factor prices nor to defense reviews (Lynk and Hartley, 1985). An example of an estimated log-linear employment model for the UK aerospace industry is shown below

$$L_t = 0.94 - 0.005t + 0.20Q + 0.66L_{t-1} + 0.025DV, \quad (7.3)$$
$$(0.56) \quad (0.717) \quad (2.29) \quad (2.74) \quad (1.774)$$

where L_t is employment in the UK aerospace industry; t is a time-trend for 1959–76; Q is output; L_{t-1} is a lagged dependent variable; DV is a dummy variable (1, 0) for UK defence reviews; variables L, Q, and L_{t-1} are logs; t statistics are in parentheses and $\bar{R}^2 = 0.96$ (Hartley and Lynk, 1983b).

Performance can also be influenced by ownership. In a number of countries, such as France, India, Italy, and Spain, defense industries are state owned. Elsewhere in the 1980s, particularly in the UK, state owned defense companies were privatized (e.g., British Aerospace, Royal Ordnance, Rolls-Royce, the warship builders). The UK experience suggests that privatization in general results in improved performance measured in terms of labor and total factor productivity. Similar empirical tests for British Aerospace confirmed a deterioration in performance following nationalization and an improved performance with privatization (Dunsire et al., 1991).

British experience provides an indication of the likely impact of competition on the unit costs and prices of defense equipment. The UKs competitive procurement policy, introduced in 1983, resulted in the Ministry of Defence, becoming a more demanding customer introducing and extending competition, making a greater use of firm or fixed-price and incentive contracts rather than cost-plus contracting and shifting risks to industry. By the late 1980s, competition was extended to embrace a greater willingness to buy from abroad. At the outset of the new policy, a target was announced for achieving cost savings of 10 percent on the total equipment budget. Some of the actual results of competition have been impressive with cost savings ranging from 10 percent to 70 percent, all of which might be taken as indicators of monopoly pricing and/or X-inefficiency in UK defense industries (HCP 189, 1991). Empirical tests show that the new UK competition policy has resulted in a large reduction in the concentration of Ministry of Defence purchases (Smith, 1990a). There remain, however, concerns about collusive tendering and that domestic monopoly might be the long-run outcome of competition.

Supporters of a national DIB often stress its dynamic benefits through promoting high technology work and in providing valuable spin-off to the civil sector of the economy (e.g., military to civil aircraft; laser technology from defense used in ophthalmic surgery). Critics of defense R & D argue that it "crowds-out" valuable investment in the civil sector, that it acts as a magnet attracting scarce scientists away from civil industries, and that there is "too little" spin-off to the civil sector. As a result there are believed to be adverse effects on industry's ability to compete in world markets, particularly in the markets for civil high technology products (Buck *et al.*, 1993). Much of the literature on spin-off has tended to rely on anecdotal evidence, lacking analytical and empirical rigor. One empirical study of spin-off from US defense and space expenditures found no evidence of spin-offs at the firm level and concluded that such expenditures "are hardly conducive to promote technical and economic performance" (Chakrabarti *et al.*, 1992, p. 187). An alternative approach to assessing spin-off and crowding-out involves monitoring the mobility of scientists and engineers between defense and civil activities. One such study found that the most interesting result concerned dual-use industries: "in industries in which defense and civil activities were roughly balanced, defense-to-civil transfers were more likely, but no comparable pattern existed to civil-to-defense transfers" (Lerner, 1992, p. 238).

Profitability is a standard measure of industrial performance. In defense procurement, though, profits are often subject to government regulation and might also be the result of protectionism and support for the country's DIB (see chapter 5). Nor are data publicly available on the profitability of specific defense projects as distinct from the overall profitability of a company's complete range of activities. Critics claim that defense contractor's profitability is dependent on wars and reflects favorable treatment by governments. Others suggest that defense profits reflect a risky business and the return needed to induce firms to remain in the industry so as to retain a DIB. These various assertions can be formulated into testable hypotheses examining the impact of wars, rearmament, government regulatory agencies and competition on profitability, and comparing the profits of defense contractors with those of civilian firms (Fox, 1974; Gansler, 1980; Hartley and Hooper, 1991a). Such studies suggest that competition reduces profitability and that wars (e.g., World War II; Korean War) can lead to higher profits (Agapos, 1975; Dunne, 1993; Hartley and Watt, 1981). Often, though, these studies rely on descriptive statistics with all the problems of allowing for other relevant influences on profitability. Or, where estimating equations are used they tend to be *ad hoc*, lacking standard economic variables such as concentration ratios (although data problems often determine the form of the equation). An example of the general estimating equation used in such studies is (Agapos, 1975)

$$\Pi = \Pi \ (D, \ W, \ R, \ t) \tag{7.4}$$

where Π = a measure of company profitability,
   D = national defense spending,
   W = a dummy variable (1, 0) representing a war,
   R = a dummy variable (1, 0) representing government regulation of profits,
   t = a time-trend.

Do large defense contractors earn greater returns than other companies? A US study found that for the period 1948–89, the financial performance of the leading defense contractors was, on average, much better than that of comparable large corporations. Such differences did not reflect variations in riskiness between the defense and civil sectors (Trevino and Higgs, 1992; also Stigler and Friedland, 1971; Kaun, 1988).

7.7   Conclusion

There remains a general lack of published, independent, and authoritative studies of the world's defense industries. There is a need for good theoretical and empirical industry studies on a comparative basis. In particular, much more knowledge is required on the conduct of defense contractors: how do firms behave and compete? For instance, how do they respond to different types of contracts, to profit controls, to collaborative projects, to competitive procurement policies and to conversion policies? Complications arise where weapons firms are conglomerates with different activities in both military and civil sectors. In such cases, a careful search and analysis of company reports might provide useful information. At the same time, such companies might provide valuable case study material on spin-off from defense R & D. There is also a need for reliable estimates of cost–quantity relationships and the minimum efficient scale for major air, land and sea equipment. Ideally, long-run cost curves need to be estimated to determine the cost implications of departing from the minimum efficient scale. Such cost estimates are an important component of any cost–benefit analysis of the DIB.

8 Economic growth, development, and military expenditures

In two provocative and important contributions, Emile Benoit (1973, 1978) uncovered a net positive association between defense spending and economic growth for forty-four less-developed countries (LDCs) during the 1950–65 period. Apparently a larger defense burden (as measured by the share of GDP devoted to defense) *may* have promoted growth (as measured by the growth in civilian product) for these countries. This finding was surprising and generated a flurry of research activity that fell into two broad categories: studies that found fault with Benoit's methodology,[1] and studies that investigated the relationship of economic growth and defense with an alternative methodology.[2] The issue raised by Benoit has considerable policy relevance. If, for example, defense is growth promoting, then the share of defense devoted to GDP can be used as a policy instrument for inducing development. If, on the other hand, defense is growth inhibiting, then a reallocation of resources from defense to civilian uses may be conducive to growth and development.

In the case of developed countries, the impact of defense expenditures on growth is also of current policy interest. Consider the case of the US and the ex-Soviet Union. During the cold war, the US defense commitment varied between 5 and 9 percent of GDP, while the USSR probably allocated as much as 15–20 percent of GDP to defense (see, e.g., Brada and Graves, 1988; Kaufman, 1983). The answer to whether a peace dividend can emerge as the US and the Commonwealth of Independent States reallocate resources from defense to civilian uses hinges, in part, on the impact of defense on growth. *If defense spending is supportive of growth*, then any peace dividend that emerges from the anticipated reallocation of resources will be attenuated by a negative

---

[1] Examples include Chan (1985), Deger (1986a, 1986b), Deger and Smith (1983), Rothschild (1973), and Smith (1980).

[2] Examples include Biswas and Ram (1986), Chowdhury (1991), Faini, Annez, and Taylor (1984), Joerding (1986), Landau (1986), Lim (1983), and Stewart (1991). Some studies fall into both categories.

impact on growth. Conventional wisdom, however, argues that defense commitment on the scale of the superpowers during the cold war hampers growth owing to defense expenditures crowding out private and public investment. Moreover, defense is often thought to siphon off R & D resources that can be more fruitfully applied to civilian applications directly.

To ascertain the extent of a peace dividend, a researcher must be able to determine the relationship among macroeconomic aggregates (e.g., defense expenditures, nondefense public investment, private investment, exports, and consumption) and the country's growth rate. If this relationship can be adequately formulated and tested for individual nations and/or a cross section of similar nations, then the estimated relationship can be used for forecasting purposes to indicate how a peace dividend will influence an economy. The purpose of this chapter is to survey the literature on the impact of defense on growth. A secondary purpose is to distill a basic conclusion from the diverse results found in the literature.

8.1   Benefits and costs of military expenditures

By way of an overview, the alleged benefits or costs that defense expenditures confer or impose on economic growth are reviewed.[3] The list of conceivable benefits can differ between developed and less-developed countries. First, both types of countries can experience a stimulative effect from defense expenditures during periods of unemployment, caused by underconsumption or underinvestment demand. This stimulative effect, of course, ends once an economy is at or near full employment. Such a stimulative benefit requires a disequilibrium in the economy.[4] Second, nations can experience direct technological effects and spin-offs from the defense sector. When spin-offs are later applied to the civilian sector, growth is promoted. Third, defense expenditures can enhance growth if some of the expenditure is used to provide social infrastructure (e.g., dams, roads, airports, communication networks) and other forms of public goods. This third class of benefits is more likely to apply to LDCs, where infrastructure is in short supply (Benoit, 1978). Fourth, defense expenditures can promote growth, especially in LDCs,

---

[3]   This section draws from the work of Benoit (1973, 1978), Chan (1985), Deger (1986a, 1986b), Deger and Smith (1983), Faini, Annez, and Taylor (1984), Grobar and Porter (1989), Mintz and Huang (1990), Ram (1986), Rasler and Thompson (1988) and Rothschild (1973).

[4]   Marxist economists argue that defense expenditures are needed to make up for underconsumption that plagues mature capitalist economies. Little empirical support has been found for this hypothesis (Chan, 1985).

by providing nutrition, training, and education to a segment of the population. These human capital enhancing activities may later impact the civilian sector. Fifth, defense expenditures can indirectly support growth by maintaining internal and external security, since a secure environment may be conducive to promoting market exchange opportunities and attracting foreign investment. Often the inflow of foreign capital may provide the transfer of advanced technology.

Other considerations may cause defense activities to have a growth-inhibiting influence. Foremost, defense may divert resources away from public and private investment that are more growth promoting than defense. If defense competes for resources intended for private investment, then any resulting crowding-out of private investment will have a long-run impact on economic growth. If, in addition, a nation imports much of its arms, then defense activities can lead to an adverse balance of payments that can have a negative impact on potentially growth-promoting capital inflows. Growth is also inhibited when defense diverts R&D activities from the private sector. Though technological spin-offs can come from either the civilian or defense sector, the application of technological breakthroughs to the private sector is often faster and more direct if they originate there. Many R & D findings in the defense sector may not have a useful application in the civilian sector (e.g., stealth). Defense can inhibit growth by diverting resources from the export sector (Feder, 1983; Rothschild, 1973), which is often a stimulus to growth as it tends to employ advanced technology and efficient management techniques in order to compete abroad. In many LDCs, the export sector is more technologically advanced than other sectors of the economy. According to Feder (1983), the export sector generates positive externalities through technology transfers. In some LDCs (e.g., Brazil and India), defense production is in the export sector using technologically advanced methods. For these countries, defense would channel, rather than divert, resources to the export sector and promote growth. Finally, the defense sector limits growth through inefficient bureaucracies and excess burdens created by taxes used to finance the military expenditures. Of course, this last factor can also apply to the public sector in general.

Since defense can both stimulate and inhibit growth, the net impact of defense depends on the relative strength of opposing influences. If defense has a net beneficial effect on growth, then this is more apt to occur in LDCs where there are more avenues from which benefits can be derived.When building a theory to show the relationship of defense on growth, the researcher needs to account for the supply-side influences (e.g., technology spin-offs, positive externalities from infrastructure) and the demand-side factors (e.g., the crowding-out of investment or exports). A full blown model is likely to be characterized by sufficiently complicated interrelationships between the defense sector and the rest of the economy, so that the net impact of defense on growth will be ambiguous and, hence, an empirical question.

8.1.1   The past record for 1979 – 1989

Before reviewing the analysis of growth and defense, we thought it constructive to examine briefly the empirical record for the share of gross national product (GNP) devoted to defense for the decade 1979–89 and the level of military expenditures in constant 1989 US dollars.[5] For the entire period, the developing countries increased their military expenditures by only 0.3 percent. In the first third of the period, these countries increased their military expenditures in real terms; but after 1983, military expenditures declined in the developing world. The military expenditures of the NATO allies grew at a rate of 3.6 percent during the decade, but slowed significantly toward the end of the decade (see Hewitt, 1992, on trends for 1972–88). Declines in military expenditures are anticipated in the 1990s owing to the end of the cold war. The same decrease is expected of the ex-Warsaw Pact nations. The bulk of the world's military expenditures, some 93 percent, are accounted for by the ex-Warsaw Pact, NATO, East Asia (especially China and Japan), and the Middle East in 1989; hence, the rest of the world (Africa, South America, South Asia, Oceania, and the rest of Europe) only account for 7 percent of military expenditures. Military expenditures continue to grow in real terms in China, Japan, India, and Pakistan. In fact, the most rapid rate of growth is in South Asia, owing to increased expenditures in India, Pakistan, and Sri Lanka.[6]

In table 8.1, military expenditures (in constant 1989 US dollars) for NATO, the Warsaw Pact, the Organization of Petroleum Exporting Countries (OPEC), and the Organization for Economic Cooperation and Development (OECD) are given for two points in time – 1979 and 1989. The two right-hand columns indicate the share of GNP devoted to military expenditures at these two points in time. The share of GNP going to military expenditures varies widely over the sample. On average, nations devote about 3–4 percent of GNP to defense. Based on this average, OPEC nations allocate a relatively large share of GNP to

[5]   The information presented in this paragraph is drawn from the US Arms Control and Disarmament Agency (1991, pp. 1–7) annual report.
[6]   On India, see the country survey by Ward et al. (1991); on Sri Lanka, see the country survey by Grobar (1992).

Table 8.1 *Military expenditures in constant 1989 dollars and share of GNP devoted to military expenditures: 1979, 1989 selected alliances, organizations, and countries*

Organization	Military expenditures[a]		Military expenditures/GNP	
	1979	1989	1979	1989
NATO	331.2	462.3	4.1	4.5
Warsaw Pact	332.3	365.7	11.7	10.9
OPEC	47.8	46.3	8.8	8.9
OECD	371.6	517.8	3.4	3.6
Selected countries	Military expenditures[b]		Military expenditures/GNP	
	1979	1989	1979	1989
Algeria	1,361	2,313	3.9	5.1
Argentina	2,039	1,858	3.2	3.4
Bahrain	231	196	6.4	6.5
Bangladesh	208	323	1.4	1.6
Botswana	36	62[c]	4.7	2.8
Brazil	2,661	5,966[d]	0.8	1.3
Burma	476	611[c]	3.6	3.7
Cameroon	107	148	1.5	1.3
China(PRC)	26,950[c]	22,330	10.4	3.7
China (Taiwan)	4,539	8,060[c]	6.6	5.4
Costa Rica	29	22	0.7	0.5
Egypt	5,187[c]	3,499[c]	12.5	5.0
Ethiopia	408	763	8.7	12.8
Gabon	82	140[c]	2.7	4.5
Ghana	29	30[c]	0.7	0.6
Haiti	29	45[c]	1.2	1.9
India	5,132	8,174	3.3	3.1
Indonesia	1,538	1,510	3.3	1.7
Kenya	248	210[c]	4.7	2.7
Korea, South	5,011	9,100	5.2	4.3
Libya	5,373[c]	3,309[c]	13.2	14.9
Madagascar	83	35[c]	3.4	1.5
Malawi	59	35	4.7	2.3
Malaysia	787	1,039	3.8	2.9
Mexico	723	875	0.5	0.5
Morocco	836	1,203[c]	5.8	5.5
Nigeria	663	130	2.4	0.5
Pakistan	1,036	2,488	5.4	6.8
Philippines	833	960	2.3	2.2
Saudi Arabia	19,910	14,690	18.1	16.0
Somalia	62	NA	5.9	NA
Sri Lanka	72	223	1.5	3.2
Sudan	449[c]	339[c]	3.4	2.2
Tanzania	207	110	9.1	4.1
Zambia	520[c]	65[c]	13.2	1.4

Notes: [a]Military expenditures in billions of constant 1989 US dollars.
[b]Military expenditures in millions of constant 1989 US dollars.
[c]Estimate based on partial or uncertain data.
[d]Figure listed for 1988 since 1989 figures not available.
NA means not available.
Source: US Arms Control and Disarmament Agency (1991, table 1).

defense, while the NATO nations are somewhat above the average. The ex-Warsaw Pact nations are far above the average, mainly because of the ex-Soviet Union. Most of the selected countries, displayed in table 8.1, are developing countries. It is easy to find nations with good (e.g., Brazil, Indonesia, and Malaysia) and poor (e.g., Bangladesh and Haiti) economic growth records that allocate relatively small amounts of GNP to defense. Moreover, some nations (e.g., South Korea, Taiwan, China, and Saudi Arabia) have good growth records in recent years, but allocate higher than average shares of GNP to defense. Hence, a cursory examination of the record for 1979–1989 indicates a wide variety of experiences regarding defense and economic growth.

8.2   Supply-side models

Supply-side explanations of the relationship between defense and economic growth derive from the aggregate production function. At the most general level, national income or output, Y, can be expressed as a function of the inputs and technology

$$Y = F(L, K, T_c), \tag{8.1}$$

where L is aggregate labor, K is aggregate capital, and T_c is a technology index (Deger and Smith, 1983). The technology parameter may be embodied within the inputs, in which case *effective* input levels, say L^* for labor, can be made to depend on input levels and a technology parameter, so that $L^* = A(T_c)L$. If technology is disembodied, then T_c affects the relationship between inputs and output, but is not specifically attached to one input or the other (see Mueller and Atesoglu, 1993). In this latter case, a total differential of (8.1) gives

$$dY = F_L dL + F_K dK + F_T dT, \tag{8.2}$$

where subscripts on F denote partial derivatives, so that $F_L = \partial F/\partial L$, $F_K = \partial F/\partial K$, and $F_T = \partial F/\partial T_c$. By dividing both sides of (8.2) by Y, we derive

$$y = F_L l(L/Y) + F_K k(K/Y) + F_T t_c(T/Y), \tag{8.3}$$

where lower-case letters correspond to a relative change (e.g., $k = dK/K$, $l = dL/L$). If equation (8.1) were expressed in terms of time, so that each variable were a function of time (e.g., $Y = Y(t)$, $K = K(t)$), then taking a time derivative and finding relative changes would yield an expression in terms of growth rates

$$\dot{Y} = F_L \dot{L}(L/Y) + F_K \dot{K}(K/Y) + F_T \dot{T}_c(T_c/Y), \tag{8.4}$$

where $\dot{Y} = [(dY/dt)/Y]$ and so on. This then gives an expression decomposing output growth into component parts. Further disaggregation can result if, say, K is decomposed into military and nonmilitary capital. National income accounts can then be used to measure empirically the contribution of these components to growth.

As a partial relationship, the supply-side production-function approach is expected to uncover a significant positive effect of defense on growth, since defense is simply a component of the output whose growth is being measured. Increases in the defense component are a positive influence on measured output.

A more interesting supply-based model of defense and growth derives from the work of Feder (1983), Ram (1986), and Biswas and Ram (1986). This approach allows for a network of externalities among sectors as well as productivity differences. A host of variations of the model exist in the literature,[7] depending on the pattern of externalities and the number of sectors included. For illustration, we present a three-sector model with a private sector, a nonmilitary public sector, and a military sector.

The following three production functions apply

$$N = N(K_n, L_n) \tag{8.5}$$
$$D = D(K_d, L_d, N) \tag{8.6}$$

and

$$C = C(K_c, L_c, N, D), \tag{8.7}$$

in which N denotes nonmilitary public-sector output, D indicates military output, and C is private-sector output. In the above equations, the nonmilitary sector implies positive externalities ($\partial D/\partial N > 0$) for the defense sector, while both the defense and nonmilitary sector provide positive externalities ($\partial C/\partial D > 0$ and $\partial C/\partial N > 0$) for the civilian sector. Externalities can arise from the provision of infrastructure, training, education, nutrition, and other human capital enhancing activities. A positive externality exists when the activity of one sector augments the output in another, and this positive interdependency is uncompensated by market activities. Subscripts on the inputs denote the allocation of inputs among sectors, so that

$$K_n + K_d + K_c = K, \tag{8.8}$$
$$L_n + L_d + L_c = L, \tag{8.9}$$

[7] The following articles use a variant of the Feder–Ram model: Adams, Behrman, and Boldin (1991), Alexander (1990), Atesoglu and Mueller (1990), Carr (1989), Huang and Mintz (1990), and Mintz and Huang (1990), Ram (1986, 1987, 1989), and Rao (1989).

in which K and L denote total input supplies available at a given point in time. Total output, Y, or GDP is composed as follows

$$Y = N + D + C. \tag{8.10}$$

Differential productivity in the defense and nonmilitary public sector is captured by the following relationships

$$D_L/C_L = D_K/C_K = (1 + \delta_d), \tag{8.11}$$
$$N_L/C_L = N_K/C_K = (1 + \delta_n), \tag{8.12}$$

in which subscripts on D, C, and N represent partial derivatives or marginal products of labor and capital. If the productivity index δ_d is positive (negative), then the defense sector is more (less) productive than the civilian sector. In (8.12), δ_n denotes the differential productivity index for the nonmilitary sector.

To relate the growth or relative change in income to the defense burden (D/Y) and other determinants, we first take a total differential of (8.10), while using the total differentials of (8.5)–(8.7) to give

$$dY = N_K dK_n + N_L dL_n + D_K dK_d + D_L dL_d + D_N dN \tag{8.13}$$
$$+ C_K dK_C + C_L dL_C + C_D dD + C_N dN.$$

Next use (8.11) and (8.12) to express N_K, N_L, D_K, and D_L in (8.13) in terms of C_K and C_L, and then regroup terms using the aggregate input relationship in (8.8)–(8.9). This yields

$$dY = C_K dK + C_L dL + \delta_n C_K dK_n + \delta_n C_L dL_n \tag{8.14}$$
$$+ \delta_d C_K dK_d + \delta_d C_L dL_d + D_N dN + C_D dD + C_N dN.$$

With repeated use of (8.11) and (8.12) as well as the differentials of (8.5)–(8.6), we can derive[8]

$$dY/Y = C_K(I/Y) + C_L(dL/L)(L/Y) + \delta'_d(dD/D)(D/Y) \tag{8.15}$$
$$+ \delta'_n(dN/N)(N/Y),$$

where $\delta'_d = \{[\delta_d/(1 + \delta_d)] + C_D\}$, $\delta'_n = \{[\delta_n/(1 + \delta_n)] + [D_N/(1 + \delta_d)] + C_N\}$, and $I = dK$ or investment.

[8] This result follows by first substituting $C_K = D_K/(1 + \delta_d)$, $C_L = D_L/(1 + \delta_d)$, $C_K = N_K/(1 + \delta_n)$, and $C_L = N_L/(1 + \delta_n)$ for the relevant terms in the third, fourth, fifth, and sixth right-hand terms of (8.14). This gives

$$dY = C_K dK + C_L dL + \left(\tfrac{\delta_n}{1+\delta_n}\right)(N_K dK_n + N_L dL_n) + \left(\tfrac{\delta_d}{1+\delta_d}\right)(D_K dK_d + D_L dL_d) + D_N dN$$
$$+ C_D dD + C_N dN.$$

Next we modify the above expression by using the differentials, $dN = N_K dK_n + N_L dL_n$ and $dD = D_K dK_d + D_L dL_d + D_N dN$ from (8.5)–(8.6). This gives

$$dY = C_K dK + C_L dL + \left(\tfrac{\delta_n}{1+\delta_n}\right)dN + \left(\tfrac{\delta_d}{1+\delta_d}\right)(dD - D_N dN) + D_N dN + C_D dD + C_N dN.$$

Substituting I for dK, regrouping terms, and dividing both sides by Y yields (8.15).

In equation (8.15), the relative change in output depends on the income share of investment, the relative change in labor, the relative change in defense, and the relative change in nonmilitary expenditures. Each of the last three expressions are weighted by the sector's share of income. If time is explicitly brought into the problem, relative changes can be reinterpreted as growth rates – e.g., dL/L is replaced by $(dL/dt)/L$. The coefficients, δ'_d and δ'_n associated with the last two right-hand expressions in equation (8.15), indicate the combined productivity and externality influences. The latter influences are the C_D and C_N components of the δ'_d and δ'_n terms. Unless further restrictions are placed on the problem, estimates of the four coefficients in (8.15) are not able to distinguish between the productivity and externality influences. This can be especially troublesome if the two influences are in opposite directions, since the coefficient estimate will not reveal the directions of the component effects. To disaggregate these influences, the production function for the private sector can be assumed to be of the following form

$$C = D^{\theta} N^{\psi} f(L_c, K_c), \tag{8.16}$$

where θ and ψ are constant elasticities of productivity with respect to defense and nonmilitary output, respectively.[9] Unfortunately, the resulting growth equation to be estimated is likely to suffer from multi-collinearity (see, for example, Huang and Mintz, 1991; Ram, 1986).

To date, the most elaborate representation of the Feder–Ram model is that of Alexander (1990) with four sectors – a nonmilitary public sector, a military sector, an export sector, and a private sector. Alexander (1990) indicated that the nonmilitary public sector can provide positive externalities for the other three sectors. This is a reasonable assumption because the nonmilitary sector provides public inputs such as infrastructure that can benefit a wide variety of activities. In Alexander (1990), both the defense and the export sectors are also viewed as providing externalities for the private sector.

The Feder–Ram model has much to offer, since it is developed from a consistent theoretical structure. There are, nevertheless, two potential theoretical problems. First, the theoretical analysis ignores the interaction between the demand and supply sides of the economy. For example, the sources of the resources for the various activities are ignored along

---

[9] With this production function, equation (8.15) can be transformed to

$$dY/Y = C_K(I/Y) + \beta(dL/L) + [\delta_d/(1 + \delta_d)](dD/D)(D/Y) + \{[\delta_n/(1 + \delta_n)][D_N/(1 + \delta_d)]\}$$
$$\cdot (dN/N)(N/Y) + \theta(dD/D)(C/Y) + \psi(dN/N)(C/Y),$$

where $\beta = C_L(L/Y)$.

with sources of the demand for the various activities. With a pure supply-side explanation, defense is apt to stimulate the growth of output unless its productivity is significantly less than other sectors or its externalities are detrimental. The relationship between defense and private investment is also an important piece to the puzzle left out. Second, the pattern of externalities among sectors is difficult to fix at the outset. A better procedure might be to allow for a rich set of interactions among sectors in terms of externalities and then to use the data to test for the underlying pattern of externalities.

There are a couple of econometric considerations to be resolved with respect to testing the Feder–Ram model. To date, all of the studies use ordinary least squares (OLS) or ordinary ridge regression (ORR) (Huang and Mintz, 1990, 1991; Mintz and Stevenson, 1993) to test the model. Thus, for example, investment is treated as an exogenous variable. Possible interactions between investment and, say, defense or nonmilitary public expenditure through either supply-side or demand-side considerations are assumed away. In addition, defense may itself be determined by the growth of output. By fixing the direction of the externalities, the Feder–Ram model does not allow reverse causality. The use of causality tests can help identify whether causation is unidirectional.

Another empirical issue involves the type of data appropriate for estimating the equations associated with the model. Three alternatives exist: time-series or longitudinal data, cross-sectional data at a point of time, or pooled time-series, cross-sectional data. Chan (1985) and Mintz and Stevenson (1993) argued that time-series data for a single country are most appropriate, since cross-sectional data aggregate across countries with vastly different economic, political, and strategic characteristics. Although we are sympathetic to many of the issues raised by Chan, we take a more moderate position. At times, insufficient data exist to do a longitudinal study, so that a cross-sectional study is the only feasible alternative. Pooling across countries is acceptable if initial time-series runs are performed for a set of countries and pooling restrictions are tested to determine the equality of coefficients among the estimated equations for the individual countries. If these restriction tests cannot be done, then cross-sectional analysis may be justified when countries are grouped by cohorts based on similar economic, political, or strategic considerations.

8.3 Demand-side models

The demand-side models are based on the Keynesian representation of aggregate demand, in which actual output, Y, or potential (full-employment) output, Q, is the sum of the component real demands for goods and services. An example of the Keynesian demand relationship is

$$Y = Q - W = C + I + M + B, \qquad (8.17)$$

where W is the gap between actual and potential output, C is aggregate consumption, I is private and public investment, M is real military expenditures, and B is the balance of trade (i.e., exports minus imports). When Keynesian demand is the focus of the model, the researcher is often concerned with the notion of crowding-out, in which one source of demand competes for scarce resources with another source. Ron Smith (1980b) examines the possibility of crowding out by expressing (8.17) in terms of the share of potential output

$$i = 1 - w - c - m - b, \qquad (8.18)$$

where lower case letters denote the ratio of the variables to Q. With some further transformations, Smith (1980b, p. 21) derives[10]

$$i = (1 - \alpha_0) - (\beta - \alpha_1) u + \alpha_2 g - m, \qquad (8.19)$$

where the αs are parameters associated with the consumption share function, u is the unemployment rate, and g is the growth rate of actual output.

In (8.19), an increase in the share of potential output devoted to military output is expected to crowd out investment. Using data for fourteen OECD countries,[11] Smith (1980b, p. 31) finds a significant negative association between military expenditures and investment for the majority of runs. Smith reports cross-sectional runs for the fourteen-country cohort as well as time-series runs for each of the fourteen countries. Though the influence of the military share term on investment varies somewhat among runs, a convincing case for crowding-out emerged from the study. Smith tests whether the coefficient on the military term is insignificantly different from -1 and finds that, in all but two cases, it is different from -1, thus implying that crowding-out is not on a dollar-for-dollar basis. When the sources of demand are

---

[10]   In particular Smith substitutes the following relationship for c in (8.18)

$c = \alpha_0 - \alpha_1 u - \alpha_2 g$,

where $c = C/Q$. The consumption share falls with unemployment and with the growth in actual output. An increase in the latter decreases the consumption share of potential output. Finally, Smith assumes that the balance between domestic demand and potential supply is directly related to the unemployment rate, so that $(w + b) = \beta u$. These assumptions are sufficient to give (8.19).

[11]   The sample included Australia, Austria, Belgium, Canada, Denmark, United Kingdom, France, West Germany, Italy, Japan, the Netherlands, Sweden, Switzerland, and the United States.

expressed as a share of potential output, crowding-out is likely to show up from the way in which the empirical test is formulated. If, however, shares are computed based on *actual* output, then crowding-out would be automatic and the exercise would be tautological. Smith (1980b) uses potential output to break the identity problem, where share must identically add to one. The problem would, however, resurface for full-employment years. Clearly, military burdens are apt to have a negative effect on investment and, hence, growth when regressed on investment shares, since both demands are in competition for the same resource pool and comprise the components of actual outputs.

Thus far, we have seen that supply-side models are, by their nature, associated with a positive impact of defense on growth, unless the defense sector has a strong negative productivity effect compared with the other sectors. In contrast, the demand-side models are apt to be associated with a negative impact on growth as military expenditures crowd out private and public investment. To give a more accurate analysis of the impact of defense on growth, a model must be constructed that includes both the demand-side and supply-side influences. The former can be captured in a Keynesian aggregate demand function; while the latter is embodied in a growth function. Equilibrium is often assumed, so that investment is equal to saving plus capital inflows. Moreover, the growth function is derived from a production function, as is the case in the supply-side model. Since the military impact on growth is the focus of the exercise, a separate equation is given for real military expenditures.

To date, the best example of this type of analysis is the work of Deger and Smith (1983) and Deger (1986a, 1986b). For instance, the Deger and Smith (1983) model contains three equations, that include growth, savings, and military expenditures relationships. The growth equation is

$$g = \alpha_0 + \alpha_1 s + \alpha_2 m + \alpha_3 n + \alpha_4 a + \alpha_5 y + \alpha_6 r, \qquad (8.20)$$

where: g = growth rate of output,
α_0 = a constant,
s = domestic savings as a share of output,
m = military expenditures as a share of output,
n = growth of population,
a = the ratio of net foreign capital flows to domestic output,
y = per capita output,
r = growth rate of agriculture,
$\alpha_1, \ldots, \alpha_5$ = constant coefficients.

In equation (8.20), investment share, i, is assumed equal at an equilibrium to the domestic savings share plus net foreign capital flows. The population growth rate serves as a proxy for the growth of the labor force; data are frequently not available for the latter and must be proxied. Starting with a Keynesian aggregate demand function, Deger and Smith (1983, pp. 342–3) express the equilibrium savings function as

$$s = (1 - \beta_0) + \beta_1 g + \beta_2 yg - (1 - \beta_3)m - \beta_4 a + \beta_5 \dot{p}, \qquad (8.21)$$

where $(1 - \beta_0)$ is a constant, the βs are coefficients, and $\dot{p}$ is the rate of inflation.[12] In (8.21), the saving share of output is expected to vary positively with growth, per capita income, and inflation, while it is expected to vary negatively with military burdens and net foreign inflows. The third equation of the system concerns the determinants of the output share for military expenditures and is more speculative. It is denoted as

$$m = \gamma_0 + \gamma_1 y + \gamma_2(q - y) + \gamma_3 N + \gamma_4 D, \qquad (8.22)$$

where γ_0 is a constant, the γs are constant coefficients, q is the per capita income at some purchasing power parity level, N is total population, and D is one or more dummy variables.

Using cross-sectional data for fifty LDCs and average values of the variables for the 1965–73 period, Deger and Smith (1983) estimate equations (8.20)–(8.22) and compute a military multiplier. A three-stage least squares (3SLS) estimation is employed, since the component equations display simultaneity problems and there is high covariance among equations. On the supply side, military expenditures display the anticipated positive effect on growth, while, on the demand side, they display the expected negative effect on savings and, hence, investment. The latter influence outweighs the former effect. Deger and Smith (1983, p. 346) compute a *net* negative multiplier effect on growth with $dg/dm = -0.201$ when all effects are taken into account in the three-equation system. When the sample is disaggregated into different income cohorts, the high-income countries possessed the greatest negative multiplier in absolute value, the low-income countries have the next largest multiplier, and the middle-income countries have the smallest negative multiplier.

The important studies by Deger and Smith (1983) and Deger (1986a, 1986b) have both strengths and weaknesses. In terms of their strengths, these studies are noteworthy because they are the best efforts to date to combine the two sides of the analysis to estimate a net impact of military

---

[12]   An increase in inflation drives down the real balance of savings and, hence, increases the desire to save more.

burdens on growth. These studies also use sophisticated econometric tests and not rely on OLS estimations when simultaneity is an obvious problem. In terms of weaknesses, the theoretical derivation of the estimating equations is not always clear. At some points in their analysis, the estimating equations are explicitly related to the underlying theoretical constructs, while, at other points, variables are introduced in a more or less *ad hoc* fashion. In addition, the growth equation does not include endogenous influence, such as human capital terms.[13] Furthermore, the causation is assumed without first performing some pre-tests to determine the direction of causation. Finally, alternative forms and representations for the equation system are not investigated. In the case of time-series data, the need to use shares may no longer be justified in which case real totals can be used. Despite some of these potential shortcomings, these studies are the best to date and should serve as a starting point for new studies.

8.4 Causality

In the approaches reviewed thus far, military expenditures were assumed to influence growth rather than the other way around. The reverse causality would apply if the growth of output is itself a determinant of military expenditures. In the theory of the demand for military expenditures (see chapters 2–3), a country's income level is a significant determinant of military expenditures; hence, the growth of income may also determine military expenditures. Granger-causality tests can be employed to ascertain the presence and direction of causation between defense and growth.[14] In essence, the Granger-causality test indicates whether the current value of X_t is related to the lagged values of X and some other series, Z_t. If the lagged values of time series X and Z are better predictors of X_t than just the lagged values of X, then Z Granger causes X. If, instead, the lagged values of X and Z are better predictors of Z_t than just the lagged values of Z, then X Granger causes Z. The tests may be inconclusive if either no causality is uncovered or the causality is in both directions.

Consider two linear time series, denoted by X and Z, and written as

$$X_t = \sum_{i=1}^{m} a_i X_{t-i} + \sum_{j=1}^{n} b_j Z_{t-j} + \epsilon_{1t}, \tag{8.23}$$

$$Z_t = \sum_{i=1}^{s} c_i Z_{t-i} + \sum_{j=1}^{k} d_j X_{t-j} + \epsilon_{2t}, \tag{8.24}$$

[13] On endogenous growth see Barro (1991) and De Long and Summers (1991).
[14] The following recent studies apply Granger-causality tests to the study of military expenditures: Chowdhury (1991), Dunne and Smith (1990), and Joerding (1986).

where the error terms are independent and identically distributed with mean zero. In these equations, the current value of each series is linearly related to its own lagged values and those of the other series. Prior to performing the Granger causality test the component series must be stationary, so that the covariance function for *any* given lag is independent of time. If the series are not stationary,[15] then they must be made stationary by the appropriate procedures, such as first differencing in the case of linear trend. Also the lag structure of each of the variables must be ascertained in (8.23)–(8.24) prior to applying the Granger causality test. When (8.23)–(8.24) is in the appropriate form, an *F*-test is used to test whether $b_j = 0$ for $j = 1, \ldots, m$. If this test is rejected, then Z Granger causes X. A similar test that $d_j = 0$ for $j = 1, \ldots, k$ determines whether X Granger causes Z.

Chowdhury (1991) recently applies this procedure to longitudinal data drawn from fifty-five LDCs. Causality is tested for each country, with military burdens measuring the share of GDP devoted to defense, and with economic growth measured by the growth rate of GDP. For fifteen countries, military burdens Granger cause growth, consistent with the causation implicitly assumed by Deger and Smith (1983). In no cases do military burdens foster growth as in the Benoit (1973, 1978) studies. Moreover, in over half of the sample, Chowdhury (1991) finds no causation between defense spending and economic growth. Economic growth Granger causes military burdens in seven countries of Chowdhury's sample. This reversed causality is found in Joerding (1986).

Granger-causality tests can be applied in more complex situations where more than two series are involved. Vector autoregressive (VAR) systems of equations can be built where military burdens and economic growth are only two of the time series that are related to the series' own lagged values and to those of all of the other series. Granger-causality tests are then used to reduce the number of terms in each equation. Kinsella (1990) is a recent example of this methodology.

When used by itself, Granger-causality VAR studies are atheoretical exercises. Equation systems are constructed with any reasonable source of interrelationship among series included. Statistical tests then allow the data to determine the form of the pattern of interrelationships. A more acceptable approach is to construct a structural VAR model (see, e.g., Baek, 1991), in which theory is first used to formulate the equation system and then causality tests are employed to reduce the system further.

---

[15] Cointegration tests between variables may have to be performed as well when two or more variables are not stationary

8.5 A review of empirical results

In table 8.2, many of the noteworthy studies since Benoit's (1973, 1978) provocative findings are highlighted. We list the underlying model, the sample, some remarks and the conclusion for each entry. For the conclusion, we are primarily interested in whether military expenditures (ME) had an impact on growth and, if an impact is found, whether it was positive or negative. A cursory examination of table 8.2 indicates a wide range of samples and conclusions. Thus, this literature is, often, described as inconclusive, a characterization that we do not entirely agree with. Some consistent findings exist when papers are placed in cohorts based on their underlying model.

For the most part, models were either supply side, demand side, or some combination of the two. The overwhelming majority of demand-side models uncovered a negative impact of defense on growth due to the competition of defense with investment for resources. Only Stewart's (1991) simulations went against this general finding for demand-side models. Since the defense share of GDP is usually small relative to the other components of demand, such as investment, it is not surprising that the overall effect of defense is modest. When both the demand and supply side are included, the former leads to a negative effect, while the latter leads to a positive effect with the former dominating the latter. Prime examples of this analysis and outcome are Deger (1986a, b), Deger and Smith (1983), Lebovic and Ishaq (1987), and Scheetz (1991). Thus, there seems to be little question that demand-side influences of defense on growth are negative.

When, however, a supply-side approach is employed, then defense may have a positive influence through spin-offs and externalities. Moreover, the productivity effect may be positive for some LDCs, but this is not expected to be the case for developed countries. In a few cases (e.g., Atesoglu and Mueller, 1990; Ram, 1986; and Ward et al., 1991) a positive impact is uncovered, which implies that the positive externality effect outweighed any negative productivity influence. Since important demand-side elements were excluded from these supply-side studies, it is premature to conclude that defense had a *net* stimulatory impact on growth. For the bulk of the supply-side studies, defense had no significant influence on growth. This conclusion also characterizes Mintz and Stevenson's (1993) recent supply-side study of 103 countries. In most cases, military expenditures have a small positive or else a zero externality effect.

Table 8.2 *Review of literature on growth and defense*

Author(s)	Model	Sample	Remarks	Conclusion
Adams, Behrman, and Boldin (1991)	Feder–Ram	LDCs, 1974–86	Three sectors: military, nonmilitary, export. Cross-sectional time-series estimation.	No defense effect on growth. Exports had positive effect.
Alexander (1990)	Feder–Ram	9 Developed countries 1974–85	Four sectors: military, nonmilitary public, private, export. Cross-sectional time-series estimations.	No defense effect on growth.
Atesoglu and Mueller (1990)	Feder–Ram	US, 1949–89	Two sectors: defense and civilian.	Small positive and significant effect of defense on growth.
Benoit (1973, 1978)	*Ad hoc* equation	44 LDCs, 1950–65	Correlations and OLS estimations.	Positive and significant defense effect on growth.
Biswas and Ram (1986)	Feder–Ram	LDCs, 1960–70, 1970–7	Cross-sectional time series estimations.	Most estimates of the impact of defense on growth insignificant.
Chowdhury (1991)	Granger causality	55 LDCs, period varies by country	Defense measured by ME/GDP. Time series estimates for each country.	30 countries: no causality. 15 countries: defense negative effect on growth. 7 countries: economic growth causes defense. 3 countries: bi-directional causality.
Deger (1986a, 1986b)	Demand-side and supply-side (*Ad hoc*)	50 LDCs	Three equation model: defense equation, savings equation, and growth equation. Cross-sectional estimations (3SLS).	Positive direct effect of defense on growth; negative indirect effect. Net effect is negative.

Study	Model/Approach	Sample	Methodology	Results
Deger and Smith (1983)	Demand-side and supply-side	50 LDCs, 1965–73	Three equation model. Cross-sectional time-series estimations. 3SLSs.	Positive direct effect of defense on growth; negative indirect effect. Net effect is negative.
Faini, Annez and Taylor (1984)	Demand-side	69 countries, 1952–70. Mostly LDCs in sample	Single equation estimation. Cross-sectional time series. Subgroupings by region and income.	Except for some developed countries, defense had a negative impact or growth.
Huang and Mintz (1990)	Feder–Ram	US, 1952–88	Single equation ridge regression. Three sectors: civilian, defense, and nonmilitary public sector.	No defense effect on growth.
Huang and Mintz (1991)	Feder–Ram	US, 1952–88	Same as above, but disaggregates externality and productivity effects.	No defense effect on growth.
Joerding (1986)	Granger causality	LDCs	Two different measures of military expenditure (ME) used.	No evidence that ME Granger causes growth. ME is potentially endogenous.
Landau (1986)	Production function (Ad hoc)	65 LDCs, 1960–80	Cross-sectional time-series OLS. Defense measured by ME/GDP, growth measured by growth of per capita income.	Defense had little, if any, effect on growth.
Lebovic and Ishaq (1987)	Production function. Keynesian demand	20 Middle Eastern nations, 1973–82.	Three-equation Deger–Smith (1983) model. Pooled cross-sectional time-series analysis.	Defense had a negative impact on growth.
Lim (1983)	Harrod–Domar growth model	54 LDCs	Lim may have had an identity in the equation that he was estimating.	Defense had a negative impact on growth.

Table 8.2 (*Cont.*)

Study	Model	Sample	Method	Findings
Mintz and Huang (1990)	Flexible accelerator model (demand-side)	US	OLS estimation of a three-equation model.	ME dampened investment and, hence, growth.
Mintz and Stevenson (1993)	Feder–Ram	103 countries. Time interval varies by country, but most intervals are 1950–85	Longitudinal estimates for each country. Three sectors: civilian, defense, and nonmilitary public sector. Ridge regressions used to break multi-collinearity.	No strong short-term relationship between ME and economic growth. ME has no externality effect.
Mueller and Atesoglu (1993)	Feder–Ram with technological change	US, 1948–90	Single equation estimates. Two sector: defense and civilian. Technological change aspects included.	Small positive and significant effect of defense on growth. No ME externality effect.
Ram (1986)	Feder–Ram	115 countries	Cross-sectional time-series estimations. Also time series estimations for each country. Defense not disaggregated from government sector.	Government sector had a positive impact on growth.
Raster and Thompson (1988)	Demand-side	Hegemonic leaders in 19th & 20th century	Take off on Smith (1980b). Relates share of capital to military burdens.	Some evidence of a defense investment trade-off.
Scheetz (1991)	Demand-side and supply-side Deger model	Chile, Argentina, Peru, Paraguay 1969–87	Pooled cross-sectional time-series estimation. Time-series estimations.	ME had a negative impact on investment.
Smith (1980b)	Keynesian demand	14 OECD nations, 1954–73	Pooled cross-sectional time-series estimations, and time-series estimations.	ME had a negative impact on investment.

Stewart (1991)	Keynesian demand	LDCs	Simulations used since estimating equations are not reduced-form.	ME is conducive to growth, but nonmilitary expenditure is more conducive to growth.
Ward *et al.* (1991)	Feder–Ram	India, 1950–87	Time-series estimation. Separate externality and productivity effects. Three sector model.	ME had a positive impact on growth.
Ward and Davis (1992)	Feder–Ram	US, 1948–90	Time-series estimation. Separate externality and productivity effects. Three sector model.	ME had a net negative impact on growth, even though externality effect is positive.

8.6 Concluding remarks

Although individual studies on the impact of defense on growth contain *seemingly* contradictory findings, there is greater consistency in the findings than is usually supposed. Models that included demand-side influences, whereby defense can crowd out investment found that defense had a negative impact on growth. In contrast, almost every supply-side model either found a small positive defense impact or no impact at all. The findings are amazingly consistent despite differences in the sample of countries, the time periods, and econometric estimating procedures. Since we suspect that these supply-side models exclude some negative influences of defense on growth, we must conclude that the net impact of defense on growth is negative, but small. In our view, defense reallocations are not the desired pathway to growth.

Future research should refine the Feder–Ram model in a number of directions. First, the simultaneity issue needs to be addressed more fully. Second, demand-side elements must be integrated into the analysis in a fuller manner. Third, more thought needs to be given to the pooling decision. Tests for pooling restrictions should be performed prior to determining each cohort. Fourth, alliance spillovers should be taken into account when relevant.

III   Defense policies, trade, disarmament, and
       conversion

9   Industrial and alliance policies

Much of the literature on the economics of military alliances has focused on the demand side, stressing the public good benefits of club membership with the associated problems of burden sharing and free riding (see chapter 2). Less attention has been given to the supply side of military alliances. And yet, in principle, members of a defense club should be able to reduce total costs through, for example, standardization of arms and equipment and through international specialization and trade with each member of the alliance concentrating on the supply of military skills and weapons in which it has a comparative advantage. An incentive to reach collective agreement on alliance supply policies results from the possibility of technical economies of scale (see chapter 7).

Within NATO, the policy problem is seen to be a failure of the allies to agree on common tactics, common training and common weapons with adverse impacts on military effectiveness and a waste of resources. In other words, in its present form, NATO is believed to be an inefficient organization in both its armed forces and its weapons markets. Equipment is not standardized nor interoperable, whilst weapons production is "uncoordinated," with wasteful duplication in costly programs. Interestingly, the former Warsaw Pact was often regarded as an ideal model for achieving the industrial benefits of standardization, through avoiding duplication and obtaining the scale economies from long production runs of each type of equipment (see chapter 7).

This chapter starts by reviewing the literature on inefficiency in NATO, standardization and the opportunities for creating a European procurement policy, a European defense industrial base, and a Single European Market for defense equipment. Inevitably, nationalism is a major barrier to creating either a Single European Market or a NATO Free Trade Area in defense equipment. In the circumstances, policy has progressed through a series of *ad hoc* initiatives involving collaborative ventures, licensed or coproduction of foreign equipment and offsets: each of these provides some degree of standardization of equipment for a number of members of the NATO alliance (Cooper, 1985). Although the emphasis is on NATO and especially European experience, the principles, problems, and lessons of this analysis could be applied to other regional groupings where neighbors or allies could form collective industrial policies and free trade areas (e.g., North America, Middle East, Asia).

9.1   NATO and Europe: standardization, free trade and managed competition

NATO is often criticized for being inefficient because its members operate different types of defense equipment which require different training and support systems; there is a failure to obtain the industrial benefits of standardization; and each member state provides an independent capability. For example, if NATO members were certain that in the event of an attack their allies would respond, each nation would have an incentive to specialize in its force structures rather than create a totally independent capability (each nation with an army, navy, and air force). Similarly, to give effect to the doctrine of comparative advantage so as to reduce combined defense costs, members of an alliance would have to agree to allow free trade in arms and equipment among themselves. However, there are at least two barriers to the creation of a NATO Free Trade Area. First, it would involve major shifts in the existing distribution of production between countries which would result in large potential gains to the USA with fears that Western Europe would be left with "metal bashing." Second, it is part of the conventional wisdom of industrial policy in several NATO countries that their future comparative advantage lies in advanced technology sectors such as aerospace: hence government support for national defense industries having a high technology input and forming a "leading" sector. Instead of a NATO Free Trade Area, the USA has negotiated a series of bilateral agreements, known as Memoranda of Understanding (MoUs) with its NATO allies. Typically, the MoUs are designed to promote standardization and interoperability by opening up the national defense markets of each party to the agreement but with the aim of achieving a "balance" in defense sales between the two countries. As a result, the benefits of standardization of weapons are to be achieved through the normal political bargaining process reflected in MoUs and not by competition and market forces (Drown, et al., 1990; Hartley and Peacock, 1978; Matthews, 1992; Taylor, 1993b; Walker and Willett, 1993).

A chronological survey of the literature on alliances and industrial policies shows the development of theory, applied work, and policy in the field. This is an underdeveloped and underresearched part of defense economics. A starting point is the classic text by Hitch and McKean which devoted a chapter to "The Economics of Military Alliances" with a mere four pages on equipment specialization (Hitch and McKean, 1960, pp. 290–3)! The authors argued that the potential for mutual gain through specialization and international trade in defense equipment is probably great for two reasons. First, nations can pursue their comparative advantages in different spheres of production. Second, there are further gains from the economies of scale and learning associated with concentrating production in one or a few suppliers (see chapters 5 and 7). This is most likely for costly high technology equipment produced on a relatively small scale (e.g., aerospace equipment). There are exceptions, namely, equipment which is simple and cheap to produce in quantity and where production is often undertaken in large quantities (e.g., artillery shells). Their argument is illustrated with an example showing a 40 percent cost saving if the output of a fighter aircraft were increased from 100 to 1,000 units (e.g., by ten allies concentrating production rather than splitting it evenly amongst themselves). And further cost savings are available by concentrating aircraft production in the most efficient industry within the alliance. However, the approach is simplistic. It does not address the issue of monopoly versus competition and the possibility that the price of efficient scale might be monopoly; the example is not supported by empirical evidence on scale and learning economies; and no consideration is given as to how the cost savings are to be shared between buying nations and the suppliers (or indeed whether the savings might be appropriated by monopoly suppliers).

A pioneering contribution was made by Thomas Callaghan with his study of *US–European Economic Co-operation in Military and Civil Technology* (1975). Callaghan argued that NATO was characterized by massive duplication leading to a waste of Allied resources exceeding $10 billion per annum (1975 prices). This waste was reflected in the duplication of research and development, short production runs failing to exploit scale economies, and the associated wasteful duplication in logistics support. Callaghan's solution was standardization with defense industry rationalization and specialization throughout NATO. He proposed a North Atlantic common defense market, open government procurement for military and civil goods and services, and the extension of Allied cooperation to embrace civil technology. Standardization of NATO's equipment through two-way trade in a North Atlantic Common Defense Market was also expected to improve military effectiveness by 30–50 percent for most units and by as much as 300 percent for some tactical air units (Callaghan, 1975, p. i). Although the estimates of waste appear attractive, they are based on simple, unsubstantiated assumptions that all European defense R & D and 25 percent of its procurement expenditures are a waste of resources; it is assumed that without European competition US firms would continue to be efficient; and the general belief is that all standardization is good, regardless of costs. Indeed, the Callaghan study and others in this field rarely address a fundamental methodological issue, namely, their standard of comparison. Are they comparing an existing situation with some ideal, but never defined and never achieved model of standardization; or are they comparing two ideal procurement models, neither of which exists? In addition to developments within NATO, a series of initiatives were emerging within Europe (Matthews, 1992; OTA, 1990).

In 1978, the European Parliament produced a Report on *European Armaments Procurement Co-operation* (Klepsch, 1978). Like the Callaghan study, this Report identified a waste of defense resources due to the duplication of costly R & D, uncoordinated purchasing leading to short, inefficient production runs, and the duplication of training, repair, and maintenance associated with nonstandardized equipment. The Report also focused on the relationship between military and civil technology. Indeed it argued that "as far as the aircraft, shipbuilding and electronics industries are concerned, it is not possible for these industries to survive without military as well as civilian work. The future of these industries can only be viewed as the development of overall civilian/ military operations within each sector" (Klepsch, 1978, p. 30). The Report recommended the creation of a European Armaments Procurement Agency, based on the Independent European Program Group (IEPG). The aim was the creation of a single, structured European Community market in defense equipment which would, by incorporating the civilian aspects of defense industries, "constitute a major element or building block in the development of an overall common industrial policy" (Klepsch, 1978, p. 30). However, the Report recognized that its proposals would encounter a variety of political, economic, military, and technical problems. Foremost amongst these remains the national commitment to independent defense. In addition, the structural adjustments required will involve some nations and their industries incurring short-term costs for longer-term benefits: the potential losers will need to be given firm guarantees about compensating benefits. And there are the inevitable differences in strategic and tactical doctrines which hamper cooperation and obstruct the choice of common defense equipment. The Report also recognized that the early stages of cooperation will inevitably involve extra "set-up" or "start-up" costs. As an example, it estimated that a two-nation military aircraft project involved a collaboration premium of 50 percent on R & D and 5 percent on manufacturing; but doubling the market due to collaboration might result in savings in unit costs of between 10 percent and 20 percent (Klepsch, 1978, p. 28). But the Report never addressed some of the fundamental choice issues which are likely to be confronted by a European Armaments Procurement Agency. Here, it is possible to envisage four different roles for such a European Agency. First, it might act as a policing agency enforcing the rules for an EU common market in defense equipment. Second, it might act as a central purchasing authority for all EU states' national requirements: here it might obtain savings from its monopsony powers and from possible coordinated purchasing. Or third, it might be a purchasing agency for standardized equipment bought for all EU members (so replacing national defense ministries). Fourth, it might be a management agency for collaborative projects. All of which suggests that proposals for a European Procurement Agency need to be specified in much more detail and subject to critical scrutiny.

Policy formulation requires information. In 1979, a Report was submitted to the EC on European Technological Co-operation and Defense Procurement (known as the Greenwood Report[1]). This Report provided a statistical and institutional description of the arrangements for defense procurement and production in the nine member states of the EC. The study was designed to provide information for debate on the policy issues. In this context, it considered opportunities and obstacles for the rationalization of procurement and the structuring of the West European defense market, including suggestions of a European Defense Procurement Agency on the demand side and a European Defense Industrial Management Authority on the supply side of the market. It recognized, though, that such proposals were unrealistic in the late 1970s and, instead, it expected policy to evolve on a project-by-project basis – i.e., involving partial coordination of demands and *ad hoc* cooperation of producers to satisfy these demands. Once again, no effort was made to explore the economic implications of these proposals; nor whether the evolution of policy on a project basis was consistent with the eventual creation of a European Procurement Agency and Industrial Management Authority.

The next major policy initiative was the Report of the Independent European Program Group (IEPG) study group which made proposals for improving the competitiveness of the European defense equipment industry (IEPG, 1986; known as the Vredeling Report). The IEPG Report recommended:

[1] In this chapter, references to the European Community (EC) are used where this was correct at the time; otherwise, the former EC is now known as the European Union (EU).

a)   That Europe's defense industries be exposed to normal market forces requiring that national governments adopt a policy of competition across Europe without direct or indirect distortions.
b)   A more extensive use of competing consortia with partners selected on commercial criteria. For work-sharing arrangements, the European Space Agency model was recommended as an effective mechanism for providing *juste retour* opportunities over a package of projects.
c)   Competitive fixed-price contracts for all stages of projects, including development, with no restrictions on profit levels.
d)   That European nations exchange information about their equipment requirements and that IEPG maintains a central register of bidding opportunities.
e)   The strengthening of Europe's technology base and the creation of a common European defense research program.
f)   Interproject compensation favoring the less-developed defense industry nations.

Whilst the 1986 IEPG Report favoured competition, it recognized constraints (boundary conditions) on its proposals in the form of each government's concern with employment objectives, the desire to maintain a national industrial and technology base, the special position of countries with less-developed defense industries, a reluctance to transfer technology and the need for a fair share of defense work (*juste retour*). The worry is that these constraints will prevent the achievement of the main objective, namely, a more open competitive market. Nonetheless, the main recommendations of the IEPG (Vredeling) Report were accepted and incorporated in the Action Plan for a step by step opening up of the European defense market and for a better coordinated European approach to defense research and technology (IEPG, 1988). To date, the emphasis on opening European defense markets has achieved modest results reflected in the publication of a contracts bulletin for IEPG nations. Concern remains about the need for a "level playing field" when opening up national defense markets (e.g., problems of subsidies and state-owned firms), and the lack of a judicial procedure for enforcement. There is a more fundamental problem. Whilst the IEPG Action Plan aims to open up national markets and create a single European Armaments Market, it has some worrying features which suggest a model of "managed competition" which is unlikely to correspond to a genuine competitive market. The worrying features are the continued stress on *juste retour*, the position of the less-developed defense industries, and the search for better coordination and management of Europe's defense R & D activities. On this basis the Action Plan seems designed to benefit producers rather than consumers and taxpayers!

The 1986 IEPG Report (Volume II) presented some useful information on the competitive position of Europe's defense technologies and on experience with collaborative projects. In reviewing defense technologies, the Report suggested that, in the mid 1980s, Europe's competitive position in tanks was "quite good" and that it was competitive in engineer equipment (e.g., bridge layers) and large calibre weapons and mortars, and very competitive in small arms and conventional submarines. In contrast, the USA had a highly competitive technology in torpedoes, electronics, and aerospace equipment. The Report also presented information on the management, technical aspects, and financial consequences of collaboration for four projects: Tornado, FH 70 howitzer, tripartite mine-hunter, and the RITA battlefield communication system. Unfortunately, most of the material was qualitative, impressionistic, and based on technical judgments, with no quantitative evidence and no consideration of economic comparative advantage.[2]

The 1988 European Parliament Report on "The Institutional Consequences of the Costs of Non-Europe" included a section on defense procurement. This estimated the savings from opening-up national defense markets in the EC at some 10–20 percent or more as a broad ball park figure, equivalent to some ECU 5 billion (EC, 1989). It was, however, recognized that relatively little was known about the defense markets of EC states (see chapter 7; Matthews, 1992).

Increasingly, within the EU, debates about defense industrial policy are presented in a European rather than a national context. The concept of a European defense industrial base (DIB) is seen as a means of rationalizing Europe's defense industrial capabilities, promoting collaboration, and creating a European defense industry capable of competing with the USA (Taylor, 1993b; Walker and Willett, 1993). Whilst proposals for a European DIB seem attractive, they are often vaguely specified and they need to be subject to critical scrutiny. Answers are required to the following questions:

a) What is meant by a European DIB, and why is it required (see chapter 7)?

b) What is the minimum size and industrial composition of a European DIB? Should it include a capability in air, land, sea, and nuclear equipment; and should the capability be restricted to R & D or include production? Moreover, within the European DIB will

---

[2]   IEPG was later known as the Western European Armaments Group (WEAG) and in December 1992, the functions of the Group were transferred to the Western European Union (WEU).

nations specialize by comparative advantage (e.g., Germany specializing in tanks, the UK in VTOL aircraft, France in missiles and helicopters)? Will contracts be awarded on a competitive firm or fixed price basis, or will work be shared using *juste retour* and cost-plus contracts?

c)   Will the European DIB support a competitive industrial structure or will it be dominated by cartels and monopolies? And will non-EU firms be allowed to compete for EU defense contracts?

d)   Will parts of the European DIB be privately owned and parts state owned and what are the implications of such mixed ownership for competition?

e)   What are the costs of supporting a European DIB; are EU nations willing to pay the price; and how will the costs be distributed between member states (burden sharing)?

f)   How is the European DIB to be created; who will make the choices, including procurement decisions; will the losers be compensated and, if so, how?

Issues about the European DIB will be determined by the possible extension of the Single European Market to defense equipment (Article 223 of the Treaty of Rome excludes arms production and trade). Here, it is possible to envisage at least four EU scenarios for such a development of the Single European Market (Hartley and Cox, 1992). For each scenario there is assumed to be a nondiscriminating liberalized competitive market, either restricted to the EU or open to the world. The four scenarios are as follows (table 9.1):

(i)   **Scenario I**. A liberalized competitive market with national procurement by national defense ministries and agencies.

(ii)   **Scenario II**. An EU centralized purchasing agency buying common, standardized equipment with the agency replacing national defense ministries.

(iii) **Scenario III**. Limited liberalization. This is similar to scenario I but certain equipments are excluded (e.g., nuclear systems).

(iv)   **Scenario IV**. A twin track approach with competition for small- to medium-sized projects purchased by national defense ministries (e.g., small missiles, ordnance), with large projects undertaken on a collaborative basis [e.g. aircraft, helicopters, large missiles, tanks, and warships (Crothier and Moravcsik, 1991; Moravcsik, 1989)].

Cost savings of a least 10–15 percent on the EC's total defense equipment budget have been estimated for the scenarios outlined in table 9.1 (Hartley and Cox, 1992). The savings are likely to result from greater competition, both within and between nations; from less duplication of R & D leading to savings in R & D costs; and from economies of scale

Table 9.1 *Scenarios for a single market*

		Liberalized competitive markets (estimated annual savings)	
Scenario		EU-wide	World-wide
I	National procurement		
II	Centralized procurement of common equipment		
III	Limited liberalization		
IV	Twin-track approach: competition and collaboration		

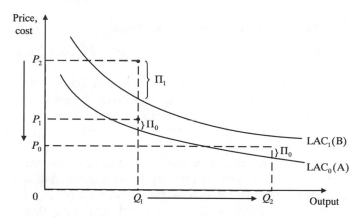

Figure 9.1 Competition, scale, and the single market

and learning resulting from longer production runs. A simple example is shown in figure 9.1. Initially, nation B with a closed market is purchasing from a domestic monopolist a quantity Q_1 on the long-run average cost curve LAC_1 at a price P_2 and a profit margin of Π_1. Opening up the national market to competition for Q_1 enables a lower cost supplier to enter the market (i.e., firms from another nation A can enter B's market). Competition leads to lower prices of P_1 reflecting lower costs (LAC_0) and lower profit margins (Π_0): this is the competition effect reflected in a price reduction from P_2 to P_1. It is then assumed that with lower prices, the successful firm in nation A will attract additional orders from other EU member states which, in the long run, will lead to a larger output of Q_2 and a further price reduction to P_0: this is the scale effect (profit margins are assumed to remain unchanged at Π_0).

Proposals for a Single European Market or a NATO Free Trade Area for defense equipment appear attractive and provide models of ideal cases with potential applications to other regions of the world. There are, though, substantial barriers to radical change in the form of nationalism, the desire for independence and opposition from the industries, regions, and countries likely to lose. Nonetheless, pressures to reduce defense budgets will increasingly expose the costs of independence and bring reality to these single market and free trade visions. Change is likely to be gradual and long term, but, in the meantime, various alliance industrial policies can provide mechanisms for moving toward more efficient alliance procurement arrangements. Can collaboration, licensed production, and offsets contribute to greater efficiency within alliance weapons markets?

9.2   Policy options: a framework for choice

When purchasing weapons, nations are faced with four broad policy options:

(i)   At one extreme, there is complete independence where a country purchases all its defense equipment from domestic firms only. Complete independence is costly, involving the sacrifice of potential gains from international trade based on specialization by comparative advantage (see chapter 7).

(ii)   International collaboration involving joint development and production. Joint projects contribute to equipment standardization. Typically, they involve two or more nations agreeing a common requirement, sharing R & D costs, and combining their national orders.

(iii) Licensed production and coproduction. These involve the domestic manufacture of another nation's weapons, either wholly or in part.

(iv)   A nation could act as competitive buyer purchasing from the lowest cost suppliers in the world market (e.g., buying off the shelf). In this case, a nation could either import defense equipment directly or it could link its overseas purchase with arrangements that provide some work for the importing nation's industry (offsets).

Cost–benefit analysis provides a framework for choosing between these policy options. A government needs to know the costs of each option and its benefits in relation to the military-strategic features of the equipment and its contribution to any wider economic benefits. Table 9.2 presents an information framework which shows policy makers the costs and benefits of the alternative policies. Usually, the options are reflected in specific equipment choices such as whether to build a combat aircraft

Table 9.2 *Policy options: a framework for choice*

Policy options	Costs				Benefits									
	Acquisition price		Life-cycle costs		Military/strategic features					National economic benefits				
	Unit	Total fleet	Unit	Total fleet	Perfor-mance	Number	Delivery schedule	Standard-ization	Others (e.g. DIB)	Jobs	Tech-nology	Balance of payments	Exchequer	Others
1 National project (independence)														
2 Collaborative project (two or more nations)														
3 Licensed or coproduction														
4 Imported equipment: (i) Off-the-shelf (ii) With offset														

or a tank independently, or collaboratively, or under licensed production or to import. For each option, information is required on acquisition and life-cycle costs, its military and strategic features, and its wider economic benefits. The table is illustrative: variants of the policy options can be included; more information can be added on specific costs and benefits; and, in some cases, policy makers might ignore apparent benefits. Not surprisingly, in view of the data problems, there is little published work by economists in this field, but an example of the approach is found in Hartley and Hooper (1993).

9.3   International collaboration

The increasing costs of national development programs for high technology defense equipment together with relatively small production runs for domestic markets has provided an economic incentive for international collaboration. France, Germany, Italy, and the UK have been variously involved in two or more nation programs involving shared development and production. Many of these programs have been for aerospace projects, namely, aircraft, helicopters, aero-engines, and missiles [e.g., French–UK Jaguar strike aircraft; British–German–Italian Tornado combat aircraft (Draper, 1990; Latham and Slack, 1990; Matthews, 1992)]. Supporters of European collaboration stress three major benefits:

(i)   Cost savings for both R & D and production. Partner nations can share costly R & D outlays and, by combining their national orders, they can achieve economies of scale and learning from a longer production run. A typical case might be two nations each producing a combat aircraft with development costs of £10 billion (duplication), each with domestic requirements of 300 units. *Ceteris paribus* a joint venture with equal sharing would save £10 billion on development (£5 billion for each nation and no duplication) and result in learning economies which would reduce unit production costs by 10 percent as output is doubled from 300 to 600 units (see chapters 5 and 7). This example of the ideal model of two-nation collaboration is shown in figure 9.2. Average development costs for a national venture are ADC and for a two nation project 0.5 ADC [a rectangular hyperbola (figure 9.2a)]. Unit production costs (APC) are based on a 90 percent unit cost curve showing a 10 percent saving for a doubling of cumulative output (figure 9.2b).

(ii)   Industrial benefits. Partner nations can retain a domestic defense industrial capability in high technology equipment (e.g., aerospace). Also, collaboration creates larger industrial groups able to compete with the USA.

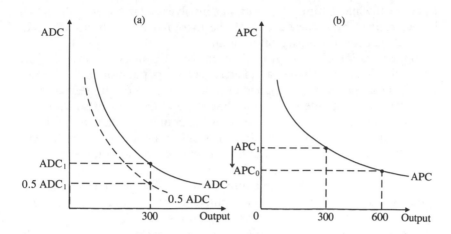

Figure 9.2 Collaboration: the ideal model

(iii) Military and political benefits. Collaboration leads to a greater standardization of equipment and demonstrates Europe's commitment to the NATO Alliance (Hartley and Martin, 1993; Kapstein, 1989; Martin, 1991; Matthews, 1992).

However, collaboration has its costs, leading to departures from the "ideal model." Bargaining between partner governments, their bureaucracies, and armed forces, together with lobbying from interest groups of scientists, engineers, and contractors can lead to inefficiencies. Work is often allocated on the basis of political, equity, and bargaining criteria and not on the basis of efficiency, comparative advantage, and competition. For example, on aircraft development work, each partner will insist upon a share of the high technology work in the airframe, the engine, and the avionics (*juste retour*); each partner nation will want its own flight testing centre and its own final assembly line for production work. Such arrangements are probably best analyzed using public choice models which incorporate bureaucracies, interest groups, and the possibility of government failure (Hartley, 1986). Collaboration also involves substantial transaction costs reflecting duplicate organizations, management by consensus, excessive bureaucracy, and delays in decision making. Further transaction costs arise from the need to harmonize operational requirements and delivery schedules to meet the different military and budgetary demands of each partner nation. As a result, it is predicted that collaborative projects involve higher costs and take longer to develop than a national program (HCP 247, 1991; IEPG, 1986, volume II). Nevertheless, like any club, members will join so long as membership is expected to be worthwhile. Ultimately, a nation's involvement in collaboration will be determined by a comparison of the marginal transaction costs and transaction benefits from a joint program.

Any evaluation of European collaborative programs encounters major difficulties. There is a limited and heterogeneous population of collaborative defense projects (e.g., combat and trainer aircraft, helicopters, missiles) involving different partner nations and different organizational arrangements. Problems also arise with the counter-factual: without the joint venture, which type of equipment would a nation have purchased? Nonetheless, there is evidence on the impact of collaboration on costs, on development time, and on scales of output (Hartley and Martin, 1993).

Evidence suggests that unit production costs are unchanged by collaboration and that total development costs are multiplied by the square root of the number of partner nations. An alternative estimate was that two-nation collaboration increased development costs by 30 percent and production costs by 5 percent compared with a national project (Harvey, 1980; Pugh, 1986, p. 357). Even so, collaboration offers each partner substantial savings compared with a single-nation venture. For example, after allowing for collaboration costs, a two-nation collaborative aircraft project with a total output of 300 units could lead to cost savings in the range of 10 percent to 20 percent compared with a national venture (Pugh, 1986, p. 358). The impact of collaboration involving different numbers of partners on total development costs and on the development costs per partner (assuming equal partners) is shown in figure 9.3. The total development cost curve is based on the square root rule. In fact, company experience suggests that the square root rule probably overestimates the cost of collaborative development work.

There is a widely held view that compared with similar national programs, European collaborative projects take longer to develop and make schedule slippages more likely (Lorrell, 1980). This hypothesis has been tested using descriptive statistics, pairwise comparisons, and regression methods. A typical estimating equation for aircraft development time scales is

$$T = T(P, C, N, DV, Z, t) \tag{9.1}$$

where T = development time (months),
$\qquad P$ = aircraft performance characteristics such as weight, speed, and range,
$\qquad C$ = development cost,
$\qquad N$ = number of partner nations,
$\qquad DV$ = dummy variables (1, 0) for US aircraft and for previous experience,

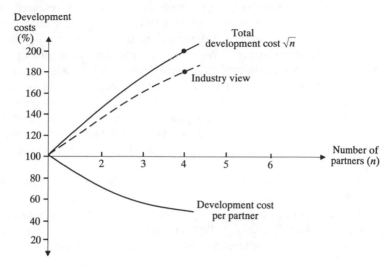

Figure 9.3 Collaboration and development costs

> Z = other relevant factors – e.g., number of aircraft developed since 1945,
>
> t = a time-trend.

Empirical work on development time scales is limited by the availability of data. There are, for example, problems in obtaining reliable data on project development costs. However, the evidence suggests that American military aircraft have shorter development periods, possibly some two years shorter. Interestingly, despite the beliefs about delays, the regression results show that, in general, collaboration had no statistically significant effect on total development times for military aircraft and helicopters (Hartley and Martin, 1993; Crothier and Moravcsik, 1991). For aircraft, an example of the estimated equations using OLS is shown below

$$TT = 34.6 + 0.02S + 0.005R - 1.1PN - 22.6DUS - 1.0EX - 19.1DVP + 0.08t, \quad (9.2)$$
$$\quad (1.7)\ (3.0)\quad (2.6)\quad (0.2)\quad (2.2)\quad (1.5)\quad (2.2)\quad (1.7)$$

where TT is total aircraft development time (months); S is speed; R is range; PN is the number of partner nations involved in developing the aircraft; DUS is a dummy variable for US aircraft (1,0); EX represents the number of aircraft the firm has developed since 1945; DVP is a dummy variable if the firm has developed a similar aircraft in the previous fifteen years; t is a time trend, with January 1945 = 1; figures in parenthesis are t-statistics; $\bar{R}^2$ is 0.42 (Hartley and Martin, 1993).

There remain substantial opportunities for further research on the economics of collaboration. For example, the organizational arrangements might be an important determinant of their success or failure. In some cases, collaborative ventures involve the creation of a new international organization (e.g., Eurofighter), or a prime contractor–subcontractor model might be used, or the program might be managed by joint committees of industrialists and government representatives. A strategic management analysis of collaboration in aerospace and defense found some tentative support for a relationship between the commercial success of a project and its organizational arrangements (Dussauge and Garrette, 1993).

Opportunities also exist for subjecting collaborative ventures to a broader economic evaluation. Evidence showing that collaboration leads to cost savings and greater scales of output needs to be incorporated into a proper cost–benefit analysis. But international collaboration is only one form of work sharing: alternative forms are licensed production and offsets.

9.4   Licensed production and coproduction

Standardization requires a group of nations within a military alliance to buy the same equipment. This could be achieved if all members of the alliance agreed to buy from the same country. However, rather than purchasing directly off the shelf, nations buying foreign defense equipment often demand some form of "offsetting" economic activity by the supplier in the importing country. Offsets form part of the product and its price. Licensed production is the traditional form of direct offset where the purchasing nation builds foreign designed equipment under licence in its own country (e.g., Canadian, European, and Japanese production of the US F-104 aircraft, and Japanese production of US F-15 aircraft). For the licensed producer, the aim might be to build all the equipment locally or to build some parts and undertake final assembly.

Coproduction has been the victim of various definitions. A Rand study defined it as "any international collaboration during the production phase of a major weapon system acquisition program" (Rich et al., 1981, p. 1). On this definition, licensed production is a variant of coproduction. However, the classic case is fully integrated coproduction in which each participating nation purchases the same equipment and produces parts of each other's order. An example was the four-nation European consortium purchase of US F-16 aircraft whereby European industry was awarded work on 10 percent of the 650 F-16s bought by the USAF, 40 percent of the 348 F-16s bought by the Europeans, and 15 percent of export sales. This guaranteed European industry 58 percent of the value of the European order. The Japanese FSX aircraft program is a further variant of coproduction involving some codevelopment. In this case, Mitsubishi Heavy Industries (MHI) and General Dynamics will codevelop and coproduce a substantially modified F-16. MHI will be the prime contractor and General Dynamics and other US companies will receive 40 percent of the development and 40 percent of the production work (Trice, 1989).

Licensed production and coproduction generally involves cost penalties compared with buying directly "off the shelf" from the main manufacturer. These cost penalties reflect entry costs, the costs of transferring technology, relatively short production runs, and the absence of learning economies. Interview–questionnaire studies estimate cost penalties of up to 50 percent for licensed and coproduction, with a typical penalty of 10–15 percent (Chinworth, 1992; Hartley, 1983; Hartley and Cox, 1992). On the US-European coproduction of the F-16 it has been estimated that the Europeans incurred a 34 percent cost penalty compared with a direct buy from General Dynamics. On the same program, it was estimated that coproduction added about 5 percent to the USAF program costs for its first 650 F-16s (Rich *et al.*, 1981). There are some exceptions. A Rand study of Japanese experience with the licensed production of the Lockheed F-104 aircraft estimated that the unit costs of the Japanese aircraft were 88 percent of US costs for a comparable aircraft (Hall and Johnson, 1967). This result arose because Lockheed transferred a significant portion of its accumulated learning on the F-104 to Mitsubishi: since US firms were paid for data, data rights, and technical assistance, "they had clear incentives to provide Japanese firms with the fruits of US experience" (Hall and Johnson, 1967, p. 187).

Licensed and coproduction have their benefits. These include support for a nation's defense industrial base, technology transfer (e.g., management, production manufacturing), employment, import savings, and military standardization. In addition, manufacturing under license saves substantial R & D resources which would have been required for an independent national venture. Unfortunately, there is little quantitative evidence on the likely magnitude of these benefits. A case study of Japanese experience with licensed production estimated that Japanese work content ranged from 60 percent on the Patriot missile to 70 percent on the F-15 and 90 percent on the F-4 (Chinworth, 1992). The remaining alternative is to seek an offset deal.

9.5   Offsets

Offsets are a growing feature of the international trade in defense equipment, particularly aerospace equipment, and, once again, this is a field which is relatively unexplored by economists. Offsets impose conditions on the foreign seller of defense equipment enabling the purchasing government to recover or offset some or all of its purchase price (Udis and Maskus, 1991). Offset schemes are usually designed to achieve a relocation of economic activity, namely, from the country of the equipment supplier to the purchasing nation. Such relocation resembles trade diversion and has been criticized by economists as welfare reducing. For the seller, offsets reflect the desire of profit-seeking firms for "doing business" with governments: they can be regarded as part of the sales package and as an alternative to price discounts. For the supplying nation, particularly the USA, there are concerns about the impact of offsets on US defense industries, on employment, and on technology transfer to potential rivals. For the buying nation, offsets provide industrial benefits in the form of jobs, technology transfer, support for the defense industrial base, and foreign currency savings (Hall and Markowski, 1994; OMB, 1987).

Offsets may be direct or indirect. Direct offsets involve participation of the buying nation's industry in some aspect of the contract for supplying foreign defense equipment. For example, if nation A purchases a foreign tank, its firms might be involved as subcontractors and suppliers, or there might be a fully integrated coproduction program, or it might manufacture the foreign tank under license. Indirect offsets involve goods and services unrelated to the purchase of the specific foreign defense equipment. For example, the sale of American F-18 aircraft to Spain allowed aid to Spanish tourism to count as part of the offset agreement. Indirect offsets can include foreign investment and counter-trade transactions such as barter, counter-purchase, and buy-back (Caves and Marin, 1992; Udis and Maskus, 1991).

Offsets need not necessarily be inefficient and welfare reducing. In some circumstances, offsets might contribute to efficiency improvements if they remove nontariff barriers and lead prime contractors to search for, and to discover, more efficient subcontractors located overseas (i.e., by extending market information and knowledge and removing barriers to the use of foreign subcontractors). Alternatively, defense offsets can be viewed as a subset of the price–quality–quantity trade-offs which characterize negotiations surrounding complex transactions. In a world of imperfect markets, oligopoly rents, complex transactions, and asymmetrical information, offsets might enhance the welfare of the purchaser (e.g. by economizing on transaction costs). On the other hand, some forms of mandatory offset obligations may inhibit the buyer's flexibility in negotiating advantageous deals and so result in inefficient procurement (Hall and Markowski, 1994).

Clearly, in competitive bidding for foreign defense contracts, overseas firms have every incentive to offer an attractive offset package as part of their bid: maximizing offsets becomes part of the competitive process, with firms seeking new and ingenious methods of satisfying their contractual obligations. They might, for example, use specialist agencies, such as banks, as well as their suppliers to achieve their offset targets; and they will try to claim as much business as possible as offset. At the same time, vote-sensitive governments have every inducement to claim the maximum size of offset deal so that they can justify the import of defense equipment in terms of protecting the national defense industry, jobs, and technology. There are, though, real worries about the extent to which offset business represents genuinely new work which would not otherwise have been obtained without the offset agreement. Some commentators have suggested that genuinely new business might be 25–50 percent of the total offset (Hartley and Hooper, 1993).

9.6   Conclusion

Industrial and alliance policies is a topic where there are extensive opportunities for theoretical and empirical work and for critical evaluation. Game theory, international trade theory, and public choice analysis can be applied to the various policy options. Case studies are needed of the benefits and costs (gains and losses to each nation in the transaction) of the different policies and the whole range of work-sharing arrangements need to be evaluated. In particular, some of the claims and myths about work sharing need to be tested and subjected to critical evaluation by economists.

10   The arms trade

The international trade in arms represents a paradox in that it is a topic which attracts considerable attention from governments, politicians, the United Nations, and the media, but it is a topic on which little theoretical and empirical work has been undertaken by academic economists. Much of the published work has been descriptive and polemical (Hartley and Hooper, 1990, references 242–308). Nevertheless, the arms trade raises a set of theoretical, empirical, and policy issues. The standard methodology of economics suggests three related questions about the arms trade. First, what are the causes of the arms trade; second what are its consequences; and, third, what are the implications for public policy?

An interest by governments and international agencies in the arms trade reflects a continued concern that arms exports will promote regional arms races so increasing the possibilities of local and even global conflict. Further concern arises because some of the countries vulnerable to regional arms races are amongst the developing nations of the world. These nations are characterized by poverty, starvation, famines, ill-health, high mortality rates, homelessness, and illiteracy. For such nations, major arms imports and an arms race are costly (see chapters 4 and 8).

The policy interest in the international arms trade requires an understanding of its causes. The arms trade involves military, political, and economic elements for both suppliers and buyers in the international market. Arms-producing nations might export arms to their allies and friends, and to other countries which they wish to support or influence (political leverage). Economic factors are also relevant. Disarmament in NATO and in the former Warsaw Pact countries has created excess capacity in their defense industries: hence, defense contractors are actively seeking export sales to compensate for declining domestic procurement. As a result, disarmament in one part of the world might actually promote arms exports, regional arms races, and possible instability elsewhere in the world. To the supplying nation, arms exports can be a source of employment, of foreign currency earnings, of spreading high fixed R & D costs over a larger output, and of achieving economies of scale and learning. It might also be the case that for defense companies, arms exports might be more profitable than domestic sales which are subject to profit regulation (see chapters 5 and 7). However, it does not follow that arms exports are always beneficial to the exporting nation as distinct from the exporting company.

To the purchasing nation, arms imports might be more efficient than developing a costly independent defense industrial base. But arms imports make the buying country dependent on overseas suppliers and vulnerable to political leverage; they require foreign currency and can lead to an increase in international borrowing and external debt. On this basis, both buying and selling nations need to be aware of the benefits and costs involved in transactions in the international arms market.

Various policy solutions have been proposed involving suggestions for monitoring, regulating, reducing, or abolishing the international arms trade. Buying and supplying nations can adopt unilateral or multilateral restrictions on the buying or supplying of certain types of defense equipment with the restrictions applied to specific countries and regions of the world. Inevitably, efforts to regulate the arms trade will lead to cheating, black markets, and illicit transfers.

Data are a starting point for thinking about the policy issues. What is known, what is not known and what is it necessary to know for formulating sensible policies on the international arms trade? After outlining the stylized facts, consideration will be given to their theoretical explanation and to empirical research results. Finally, policy proposals are reviewed.

10.1   Data

Ideally, data are needed which capture the magnitude and variety of international transactions in arms. Which countries are buying which items of defense equipment from whom, and what are the terms of exchange? The international trade in defense equipment is reflected directly in arms exports and imports. There is also an indirect trade reflected in international supplier relationships (e.g., US and European prime contractors purchasing parts and components from, say, Asia and Japan), in technology transfer and in a variety of international transactions in the form of collaborative programs, licensed and coproduction agreements, and offsets (Willett, 1991; see also chapter 9). How far is such variety of transactions reflected in the available statistics?

First impressions suggest that a good data set is available. Regular annual data by arms exporting and importing countries are provided by the Stockholm International Peace Research Institute (SIPRI) and by the US Arms Control and Disarmament Agency (ACDA). There are, however, differences between these sources. SIPRI focuses on five categories of major weapons (aircraft, armor-artillery, guidance-radar systems, missiles, and warships) and excludes trade in small arms, ammunition, support items, services, and components (SIPRI, 1993). ACDA reports international transfers of conventional military equipment, including parts, small arms, the building of defense production facilities, and some military services (ACDA, 1993). As a result of different definitions, the ACDA figures are higher than the SIPRI data. For example, in 1989, world arms transfers were estimated at $45 billion (1989 prices) by ACDA and $38.1 billion by SIPRI [1990 prices (Blackaby and Ohlson, 1987)]. A more recent addition has been the United Nations Register on Conventional Arms, first introduced in 1992 (Chalmers and Greene, 1994). For the UN Register, member governments are requested to provide annual data on their imports and exports of seven categories of weapons systems, namely, battle tanks, armored combat vehicles, large calibre artillery systems, combat aircraft, attack helicopters, warships, and missiles. By increasing transparency and openness on arms transfers, the UN Register aims to promote peace and stability. In addition, the Register might highlight important discrepancies; it could serve as a confidence-building measure in regional efforts to reduce arms imports; and it represents a step in a possible process of further international cooperation on arms trade restraints. However, since the Register only provides data on numbers and not on the value of transactions and their financing, its contribution to understanding the economics of the arms trade will be somewhat limited (SIPRI, 1993).

A reading of the sources and methods used to estimate the world's arms trade soon reveals their limitations. Data problems abound. International arms agreements are often secret and there is some black market trading. Exact numbers of weapons ordered and delivered may not be available in the public domain. Price data are even more difficult to obtain and vary in their coverage of equipment, spare parts, training, support, infrastructure, and offset arrangements. The international arms trade is also characterized by a variety of payment arrangements involving military aid including gifts, interest-free loans, buy back, and payment in kind (e.g., oil for missiles). The financing arrangements raise questions about the true costs of the arms trade, particularly arms imports by developing countries. The data usually focus on physical transfers and their monetary representation, so ignoring the question of whether and when the weapons are paid for. Unfortunately, little is known about the financial aspects of the arms trade. One study using an opportunity cost approach and some heroic assumptions estimated that the financial burden from arms imports (new imports plus debt repayment for earlier imports) grew in the 1980s whilst transfers as measured by the available data decreased. As a result, the available data are of only limited use in the analysis of the economic effects of arms imports (Brzoska, 1994). Complications also arise because bribery, side payments and rent seeking are not unknown (Sampson, 1977, 1992; Treddenick, 1987). Indeed, SIPRI summarizes the data problems succinctly: "Published information cannot provide a comprehensive picture because the arms trade is not fully reported in the open literature" (SIPRI, 1993, p. 519).

Further difficulties arise in defining defense equipment. For example, transport helicopters can be quickly converted into attack helicopters and oil tankers can be similarly converted into landing platforms for military helicopters and vertical take-off combat aircraft. The UN Register on Conventional Arms excludes an entire range of weapons, including small arms, noncombat planes and helicopters, and surface to air missiles. It can also be misleading to focus solely on arms transfers. There is a major international trade in civil goods, services, and technology which have potential military applications currently or in the future (i.e., dual use). The international mobility of scientists is a further source for the transfer of military technology (UN, 1993). In total, major data limitations raise problems for both economists in their empirical work on arms transfers and for policy makers in their efforts to monitor the international trade in defense equipment (Blackaby and Ohlson, 1987).

10.2   Modeling the arms trade

Traditional trade theory predicts that international trade will be based on differences in comparative advantage between nations and that competitive market prices will determine the volume and value of overseas trade. As a starting point, this competitive model explains the arms trade in terms of market forces: the demand for arms (imports) is determined by prices, incomes, tastes and preferences (e.g. threat perception), whilst supply (exports) is based on technology and comparative advantage with supply prices reflecting costs. Reality is different. International arms markets are heavily influenced by governments which can control the exports of their defense contractors and determine prices through offering subsidies and generous financial terms. Furthermore, arms exports and imports have traditionally been highly

Table 10.1 *The arms trade*

Leading exporters of major conventional weapons	US $ m (1990 prices) 1988–92
USA	54,968
USSR/Russia	45,182
France	9,349
Germany	9,313
China	7,658
UK	7,623
Czechoslovakia	3,163
Netherlands	2,048
Italy	1,613
Sweden	1,416
Brazil	1,028
Spain	1,014
Switzerland	874
Israel	777
Others	4,987
Total exports	151,013
Leading importers of major conventional weapons	
India	12,235
Japan	9,224
Saudi Arabia	8,690
Afghanistan	7,515
Germany	6,372
Greece	6,197
Turkey	6,167
Iraq	4,967
Spain	3,747
Iran	3,632
South Korea	3,524
Czechoslovakia	3,501
Others	77,143
Total imports	151,013

Source: SIPRI (1993).

concentrated amongst a few sellers and a few buyers (oligopoly and oligopsony). In principle, such small numbers of countries should make it easier to reach agreements to control the arms trade. In recent years, though, there has been the emergence of new major weapons exporters (e.g., China, Brazil), together with the entry of a number of small arms producers and the potential for minor arms exporters to have a major impact via high technology weapons exports (e.g., North Korea's export of Scud missiles).

Some of the stylized facts of the arms trade are shown in table 10.1. For the period 1988–92, the USA and former USSR accounted for 66 percent of the world's arms exports and the top six exporting nations accounted for almost 90 percent of the world total. On the buying side, between 1988 and 1992, the top six countries accounted for one-third of total world imports. There have, though, been changes in the international arms trade. In the 1950s and 1960s, much of the arms trade involved arms transfers as military and economic aid. The trade was dominated by the two superpowers with mainly political aims in their arms transfer policies. Since the early 1970s, with the rise in oil prices, the trade has become more commercial, with transfers of the most advanced weapons systems and the transfer of arms production capabilities (e.g., via offsets). As a result, new suppliers have entered the market. An increasing number of developing countries have acquired an arms production capability and some of these are major arms exporters [e.g., China, Brazil, Egypt, North Korea (Brzoska, 1987a; Treddenick, 1987)].

Efforts by economists to explain the facts of the arms trade have often involved a political economy framework. Notions of comparative advantage as a major determinant are rejected as governments pursue national security and independence (Treddenick, 1987). Simple market analysis predicts that with world oversupply, there will be intense price competition and eventual capacity adjustments on the supply side – unless, of course, governments intervene to support their domestic defense industries (see chapter 7). The political economy approach to arms transfers stresses the role of both political and economic factors. The demand from importing countries is motivated by security considerations with economic factors forming a constraint (e.g. arms imports rising with an oil or commodity price boom). Supply by the arms exporters also reflects political factors in such forms as "making friends and influencing people," together with economic factors, namely, profitability for companies and wider economic benefits for the exporting country. Using this approach, one estimate suggests that the economic motivation could account for 50 percent of total arms exports (Deger, 1989).

A cost–benefit approach to the arms trade suggests a divergence between private and social benefits and costs for the arms exporting country. It is not unknown for arms exports to be sold at a loss, for R & D costs to be waived and for governments to underwrite credits, marketing efforts, offsets, and counter-trade agreements. Examples have also arisen where payments have not been made (Smith *et al.*, 1985). In contrast, private firms will only be willing to continue with arms exports so long as they are profitable. Here, a public choice analysis suggests that income-maximizing defense contractors and budget-maximizing defense departments will lobby and seek to persuade governments of the economic and political benefits of arms exports. Vote-conscious governments can stress the economic benefit of arms exports in the form of jobs, exports, support for high technology industries, and for the nation's defense industrial base, as well as political benefits in the form of power, influence, and political leverage in foreign policy. Furthermore, defense contractors can support their case by stressing that exports will enable the firm to obtain scale and learning economies from a larger output (Deger, 1989). If governments pay for fixed R & D costs through their domestic orders, and waive any R & D levy on overseas sales, then profit-maximizing defense contractors can offer exports at a price determined by their average variable costs, so increasing their competitiveness in world markets. Or, with decreasing costs, a defense contractor might persuade its government to offer a subsidy to achieve the social benefits of marginal cost pricing. Furthermore, having offered the original equipment at an attractive price, the defense contractor can use its monopoly position to charge high prices for spares and "essential modifications" (Chinworth, 1992). The outcome of these various social and private costs and benefits is that the return to the exporting country might be lower than the return to the defense exporting company, with the possibility that the returns to the arms exporting country might even be negative (Smith et al., 1985).

An original contribution to modeling the international arms market is provided by Levine, Sen, and Smith (1994). Their model incorporates both economic and political (security) factors, with the arms market treated as a case of international trade in an imperfectly competitive market, where intertemporal contracts are important and an externality is associated with the product (e.g., arms sales to an ally increase the suppliers' security). The model focuses on a set of forward-looking, competing supplier governments each deciding on the quantity of arms to sell to a generic recipient, and considering the economic benefits of arms exports and the security implications (positive or negative) of changes in the recipient's behavior following its acquisition of weapons. Recipient demand depends on its security and budgetary positions. Nash equilibrium conditions are derived, with suppliers maximizing an intertemporal welfare function which depends on profits from the sale and the security repercussions.

The basic model of Levine et al. (1994) is summarized in a set of equations. The amount of arms which supplier i delivers to the recipient at time t is represented by q_{it}, $i = 1, \ldots, n$. The aggregate total of arms supplied to a particular country per period is shown by $Q_t = Q_{it} + q_{it}$, where Q_{it} is the quantity supplied by all nations other than country i. The end of period aggregate stock of defense equipment S_t is defined by

$$S_{t+1} = (1 - \delta)S_t + Q_t, \tag{10.1}$$

where δ is the depreciation rate. The aggregate stock determines the military capability and hence the behavior of the recipient nation. The recipients' demand for weapons is summarized in a linear demand function, where P is the price of arms

$$P_t = a - bQ_t = a - b(Q_{it} + q_{it}). \tag{10.2}$$

The various security implications of international arms transfers (e.g., as reflected in the guidelines used by the five Permanent Members of the UN Security Council) are reflected in a single index of security. It is assumed that the objective function of supplier i, namely U_i, depends on the profitability of the sale, Π_i, and the security repercussions, $V(S)$, which depend on the stock of arms held by the recipient, S. These assumptions result in

$$U_{it} = \Pi_{it} + V(S_t) \tag{10.3a}$$

where

$$\Pi_{it} = P(Q_t)q_{it} - C(q_{it}) \tag{10.3b}$$

where $P(Q_t)$ is the recipients' demand function and $C(q_{it})$ is the suppliers' cost function (assuming constant marginal costs). The variety of possible impacts of the recipients military capability on supplier security, $V(S)$, is represented by a quadratic security function

$$V(S_t) = dS_t + eS_t^2. \tag{10.4}$$

An illustration is provided by taking the case of a pure adversary with $d < 0$, $e = 0$, so that there are negative security externalities in both the short and long run. Corresponding to (10.4) is an intertemporal welfare function for the supplier at time τ, where r is the discount rate

$$W_{i\tau} = \sum_{t=0}^{\infty} \left[\frac{1}{1+r}\right]^t [P_{\tau+t}q_{i\tau+t} - C_i(q_{i\tau+t}) + V(S_{\tau+t})]. \tag{10.5}$$

With the market characteristics as described above the next task is to determine price and quantity as the symmetric Nash equilibrium between the competing suppliers. By substituting (10.2) and (10.4) into (10.5) and letting $C(q_{it}) = cq_{it}$ plus fixed costs, the supplier's optimization problem at $\tau = 0$ is to maximize

$$W_{i0} = \sum_{t=0}^{t=\infty} \lambda^t[(a - c)q_{it} - b(Q_{it}q_{it} + q_{it}^2) + (dS_t + eS_t^2)]$$

(10.6)

where $\lambda = 1/(1 + r)$, subject to the dynamic constraint in (10.1); the nonnegativity constraint $q_{it} \geqslant 0$; and S_0 is given as the initial condition.

A number of propositions result from the model. One suggests that the steady-state levels of output and military stock exceed the pure profit-maximizing levels, and another proposition states that increasing competition increases supply. The authors recognize that their model needs extending to capture other features of the arms trade. For example, different strategic relationships are possible with the USA acting as a Stackelberg leader with world-wide security interests whilst a number of small followers (France, UK) are motivated by economic returns (Levine et al., 1994).

There have been other contributions to understanding the arms trade. Arms re-supply during conflict is an underresearched aspect of the arms trade and Harkavy (1987) provides a classification system illustrating the myriad dimensions of the subject. International trade has also been incorporated into models of military alliances (Wong, 1991; see chapter 2). McGuire (1990a) has considered the analytical issues involved in nations intervening to reduce their dependence on foreign trade. Military equipment is one class of products for which many countries seek to maintain greater independence than would result from competitive markets. The analysis compared the relative efficiency of trade controls (i.e., protection of domestic industries) with one alternative namely stockpiling (i.e., storage, including maintaining standby production capacity). Unexpectedly, the analysis shows that even when stockpiles can be accumulated at world prices and stored at zero interest with no loss or deterioration, some degree of protection may still be justified (McGuire, 1990a, 1991).

Finally, a number of world models have incorporated the arms trade. Examples include the Leontief world input–output model, computable general equilibrium models, and world econometric (LINK-type) models. Such models are used to identify and to forecast the impact of military expenditure on various parts of the world and, at the same time, "to expose as much as possible the arms trade component of that trade matrix and project it since such data and projection can be critical information in negotiation processes" (Isard, 1988, p. 327).

10.3   Empirical work

The empirical work on arms transfers can be arranged in three groups concerned with country studies of the economic importance of arms exports, econometric results, and the economic implications of arms imports for less developed countries.

The study by Wulf (1993a) describes the economic importance of arms exports for both the USA and the former Soviet Union, with further information for the EU, Poland, Czechoslovakia, China, and Australia. Some of the descriptive statistics for the USA and former USSR are impressive. In 1991, the USA accounted for 51 percent of total deliveries of major conventional weapons compared with 30 percent in 1987. The USA achieved this dominant position as a result of the dramatic decline in the volume of arms exports from the former USSR. Over 95 percent of US arms exports were to Western Europe, the Near East and East Asia, with American defense industries dominant in aircraft, helicopters, and armored vehicles, but not in naval vessels. For the USA, a major issue is whether some of its defense equipment is too sophisticated for export markets [e.g., warships, stealth aircraft (Anthony, 1993)]. This contrasts with China which has substantial arms exports of inexpensive equipment involving simple technologies (Frankenstein, 1993). The relative export performance of the USA and China is consistent with their perceived comparative advantages based on technology and labor, respectively.

The USSR accounted for about 40 percent of the world trade in major conventional weapons for most of the 1980s, but, by 1991, its share had fallen to less than 20 percent with drastically reduced exports to Third World countries. Unlike Western arms suppliers, the Soviet government restricted the supply of arms production technology to many recipients. Interestingly, though, "there is no evidence that arms sales brought significant benefits to the Soviet economy as a whole. Several of the key recipients of Soviet weapons were not in a position to pay for the imported weapons, let alone in hard currency" (Wulf, 1993a, p. 128). The main Soviet arms exports were in tanks, fighter aircraft, warships, and small missiles. Following the end of the cold war, Russian arms exports were seen as a means of obtaining foreign currency, maintaining employment, and avoiding the need for conversion (Wulf, 1993a).

Between 1988 and 1992, France was the world's third largest arms exporter. A definitive study of the French case is provided by Kolodziej (1987). From 1945 to the 1960s French arms production and transfer policy was determined by strategic and foreign policy considerations. From the 1960s, economic, and technological factors were the principal determinants of French arms transfer behavior, with its defense industry

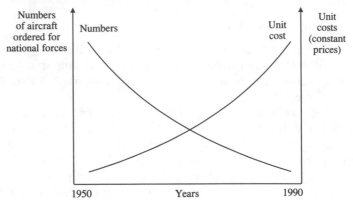

Figure 10.1 Unit costs and numbers

becoming export dependent. For example, between the 1950s and 1980, over 60 percent of most types of helicopters and military aircraft were exported (e.g., Mirage aircraft) and over 50 percent of vehicles and tanks were sold abroad. The pressures to export came from rising unit costs and a limited domestic market. An example of the trade-off between the rising unit costs of combat aircraft and numbers ordered annually for the domestic armed forces is shown in figure 10.1. The upward-sloping curve shows the unit costs of successive generations of French fighter aircraft; and the downward-sloping curve shows the decreasing numbers of these aircraft which can be purchased annually by the French Air Force (Kolodziej, 1987, p. 142). Part of the French success in arms export markets arose because they offered serviceable, battle-tested products with few political strings attached; they kept their promises and they offered a wide range of effective weapons at competitive prices (Kolodziej, 1987, p. 183). This success resulted from an arms complex which enjoyed considerable prestige with major claims on resources within the defense community, particularly for its most technically advanced sectors in aerospace, electronics, and nuclear energy. There was government support for national champions such as Aerospatiale, Dassault, and SNECMA in the aerospace industry, Thomson-CSF in electronics, and GIAT for land equipment. As a result of their success, French arms exports in 1983 employed 110,000 persons or some 35 percent of total French defense industry employment (Kolodziej, 1987, p. 189).

Whilst the benefits appear attractive, French arms exports have not been costless. Conflicts have arisen between arms exports and national military requirements, with the French armed forces sometimes having to accept equipment in order to support exports, as well as having to accept slower deliveries to the French forces. Indeed, with the increasing dependence of the French defense industrial base on exports, there is concern that the military requirements of arms exports more than French national military requirements will determine weapons design, development, and production priorities. Arms exports have also meant that France has acquired unwanted and potentially costly and dangerous security obligations. Finally, there are external costs in that French experience and success in arms production and exports is being emulated in other nations of the world, resulting in greater international instability and less-developed countries allocating scarce resources to creating national defense industries (Kolodziej, 1987, p. 407).

Japan is a completely contrary case to France. Japan is committed to building up its national defense industry based on a limited domestic market with major constraints on its arms exports which means dearer arms for Japan (Taylor, 1993a). Its arms export policy is based on three principles, namely, that Japan would not supply arms to communist countries, to states subject to United Nations arms embargoes, or to countries involved or likely to be involved in international conflicts. The export of complete defense systems is prohibited so that between 1984 and 1988 Japan's arms exports were half those of Switzerland (Taylor, 1993a). The policy has its problems particularly in relation to dual-use products and technologies (e.g., machine tools, electronics) and the agreement to transfer military technology to the USA.

Some of the economic arguments favoring arms exports are not without their critics. The standard economic argument is that for costly defense equipment, arms exports enable longer production runs so spreading development costs and exploiting economies of scale and learning. However, the claim that foreign sales reduce unit costs is weakened "if suppliers fail to charge their customers a proportional share of R & D and other fixed costs, if they export weapons towards the end of the production run (when economies of scale and learning do not promise large gains) and if the savings in unit production costs are largely eaten up by price reductions that are necessary to compete with other suppliers ..." (Catrina, 1988, p. 358). Nevertheless, arms exports can be an important source of employment. For example, in the mid-1980s, it was estimated that the jobs of at least one-quarter of Western Europe's 1.5 million arms workers depended on exports to the Third World alone, with some countries, companies, and regions highly dependent on overseas sales (Renner, 1992, p. 129). With substantial job losses forecast for the 1990s, such groups are likely to oppose efforts to restrict the international arms trade. Nor should it be assumed that arms exporters are all developed nations. Some Third World countries are major arms exporters (see table 10.1 and Lasso, 1987).

Whilst there is no shortage of descriptive accounts of the arms trade, good quality empirical work has been conspicuous by its absence. Admittedly, there are major data problems, but such problems have not prevented extensive econometric work in other parts of defense economics (see chapters 3, 4, and 8). For the arms trade, a study by Smith *et al.* (1985), estimated a regression equation of the following form

$$Wi = a + bD + cW + dMi + eDMi, \qquad (10.7)$$

where

$Wi =$ log of weapons exports by country i,
$D =$ oil price dummy (1,0) representing the 1973 oil price rise,
$W =$ log of total weapons exports,
$Mi =$ log of military expenditure in country
$DMi =$ change in military expenditure in country

The equation was estimated for five countries for the period 1958–82. Significant coefficients were obtained for W and sometimes for DMi, the main result being that military expenditure had contradictory results on arms exports. However, the authors stressed the preliminary nature of the results reflecting an highly simplified model with problems about the direction of causation (Smith *et al.*, 1985).

Regression analysis was also used by Pearson (1989) to explain arms imports. The estimating equations included variables for national characteristics (e.g., geographical area, population), military characteristics (e.g., defense expenditure, numbers of military personnel, nuclear status), government characteristics (regime type), economic characteristics; involvement in a foreign or domestic conflict, and alignment patterns (e.g., alliances). The analysis explained over one-third of the variance and the main predictors of arms imports were military spending and ambition, foreign policy alignment, and economic variables (Pearson, 1989). Another econometric study of Third World countries by McKinlay (1989) found evidence of a strong relationship between arms imports and military expenditure although the results can be criticized for the *ad hoc* nature of the estimating equations.

Alternatively, a disaggregated approach is possible using industry- or firm-level data. One example attempted to explain the export performance of the defense-intensive British aircraft industry. It was hypothesized that variations in the pressure of domestic demand would have an inverse effect on the industry's export performance (Hartley, 1972). Both levels and shares models were estimated for the period 1948–67 (a fixed exchange rate regime) and the basic estimating equations were

$$X = f(W, D, t) \tag{10.8a}$$

$$S = f(D, t), \tag{10.8b}$$

where

X = level of UK aircraft exports over time,
W = value of total world aircraft exports,
D = pressure of domestic demand,
S = British aircraft industry's share of world trade in aircraft,
t = a time trend, 1948–67.

The level of exports equation (10.8a) was estimated using both linear and log-linear regressions. The overseas demand variable was significant and positive with a partial elasticity of British aircraft exports with respect to overseas demand varying between 0.7 and 1.2. There was also some support for the pressure hypothesis showing that domestic demand had a significant effect on both levels of exports and shares, with the predicted negative sign (Hartley, 1972).

A substantial part of the literature on the arms trade focuses on its potential for causing regional conflicts, especially in the Third World. This literature raises interesting questions about the direction of causation and the need to recognize that arms transfers are only one element in a complex set of factors explaining rivalry and conflict in the Third World (e.g., religious and ethnic factors; territorial disputes). Work by Chadwick (1986), suggested that arms transfers to Asian countries led to an increase in the military expenditure of their neighbors. A study by Kinsella (1994) used cross-correlation analysis, Granger-causality tests, and vector auto-regression techniques to estimate the impact of super-power arms transfers on conflict in the Middle East. The results show that Soviet arms transfers to the Middle East, more than American transfers, have exacerbated interstate rivalry in the region; and that Soviet, more than American, arms transfers have encouraged compensatory arming by the other superpower (Kinsella, 1994).

A third strand of the literature on the arms trade has focused on arms imports by developing countries. Often, a broad benefit–cost framework is used. On the benefits side, less-developed countries demand arms imports for security, the needs of warfare, for prestige (operating modern weapons), and to satisfy the demands of the military for modernization. Spin-off arguments are also used, whereby arms imports lead to the acquisition of advanced technology which might be used in the civil sector (Brauer, 1991; Deger, 1986; Whynes, 1979). But costs are involved. The imports of advanced weapons can distort manpower training to meet military demands with no civil applications. There are worries about regional arms races. Arms imports can also involve substantial life-cycle costs considerably in excess of the initial acquisition price and foreign currency is needed which might otherwise be used to import civil investment goods of more immediate use for improving living standards. One estimate has shown that for a sample of less-developed countries, if all military imports were stopped, then growth would rise by about three-quarters of 1 per cent (Deger, 1986, p. 146). For countries such as India, Pakistan and Turkey, where imported capital goods have important productivity linkages with growth, arms imports are very costly: respectively, 27 percent, 18 percent, and 13 percent of engineering imports were potentially diverted to arms (Deger, 1986, p. 147).

Both economic and military aid to developing countries (including concessionary arms sales) raise issues of fungibility (transferability) and leakages whereby aid designed for one purpose releases resources to finance greater military spending and arms imports. General aid programs for government expenditure are clearly more fungible: such aid can be used for military spending and arms imports (Deger, 1986; Deger and Sen, 1991). McGuire (1987) estimated a model of US foreign assistance, Israeli defense spending, and the Middle East arms race. Allowing for interdependencies, he estimated that Israel allocated about 23 percent of US military aid to non-defense purposes and that some 40 percent of US economic assistance filtered through to defense spending. So, for equal amounts of US military and economic aid, about 60 percent ends up as increased defense outlays, some of which will be used for arms imports (McGuire, 1987).

Arms imports by developing countries can also add to their foreign debt problems. One estimate has suggested that if the non-oil-developing countries had not purchased foreign arms during the period 1972–82 they would have needed to borrow 20 percent less each year and their accumulated long-term debt by 1982 would have been about 16 percent smaller (McWilliams-Tullberg, 1987). It is, however, possible that the debt burden may force Third World countries to reevaluate their priorities and seriously consider whether their military expenditures are "too large." The possibility arises that following the end of the cold war superpower arms race, the debt burden provides "a window of opportunity through which Third World countries can reduce military expenditure, concomitant arms procurement and transfer as well as foster an atmosphere of arms control" (Deger and Sen, 1990a, p. 142).

10.4   Policy issues: controlling the arms trade

There is continued national and international interest in controlling the arms trade. Some nations have adopted voluntary unilateral controls refusing to export any arms or certain types of weapons (e.g., nuclear, chemical), or refusing to export to specific countries and regions (e.g., Middle East). Some countries, such as Japan, have decided that economic aid will not be forthcoming to countries which have imported arms to excess (Taylor, 1993). Elsewhere multilateral initiatives to control the arms trade have been, and are being, pursued through the UN, the EU, the Conference on Security and Cooperation in Europe (CSCE), and the Group of Seven. In addition from time to time the UN imposes mandatory arms embargoes on specific countries (e.g., Yugoslavia in 1991). A description of the various initiatives to control arms transfers is provided in the SIPRI Yearbook: *World Armaments and Disarmament*. Brzoska (1987b) has suggested a taxonomy in which the variety of arms transfer initiatives can be grouped into unilateral or multilateral supplier restraints and limitations on arms exports, and unilateral or multilateral buyer or recipient restraints.

Despite the level of concern, international efforts to control the arms trade have generally failed (Wulf, 1987). Failure is not surprising once some of the problems of reaching a multilateral agreement are recognized. There are problems of definition; of verifying and enforcing an agreement, particularly one involving a large number of nations; there are economic pressures to export; there are substitution effects whereby nations unable to import arms for security and protection might create a domestic defense industry (e.g. Israel, South Africa); and there are always black market pressures and incentives to cheat (UN, 1993). As one authority has stated "The problem is how to make governments do something they do not want to do and, for the most part, have steadfastly resisted doing . . ." (Wulf, 1987, p. 204).

Any evaluation of proposals to control arms transfers needs evidence on their likely benefits and costs. Who are the likely winners and losers from controls on the arms trade? Here, two studies provide valuable quantitative estimates of the likely economic impacts of controls on arms transfers. First, the Michigan Model of World Production and Trade has been used to assess the impact of the export of armaments on sectoral trade, employment, and other economic variables in the major Western trading nations, using 1980 data. The Michigan Model comprises two parts, namely, the country system and the world system. The country system is represented by separate blocks of equations for the individual tradable and nontradable sectors for each country, whilst the world system contains a single set of equations for individual tradable sectors for the whole world. The model was based on twenty-two tradable and seven nontradable industries in eighteen industrialized and sixteen developing countries, together with an aggregate sector representing the rest of the world. Typically, the coefficients of explanatory variables that appear in the model are calculated from data on production, trade, and employment by sector in each country, from input–output matrices, and from published estimates of demand and substitution elasticities. The Michigan model differs from full Walrasian general equilibrium models. Instead, in the Michigan model, the equations of the model are first differentiated and the resulting linear system is then solved computationally.

The Michigan model was then used to forecast the effects if the arms trade were subject to embargo, either unilaterally by the USA or multilaterally by all the major Western trading nations. For a unilateral US embargo, it was estimated that there would be a small amount of employment displacement in the aggregate in the USA, mostly in the transport equipment and electrical machinery sectors. For a multilateral embargo on the arms trade, the effects on the USA were again fairly small and similar to the unilateral American embargo. However, the employment effects in several other industrialized and developing countries (e.g., South Korea, India, Brazil, France) were estimated to be much larger, suggesting major adjustment problems in some labor markets (Grobar *et al.*, 1990). Although the model has its limitations (e.g. it assumes perfect competition in producing sectors with constant returns to scale) and is based on 1980 data, the approach is potentially useful as a guide to policy makers seeking information on the likely economic impacts of various controls on arms transfers.

The second study undertaken in the USA estimated the economic, military, and political effects of multilateral supplier limits on conventional arms transfers to the Middle East. It was assumed that the sales of major weapons to the Middle East would be reduced by about 50 percent relative to typical 1980s levels. The macroeconomic effects on the USA and other developed countries which supply arms were estimated to be tiny; but there might be short-term adjustment problems for the former Soviet Union. In contrast, the Middle Eastern countries would benefit from substantial increases in their domestic aggregate demand and nonmilitary imports and, under some circumstances, significant long-run increases in real GDP (CBO, 1992b). However, for the arms suppliers, there are likely to be more pronounced effects at the level of industries, firms, and local areas. For the USA, as many as 75,000 jobs might be lost in the defense sector, with the tank industry severely affected (e.g., General Dynamics). Even so, the CBO study concluded that the benefits of limiting the arms trade to the Middle East may justify the costs. An effective system of limits could lead to a safer and more prosperous period in Middle East history and also a possible easing of the burden military spending imposes on the US economy (CBO, 1992b, p. xviii).

10.5   Conclusion

This survey has shown the considerable opportunities for further work on the theoretical, empirical, and policy aspects of the arms trade. The field is rich in its potential for applying game theory, industrial economics, the economics of regulation and public choice models; as well as providing opportunities for interdisciplinary approaches. Empirical work needs to undertake industry and firm-level studies of export performance. Interview–questionnaire techniques and case studies need to investigate export pricing and profitability. For example, do firms use discriminatory pricing; how profitable are exports compared with home sales; and do firms offer exports at low prices only to recover their profits through spares pricing?

Policy-relevant studies are also needed. Policy makers need reliable quantitative estimates of the likely economic impacts on buyers and sellers of various types of controls on arms transfers. They also need guidance on the costs of creating and policing effective international controls on arms transfers. With any control regime, there will always be incentives to cheat and undertake some illegal trading – and this is an area where data problems abound!

11   Arms control and disarmament

Since the late 1980s, there have been dramatic changes in the world political scene, especially in Europe. The end of the East–West cold war arms race has raised the prospect of genuine disarmament associated with sizable arms reductions. The new climate for international relations reflects changes in eastern and central Europe and in the former USSR. There have been international arms control agreements [1987 INF Treaty, 1990 CFE Treaty, and the 1993 START II (see table 11.1)], followed by voluntary unilateral cuts in defense spending. Increasingly, the United Nations is regarded as an international peace-keeping, peace-making, and peace-enforcing agency in a new world order [e.g. Iraq's invasion of Kuwait; Yugoslavia, 1992–4 (McNamara, 1991)]. There are now real prospects of a disarmament race replacing the cold war arms race as nations and their electorates seek the benefits of the peace dividend.

Real disarmament offers a range of opportunities and potential economic benefits. Disarmament is likely to contribute to peace, and, in turn, peace itself makes an immediate contribution to the peace dividend. In addition, resources released from defense will eventually become available for alternative uses elsewhere in different economies. There is no shortage of alternative uses. Nations need to alleviate poverty and have increasing demands for health, education, and housing. The problems of hunger and poverty are especially severe in the developing nations of the world. There are also major scientific challenges to protect and improve the environment, to explore space, to develop future sources of energy, and to eradicate some of the major health hazards (e.g., cancer, AIDS). On this basis, there are numerous high technology problems requiring scientific manpower of the type currently used in military R & D. However, it would be misleading to suggest that disarmament alone will solve all the world's problems. It can help, but there are no free lunches nor magic wand solutions. It has also to be recognized that this is a controversial field, dominated by myths, emotion, and ideology, often lacking in economic analysis, critical evaluation, and the empirical testing of hypotheses (Schmidt, 1993).

Expectations of a peace dividend have already created a set of myths which need to be challenged. There are beliefs that the peace dividend will be large; that it will solve a nation's economic and social problems, and that any adjustment problems will be small and can be ignored. Such claims are typical of the rich research agenda in this field. There is no shortage of research questions: this is a relatively underresearched area which offers extensive opportunities for applying economic analysis (UN, 1993; Fontanel and Ward, 1993).

The chapter views disarmament as an investment process involving short-term costs in return for longer-run benefits. On this view the economic dividends of peace are likely to be small in the *short term* and dominated by the adjustment costs associated with unemployment and a reallocation of resources from military to civilian uses needed to obtain *long-term* benefits in the form of a larger output of civil goods and services. But not all investments are successful: some fail. If, for example, disarmament involves high conversion costs and leads to relatively low benefits, then society's rate of return from disarmament will be low or even negative (Intriligator, 1992).

The chapter starts by defining disarmament and considering the likely burdens and benefits of both defense spending and disarmament. There follows an analysis of arms control and arms limitation issues. This will embrace arms control in the context of arms race models and a taxonomy of arms control and arms limitation initiatives. There is an evaluation of likely problems in the form of substitution effects, uncertainty, cheating, and the possible opposition from established interest groups. Public choice analysis, economic models of regulation, and cost–benefit analysis will be applied. Finally, the concept of the peace dividend is evaluated.

11.1   Definitions, burdens, and benefits

Disarmament can be defined to involve one or more of the following:
(i)   Reductions in military expenditure due to unilateral initiatives or to bilateral and/or multilateral international agreements.
(ii)   The reduction or destruction of stocks of specific weapons (e.g., nuclear, chemical, biological, and offensive weapons, etc.).
(iii)   A ban or limitation on the production of certain types of military equipment (i.e., acting on flows as a means of affecting stocks of equipment).
(iv)   Controls on defense R & D for military purposes.

(v)   A reduction in the numbers of military personnel and in their
      geographical location (e.g., withdrawal from foreign bases).
(vi) Limitations on arms transfers.
(vii) A monitoring and verification process.

   Inevitably, questions arise as to whether disarmament will be a burden
or benefit? It might be a burden if defense spending offers worthwhile
benefits. To its supporters, defense spending is viewed as a form of
insurance policy providing security and protection. Nations require
military expenditures to respond to actual or perceived threats to their
national interests. Threats can reflect a struggle for power or for
resources (e.g. for land, minerals, oil), or they can reflect differences in
ideology, race, or religion, or any kind of difference perceived as
weakening a nation's security. The greater the perceived threat to a
nation's interests, the more willing it will be to allocate resources to
defense rather than civil goods (i.e., it will sacrifice butter for guns).
Defense, though, has a unique feature in that two nations in an arms race
might not succeed in increasing their national security by increasing their
military expenditures. This is in contrast to the benefits which result
when two nations each increase their expenditures on education, health,
or housing. Indeed, defense spending by two nations in an arms race
resembles a situation where both nations become trapped in an high
spending equilibrium as in the well-known Prisoner's Dilemma problem
of game theory. Each nation would be better off if it switched to a lower
level of defense spending but they would need to cooperate and possibly
trust one another for the agreement to work: this was the role of classical
arms control (Schelling, 1966). However, trust might not be necessary if a
strong verification regime can compensate for intense rivalry and mistrust
between nations.

   There are, though, major problems and limitations in applying game
theory to defense spending and disarmament. Zero sum game models are
probably more applicable to tactical situations such as a duel between
two aircraft or two tanks (Shubik, 1987). At the strategic level (e.g., arms
race, threats, crisis management) and where the games are not zero sum,
modeling becomes extremely complex. Who are the players, what are
their society's preferences and what does each player know about its
potential adversary? There are problems of modeling the highly complex
behavior and motivations of nation states, with various interest groups
and different interpretations of national behavior, and with different
attitudes to, and preferences for, risk taking, different valuations placed
on human lives, and different information on the "rules" of the game (see
chapter 4).

   Supporters of defense spending also claim that it provides economic benefits in the form of manpower training (adding to a nation's stock of human capital), jobs, balance of payments contributions (e.g., exports of defense equipment), support for high technology, and spin-off to the civil economy: hence it is suggested that such benefits will be lost through disarmament. But these benefits are not free gifts. Civil goods and services have to be sacrificed and there are potential adverse effects on a nation's economic growth and its international competitiveness. To quote Paul Kennedy's influential study on the rise and decline of nations "by going to war or by devoting a large share of the nation's manufacturing power to the expenditures upon unproductive armaments, one runs the risk of eroding the national economic base *vis-à-vis* states which are concentrating a greater share of their income upon productive investment for long-term growth" (Kennedy 1988, p. 697; for an annotated bibliography of relevant literature, see Hartley and Hooper 1990, references 736–932). Disarmament leading to lower defense budgets usually requires a reduction in the actual or potential current or future threats to national security (i.e., a more peaceful world scenario). The resulting economic benefits of disarmament would be reflected in the release and reallocation of resources from military to civil uses and possibly favorable effects on growth and international competitiveness. There could, though, be some adverse effects if, as is sometimes argued, defense spending promotes technical advance. Moreover, reallocating expenditure and resources away from the defense sector takes time and there are costs involved in adjusting to change.

A framework showing the effects of defense spending and disarmament is shown in figure 11.1. This shows the interrelationships between defense spending, the purchase of factor inputs (labor, capital, energy, materials, services, and management), the resulting outputs of the defense industries and the armed forces, and the consequent macroeconomic impacts. It shows how cuts in defense spending impact on various factor inputs and how disarmament could be targeted at other elements of the military production function. For example, cuts in defense spending will reduce the demand for manpower and capital in both the armed forces and the defense industries. The result will be job losses and the closure of military bases and facilities, as well as some factories and plants in defense manufacturing industries. Some of these military base and plant closures will be concentrated in specific towns and regions. Elsewhere, the ways in which the inputs of labor and capital are assembled to produce an output in the form of defense shows that disarmament might focus on other elements in the military production function, such as defense R & D or the types of military equipment acquired by the armed forces or limitations on the numbers of armed

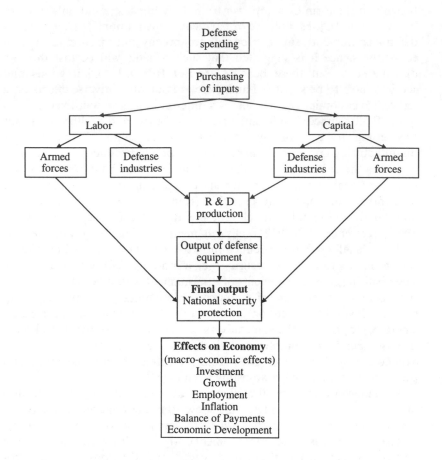

Figure 11.1 The effects of defense spending

forces personnel. Nonetheless, reallocating expenditure and resources away from defense to the civil sector of an economy takes time and involves costs in adjusting to change. What is the contribution of economics to understanding the problems of disarmament?

11.2   The contribution of economics

Interest by economists in the burdens and benefits of defense spending and in disarmament is not new. Some of the early economists addressed issues of the "proper" role of the state, the economic causes of war and the short- and long-run impacts of military expenditure. Marxists have also argued that military expenditure is necessary for the maintenance of capitalism as a viable economic system (Baran and Sweezy, 1966; Fontanel, 1994; Smith and Smith, 1983).

Often the starting point in analyzing defense, disarmament, and peace issues has been standard macro- and microeconomics, usually Keynesian and neo-classical economics. Keynesians focus on defense spending as a component of aggregate effective demand. With unemployment in an economy, higher military spending adds to aggregate demand resulting in a greater national output and higher employment. However, in a full-employment economy, higher military spending might be inflationary, or could be associated with balance of payments problems (Smith and Smith, 1983). Similarly, where an economy is already in recession with large-scale unemployment, then disarmament leading to sudden, large reductions in military spending without any compensating increases in aggregate demand will add to unemployment. In contrast, reduced defense spending in conditions of economic expansion and tight labor markets might provide the additional resources needed for sustained economic growth. This suggests that to minimize the dislocations and unemployment effects of disarmament, there might need to be compensating aggregate demand policies with reductions in defense spending which are gradual and predictable (Benoit and Boulding, 1963; Hartley, 1994).

Neo-classical economics focuses on opportunity costs and market adjustments. Opportunity costs reflect the fact that resources are scarce and their use in defense means that they cannot be used for something else (e.g. education or health). A classic example is the "guns versus butter" trade-off as shown in figure 11.2. Where an economy's resources are fully and efficiently employed, then an increase in defense spending from D_0 to D_1 involves a sacrifice of C_1 to C_0 of civil goods and services (e.g., schools, hospitals, housing, etc). In addition, neo-classical economists use demand and supply analysis to assess the impact of changing demands between military and civil goods by focusing on the changes in prices and quantities in product and labor markets. In these simple models, prices are assumed to clear all markets leaving neither shortages nor surpluses of labor, capital, and goods and services. However, market adjustments are not always smooth and instantaneous: we do not live in a world of magic wand economics where resources can be reallocated instantly and without cost. Adjusting to change takes time and is likely to involve costs as reflected in dislocations, unemployment, and the underemployment of labor, capital, and other resources. An example is shown in figure 11.2. Disarmament involving a reduction in defense spending from D_1 to D_0 will eventually be associated with a greater

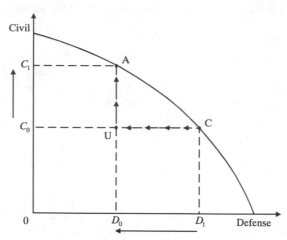

Figure 11.2 Guns and butter

output of civil goods and services. Effectively, the move from C to A reflects a change in society's preference function and a move to a new preferred position. But as the economy moves from position C to position A it is likely to proceed via point U which will be associated with unemployment.

The likelihood that disarmament involves costs as well as benefits suggests that it should be regarded as an investment process. There are initial costs reflected in unemployment and the underemployment of the resources used to produce military goods and services (labor, capital, land). This unemployment occurs during the transition period (which may last for years), as resources are reallocated from the defense sector to obtain long-term benefits in the form of a larger output of civil goods and services. The issue is whether these unemployed resources can be employed elsewhere and, if so, where, when, and how. The costs of conversion can be very substantial and last a long time, involving structural rather then frictional unemployment (Richards, 1991). Indeed, the groups and local communities likely to lose from defense cuts will form major barriers opposing disarmament. Additional costs are incurred in restoring land at military bases (e.g., environmental hazards) and in destroying weapons, especially nuclear systems. Eventually, though, benefits will flow as the inputs released by the armed forces and defense industries are reallocated to increase the output of civil goods and services. Since both benefits and costs occur over time, they need to be discounted and expressed as present values, so enabling the peace dividend to be regarded as the social rate of return to disarmament. For policy makers, the relevant question is how to maximize the return from disarmament by minimizing unemployment, conversion and reallocation costs, and maximizing the economic benefits of disarmament. And the economies of Eastern Europe and the former USSR face real difficulties in simultaneously disarming and shifting to a market economy (Wiseman, 1991). However, before addressing policy issues, a review is needed of the empirical work on disarmament.

11.3   Empirical work

Given the variety of economic models offering alternative insights, explanations, and predictions, it might be expected that the differences between them could be resolved through empirical studies. Which economic theory is best fitted to understanding and predicting the economic effects of disarmament? Here, there are at least two approaches, namely, qualitative and quantitative.

First, historical studies and case studies can provide useful insights. For example, studies of previous experience following defense cuts can identify how well and how quickly economies adjusted to change. Examples include the experience of economies following the end of World Wars I and II and of the US economy following the end of the Korean and Vietnam Wars (Hartley and Hooper, 1990). Of course, following the end of World War II, the UK economy, for example, was faced with a massive rebuilding programme to restore its damaged infrastructure, so there was no shortage of demand. For UK defense firms, government orders for, say, housing replaced orders for defense equipment. The disarmament of the early 1990s is different in that it is occurring without a prior major war. At the same time, in several countries, disarmament is occurring simultaneously with a shift from a centrally planned to a market economy. Case studies of defense contractors can also contribute to an understanding of firm behavior and the problems of conversion (Southwood, 1991). Some country case studies, such as those of Germany and Japan since 1945, suggest that economic success does not require large military expenditures. However, the cases of Germany and Japan show the temptations of confusing simple correlations with causation. A variety of factors determine economic performance and success with military spending as only one amongst a number of determinants (Fontanel, 1994).

Second, various quantitative techniques are available, including input–output analysis, simulation studies and statistical-econometric methods. One major study applied an input–output model to forecast the implications for the world economy by the year 2000 under different assumptions as to military spending, the arms trade, and aid transfers from rich to poor nations (Leontief and Duchin, 1983, p. 66). The results show that, with reduced military spending, almost all economies are able to increase total output and per capita consumption. Furthermore, this study predicted that whilst lower defense expenditures throughout the world accompanied by aid transfers from the rich nations would improve the living standards of the poor nations by the year 2000, the gap in economic well being between the rich and poor nations would be barely narrowed.

Econometric and quantitative techniques are extremely attractive with their emphasis on elaborate models and quantification. A number of recent examples illustrate some of the findings relevant to this chapter:

(i)   An econometric study based on a two-sector production function model (defense and civilian sectors) applied to the USA, found a positive and significant relationship between defense spending and economic growth; but the findings also showed that the responsiveness of economic growth to changes in defense spending is small. Thus, for the USA, if there are significant cuts in defense spending, the adverse effects on economic growth should not be large (Atesoglu and Mueller, 1990; Mueller and Atesoglu, 1993).

(ii)   The economic effects of reducing US defense spending over the period 1990–5 have been simulated using both macroeconomic and input–output models. Assuming the defense cuts were used to reduce the Federal government deficit, it was estimated that there would be reductions in real output, the price level, and employment (with civilian job losses of up to 850,000 plus 270,000 military personnel released from the services). Defense-dependent industries were particularly vulnerable, namely, tanks, guided weapons, and shipbuilding (Thomas et al., 1991).

(iii) A study using a four-sector production function model (with the sectors comprising defense, government, exports, and the rest) applied to a group of developed nations concluded that the gross effect of military spending on growth is neither significantly positive nor negative, although the defense sector is much less productive than the rest of the economy (Alexander, 1990).

(iv)   A substantial number of econometric studies confirm an inverse or negative relationship between military expenditure and investment (Smith, 1980b).

(v)   A study of defense spending and US economic performance found no substantial relationship, in either causal direction, between defense spending and the price level, the unemployment rate or the interest rate: hence, those arguments which link defense spending to poor economic performance receive little empirical support (Kinsella, 1990; Baek, 1991; Payne and Ross, 1992).

(vi) Evidence from the UK, USA, and eleven OECD countries does not suggest that the share of military expenditure is a significant influence on the unemployment rate. Thus, in analyzing unemployment, no special account needs to be taken of military expenditure (Dunne and Smith, 1990).

Persuasive though econometric results appear, they have their limitations. For example, they might be *ad hoc* models, lacking a satisfactory theory. Few compare the relative impacts of defense with civil expenditures (e.g. do civil expenditures have crowding-out effects and adverse effects on economic performance?). Data problems are ignored and much of the empirical work is highly aggregative ignoring the underlying micro-economic foundations of macro-economics; and the results can be conflicting, being sensitive to equation specification, to time periods and to the sample of nations included in the estimation (e.g. the inclusion or exclusion of Germany and Japan). In the circumstances, it is prudent to adopt a combination of economic theories and methods of testing to obtain satisfactory insights into the economic aspects of defense spending and disarmament (Kirby and Hooper, 1991; Sur, 1991). More significantly, questions arise as to how disarmament can be achieved.

11.4   Arms control and limitation

Arms limitation is the means of achieving the disarmament needed to release resources for increasing the output of civil goods and services. Arms limitation embraces both treaty-based international arms control agreements as well as unilateral limitations on, and reductions in, arms. Major developments in arms limitation have occurred since 1986. Agreements on nuclear and conventional forces and the political changes in Eastern Europe and the former USSR have resulted in the prospects of a disarmament race replacing the cold war arms race (Intriligator, 1994).

Classical arms control aimed to change the international security situation by promoting security and stability at lower levels of risk and cost. But classical arms control has two features. First, the greater its success in achieving security and stability, the less important it tends to become. This is an achievement of arms control: if the tool is successful and puts itself out of business, then the arms control bureaucracy and associated resources are released for alternative uses (the peace dividend). Second, arms control is only needed in a hostile, adversarial international environment; but if the international environment is too antagonistic and hostile, then the levels of trust and confidence needed for arms control negotiations will not exist. This is the second feature of arms control: when it is achievable, it does not seem to be needed; and when it is needed, it cannot be achieved! These features have been reflected in the rise and fall of classical arms control over the period 1987–94. From the late 1980s, the emphasis has been on national disarmament initiatives through *unilateral cuts* rather than treaty-generated cuts (e.g. INF, START, CFE). Such unilateral cuts, especially those in the former Soviet Union, in the other former Warsaw Pact nations, in the United States and other NATO states have become much more important than bilateral or multilateral treaties in generating reductions in defense expenditures (Sur, 1992).

Arms limitation aims to reduce the risks of regional or global conflicts by reducing or ending the arms race between nations. Examples include the USA and former USSR cold war arms race between the late 1940s and 1990 and the regional arms races in the Middle East, India and Pakistan, North and South Korea, Central and South America. For the 1990s, there are worries that new technology will create future arms races (e.g., SDI) and that nations will be reluctant to sacrifice their latest technology for fear of losing a military advantage. There are further concerns about new regional arms races; about the proliferation of nuclear, chemical, and biological weapons; and about international terrorism and fears of instability leading to wars. But reducing the probability and the risk of war is not the only aim of arms limitation. It can reduce death and destruction if war does occur and there are further economic benefits. Arms control saves money and releases resources that can ultimately be used for producing valuable civil goods and services. There might, however, be trade-offs between these various benefits of arms control. For example, an expensive arms race might lead to a lower probability of war occurring but great destruction if war does occur. Or, weapons reductions which result in resource savings might increase the probability of war (Schelling, 1966; Schelling and Halperin, 1985; UN, 1989; also chapter 4).

An understanding of why nations acquire arms is central to explaining the arms race and to formulating appropriate arms limitation measures. Models of the arms race start from the simple proposition that nations arm in response to the threats which they believe to come from rival states. The Richardson model shows that a nation will increase its defense spending in response to the higher military spending of its rivals and that its response is also affected by grievance and fatigue or economic factors (Richardson, 1960; chapter 4; Fontanel, 1994).

Arms race models are an obvious starting point in analyzing the outbreak of war. Some analysts have claimed that a continuous upward spiral of armaments in two rival nations must inevitably result in war (Richardson, 1960). However, alternative models have suggested that in various situations a two-nation arms race might lead to either war or peace and that, conversely, disarmament can preserve peace or result in war. For example, an arms race could lead to peace and stability if it resulted in both sides reaching a position of mutual deterrence with each nation deterring the other (e.g,. the arms race between the USA and USSR in the 1960s and 1970s). Alternatively, disarmament could lead to war if both sides move from a stable position of mutual deterrence to an unstable one in which each can attack the other (Intriligator and Brito, 1984). Examples where disarmament was eventually associated with war included Europe in the 1930s and the Falklands Islands (Malvinas) in the early 1980s. Difficulties arise, however, because the world is dominated by uncertainty: situations of instability are usually identified with hindsight. Uncertainty is increased by technical progress (via military R & D) which provides an opportunity for one side to obtain a temporary military advantage (e.g. US nuclear monopoly after 1945). Further potential for instability arises in a multi-polar rather than a bi-polar world: hence, it is possible that reductions in tension between the big powers could increase regional tensions and instability (chapter 4).

11.5   A taxonomy

References to arms races and arms limitation often tend to oversimplify a complex situation. Arms limitation involves any initiative to reduce or limit defense spending, weapons, and armed forces. The initiative can be unilateral, bilateral, or multilateral, it can be global or regional, and it can be voluntary or compulsory (e.g., after a war, the victors might impose disarmament on the defeated nation as in the case of Iraq and the UN Security Council Resolution 687 of 3 April 1991). Recent examples of unilateral, bilateral, and multilateral arms limitation agreements are shown in table 11.1. The table is illustrative rather than comprehensive. Other examples include the 1963 Partial Test Ban Treaty (limitations on nuclear weapons testing: 120 signatories); the 1967 Outer Space Treaty, with restrictions on weapons of mass destruction and military bases in space (ninety-three signatories); the 1970 Treaty on the nonproliferation of nuclear weapons (156 signatories); the 1972 bilateral Treaty on the limitation of anti-ballistic missile systems (ABM Treaty); the 1972 Sea Bed Treaty which prohibits weapons of mass destruction being placed on the sea bed (eighty-eight

Table 11.1 *Recent arms limitation initiatives*

Initiative	Participating Nations	Major Features
CSCE: Conference on Security and Co-operation in Europe (Stockholm 1986; Vienna 1990, 1992; Helsinki 1992).	53 nations of Europe and North America	Confidence and security building measures (e.g., advance notification of military exercises; visits to air bases; observation of exercises).
INF: Intermediate Range Nuclear Forces Treaty, 1987.	USA USSR	Elimination of all intermediate range ground launched nuclear missiles (ballistic and cruise missiles).
MTCR: Missile Technology Control Regime, 1987.	7 originally: now 17 nations	Limits exports of nuclear-capable missiles and missile technology.
CFE: Conventional Forces in Europe Treaty, 1990.	29 members of NATO and former Warsaw Pact	Limitations on major conventional equipment holdings in Europe.
BWC: Biological Weapons Convention – Review Conference, 1991.	126 states	Ban on development, production and stockpiling of biological weapons.
START: Strategic Arms Reduction Treaty, 1991.	USA former USSR	Reductions in strategic nuclear arsenals of about one-third. Overall ceiling of 6,000 accountable warheads for each party.
Open Skies Treaty, 1992.	25 nations	Rights to overfly one anothers' territory.
CFE 1A Agreement, 1992.	29 states	Limitations on military manpower.
CWC: Chemical Weapons Convention, 1993 (Paris): for implementation in 1995.	150+ nations.	An international treaty to ban chemical weapons.
START II Treaty, 1993.	USA Russia	Aims at further cuts in nuclear arsenals. Elimination of MIRV ICBMs and ceiling on strategic nuclear warheads of 3,000–3,500 each by 2003.
Other nuclear arms control initiatives.	USA Former USSR	Proposals for a comprehensive Test Ban Treaty and widening membership of the Non-Proliferation Treaty (NPT).
Unilateral initiatives 1988 onwards.	USSR USA European nations	Announcements of unilateral cuts in defense budgets and military forces – e.g. Mr Gorbachev's UN Speech 1988, President Bush 1991.

Source: SIPRI, 1993.

Table 11.2 *Classifying arms limitation*

Type of arms limitation initiative, affecting	Number of nations to agreement or initiative (with examples)		
One	Two		Many
1 Total defense spending	USA, Russia UK, Germany		
2 Military R & D (inc. nuclear testing)	France		PTBT 1963
3 Type of weapon, e.g.			
(i) Nuclear	UN–Iraq 1991	START 1991 START II 1993	PTBT 1963 NPT 1970
(ii) Conventional			
(iii) Biological	UN–Iraq 1991		BWC 1991
(iv) Chemical	UN–Iraq 1991		CWC 1989
4 Delivery system, e.g.			
(i) ICBMs (land or submarines)			⎫
(ii) Intermediate range missiles		INF 1987	⎬ MTCR 1987
(iii) Aircraft			⎭
5 Conventional forces			
(i) Number of personnel	⎫		CFE IA
(ii) Number of equipment	⎬ Russia		
(iii) Geographical distribution of forces	UK USA ⎭		CFE 1990
6 Arms exports			UN Register 1992
7 Regional agreements			Antarctic Treaty 1961

Notes: For details, see table 11.1.
        PTBT = Partial Test Ban Treaty.
        NPT = Non-Proliferation of Nuclear Weapons Treaty.

signatories); and the South Pacific Nuclear Free Zone Treaty of 1985 (Treaty of Rarotonga: SIPRI, 1993)

At the outset, governments and their arms control negotiators have to decide which aspects of defense expenditure, force structures, and weapons they wish to regulate. Here, problems arise in applying models of the arms race so that they can guide arms control negotiators: what are the likely effects on peace and stability of different types of initiatives and agreements involving, say, manpower or nuclear or conventional equipment? Table 11.2 presents a framework outlining the range of defense variables which could be the focus of arms limitation initiatives and agreements (Sur, 1991a). The possible variables for control include total defense spending, military R & D, type of weapon, delivery system, manpower, exports, and the geographical distribution of military spending. Such variables embrace a variety of different inputs and intermediate outputs, all designed to affect final outputs in the form of peace, protection, and security.

11.6   Some problems for arms limitation: substitution, technical progress, uncertainty and cheating

Economic agents in the military-industrial complex (i.e., armed forces, defense ministries, and contractors) are always seeking alternative ways of ensuring national security, of making money and protecting their incomes and budgets. Thus, a successful arms limitation agreement for one class of weapons might lead to the search for new weapons (via defense R & D) and the continuation of the arms race in new and different forms. For example, controls on nuclear weapons might lead to an expansion of conventional weapons; or controls on cruise and ballistic missiles might lead to the purchase of more bomber aircraft; whilst restrictions on military manpower might lead to the purchase of more equipment [substituting capital for labor (Brito and Intriligator, 1981; Intriligator, 1994)].

Technical progress makes life even more difficult for arms control negotiators. It increases uncertainty so that no one can predict accurately the future. New weapons resulting from *current* military and/or civil R & D could create *future* instabilities and threats to world peace (e.g., MIRV, SDI). Who, for example, in 1930 forecast that within fifteen years, a nation (the USA) would have developed an atomic bomb and that another country (Germany) would have deployed the first genera-tion of cruise and ballistic missiles (V1 and V2 rockets)? However, the major powers are reluctant to include new defense technologies in any arms limitation agreement for fear of losing a military advantage which might threaten national security. It is also possible that nations might sign an agreement knowing that they can break out of it at a later date (Nadal, 1994).

Compliance with arms limitation agreements is also a major problem, which is why nations insist upon adequate verification arrangements. Some agreements are more easily verified. For example, the 1987 INF Treaty can be verified by observing the missiles being destroyed – assuming that both sides have provided accurate data on their stocks. National technologies such as space satellites can also be used to detect cheating and noncompliance. However, the verification problems are much greater where large civil sectors and civil firms are affected by arms limitation agreements, as in the case of chemical weapons. Any country with a chemical industry has a *de facto* chemical warfare potential. The differences between chemical weapons and domestic and industrial chemical products can be small: for example, some fly sprays are derived from technologies similar to those used to produce nerve gas. Understandably, civil firms will also wish to protect legitimate technological and commercial secrets resulting from their R & D activities and will resist verification for fear of industrial espionage. Furthermore, verification can impose substantial costs on firms in the affected area, as they have to deal with the requirements of reporting and site visits (Sur, 1991a, 1992).

Arms limitation agreements and initiatives appear to offer substantial economic benefits. In addition to contributing to a more peaceful world, they can end an arms race. There are also indirect effects as companies associated with the military-industrial complex acquire a culture of dependency on government defense contracts, rather than a culture of enterprise in which firms have to survive in competitive markets; and a culture of dependency could adversely affect an economy's international competitiveness (Melman, 1974). These costs of the arms race show the potential benefits of arms control leading to disarmament: the release of resources for alternative civil uses. But arms limitation agreements are not costless. There are direct costs associated with negotiation, implementation, destruction, and ensuring compliance through verification and inspection, as well as the costs of adjusting to change. Arms limitation agreements which involve high verification, inspection, and destruction costs need to be subject to critical cost–benefit scrutiny to determine that they are worthwhile. For example, with chemical weapons, an elaborate and resource-intensive inspection system might be too costly and a much lower level of inspection could produce substantial savings and make an agreement worthwhile (i.e., where the benefits exceed costs). In other words, a less than complete and comprehensive inspection system might be the best solution (Sur, 1991, part IV). Nor should the environmental costs of destroying weapons be ignored. The destruction of nuclear and chemical weapons involves major environmental problems. At the same time, the business of destroying weapons will create new market and employment opportunities to replace some of the job losses in defense industries. A study of the environmental costs of cleaning up at US military bases due to be closed estimated clean-up costs of some $900 million over the period 1990–5 [e.g., buried ammunition, ground water contamination (CBO, 1992a)].

Table 11.3 *US compliance and inspection costs*

Treaty of agreement	$ million (1990 prices)		
	One-off costs	Annual costs	Annual savings
START	410–1,830	100–390	} 9,000
CFE	105–780	25–100	
Threshold Test Ban Treaty & Peaceful Nuclear Explosions Treaty	85–200	50–100	} 200
Chemical Weapons Agreement	45–220	15–70	
TOTAL	645–3,030	190–660	9,200

Source: CBO 1990.

Some US studies have estimated the costs to the USA of verification and compliance associated with five arms limitation agreements. One study undertaken by the Congressional Budget Office (CBO) analyzed START, CFE, a Threshold Test Ban Treaty, a Peaceful Nuclear Explosions Treaty, and a Chemical Weapons Agreement (all but CFE were between the USA and the former USSR). The cost estimates distinguished between one-off and recurring annual costs. One-off costs included the destruction of equipment and facilities and creating the facilities for on-site inspection: these costs are likely to be incurred over a period of five to ten years from the treaty agreement. Annual or recurring costs, continuing indefinitely, included routine inspections, continuous monitoring of some sites and inspections at sites suspected of hiding treaty limited equipment. The CBO cost estimates for the five agreements are presented in table 11.3. US compliance and inspection costs ranged from $0.6 billion to $3.0 billion for one-off costs and $0.2 billion to $0.7 billion for recurring costs [1990 prices (CBO, 1990)]. More than half the costs were associated with the START Treaty. In return, there will be substantial savings for the USA. The START and CFE Treaties were eventually expected to reduce defense expenditure by at least $9 billion per annum below its 1990 level (CBO, 1990). Further substantial savings were estimated to be available from more nuclear arms control agreements. For example, according to the CBO, a post-START option to reduce the number of strategic warheads to 3,000 might save the USA over $15 billion annually (CBO, 1991).

11.7 The peace dividend

The peace dividend has at least three interpretations:

(i)   A simple reallocation of public expenditure from defense to other budget headings (the uninformed view).

(ii) Perfect substitutability between defense and other economic activities (the simple view).

(iii) It requires a major reallocation of resources involving costs and taking time: adjusting to change is not instantaneous (the informed view).

At least three myths surround the peace dividend. *First*, it is reputed to be large and available instantly. According to this myth, disarmament leads to an immediate peace dividend which can be paid out to the citizens of the disarming nation or used in some other way, such as reducing taxes, paying off the national debt, building or rebuilding infrastructure, funding social services, or it can be transferred to a development fund for developing countries. This naive view treats military expenditure as a category of social spending which can be shifted to another category (e.g. like shifting money from one pocket to another). It ignores the fact that conversion and adjustment requires a fundamental reallocation of resources in the economy, with real adjustments to be made in employment patterns, capital utilization, in the size, structure, and location of industries, and in land use.

The second myth is that the peace dividend will solve a nation's economic and social problems. It might help, depending on the size of the dividend and how it is used. For example, will it be used for public or private consumption or for investment? However, there is a danger that analysis of the relationship between defense spending and poor economic performance will confuse correlation with causation. Even a simple and illustrative model shows that the possible relationship between disarmament and economic performance involves a complex set of linkages, as shown in figure 11.3. At the outset, defense cuts will produce budget savings which may be used to meet alternative demands for government expenditure (e.g. health or eduction) or returned to citizens in the form of lower taxation. These financial adjustments will lead in turn to changes in the flows of real resources of land, labor, capital, and enterprise in the economy. Manpower of varying skills will be released from the armed forces and from defense industries; and capital will also be released in the form of surplus military bases and defense manufacturing facilities. The resources will in most cases initially be unemployed, and then eventually be taken into alternative uses in the public or private sectors (as in the informed view of the peace dividend). The extent to which the peace

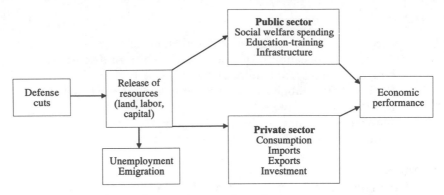

Figure 11.3 Defense and economic performance

dividend is likely to affect a nation's economic performance (employ-ment, growth, inflation, etc.) depends on how it is allocated between the public and private sectors and between investment and consumption. Allocating the peace dividend to private investment in new plant and machinery, or to public investment in education and training (human capital) and infrastructure may be more likely to improve economic performance, particularly growth, compared with expenditure on, say, social welfare payments (although these will contribute to social objectives).

The third myth is that adjustment problems and costs will be relatively small and localized, so that effectively they can be ignored. In fact, adjustment problems and costs may be substantial and long lasting for certain groups and communities likely to lose from disarmament, particularly in a period of recession. Without adequate adjustment policies, such as manpower and regional policies, these groups will suffer significantly from disarmament and could form barriers to change (Paukert and Richards, 1991). The opponents of disarmament will point to continuing security threats in an uncertain world, the employment implications for defense-dependent towns and regions, and the loss of high technology. These groups will seek to persuade vote-conscious governments to modify disarmament policies and to offer compensating work to the worst-affected towns and industries. But other interest groups in the political market place (e.g. education, health, and housing ministries) will favor disarmament as they seek to obtain a share of the expected peace dividend (Hartley, 1991b).

Separating myths from reality, the peace dividend can be viewed as an investment process in which present costs are incurred in the expectation of future benefits (all expressed in present values). On this

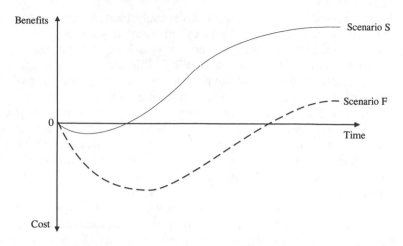

Figure 11.4 Disarmament as an investment process

view, the dividends of peace are likely to be small in the short run and dominated by adjustment costs associated with the reallocation of resources needed to obtain long-run benefits in the form of a larger output of civil goods and services. It is also possible that diminished fears of nuclear war might lead to enhanced savings and therefore more funds available for investment: hence, an unanticipated contribution to the peace dividend (Russett and Slemrod, 1993).

All investments involve possible successes and failures. Two examples are shown in figure 11.4. Scenario S represents a successful investment with low costs and a short adjustment period, followed by large benefits resulting in a high social rate of return from disarmament. The low costs and short adjustment period might reflect the availability of appropriate public policies for reallocating resources with these operating in an expanding economy. Scenario F shows a poor investment involving massive adjustment costs incurred over many years followed by relatively low benefits, so resulting in a low or even negative social rate of return to disarmament. In this scenario, the high costs might reflect an economy which relies on market forces alone, where markets are failing to work properly and the economy is in recession (Intriligator, 1992).

11.8   The role of public policies

Public policies are needed to assist economic adjustment: they help to minimize the costs of adjustment and conversion. Various public policies are available and their use will vary between different types of economies (industrialized market, transitional, centrally planned, developing countries). In formulating public policies, problems arise because of a lack of adequate information. What is known, what is not known, and what do governments need to know for making informed public choices in this area? There is little published data on the size, employment, skill composition, structure, degree of diversification, competitiveness, and location of the world's defense industries and firms (Todd, 1988). For example, what is a defense contractor, what is the network of supplier relationships with prime contractors, how dependent are suppliers on defense contracts, which type of skills are employed by which firms, how marketable are the skills, and how important are defense suppliers and subcontractors in their local labor markets? There is also a lack of information on how easily and quickly different types of defense contractors can switch resources from their traditional defense business to new markets. Often firms have production facilities and workforces which can be used interchangeably between defense and civil contracts (e.g. castings, forgings, aerospace). Similar published information is lacking on the world's defense facilities (military bases), their location and regional importance, and on the skill composition of the world's military manpower (Deger and Sen, 1990a).

Even though information might be limited, there are useful lessons from previous experience. Case studies, for example, show that some proposals for converting industrial capacity from military to civil work (examples have included tank factories producing tractors, aerospace factories producing stainless steel teapots and subway cars) often reflect the triumph of hope over experience. The conversion efforts of major defense contractors have rarely been successful (see chapter 12; Southwood, 1991).

There is also considerable experience of private firms in civil markets in Western economies adjusting successfully to changes in their traditional markets without needing any government support. Examples include the adjustments to the oil price rises of the 1970s and the response of the UK tobacco industry to a decline in its traditional markets, which involved diversification into insurance, engineering, hotels, retailing, etc. On the other hand, there are cases of firms, industries, and communities in Western economies which have not survived change, such as the coal, shipbuilding, steel, and textile industries; as well as cases where governments have not been successful at picking winners (e.g., Concorde). For example, governments in the European Union faced with job losses and unemployment due to industrial and regional decline have adopted a variety of industrial, manpower, technology, and regional policies. The results provide a

Table 11.4 *Public policies*

Types of policies	Examples
1 Manpower Policy	Training; retraining; information; mobility
2 Capital Policy	Retooling old plant-equipment; new investment
3 Technology Policy	New civil R & D programs
4 Regional Policy	Location of industry policy; infrastructure
5 A State Conversion Agency	Assisting the conversion of plants from defense to civil markets
6 Aggregate Demand Policy	Using government expenditure to avoid recessions; tax cuts
7 Income Deficiency Payments	Compensating the losers from disarmament (e.g., unemployment and redundancy pay)

wealth of experience about the efficiency of different policy measures. Some policies toward civil industries failed because they were protectionist, thereby preventing socially desirable change and resource reallocation (e.g. subsidies to preserve inefficient firms: Whiting, 1976).

A variety of public policies are available for assisting an economy to adjust to disarmament. These policies can be classified using a production function approach, as presented in table 11.4 which shows a range of possible policy options with supporting examples. In assessing various adjustment policies (table 11.4), a distinction needs to be made between those public policies which assist a reallocation of resources from the declining defense sector to civilian industries and other regions of the economy, and those policies which prevent change and resource reallocation. State subsidies are a good example. Subsidies for labor retraining, occupational guidance, and geographical mobility are methods of promoting a necessary reallocation of labor resources. In contrast, subsidies which support inefficient firms and are used to preserve the defense industrial base will prevent socially desirable adjustment and could represent a waste of resources. After all, the peace dividend cannot be obtained without a shift of resources from the defense sector to produce a greater output of civil goods and services.

In all economies, the major focus of adjustment is likely to be on how well and how quickly labor markets operate. There are, though, differences between types of economies. In industrialized market economies, labor markets provide price signals (wages and salaries) allocating manpower between different skills, different industries and different regions in an economy. For such economies, a reduced demand for manpower in the armed forces and defense industries will be reflected in job losses and relatively unattractive employment and future income prospects. These changes will affect not only the existing *stock* of workers but also the future *flow* of new entrants. Faced with future defense cuts, school leavers and graduates will undertake training for more attractive alternative occupations in the civil sector. But, of course, there are a variety of labor markets in industrialized market economies, each for different skills, industries, and locations, and they can differ in how well they might work. A satisfactory position in the aggregate labor market might conceal major adjustment problems in a particular town dependent on a defense contractor or on a military base faced with closure. In these circumstances, public policies might aim to improve the operation of local labor markets through manpower policies embracing training, retraining, job information, and labor mobility (Kirby and Hooper, 1991; UN, 1993).

Labor, though, is only one input into the production process. Capital, land, and technology also contribute to the production of goods and services. Once again, in industrialized market economies, market price signals will reallocate resources from defense to the civilian sectors. But left to themselves, private markets might fail to work properly. In such circumstances, state intervention through public policies can correct market failures and improve the operation of markets. For example, public policy might assist the reallocation of capital (plant and equipment) to alternative civilian uses, some of which might necessitate moving to another region (Renner, 1991).

In centrally planned economies, a command system reallocates resources from defense to civil uses. For example, the central plan might require labor and capital to move out of the production of ballistic missiles into the manufacture of consumer durables, such as washing machines, TVs, and refrigerators (see chapter 12). However, problems arise for the economies of Eastern Europe and the former USSR where an adequate system of properly working markets has not yet been established to replace the original centrally planned command system. Such economies will lack the appropriate markets for reallocating the resources released by reduced defense spending. As a result, there are real prospects of a costly and painful adjustment process and a failure to reap the potential benefits of disarmament. To avoid such consequences will require an unusual combination of national economic policies together with technical advice and assistance from other nations and international economic organizations (Cooper, 1991; Paukert and Richards, 1991; Wiseman, 1991).

11.9   Conclusion: some guidelines for adjustment policy

Appropriate adjustment policies are designed to minimize the costs and time involved as the resources released from defense are reallocated to the civilian economy. For all types of economies faced with disarmament, there are some guidelines for adjustment policies:

(i)   Major and rapid reductions in defense spending in recessionary conditions (e.g. large-scale unemployment) with relatively small sums available for retraining and reinvesting in new plant and equipment are likely to contribute to high adjustment costs and a long transition time.

(ii)   Certain types of public policies might actually hinder or prevent a socially desirable reallocation of resources. For example, some subsidies in market and transitional economies can be used to preserve the existing pattern of resource allocation (e.g. subsidies to support declining industries and to prevent change).

(iii)   Long-term gradual reductions in defense spending under conditions of economic expansion with supportive government policies for new investment and for retraining military personnel and defense workers for the civilian economy offer the potential for a high return from disarmament (Fontanel and Ward, 1993).

Viewed as an investment, disarmament offers opportunities and challenges. Not all investments are successful: some fail. Nor is it suggested that disarmament alone will solve all the world's problems; but it can help. Disarmament also represents a challenge to the economics profession. There is a major research agenda on the economics of arms limitation and disarmament, but solutions will require the profession to reallocate its human resources away from alternative uses!

12 Conversion

Disarmament inevitably means a reduced demand for resources in the defense sector. The military will require fewer personnel for its armed forces and will close some of its army, navy, and air force bases and facilities (e.g., communications centers, storage depots, etc.). Similarly, smaller defense industries will require fewer scientists, technologists, and production workers, together with fewer R & D establishments and manufacturing plants. For all societies and economies, the immediate challenge is to transfer successfully resources from the military to the civilian sector. Here, two general solutions are possible. First, the resources can be released and reallocated to other firms and regions in the economy. Second, efforts can be made to use the existing military resources and assets directly in the civilian sphere so that in the limiting case, there would be no job losses and no plant closures. On this view, workers and factories would simply convert their production from, say, tanks to tractors or swords to ploughshares, all at existing locations. Such conversion is attractive: it minimizes dislocations and upheaval caused by plant closures and it provides an opportunity for using apparently valuable human and physical resources which might otherwise be "wasted" through plant closure. But the apparent attraction and appeal of such examples is no substitute for critical economic evaluation and a review of the evidence.

Proposals for direct conversion often ignore the costs involved in discovering and entering new civil markets. Similarly, the fact that resources are valuable in the defense sector does not guarantee their marketability elsewhere in the economy. This chapter starts by presenting a historical overview, it defines conversion and assesses its difficulties; it develops an analytical framework, evaluates the evidence and considers some possible policy options. The focus is on the microeconomics of conversion, although it is recognized that other approaches such as input–output analysis, general equilibrium models, and macroeconomics have been used to forecast conversion impacts (see chapter 11).

12.1   Historical Overview

Conversion is not a new phenomenon. It occurred following the end of both World Wars as economies adjusted from the demands of war to their peace time requirements. Of course, following a major war, there are massive unsatisfied demands for consumer goods and services, as well as opportunities for the civil application of wartime technology. For example, in 1918 at the end of World War I, aircraft firms like Sopwith Aviation (UK) were faced with a drastic contraction of their business: suddenly overnight, no one wanted any more aeroplanes, and the market was saturated with a great stock of surplus wartime aircraft. Sopwith Aviation looked around for things to manufacture – anything to keep the factory going and bring in money to pay the wage bill (a classic short-run response by firms). It built motor cycles under license as well as kitchen utensils and several prototype aircraft, but went into liquidation in 1920 (Bramson, 1990). Other aircraft firms attempted to diversify into motor vehicles and general metal working; one firm produced milk-churns and one turned its hangers over to pig-rearing and mushroom-growing (Hayward, 1989).

In contrast, in 1945, macro- and microeconomic conditions were favorable to conversion. A number of governments were committed to Keynesian aggregate demand and full employment policies and to state intervention in the economy (e.g., UK); there was excess demand for both consumption and investment goods; there was a need to repair war damage and governments were prepared to use their buying power and their power to allocate government contracts to assist resource realloca-tion. For example, the British government assisted conversion by awarding former defense firms contracts for building prefabricated housing and, in some instances, wartime aircraft firms returned to their original peacetime business of manufacturing motor cars. Indeed, in both the UK and the USA after World War II, conversion for many companies meant a return to the pre-war situation (reconversion): such firms were familiar with the enterprise culture with its emphasis on risk-taking and searching for profitable markets (Dumas, 1977). Technolo-gical advances during the war also created new product markets, such as the electrical and electronics sector. In aviation, there were new market opportunities associated with the jet engine and the developing civil aircraft market. As a result of these macro- and microeconomic factors, conditions in countries such as the UK and USA were potentially favorable to conversion, and there is general agreement in the literature that conversion was successfully achieved in the aftermath of World War II (EIU, 1963). For other countries which suffered extensive war damage, such as Germany and Japan, the destruction of defense plants also facilitated conversion.

Not all post-1945 conversions were successful. A classic example of a failed conversion, often cited in the literature, is provided by the attempt of Vickers to convert part of its tank production to tractor manufacture. After World War II, Vickers, Rolls-Royce, and Oldings (UK) agreed on a joint venture aimed at entering the world tractor market which was dominated by American companies. After favorable trials, production was launched in 1952, but the tractors performed unsatisfactorily in service. Efforts to modify and improve the tractors were based on Vickers' experience as tank designers where costs were secondary to performance. Government support during the product development phase was also progressively withdrawn in the marketing phase, and an additional problem was the market domination of US firms (i.e., they had an established reputation). Eventually, Vickers exited the market having learned important lessons about engineering cost control, market analysis and competition in international commercial markets (Scott, 1962). By 1990, Vickers was a diversified group, with defense (tanks) accounting for under 13 percent of its sales and its other activities embracing Rolls-Royce and Bentley motor cars, lithographic printing plates, medical equipment, and marine engineering (Foss and McKenzie, 1988).

In the cold war period 1948–90, specialized defense industry sectors were sustained, often protected and supported by government policies (e.g., aerospace, electronics). Compared with the massive scale of conversion after World War II, the post-1948 defense industries were relatively small and highly specialized, characterized by a culture of dependency [a permanent defense industry (Melman, 1974)]. During the cold war, a number of defense firms diversified into a range of civil activities, often through acquisition. Examples include British Aerospace which in the 1980s acquired automobile, ordnance, and property interests. An example of unsuccessful conversion arose with the American Boeing-Vertol Company which specialized in military transport helicopters. Following the end of the Vietnam War, the company tried to enter the market for light rail vehicles for urban mass transportation. It was believed that Boeing's proven engineering and program management capability in aerospace together with state support would ensure success. In fact, a series of problems arose concerned with derailments, doors, emergency systems, and maintenance features. Boeing failed to solve the technical problems and a legal settlement between Boeing and the operator was agreed, costing Boeing $40 million. Since the technical problems were not resolved, the US operator

(Massachusetts Bay Transportation Authority) sought a foreign source of supply and, shortly afterwards, Boeing exited the light rail vehicle market. The interesting feature of this example is that a highly successful firm in both the military and civil aerospace markets seemed to have underestimated the technical tasks and overestimated its own capabilities (Melman, 1983). Such lessons are of relevance, since, with the ending of the cold war, there is likely to be a reduction in the size and structure of the permanent defense industries throughout NATO and the former Warsaw Pact countries (Ullman, 1970).

Conversion also needs to be seen in its wider context. It is not unique to the defense sector. Firms in the civil economy have to adjust to continuous change and uncertainty. Consumers have changing demands leading to new market prospects (e.g., clothing, fashion, motor cars) and firms either within a country or elsewhere in the world (e.g., newly industrializing countries) are always seeking to respond to changing market opportunities. On the supply side of the market, nations have different comparative advantages and differential access to new technology. Some firms adapt successfully to such changes and hence survive; others fail to adjust and so decline and exit with impacts on their local economies. Regions highly dependent on a single firm or industry which fails to survive are especially vulnerable: examples include coal-mining, shipbuilding, steel, textiles, and defense activities which are often concentrated in one region. In such cases, a failure to adjust or convert has industrial, employment, social, and regional implications (Kirby and Hooper, 1991).

Some companies seek to protect themselves from dependence on the fortunes of one product by diversifying into a range of products, so spreading risks across a variety of markets. The UK tobacco companies are a good example of large diversified enterprises with a wide range of other activities such as engineering, financial services (insurance), luxury consumer products, paper manufacturing, printing, and retailing. In this case, diversification partly reflects the UK industry's response to an actual and expected decline in cigarette smoking, starting with the home market in the early 1960s (e.g., health warnings; higher taxation on cigarettes; restrictions on advertising: Booth et al., 1990). In other words, there are examples of firms which have successfully survived the loss of their major market and such examples provide useful case study material for defense companies facing similar adjustment problems. For defense facilities and defense plants no longer needed by the armed forces and defense ministries, questions arise as to the possibilities for conversion (Lovering, 1993; McFadden, 1984).

12.2   Definitions

What, if any, are the alternative uses for the labor and capital resources currently allocated to, but no longer needed by, the military-industrial complex? The simple answer appears to be to look around to identify the myriad of unsatisfied demands in every nation of the world. There is a massive shopping list of demands for food, health, education, housing and better living standards. Similarly, there is no shortage of challenging scientific problems associated with future energy sources, protecting the environment, reducing illness (e.g., cancer, AIDS), improving food production, space exploration, and assisting the former command economies to become market economies (Wiseman, 1991). But in market economies, firms have to seek profitable opportunities in situations of uncertainty: they are not "guaranteed" profits; and where firms under-invest in socially desirable activities (e.g., basic research), governments might intervene to provide an optimal outcome. Even so, with scarce resources, there will always remain unsatisfied demands. On this basis, defense companies can be viewed like any other company in an economy faced with a declining market in a situation of uncertainty (e.g., bicycles, horse-drawn vehicles, motor cycles; coal, steel; cigarettes; fashion houses which miss this year's fashions). Questions then arise as to whether governments might need to intervene to correct any obvious major market failure (e.g., through manpower and regional policies). Supporters of conversion go further and argue for government involvement in assisting defense plants to convert to the manufacture of civil goods for which there are "obvious" market demands. As a starting point in assessing such claims, the term conversion needs to be defined.

Various definitions have been suggested, including the following:

(a)   **Conversion** involves "developing alternative uses of the work force and facilities currently engaged in military production in advance of changes in policy that may shut down or slow down work at the particular facilities" (Lynch, 1987, p. 13).

(b)   "**Conversion** involves new products for the former defense plants. Examples of successful conversion of defense industrial facilities are few and far between or even non-existent" (Lynch, 1987, p. 29).

(c)   **Conversion** is "the conversion of military capacity to civilian capacity. It implies that the company stops making some military products and changes over to civilian ones. People who were working on military projects then work on civil ones and factory facilities that were being used for military products are turned over to the civil work" (Voss, 1992, p. 1).

(d)   **Economic Conversion** is "the problem of how to adjust the structure of production in the economy – that is the commodity mix of total output – to shifts in the structure of total demand public and private" (Boulding, 1960, p. 848).

(e)   **Reconversion** means "the process by which certain industries, firms and other facilities return to civilian activities after a temporary involvement in military activities due to war or some other national or international crisis" (Southwood, 1991, p. 8).

(f)   **Diversification.** "The entry of a firm into a substantially different business field, either through internal changes or through acquisition, without abandoning its original business field. In the case of military firms, this implies a widening of the base of activity – alternating military and nonmilitary work for unconverted capacity" (Southwood, 1991, p. 9).

For the purposes of this chapter, conversion has at least two interpretations. First, there is the narrow interpretation of converting defense research establishments and plants directly into enterprises undertaking civil research and manufacturing civil goods (and, vice versa, converting civil plants into establishments manufacturing military goods). Effectively, this interpretation requires product substitution in which the same plant and workforce produces civilian products instead of military products (e.g., tanks to tractors). Such product substitution is not possible for the armed forces remaining within the military sector. However, with a change of ownership, there are product substitution possibilities for some of the armed forces defense facilities which can be converted into civilian uses. Military air bases, for example, can be used as civil airports or prisons or as storage facilities (e.g., for agricultural produce). Similarly, military capital in the form of defense equipment such as transport aircraft and armored vehicles have civilian uses (e.g., police forces use armor and rifles).

Second, a broader interpretation of conversion focuses on the process of reallocating resources released from the armed forces and from declining defense industries to the expanding sectors and regions of the economy. This factor reallocation process is occurring continuously in any dynamic economy and its success depends on the operation of the markets for labor and capital and on general state of the economy (e.g., whether it is in recession or prosperity). The broader definition of conversion has its attractions. As will become apparent, to adopt the narrow interpretation, it would have to be concluded that in many cases, conversion will be neither technically nor economically feasible (UN, 1993).

12.3   Reallocating resources

Conversion needs to be seen in the context of the costs of defense cuts. Disarmament involves adjustment costs resulting from the release of resources from the armed forces and from defense industries. A framework showing both the broad and narrow interpretations of conversion as part of the costs of disarmament is presented in figure 12.1. This figure shows the economic impact of defense cuts on the armed forces, on defense industries, and on industries supplying the defense sector, as reflected in the release of manpower, the closure of defense bases and defense plants, and cutbacks in the industries supplying such bases and plants. These effects will have a local or regional dimension. Thus, there are both direct and indirect implications for national economies and there will be further multiplier effects of reduced defense spending (some of which might have serious local impacts).

Questions then arise as to how well and how quickly market and centrally planned or transitional economies can adjust to cuts in defense spending [transitional economies are economies which are abandoning administrative allocative mechanisms and moving to market systems: (UN, 1993)]. Answers to this question influence whether there might be a role for public policy: if so, should policy focus on assisting the reallocation of resources from declining defense sectors to other parts of the economy, or should it assist defense contractors to convert to civil activities? But, as already explained, these adjustment problems are not new, nor are they confined to defense. The civilian economy has a long history of adjusting to change. Moreover, major reductions in defense spending have occurred previously, such as following the end of World Wars I and II (Kirby and Hooper, 1991). However, previous experience might not be useful for the current situation. Defense cuts are now taking place in a situation of peace without a buoyant demand for civilian products in contrast to the situation after World War II. In addition, since 1945 defense firms have become much more specialized, relying on technologies which are less adaptable and useful for civilian purposes so that less product substitution is possible (Renner, 1992).

A framework of the type outlined in figure 12.1 provides a starting point for evaluating the costs and benefits of cuts in defense spending. Some of the policy-relevant questions relating to the adjustment and transition aspects of disarmament can be identified:

(i)   Which industries, regions, and localities are especially vulnerable to cuts in defense spending resulting from disarmament? Cuts will affect firms and industries and their supplier networks dependent on defense markets, and will involve the closure or run-down of

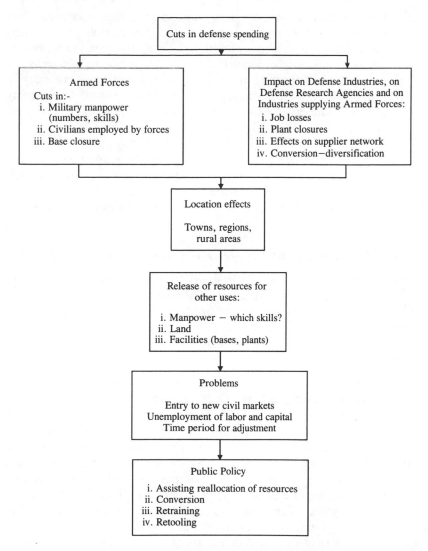

Figure 12.1   Reallocating resources

military bases with adverse impacts on spending power in towns and regions (Braddon *et al*, 1992; Paukert and Richards, 1991; EC, 1992).

(ii)   Which types of labor and skills and in what numbers will they be released by the armed forces, defense industries, and their supplier industries, and where will the employment reductions be located?

(iii)   How marketable are the labor and capital resources which are released? For example, some of the labor skills of military personnel are highly specific with value only to the military, such as torpedo and missile operatives and tank gunners. The value of general skills acquired from military service which may normally be sought by civil industry might be reduced by the sudden availability of large numbers of ex-servicemen on the job market (Hartley and Hooper, 1990). Similarly, some defense facilities such as rocket factories and submarine yards might be highly specific to defense uses, whilst other plant and facilities can be readily and cheaply converted to civil use. Examples include military airfields which can be converted to civil airports and aircraft factories which can manufacture civil airliners instead of combat aircraft (Ball, 1986).

12.4   Conversion in market economies: analysis and experience

Previous experience in the industrialized market economies suggests that very few defense manufacturing establishments will convert in the sense of making fundamentally the same product for a civilian market. Some firms will attempt to use the technology, resources, and skills developed for defense production in new civilian areas. Such efforts will face four major difficulties:

(i)   **Many defense companies are specialists, not used to operating in competitive civil markets**. Their research technology, production facilities, management, workforce, expertise, organization, marketing, and culture are highly specific to defense. The process of obtaining and fulfilling orders, the contract procedures, standards, and all aspects of doing business differ between the defense and civil markets. Some defense companies have become defense specialists because of the benefits of specialization: they are good at defense work, where the culture is different from that in civilian work (see figure 12.2: also Melman, 1971).

(ii)   **The need to identify civil markets and products** which can be made using the management, labor, and capital resources available to specialist defense contractors. What, if any, are the obvious civil market prospects for plants which have specialized in the production of large ballistic rockets?

(iii)   **The need to identify profitable civil markets**. Questions arise as to why, if there are potentially profitable civil markets available to be exploited, existing civil firms have not already moved into these markets. Also, for defense firms, new civil markets have to be

Characteristics of supply: Asset specificity		Characteristics of demand: Dependence on defense sales	
		Low	High
	Low	A relatively easy	B
	High	C	D most difficult

Figure 12.2 A framework for conversion

potentially profitable after incurring entry costs (including retooling and retraining).

(iv) **The difficulty of conversion in a recessionary period**. Even where firms are able to switch their plant and workforce quickly and easily from defense to civil production, they might be prevented by a recession in the civil sector of the economy (Hooper and Hartley, 1993).

12.4.1 An analytical framework

An analytical framework is needed to assess the prospects for converting industrial capacity from military to civil work. Two characteristics are important. First, on the demand side, a firm's dependence on defense sales with reliance on a single customer, noncompetitive cost-based contracts, state-funded research and development, a protected market, guaranteed profits, and a culture of dependency rather than a culture of enterprise (Melman, 1971). Second, on the supply side, a firm's asset specificity in the form of the transferability of its labor, capital, and technology (e.g., dependence on defense-led and defense-specific technology). Some defense technologies have extensive civil applications such as radar, aircraft, and avionics; others have few, if any, direct civil applications such as stealth, armor, and nuclear weapons. Figure 12.2 presents an analytical framework which provides a starting point for assessing the prospects for conversion (Dussauge, 1987). Firms in region A are the ones where conversion is easiest and most likely. In contrast, firms in region D

Table 12.1:*Defense-dependent firms*

Industry/Company	Country	Arms sales ($US million, 1990–1)	Arms sales dependency (%)
Aerospace			
Hindustan Aeronautics	India	500	97
Electronics			
Loval	USA	1,920	90
Land systems			
GIAT	France	1,430	97
Ordnance factories	India	1,430	97
Eidgenossische Rustungsbetriebe	Switzerland	700	95
Israel military industries	Israel	640	98
Ships and sea systems			
DCN	France	3,710	100
VSEL	UK	920	100
Devonport management	UK	470	94

Source: Wulf, 1993, pp. 23–5.

face the greatest difficulties of conversion: defense sales dominate their business, and they depend on defense-specific assets such as defense-led technology which is highly specific to the defense sector [e.g., GIAT and DCN in France, VSEL and Devonport Dockyard in the UK (table 12.1)]. Elsewhere, firms in the B region probably face greater adjustment problems than those in region C simply because of their dependence on the defense market (reflecting the difficulties and costs of entering new civil markets).

This, though, is an area requiring more analytical and empirical work. There are opportunities for applying alternative models of firm behavior in different market structures (e.g., profit, growth, sales, utility-max-imizing, and satisficing models). For example, with utility-maximizing and satisficing models of firm behavior, disarmament might provide a "shock effect," shocking a defense firm into improved efficiency and competitiveness. Similarly, the conversion problem might be modeled as a profit-maximizing discriminating monopoly facing two markets, namely, military and civil. Demand elasticities are likely to differ, with military demand being relatively inelastic. On this basis, a reduction in military demand might be associated with positive, negative, or zero effects on civil market sales, depending on the firm's cost conditions. An inverse relationship between military demand and civil sales requires a profit-maximizing firm to operate under conditions of increasing marginal costs (Cooper, Hartley and Harvey, 1970, p. 56). Such predictions provide a starting point for empirical work. The model also highlights one of the major problems of conversion. It assumes the existence of both military and civil markets when for defense firms there might be major difficulties and costs of identifying and entering appropriate and potentially profitable civil markets.

For specialist defense firms wholly dependent on defense business, direct conversion is technically difficult, costly, and probably not worthwhile. For such enterprises, the plant, equipment, managers, and workforce are highly specific to defense and nontransferable – at least at reasonable cost. In such circumstances, it is probably most efficient to close the specialist defense plant and, if there are willing buyers, redevelop the site for other purposes (e.g., housing; industrial estates shopping centers). Interestingly, outside the former USSR, there are relatively few large arms firms which are highly dependent on defense sales [i.e., 90 percent or more (see table 12.1)].

12.4.2   Problems of conversion

Advocates of direct conversion for specialist defense plants often claim that there are many civil market opportunities available to such firms. Rarely do they address the following problems:

(i)   **Reequipment and retraining**: costs are involved in converting defense plants and retraining the managers, scientists, and the workforce;

(ii) **Entry costs**: there are costs of entering civil markets, with the size of the market being an important factor; and

(iii) **Profitability**: a key question is whether the civil markets are expected to be profitable after bearing the costs of conversion and entry.

If these advocates of conversion are right and there are many opportunities not already being exploited by existing specialist civil firms, then there is the ultimate capital market test, namely, defense firms will be taken over and/or their defense plants and workforce will be marketable for other uses. In other words, when defense plants are offered for sale, they will be bought by firms which believe they can find a profitable use for the assets. Typically, however, what happens is that the original defense plant and its site are redeveloped for more appropriate alternative uses. In the meantime, though, the labor released will either be unemployed and might require retraining, or it will be reemployed elsewhere in the economy [depending on how well local labor markets work (see studies of London, Michigan, Munich and Rome in Paukert and Richards, 1991; also Ball, 1986 and Renner, 1992)].

Contrary to the assumptions of conversion advocates, adjusting to change takes time: it is neither instantaneous nor costless. Much depends on civil market opportunities but, typically, an adjustment period of up to five years might be needed. Nor should the conversion debate be dominated by the large defense prime contractors. For suppliers and subcontractors, direct conversion is less of a problem. Often, these are firms where defense might be only part of their total business and/or the firm's resources could be used flexibly and interchangeably between military and civil work. Examples include foundries, castings, and precision engineering which can produce products for either defense or civil business [e.g.. wings for combat aircraft and airliners, and gear boxes for tanks can be used for tractors and heavy vehicles (Gruneberg, 1994; Hooper and Hartley, 1993)].

Previous experience in the industrialized market economies of North America and Western Europe suggests that very few defense manufacturing establishments will convert in the sense of making fundamentally the same product for a civilian market. Amongst prime contractors, there are sometimes possibilities for direct conversion, using the firm's defense resources to produce civil goods. Aerospace is a good example, where a firm's plant and labor force are transferable and can be used to manufacture either military or civil aircraft, helicopters, aero-engines, and space satellites. Similarly, shipyards can shift from building warships to building merchant ships. Elsewhere, firms have used their military technology to develop new civil businesses such as satellite broadcasting, videophones, and security systems (e.g., GEC-Marconi, UK). Other examples of conversion have been less successful, such as Vickers' (UK) efforts at converting from tanks to tractors after 1945 and Boeing-Vertol's failure to enter the market for light rail vehicles. There are good reasons for such failures. Vickers is a defense specialist able to compete and survive only in its specialist market. Similarly, tractor firms have survived by establishing a competitive advantage in their specialism. If there are profitable opportunities in civil tractor markets, there is every reason to expect the established tractor firms to have identified and exploited such opportunities. Defense firms seeking direct conversion have to identify profitable civil markets which are appropriate for their resources. In many cases, however, the plant, equipment, management, and skills of defense firms are highly specific and nontransferable: hence the need for appropriate retraining and possibly retooling programs for both labor and capital [none of which is free (UN, 1993)].

There is a related cultural adjustment problem for specialist defense firms, particularly those wholly dependent on defense work. Difficulties arise in changing the culture of an enterprise from demanding defense requirements to the different requirements of civil markets. For example, defense products are often of high quality and such products are difficult to sell in civil markets where quality standards are different. Nor is it easy and cheap to identify possible market opportunities. In specialist defense firms, the government dominates and determines the firm's culture and that culture tends to be one of dependence on the government rather than an enterprise culture responsive to changing market demands. It is not unknown for defense contractors in non-competitive markets to be criticized for high costs, cost escalation, delays, unsatisfactory equipment performance, waste and excessive profits (Hartley, 1991a).

12.4.3 Converting defense research establishments

Much of the literature has focused on the conversion of defense industries to the relative neglect of the problems and opportunities for the conversion of specialist *defense research establishments and defense facilities released by the armed forces*. Conversion for defense research establishments raises the usual problems concerned with highly skilled and specialized man-power and defense specific assets, entry costs, and cultural adjustment (UN, 1993). For example, defense scientists and engineers have worked in a culture dominated by secrecy, high technology, and performance requirements, where costs are of secondary importance. However, in terms of possible alternative uses, there is no shortage of high-technology problems requiring scientific manpower. Examples include the environment, future sources of energy, food production in developing nations, and health problems [e.g., cancer, AIDS, etc. (IMPS, 1990)]. Here, there might be a role for government in supporting such civil R & D projects. For example, defense scientists might be offered employment in academic institutions as teachers and researchers, or governments might fund space exploration or the development of the next generation of supersonic airliners (Nadal, 1994; UN, 1993).

12.4.4 Conversion and the armed forces

Experience shows that some surplus military bases have alternative uses. Former military air bases have been converted into civil airports; some have been used as gliding clubs, motor racing circuits, and industrial trading estates; whilst some have been redeveloped as housing estates and shopping centers; and others have been returned to agricultural use.

Questions also arise about the alternative use value of military manpower. Some military personnel acquire skills which are highly marketable and transferable to the civilian economy. Examples include transport aircraft pilots, engineers, computer operators, vehicle mechanics, drivers, military police, and medical personnel. Other military skills are highly specific and not transferable having value only to the armed forces, such as missile operators, paratroopers, and the crews of nuclear-powered submarines. For these groups with nontransferable skills, disarmament renders their human capital obsolescent. Elsewhere, many servicemen, particularly those who enter without formal qualifications, benefit in later civilian life from the training received during military service. Much of the empirical evidence on the civilian employment experience of military personnel relates to US servicemen, where the results are somewhat mixed (Hartley and Hooper, 1990; see also chapter 6). Some evidence suggests that there is little difference between the benefit obtained from military service and that from civilian training. Other studies suggest that the benefits of military training are greater for disadvantaged and minority groups (Browning et al., 1973). The importance of military service and training for future employment and income is also affected by the state of the labor market at the time of reentering the civilian workforce. For example, Vietnam-era veterans reentering the labor force fared less well compared to their nonveteran competitors than those leaving the services after the Korean war. This difference reflected the rapid changes which had occurred in civilian workforce, lost seniority, and the depressed state of the labor market (Berger and Hirsch, 1983; also chapter 6).

12.5   Conversion in other economies: centrally planned, transitional, and developing economies

In principle, conversion in centrally planned economies involves the same issues of reallocating resources from defense to civil activities. However, the allocative mechanisms differ, with market economies relying on private ownership, competition, profitability, and price signals in product and factor markets. In centrally planned economies, allocative decisions involving what to produce and how are made by the state's central planning agency (e.g., the USSR after World War II). However, the former USSR is now in a transitional stage, moving from a centrally planned to a market economy which creates even greater problems for conversion and adjustment to major disarmament. The tasks of creating a private enterprise market economy or converting defense plants are *each* difficult enough. To undertake *both* tasks simultaneously is a major challenge for the former Soviet Union (Bougrov, 1994; Paukert and Richards, 1991; Renner, 1992; UN, 1993; Wulf, 1993a).

Some of the problems of conversion in developing countries will be similar to those in market, centrally planned, and transitional economies. There are, though, some distinguishing features of the problem in developing countries. Typically, developing nations have most of their defense sector employment in the armed forces. Thus, their conversion problems will involve either releasing military personnel on to the labor market or, in the case of conscription, not recruiting labor. In the short run, the result is likely to add to their substantial employment and unemployment problems. In Indonesia, for example, defense spending is more labor intensive than civilian public spending: hence, conversion from military to civil spending would increase Indonesian unemployment in the short term (Wing, 1991). However, those developing countries with centrally planned economies might be able to minimize unemployment by reallocating military personnel to alternative civil occupations. In contrast, those developing countries with market economies might experience greater conversion problems if they have to rely upon limited labor markets which are restricted geographically and which fail to provide information on relative scarcities and appropriate market price signals (i.e., characterized by major market failures).

Some developing countries have a substantial defense industrial base, particularly China, India, Egypt, and Brazil (Renner, 1992). In those countries which have created specialist defense companies and plants, without any civilian activities, conversion is considerably more difficult. An example might be Hindustan Aeronautics, India where arms sales form 97 percent of its total sales (table 12.1). Similar examples have occurred in the former USSR, where the conversion problems are even greater within the "closed cities" which were wholly dependent on military activities (e.g., Chelyabinsk 65, east of the Urals). There is a further dimension for those developing countries with a defense industrial base. Some are amongst the world's largest arms exporters, including China, North and South Korea, Egypt, and Chile. For these countries, the loss of arms exports would have an immediate impact on their ability to earn scarce foreign currency. Also, the loss of its domestic defense industry might be seen as having a major adverse effect on the ability of a developing nation to achieve economic growth through promoting its technology base (Molas-Gallart, 1992). Once again, though, it has to be recognized that for developing countries, there are alternative ways of promoting high technology in the civil sector. Possible examples include support for R & D in the agricultural sector, the development of a civil aircraft industry to improve internal communications and joint R & D projects with industrialized nations (UNDP, 1992; Wulf, 1993a). In all types of economies, there is a potential role for public policies in assisting conversion, in either its narrow or broad interpretations.

12.6   Public policies

Without adequate compensation, interest groups in the military-industrial complex will oppose disarmament. And yet, reallocating resources from defense to the civil sector of the economy is needed to obtain a peace dividend. This raises the more general issue of the role of public policies in assisting change and conversion (see also chapter 11). Welfare economics suggests that socially desirable change requires that the potential gainers from the change be able to overcompensate the potential losers.

There are a range of policy options which might be adopted by international agencies (e.g., UN, IMF, World Bank, EC), and by national, state, and city governments. Of course, governments of different political persuasions will adopt different views on the form and extent of intervention in the economy. The extremes vary between a government which leaves everything to market forces and commercial decisions by profit-seeking firms, and one which intervenes extensively through, say, a state conversion or diversification agency (Hartley and Hooper, 1991b). Here, we return to one of the themes of this chapter, namely, that conversion is a subject dominated by myths and special pleading. There is an absence of good, methodologically sound, analytically and empirically based case studies of conversion, and the policy options (see Hartley and Hooper, 1990). For example, the benefits and costs of conversion (both successes and failures) need to be evaluated against the benefits and costs of policy options such as measures to assist a reallocation of resources, especially labor, to other industries and regions in the economy. In the case of policies aimed at assisting a reallocation of resources, information is needed on how quickly redundant workers obtain new jobs following the closure of a defense plant, the types of jobs obtained, their wages and employment conditions compared with their previous defense work. Experience of adjustment, diversification, and conversion in the civil sector also needs to be evaluated (e.g., local communities in the EU and USA adjusting to the closure of coal mines, shipyards, and steel works). Inevitably, in making such comparisons, questions arise as to whether conversion assistance to defense firms should be treated differently from assistance given to civil firms (i.e., should public policy favor defense firms and workers and, if so, why?).

Within Europe and the USA, various policy-relevant proposals have been made for the conversion of both defense industries and defense-dependent areas. These include (EC, 1992; Willett, 1990; Voss, 1992):

Proposals for alternative uses of vacant sites (e.g., residential, leisure use, food superstores)

The provision of industrial premises

Funds for training of redundant military and civil personnel

Road projects to improve access to an area

Tourism developments

Researching best practice in diversification

Land reclamation

Technology transfer

A greater exchange of knowledge and experience of adjustment and conversion

Offering guidance to management

Promoting increased awareness of existing sources of assistance for new investment, training, and diversification available from the EU, central, and local governments.

Focusing assistance on a small number of firms with high defense dependency and significant employment levels

Creating enterprise zones

Venture capital investments

In Europe, many of the suggestions for conversion have been proposed by the trade unions and socialist parties (e.g., IMPS, 1990). One of the most frequently quoted studies was the Lucas Plan (UK) which was developed by the workforce (Lucas, 1976; Wainwright and Elliott, 1982). Faced with redundancies in the early 1970s, the Lucas Aerospace shop stewards' committee formulated a detailed alternative corporate plan with proposals for a series of new products needed by society and which the company had the skills to produce. In total, there were 150 products ranging from medical equipment, alternative energy technologies, and equipment for the handicapped. Despite its detailed nature, the Lucas Plan was never implemented, mainly because it was "a challenge to the status quo and required external sources of demand and finance" (Willett, 1990, p. 480).

12.7 Conclusion

Conversion offers economists extensive scope for theoretical and empirical research and for critical evaluation. It also poses the challenge of formulating cost-effective policy solutions derived from a methodologically sound research program. This survey has shown that the various ideas for direct conversion are limited and likely to fail because all too often a list of alternative products is provided, spuriously defined as socially useful, determined mainly by the available skills and industrial structures of the existing defense production facilities. Such a supply-side approach ignores the costs of conversion and of entering new civil markets, the problems and costs of changing management culture, the demand side of markets, and the uncertainties associated with the potential profitability of new civil markets. Certainly, there is scope for rigorous case studies of successful and failed conversions, identifying the reasons for success and failure. Not only are such case studies needed for market economies: comparative studies are also needed of Chinese and Russian experience with defense conversion.

IV   New developments and future directions

13 Nonconventional conflict: revolutions, guerrilla warfare, and terrorism

The post cold war era may be quite susceptible to insurgencies, terrorism, and other forms of nonconventional conflict. Consider the breakup of the Soviet Union and the democratization of Eastern Europe, which involves many republics and nations that contain significant ethnic and religious diversity. When this diversity is combined with a record of earlier atrocities committed by subgroups on one another, the ingredients for a violent conflict are present as in Bosnia. Additional risks of conflict stem from the increased arms trade of the 1980s and 1990s that flooded the world with weapons that can be used in insurrections. States bent on destabilizing other nations may view covert low-level operations, such as terrorism, as a cost-effective means for achieving political disruption. Nonconventional conflict may also be tied to population growth throughout much of the Third World that is creating more poverty and ever-increasing needs for resources. As greater demands are placed on forests, rivers, arable lands, oceans, and air, resource shortfalls may result in an impoverishment that causes sufficient discontent to erupt in revolution. Dissatisfied groups may be able to cause great havoc and impose huge costs on a strong government when such groups resort to guerrilla warfare tactics. In fact, small groups may be at an advantage over a much larger opponent when such tactics are used. According to Hirshleifer (1991, p. 178; 1994), a disadvantaged opponent is motivated to apply more effort and to fight more rigorously than its better-equipped adversary. As a result, the returns devoted to the struggle may be greater for the disadvantaged agent(s). Whatever their origins or causes, nonconventional forms of warfare pose a significant risk to individual countries as well as to the world community.

The purpose of this chapter is to provide an overview of the application of economic methodology to the study of nonconventional conflict. In particular, the chapter focuses on the literature that analyzes revolutions, guerrilla warfare, and terrorism. A vast body of literature exists in both economics and political science;[1] hence, this survey must be selective with emphasis on some key pieces and methodologies. The primary focus is on the use of rational-actor models to analyze nonconventional conflict. A rational-actor model depicts an individual or collective as optimizing some goal, usually that of utility or net benefits, subject to a set of constraints that restrict actions. These constraints indicate the limits imposed by resources, laws, institutional rules, or other considerations on the participants. Alteration in these constraints brought about, say, through government policies (e.g., increased security or stiffer penalties) should have a predictable effect on the agent's or optimizer's behavior. In some studies, the optimizing behavior of two or more classes of participants (e.g., terrorists and government) is taken into account, so that a game-theoretic approach is applied.[2]

The application of rational-actor models to the study of nonconventional conflict can throw light on many interesting questions that include the following: What motivates individuals to assume the great personal risks associated with revolution? Why are some revolts successful and others not? Are revolutions predictable? Why do guerrilla wars assume different discrete stages? Should governments precommit never to negotiate with hostage takers? What antiterrorist policies work best? Will antiterrorist policies induce terrorists to substitute between different modes of attack? Should governments share intelligence if they choose not to coordinate their deterrence in curbing terrorism? Why do nations fail to abide by treaties designed to curb terrorism? These and other policy questions have been addressed by the economic literature using a variety of methods. Many of these questions are addressed in this chapter.

13.1   Definitions

At the outset, definitions are required for each of the major terms used in this chapter. These definitions reflect the general use of the terms in the economic literature.

A *revolution* is a sudden change in government or collective choice, not brought about through legitimate institutionalized channels such as election, national succession, or retirement. Timur Kuran (1989, 1991a, 1991b) defined a revolution as a people-supported overthrow of the

---

[1] Lichbach (1992) provides a very comprehensive and up-to-date typology and list of references on the economic literature and literature relating to mathematical and statistical models of political conflict. On the political science literature in terrorism, see Crenshaw (1992) and Wilkinson (1992) for a list of references.

[2] Examples of this strategic interaction can be found in Atkinson, Sandler, and Tschirhart (1987), Brito and Intriligator (1992), Islam and Shahin (1989), Lapan and Sandler (1988, 1993), Scott (1989), and Selten (1988).

political establishment that transforms the social order within a relatively short period of time. An example is the overthrow of the government in Czechslovakia in late 1989 – the so-called Velvet Revolution. Other instances include the subsequent downfall of the governments in Romania, East Germany, and elsewhere in Eastern Europe. Revolutions frequently involve political violence or its threatened use. Any theory of revolution would require much modeling ingenuity to capture the discrete threshold aspects as well as the complex interactive effects among the participants. Revolutions may be solely supported within a country or they may draw resources from abroad.

An *insurrection* is a politically based uprising intended to overthrow the established system of governance and to bring about a redistribution of income. That is, an insurrection is a process by which a political revolution may be achieved. In recent years, the Shining Path has been carrying on an insurrection in Peru. Unsuccessful insurrections have been going on in the Philippines and Colombia during the 1980s and early 1990s. Leaders of an insurrection recruit members from the peasantry or the general population. Successful rebel operations may significantly enhance recruitment efforts and may eventually create a bandwagon effect once beyond a certain threshold of support. If an insurrection is successful and a new ruling coalition is in power, a redistribution of property rights ensues as the winners take from the losers. Dynamic and static considerations are germane and must be delineated when analyzing the interactive behavior of the government and insurgents. Dynamic issues include recruitment, time consistency considerations (e.g., the desirability of precommitting to courses of action), and reputation building, whereas static issues involve short-run optimization on the behalf of the agents. Information is either imperfect or one-sided when characterizing insurrections; e.g., the government may not know the true strength of the insurgents.

Guerrilla warfare is another tactic used by an armed movement to overturn a government for the purpose of political change. In many instances, guerrilla warfare consists of small bands of rebel forces [e.g., the Revolutionary Armed Forces of Colombia (FARC)] that attack superior government armies. These rebel bands attempt to capture and control a sector of the country from which to base their operations. In so doing, the guerrillas force the indigenous population to support logistically their operations. Ideally, the rebels try to recruit members from the territory that they hold. Guerrillas rely on surprise and cover to harass and defeat government troops. This tactic is used in both the countryside and urban centers. Guerrilla warfare is a more pervasive tactic than terrorism as many more people are put at risk.

Terrorism is the premeditated use, or threat of use, of extra-normal violence or brutality to gain a political objective through intimidation or fear. Terrorists frequently direct their violence and threats at a large target group or audience, not immediately involved in the political decision-making process that they seek to influence. Thus, terrorist incidents may injure pedestrians along a crowded street or passengers waiting to check in at an airline counter in an international airport (e.g., armed attacks in the Rome and Vienna airports on December 27, 1985). Terrorists employ a variety of attack modes that include assassinations, skyjackings, threats, armed attacks, kidnappings, and various forms of bombings. Terrorism is a tactic often used in insurrections and, as such, relies more heavily on threats than does guerrilla warfare. Individuals may, of course, resort to terrorism without engaging in an insurrection. For instance, terrorism may be used to publicize a cause (e.g., ending the Vietnam War), to achieve religious freedom, to promote an ideology, or to attain the release of an imprisoned colleague. When a terrorist act in one country involves victims, targets, institutions, governments, or citizens of another country, terrorism assumes a transnational character. Since 1967, *transnational terrorism* has plagued many countries worldwide. Spectacular acts of terrorism [e.g., the downing of Air India flight 182 (with 329 people aboard) over the Atlantic Ocean on June 23, 1985, or the downing of Pam Am flight 103 (with 270 deaths) over Lockerbie, Scotland, on December 21, 1988] capture media attention worldwide, thereby publicizing the terrorists' cause. Terrorist campaigns succeed if terrorists convince the government that the costs from capitulating are less than those from not capitulating.

Inasmuch as the legitimacy of any government depends, in large part, on its ability to safeguard the life and property of its constituency, terrorist groups that can strike at will, aided by surprise, pose a serious threat to political stability. If terrorists exert sufficient pressures on a duly elected government to capitulate to their demands, democratic principles are compromised, insofar as an unelected minority has altered policy without a voters' mandate. A democratic government must respond with care: if it uses too much force to repress the terrorists, then the government may lose popular support. But it may also lose that support if it uses too little force to gain control of the situation.

13.2   Revolutions and insurrections

The literature on revolutions and insurrections is vast and includes works from sociology, political science, public choice, and economics. In sociology and political science, a debate has raged between the rationalists and the structuralists (Taylor, 1988). The rationalists view participants in an uprising as rational actors who weigh the expected benefits and expected costs from their participation. In essence, the rationalists are employing economic methodology drawn from public choice to explain why an individual might assume great risk when engaging in revolutionary activities. A collective action problem arises as potential participants must overcome an incentive to free ride, since, once a political upheaval is achieved, everyone who wanted the change experiences the gain. That is, the overthrow of a political system provides benefits that are nonrival and nonexcludable, so that a public good is provided. The question remains: Why assume the great personal risk associated with revolutionary activities if the resulting benefits from a successful revolution are nonexcludable? Moreover, collective action that requires a large number of participants, as is the case for mass-supported revolutions, is not usually anticipated to materialize unless special circumstances are present (Berejikian, 1992; Olson, 1993; Sandler, 1992). For example, private benefits must be obtained by revolutionary leaders, who then motivate others to join.

In contrast, the structuralists (e.g., Skocpol, 1979) view the institutional environment as the crucial consideration for understanding the revolutionary process. A structuralist characterizes many societies as having the potential for revolution if a sizable portion of the population is dissatisfied with the ruling authority. What this majority needs is the opportunity or leverage to confront the rulers. Circumstances that weaken a government or draw its attention elsewhere may give aggrieved masses the opportunity they need to revolt successfully. Michael Taylor (1988) has argued that a theory is required that combines rationalist and structuralist elements. Recently, Berejikian (1992) has attempted such a synthesis by including the notion of framing to account for a participants' perception of expected gains and losses from revolutionary activities. In short, Berejikian (1992) indicated that risk attitudes may vary depending on the *initial* social state and, hence, whether gains or losses are anticipated. Although the structuralists raise some intriguing issues, our review, henceforth, concerns the rationalists.

13.2.1   Revolution participation

Tullock (1974) drew on Olson's (1965) seminal work on collective action to answer the question concerning why individuals participate in a revolution. In particular, Olson indicated that selective or private incentives that accompany a collective good may be sufficient to induce an individual to join the revolution. Since private incentives are excludable, they are not available to the nonparticipants. Successful revolutionaries can help themselves to the spoils, or else can occupy positions in the new government.

In the Tullock model, a representative revolutionary gains satisfaction from both a successful outcome and his or her participation. The overthrow of the government gives a collective benefit to everyone, while participation yields private benefits to the rebels. Of course, an individual's perceived benefits must be weighed against anticipated costs when deciding whether to participate.

Each participant contributes e^i units of effort, which can be measured in terms of the time devoted to revolutionary activities. The probability, θ^i, of a successful revolution increases with the effort of the individual and with the cumulative effort, $\tilde{E}$, of the other $n-1$ revolutionaries, where $\tilde{E} = \sum_{j \neq i}^{n} e^j$, so that

$$\theta^i = \theta^i(e^i, \tilde{E}), \tag{13.1}$$

with $\theta_1^i = \partial\theta^i/\partial e^i > 0$ and $\theta_2^i = \partial\theta^i/\partial\tilde{E} > 0$. In (13.1), one's own effort is not necessarily a perfect substitute at the margin for that of others since θ_1^i need not equal θ_2^i. A variety of different forms for (13.1) could be allowed, including that in which perfect substitution among effort levels occurs so that $\theta^i = \theta^i(E)$ with $E = e^i + \tilde{E}$. The number of participants could be added as another argument, or the probability function could be allowed to change once a threshold level of participation is reached. If the revolution succeeds, the ith agent (rebel) receives a fixed benefit of B^i. Despite the revolution's outcome, the agent obtains a private benefit of u^i that depends positively on his or her own effort and that of the collective. Other private benefits, contingent on success and the rebel's level of effort, could be included, but would not alter the basic results derived below for risk-neutral individuals.

On the cost side, each rebel can be penalized F^i if caught in revolutionary activities. The probability of capture, ϕ^i, is dependent on one's own effort, the effort of others, and the policing resources, R, of the government

$$\phi^i = \phi^i(e^i, \tilde{E}, R), \tag{13.2}$$

with $\phi_1^i > 0$, $\phi_2^i < 0$, and $\phi_3^i > 0$. The probability of apprehension falls with an increase in the participation of others, since there is safety in numbers. If, for example, a bandwagon effect occurs and revolutionary activities expand, an individual may increase his or her own effort as the marginal risk of apprehension declines. When the government expends more resources to repress and monitor, the likelihood of capture increases. The revolutionaries also experience an opportunity cost equal to foregone earnings, we^i, where w is the wage rate per unit of effort, when participating in antigovernment activities. The model could be expanded to include legitimate nonviolent protest and illegitimate violent protest (Ehrlich, 1973; Chalmers and Shelton, 1975; Sandler *et al.*, 1987). Each activity would then have its own price and payoff, so that a substitution effect would be anticipated as the relative prices change owing to government policy or environmental factors. Ironically, if the government were to increase its repression of nonviolent demonstrations, this action would, *ceteris paribus*, lower the relative price of violent acts and encourage more revolutionary activities.

With just violent acts, the risk-neutral rebel chooses e^i to

$$\text{maximize} \left\{ \theta^i(e^i, \tilde{E})B^i + u^i(e^i, \quad \tilde{E}) - \phi^i(e^i, \tilde{E}, R)F^i - we^i \right\}, \quad (13.3)$$

where $\tilde{E}$, B^i, F^i, and w are exogenous. For an interior solution, the first-order condition is

$$\theta_1^i B^i + u_1^i = \phi_1^i F^i + w, \quad (13.4)$$

where the *sum* of the rebel's marginal expected collective benefit and the marginal participation benefit equals the *sum* of the marginal expected penalty cost and marginal participation cost.

Comparative statics follow directly from differentiating (13.4) and solving for the requisite partial derivatives using standard techniques. An increase in collective benefits or the rebellion level of others will augment the ith rebel's optimizing level of revolt, whereas an increase in the penalty or the wage rate will reduce the rebel's optimizing level of revolt. If an agent is a leader, then his or her marginal expected benefits from participation are larger than those for followers, since θ_1^i and u_1^i are apt to be larger. Thus, leaders are expected to be more active than the average member, provided that wages do not vary between followers and leaders and the probability of apprehension does not increase too greatly with individual effort. If personal participatory benefits are positively dependent on government repression, then increased repression may augment rebellion if a rebel gains sufficient satisfaction from challenging an unjust or tyrannical government. The model can be extended in a number of directions; e.g., risk attitudes may include risk-loving or risk-averse agents. As the complexity of the model increases, comparative static changes tend to become ambiguous owing to opposing influences.

Perhaps the most interesting question posed by the participation decision concerns whether to participate at all. That is, the corner solution of no participation is relevant when expected marginal costs exceed expected marginal benefits at all levels of individual effort. This follows because θ^i and u^i are apt to be very small, except for leaders, so that expected marginal benefits may be tiny. In a large-scale uprising, a person may view his or her own efforts as having no effect on revolutionary success, so that θ_1^i is zero. If penalties are severe and/or wages are sufficiently high, most dissatisfied persons may not participate. A classic collective action problem arises, as the average citizen is apt to gain a very small share of the benefits (i.e., B^i is small) from a successful revolution, but, if caught, will be made to pay dearly. Mass uprisings are not adequately explained by the Tullock (1974) theory, because band-wagon effects and other dynamic aspects are not captured. Another problem concerns the one-sidedness of the theory, because the government side of the interaction is not presented and integrated with the choices of the revolutionaries. Moreover, the equilibrium presented is partial, based solely on the viewpoint of a representative individual. Leaders and followers are not distinguished, and a Nash equilibrium that accounts for the interaction both within and between these groups of participants is not addressed.

Another static approach to the participation decision is based on Becker's (1968) and Ehrlich's (1973) contributions on the economics of crime. A state preference approach is used in which an individual must allocate effort among three activities: consumption (c), a legal activity (l), and an illegal activity (i). The illegal activity may be revolutionary actions, criminal activity, or terrorism (Landes, 1978; Sandler and Scott, 1987). Suppose that the returns, W_l and W_i, from legal and illegal nonconsumption activities, respectively, increase with effort, e, or time spent in that activity (Ehrlich, 1973). An individual can divide his or her total time, E, among the activities, so that

$$E = e_l + e_i + e_c, \tag{13.5}$$

where subscripts indicate the activities and e_c, in particular, denotes time spent in consumption.

Suppose further that the illegal activity is risky with two possible outcomes: apprehension and punishment with probability p_i, and success with probability $1 - p_i$. Denote the first state as a and the second state as b. In state a, the agent suffers a penalty of $F(e_i)$, which depends on the level of illegal activity. If the individual succeeds with his or her illegal activities, then he or she receives

$$X_b = W' + W_i(e_i) + W_l(e_l), \tag{13.6}$$

in which W' indicates assets not dependent on legal or illegal activities. If, on the other hand, the individual is apprehended, then he or she receives

$$X_a = W' + W_i(e_i) + W_l(e_l) - F(e_i). \tag{13.7}$$

In choosing a time allocation, the individual maximizes expected utility,

$$EU = (1 - p_i)U(X_b, e_c) + p_iU(X_a, e_c), \tag{13.8}$$

subject to equations (13.5)–(13.7), where E is the expectations operator and U is utility. Becker (1968) and Ehrlich (1973) demonstrated that whether offenders specialize in illegitimate endeavors depends on risk attitudes and relative opportunities in legitimate activities. From the first-order conditions associated with the constrained optimization problem, an *offense function* is derived that relates the number of offenses to the following independent variables: the probability of success, the average penalty, wealth differentials among activities, environmental factors, and other considerations. The offense function is analogous to a supply function. Although the Becker–Ehrlich approach has generated many interesting insights and results, it shares many of the same weaknesses as the Tullock (1974) model. Unlike the latter model, the Becker–Ehrlich approach does not take into account the collective action aspects.

13.2.2 The Kuran approach

Timur Kuran (1989, 1991a, 1991b) offered a model that provides insights into the unpredictability of revolutions, while accounting for the bandwagon effect that often characterizes rebellions. Kuran relied on preference falsification as a foundation for his analysis of the unpredictability of revolutions. According to Kuran (1989, 1991b), people may have two sets of preferences: (1) their true private preference, which is fixed at a point in time, and (2) their public preference, which is variable. The individual's choice for his or her public preference depends on his or her valuation of reputation and his or her valuation of integrity. Reputation is solely dependent on public preference, while integrity is dependent on the "distance" between his or her true preference and the preference that he or she reveals publicly when preference falsification occurs. As public opposition to an autocratic government grows, dissatisfied individuals may place greater importance on integrity and "come out of the closet" by revealing their true preference for change. That is, integrity considerations may outweigh reputational factors once a certain threshold of opposition is achieved. The benefits from revolutionary involvement are positively related to the size, n, of the revolutionary collective. For each potential rebel, the size of n corresponds to when the threshold of participation is first ascertained; that is, the smallest n for which $e_i > 0$. Individuals are then ordered according to these thresholds; agents whose thresholds are the smallest are first in the ordering. Suppose that the threshold sequence is $S^1 = \{0, 2, 2, 3, 4, 5, 6, 7, 8, 10\}$ for a population of ten, in which each number denotes the threshold size of the revolutionary group before the relevant individual opposes the government. Thus, individual 1 has a threshold of 0 so that he or she participates regardless, while individual 10 never participates. Individuals 2 and 3 revolt once the revolution includes at least two people; individual 4 joins once the revolution grows to three or more; and so on.

With sequence S^1, an equilibrium exists with just one revolutionary because individual 2 onward will not join unless the revolt includes more than just one individual. If, however, an exogenous or structural change occurs (e.g., higher inflation or reduced freedoms) that were to lower individual 2's threshold to 1, then S^1 would imply a bandwagon effect that stops at a new equilibrium with nine revolutionaries (Kuran, 1991a, p. 122). This follows because once individual 2 joins, individual 3's threshold is then met. With three rebels in the movement, individual 4's threshold is obtained. This process continues until individual 9 enlists and a new equilibrium is obtained. Threshold sequences with numbers clustered together are conducive to this bandwagon effect. In the case of S^1, revolutions may be set off by a small precipitating cause. Since people falsify their true preference prior to attaining their threshold level, revolution may be difficult to anticipate even though it may take little to set things off. With sequence $S^2 = \{0, 1, 6, 7, 7, 7, 7, 9, 9, 10\}$, a revolution may be difficult to start owing to the large thresholds needed before a bandwagon effect occurs. For larger and more diverse populations, threshold sequences may show little clustering. The distribution of preferences over the population becomes a crucial consideration when analyzing the bandwagon phenomenon.

13.2.3   A general equilibrium analysis of insurrections

The above models focused on the participant's decision regarding his or her allocation of time to rebellion. Obviously, a more complete analysis must also include the incumbent government's decisions regarding deterrence and other choice variables within an interactive framework with the choices made by the rebels. That is, the choices of the government must be conditional on the optimizing choices of the insurgents, and the choices of the insurgents must be conditional on the optimizing choices of the government. When these choices are modeled in an internally consistent framework that accounts for strategic interactions among agents, a general equilibrium analysis has been formulated. In the nonconventional conflict literature, such strategic interactions are accounted for by Brito and Intriligator (1992), Grossman (1991, 1992), Intriligator and Brito (1988), Kirk (1983), Lapan and Sandler (1988, 1993), Sandler and Lapan (1988), Sandler, Tschirhart, and Cauley (1983), and Selten (1988). An all-important modeling decision concerns the manner in which to depict the strategic interaction. A number of possibilities exist. For static models, Nash behavior is frequently assumed so that each agent optimizes simultaneously, while assuming that his or her counterpart uses a best-response level. A second alternative is that of leader–follower in which the leader moves first and the follower second. In this framework, the follower's Nash reaction path, as derived from his or her first-order conditions, is first found, and then the leader uses the follower's reaction path as a constraint along with the leader's resource constraints.

To illustrate a representative general equilibrium model, we focus briefly on Grossman's (1991, 1992) model of insurrections and income appropriation. Because we only have space to give the general setup of the model, the interested reader is encouraged to consult Grossman (1991, 1992) for solutions and further interpretations. Unlike the models discussed above, Grossman (1991) was not interested in the collective action aspects of insurgencies.[3] Thus, the private returns of the insurgents were the motivating force; collective benefits and free-riding considerations were ignored. Grossman considered two sets of participants: a ruler who moves first in terms of decision variables, and the peasants who move second. A noncooperative solution was derived for this one-shot game in which Grossman (1991) viewed an insurrection as a means for redistributing property rights from the ruler (and his or her "parasitic clientele") to the successful insurgents. The ruler's entire income, collected from tax receipts, is captured by the rebels if the insurrection succeeds. A failed insurgency gives the rebels nothing.

A peasant family divides its time over three activities: soldiering, production, and rebellion. Following Grossman (1991, 1992), the *fractions* of the family's time devoted to the activities are as follows: l to production, s to soldiering, and i to insurrections. For the entire population, the nonnegative fractions of time that peasant families devote on average to each activity is denoted by capital letters L, S, and I, respectively. Since insurrections and soldiering do not add to output, Pareto-optimal allocation corresponds to $(L, S, I) = (1, 0, 0)$, which requires $(l, s, i) = (1, 0, 0)$ for all peasants.

The ruler lives on tax revenues, r, that derive from a fraction, x, of the total output. The production technology is linearly dependent on labor

---

[3]   Thus, Grossman (1991, 1992) contrasts with Kuran (1989, 1991a, 1991b), Roemer (1985), Tullock (1974), and others.

time, L, whereas production per family is λL, where λ is a positive measure of productivity.[4] To stay in power, the ruler must protect against insurrection by raising an army; hence, the ruler must pay each peasant family ws in soldiering fees, where w is the wage rate of soldiering. If the probability of a successful insurrection is denoted by β, with $0 \leqslant \beta \leqslant 1$, then the ruler receives $r - wS$ with probability $1 - \beta$ and zero otherwise. Hence, the ruler's maximand is his or her expected income, M

$$M = (1 - \beta)(x\lambda L - wS). \tag{13.9}$$

The representative peasant's net income from working is $(1 - x)\lambda l$. In contrast, soldiering and revolting yield an uncertain payoff depending upon the outcome of the insurrection. Soldiering gives either ws with probability $1 - \beta$ or zero with probability β; insurrection activities give either zero with probability $1 - \beta$ or ri/I with probability β. In this representation, *only* the participants to the rebellion are rewarded based upon the family's share of the total time spent in rebellion. Each family chooses l, s, and i to

$$\text{maximize } [(1 - x)\lambda l + (1 - \beta)ws + \beta ri/I], \tag{13.10}$$

subject to the time constraint

$$l + s + i = 1. \tag{13.11}$$

When finding the first-order conditions associated with (13.10)–(13.11), corner solutions must be considered, since the peasant family would devote none of its time to an activity whose expected payoff is less than the expected payoff from either of the other activities. Furthermore, the peasant family would allocate all of its time to any activity whose payoff was strictly greater than those of the alternative activities.

To characterize the ruler's problem, Grossman (1991) assumed the following technology of insurrection

$$\beta = \frac{I^{1-\gamma}}{S^{\sigma} + I^{1-\gamma}} \quad 0 \leqslant \gamma < 1, \quad 0 < \sigma < 1, \tag{13.12}$$

which relates the probability of success to a ratio relating insurrection time to soldiering and insurrection time. The resulting ratio varies between zero and one.

Because the ruler was assumed to choose his or her policies prior to the peasants' choice, a leader–follower interaction was hypothesized by Grossman. That is, the ruler must choose x, w, and S to maximize his or her expected income in (13.9) subject to the technology of insurrection

---

[4] All peasants are assumed identical; hence, the ruler only needs to optimize with respect to the average or representative net benefit derived per peasant family.

and to the first-order conditions associated with the peasants' optimization. This problem is identical to that of choosing L, S, and I to maximize expected income M subject to $L + S + I = 1$, where L, S, and I are related to x and w via the first-order conditions for the peasants. Moreover, the technology of insurrection relates β to S and I. Grossman (1991) used the Kuhn–Tucker conditions to indicate that "equilibria with more time allocated to insurrection and a higher probability of a successful insurrection have a lower production and total income but nevertheless can have higher expected income for the peasant" (p. 912). The ruler's choice of a tax rate implies an important tradeoff between the treasury and the financing of soldiering on one hand and the increased incentive to rebellion on the other.

In a follow-up study, Grossman (1992) included foreign aid flows to the country confronted with political instability. Ironically, foreign aid was shown to *augment* the threat of an insurrection, because the rebels stand to gain more from a successful takeover. If the ruler is to limit somewhat the likelihood of an insurrection, then he or she must redistribute some of the foreign aid to the subjects – i.e., an important tradeoff between the ruler's needs and those of the subjects again exists.

Although the Grossman (1991, 1992) analysis highlights important allocative and distributive effects of insurrections, many important considerations are not addressed. First, the model does not really capture the bandwagon effect that often characterizes insurrections. Second, the model is static and does not allow for dynamic considerations. The accumulation and distribution of wealth by the ruler is really a stock problem and, as such, should allow for income flows and past accumulations. To capture the accumulation and distribution of wealth, the researcher needs to formulate a dynamic representation. Moreover, the growth of rebel forces is inherently dynamic in which past successes against government forces may augment the rebel's ability to attract recruits. Third, information is unlikely to be complete. One or both sides are apt to be uninformed about crucial aspects of the confrontation, including the allocative decision of the opposing side. Fourth, other types of strategic interactions need to be investigated.

13.3 Guerrilla warfare

In a conventional war, opposing forces face off against one another along a *front*. If one side can break through, then the other will be at a decided disadvantage. For conventional warfare, the strength per mile of the perimeter or front is an important variable when determining the relative strengths of the opposing sides. Geographical factors (e.g.,

mountain ranges and passes, rivers, and oceans) are a crucial consideration. In contrast, guerrilla warfare often involves small bands of forces
that hide within a nation's borders and use the tactic of surprise to strike
at superior governmental regulars. The notion of a front loses its
importance when analyzing the initial stages and tactics of guerrilla
warfare. Three classes of participants are involved: the government, the
guerrillas, and the peasantry. Both the government and guerrillas are
competing for supporters from the peasant population. The government
draws its soldiers from the peasant population in the territory not
controlled by the guerrillas, while the guerrillas recruit their forces from
the territory that they control.

Brito and Intriligator (1992) characterized guerrilla warfare as consisting of three stages. In the first, the guerrillas attempt to raise a
formidable force. The second stage involves a stalemate in which the
guerrillas try to establish a territorial base from which to launch
operations. In the third, the guerrillas grow to sufficient strength to
mount conventional attacks. If the guerrillas can apply sufficient pressure
on the government, then the latter may collapse. In three papers, Brito
and Intriligator put forth models that correspond to each of these three
stages: the Intriligator and Brito (1988) paper concerns the first; Brito
and Intriligator (1989) the second; and Brito and Intriligator (1992) the
third. Their analysis is noteworthy because it is dynamic and includes
strategic interactions among participants. Information is, however,
assumed to be complete. We briefly present elements of Intriligator and
Brito (1988) and refer the interested reader to this series of papers for
extensions and other issues.

To characterize the initial stages of guerrilla warfare, Intriligator and
Brito (1988) combined features of the Lanchester model of tactical
warfare (see chapter 4) and a model of predator–prey interaction. This
representation of guerrilla warfare is only concerned with the dynamic
recruitment function or transition equations for the guerrillas, the
soldiers, and the size of the populace controlled by the guerrillas. Each of
these variables are denoted by:

$x_1(t)$ = the number of guerrillas at time t;
$x_2(t)$ = the number of regular soldiers at time t; and
$x_3(t)$ = the size of the population under guerrilla control at
time t.

Guerrilla recruitment is dependent on the interaction between the
guerrillas and the population that they control, whereas guerrilla losses
are determined by the interaction between guerrillas and the government
regulars. The time rate of change for guerrilla forces can be represented as

$$\dot{x}_1 = \alpha x_1 x_3 - \beta x_1 x_2 = (\alpha x_3 - \beta x_2)x_1, \tag{13.13}$$

where α and β represent positive parameters. In (13.13), the time rate of change for guerrillas ($\dot{x}_1 = dx_1/dt$) increases with the population under their control and decreases with the size of government forces. In the case of soldiers, the time rate of change is

$$\dot{x}_2 = (\gamma - \delta x_1)x_2, \tag{13.14}$$

where γ and δ are positive parameters. In (13.14), the time rate of change of regular forces is positively dependent on the stock of soldiers and negatively related to the interaction between guerrillas and regulars. Inasmuch as the government possesses the authority to raise forces, its power alone, as reflected by its forces, and not its interaction with the population, determines its recruitment ability. Finally, the time rate of change for the population under rebel control is

$$\dot{x}_3 = \varepsilon x_1 - \lambda x_2, \tag{13.15}$$

where ε and λ are positive parameters. The rate of change of this population depends positively on the guerrilla forces and negatively on the government forces.

To display the underlying dynamics, Intriligator and Brito (1988) derived a phase diagram for the three differential equations. First, they determined the steady-state locus where $\dot{x}_1 = 0$ and $\dot{x}_2 = 0$ for nonnegative values of x_1 and x_2, respectively. By (13.13), we have

$$\dot{x}_1 = 0 \quad \text{if } x_2/x_3 = \alpha/\beta \equiv \alpha' \tag{13.16}$$

for $x_1 > 0$; and by (13.14), we have

$$\dot{x}_2 = 0 \quad \text{if } x_1 = \gamma/\delta \equiv \gamma' \tag{13.17}$$

for $x_2 > 0$. The critical ratios, α' and γ', correspond to recruitment-to-loss rates. Ratio α' denotes the critical ratio of soldiers to population for there to be no change in the guerrilla camp; similarly, the ratio γ' indicates the critical size for the guerrilla force for there to be no change in government forces. Equations (13.13)–(13.15) imply the following behavior on either side of the steady-state loci

$$\dot{x}_1 \gtrless \quad \text{if } x_2/x_3 \lessgtr \alpha' \tag{13.18}$$
$$\dot{x}_2 \gtrless \quad \text{if } x_1 \lessgtr \gamma'. \tag{13.19}$$

Second, Intriligator and Brito (1988) used the information in (13.16)–(13.19) to derive the phase diagram in figure 13.1, where guerrillas are measured on the horizontal axis and government regulars on the vertical axis. The vertical line at $x_1 = \gamma'$ indicates the steady-state locus $\dot{x}_2 = 0$,

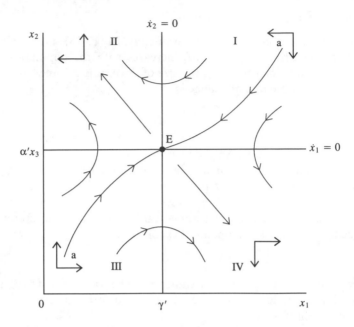

Figure 13.1 Phase dynamics of predator – prey guerrilla warfare model

while the horizontal line at $x_2 = \alpha' x_3$ depicts the steady-state locus $\dot{x}_1 = 0$. To the left of the $\dot{x}_2 = 0$ locus, $x_1 < \gamma'$ so that $\dot{x}_2 > 0$ by (13.19), while to the right of this locus, $x_1 > \gamma'$ so that $\dot{x}_2 < 0$ by (13.19). By (13.18), $\dot{x}_1 < 0$ (>0) above (below) the $\dot{x}_1 = 0$ locus for x_3 given at a point in time. In figure 13.1, the arrows in each quadrant indicate qualitatively the dynamics. Thus, in quadrant II, guerrilla forces decline to zero and government regulars grow until the guerrilla movement is crushed. In quadrant IV, the guerrillas achieve victory as the opposite dynamics occur. A stable equilibrium at E (see path aEa) may result when starting in quadrant I or III. Conflict neither escalates nor declines at the steady-state equilibrium. Instability may, however, occur in these quadrants if the trajectory crosses into either quadrant II or IV.

The likelihood of a victory for the government depends, in part, on the magnitude of γ'. If γ' increases so that the government recruitment parameter increases relative to the loss rate of regulars, then the size of quadrant II expands and this augments the chances of a government victory. Similarly, a fall in α' is conducive to a government victory. A host of different cases are possible. For example, the guerrillas can improve their fortunes by decreasing their loss rate β, increasing their recruitment rate α, or increasing the population that they control. The critical ratios in the Intriligator–Brito analysis bear a similarity with Kuran's thresholds. Moreover, the unpredictability of the outcome in the Intriligator–Brito study resembles that in Kuran (1989, 1991a).

In their other analyses, Brito and Intriligator (1989, 1992) investigated the other stages of guerrilla warfare. These subsequent models also include objective functions for the participants, so that the transition equations, which account for recruitment and losses in forces, serve as constraints. In this latter analysis, Brito and Intriligator also accounted for strategic interactions among the participants. To date, these two authors' models are the best examples of dynamic representations of nonconventional warfare. Nevertheless, their analysis could be improved. In the predator–prey model above, the parameters could be made endogenous. For example, the recruitment rate might depend on the size of the guerrilla force or the level of success achieved in guerrilla operations. Some uncertainty could be introduced and alternative forms of strategic interaction used.

13.4   Terrorism: background

Terrorism is an activity that has probably characterized modern civilization from its inception. In the last quarter century, however, terrorist activity has taken on an important, novel dimension. As advances in technology, transportation, and communication have made the world a global community, terrorism has become transnational in character. Transnational terrorist incidents involve perpetrators, institutions, boundaries, civilians, or government participants from two or more nations. The kidnappings of Americans and other Westerners from the streets of Beirut by Hezbollah or the Revolutionary Justice Organization are examples of this. Other examples include armed attacks at international airports, assassinations of diplomats on foreign soil, the takeover of an embassy, or the bombing of multi-national corporate headquarters.

Since the late 1960s, a number of data sets have been assembled concerning transnational terrorism. The most complete data set is that of the US State Department (see, for example, US Department of State, 1986, 1993); but it is not available to researchers. RAND also maintains a data set of significant incidents and has made it publicly available in recent years. Edward Mickolus (1980, 1982) developed a data set, *International Terrorism: Attributes of Terrorist Events* (ITERATE) for 1967–77, which was extended by Mickolus, Sandler, Murdock, and Fleming (1989) to cover 1978–87.[5] More recent updates include 1988–90.

---

[5]   Verbal descriptions of the incidents in the data set are found in Mickolus, Sandler, and Murdock (1989).

The working definition of transnational terrorism used by ITERATE is the use, or threat of use, of anxiety-inducing, extranormal violence for political purposes by any individual or group, whether acting for or in opposition to established governmental authority, when such action is intended to influence the attitudes and behavior of a target group wider than the immediate victims and when, through the nationality or foreign ties of its perpetrators, through its location, through the nature of its institutional or human victims, or through the mechanics of its resolution, its ramifications transcends national boundaries.

The ITERATE data set does not classify incidents as terrorism that relate to declared wars or major military interventions by governments, or guerrilla attacks on military targets conducted as internationally recognized acts of belligerency. If, however, the guerrilla attacks were against civilians or the dependents of military personnel in an attempt to create an atmosphere of fear to foster political objectives, then the attacks are considered terrorism. Official, government-sanctioned military acts in response to terrorist attacks, such as the US bombing of Libya in April 1986 or the US seizure of an Egyptian commercial airliner carrying the terrorists from the *Achille Lauro* incident in October 1985, are not themselves classified as terrorist acts. This is obviously a judgmental call that will not please everyone. ITERATE is event data that record attributes concerning the incident, its victims, the terrorists, and the outcome.

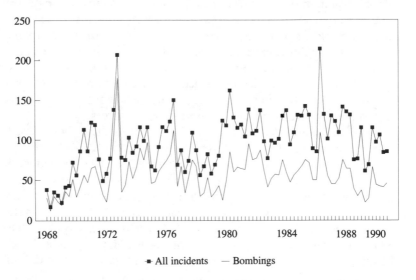

Figure 13.2 All incidents and bombings (quarterly 1968–90)

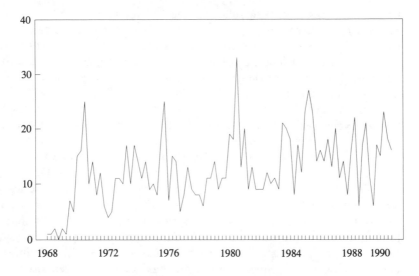

Figure 13.3 Hostage incidents (quarterly 1968–90)

In figure 13.2, the number of transnational events per quarter is depicted for 1968–90, using the ITERATE data set. This figure also illustrates the number of terrorist bombings per quarter for 1968–90. Bombings are the favorite mode of attack for the terrorists and typically comprise more than half of quarterly attacks. Any policy that severely curbs bombings could significantly reduce terrorism. Bombings assume sundry forms including car bombs, incendiary devices, letter bombs, and explosive bombs. In figure 13.3, the quarterly time series for hostage events – kidnappings, skyjackings, and barricade and hostage taking – is indicated. These events are much less frequent than bombings. Hostage events are both more risky and logistically more complex to execute. Terrorists appear aware of risks and engage in the more risky, higher-payoff modes of attack less often (see Mickolus, Sandler, and Murdock, 1989, vol. II, p. xvii). For hostage events, the terrorists often make demands of government, business, or family that might involve ransom, the release of prisoners, political concession, or media exposure.

In figures 13.2–13.3, a number of aspects of the time series are worth noting. For example, the shape of the bombing series is a prime determinant of the shape of the time series for all events. The time paths also appear to display cycles and an upward trend. Peaks in the time series often correspond to significant international events; e.g., in figure 13.2, the peak in 1972 came after a war between Israel and its neighbors, whereas the peak in 1986 followed the US retaliatory raid on Libya. Transnational terrorism began at low levels in 1968 and escalated, in part, because of Israeli victories in the Middle East. In a recent study, Enders, Parise, and Sandler (1992) examined the properties for five time series – all incidents, hostage events, bombings, threats, and assassinations – using quarterly ITERATE data drawn from 1979–89. These authors uncovered the following results: (1) All five time series display regular cycles (also see Im, Cauley, and Sandler, 1987). (2) Logistical complexity is positively related to the length of the cycles with hostage events and assassinations displaying the longest cycles of eighteen quarters and threats showing the shortest cycles of 3.6 quarters. (3) Bombings are associated with a 7.2-quarter cycle. (4) The time series for all incidents shows two periodicities – eighteen and 7.2 quarters. (5) Linear trends characterize the time series of all incidents and that of hostage events, while nonlinear trends characterize threats and assassinations. (6) Cycles are attributed to an attack–counterattack relationship between adversaries. Since 1989, there has been a marked decline in transnational terrorism, except for the first quarter of 1991 during the Gulf War. In 1992, transnational terrorism hit its lowest level since 1975. Only 361 incidents took place in 1992 (US Department of State, 1993). This downward trend coincides with the breakup of the Warsaw Pact and the dissolution of the Soviet Union, and may be caused, in part, by the loss of state sponsorship of terrorism by Eastern Europe and the former Soviet Union.[6]

In fighting terrorism, a government can choose between two general kinds of response – passive and active. Passive or defensive responses include erecting technology-based barriers (metal detectors at airports, bomb-sniffing devices), fortifying potential targets (embassies, military command posts), instituting stricter laws, augmenting intelligence, and enacting international agreements.[7] Active responses involve retaliatory raids (especially against state sponsors), preemptive strikes, group infiltration, and covert actions. Governments choose to allocate resources among antiterrorist policies to minimize its costs. Capitulation to terrorists' demands may be best if the expected costs from enduring further attacks exceed those from capitulation (Lapan and Sandler, 1993).

[6] On state sponsorship of terrorism, see Mickolus (1989).
[7] On government policies to curb terrorism see Brophy-Baermann and Conybeare (1994), Cauley and Im (1988), Cauley and Sandler (1988), Celmer (1987), Enders and Sandler (1993), Enders, Sandler, and Cauley (1990a, 1990b), Islam and Shahin (1989), Landes (1978), Lapan and Sandler (1988), Lee (1988), Lee and Sandler (1989), Ross and Gurr (1989), Sandler, Enders, and Lapan (1991), Sandler and Lapan (1988), Scott (1991), Shahin and Islam (1990, 1992), and Wilkinson (1986, 1992).

13.5   Choice-theoretic models of terrorism

A terrorist group must allocate its scarce resources, such as labor and time, between terrorist and nonterrorist activities in order to maximize its well being, which depends, among other things, on the attainment of some political objective.[8] The allocation process might further involve the assignment of resources among the various modes of attack – skyjackings, kidnappings, and bombings. The terrorist group's resource constraint equates the value of expenditures and its resources or income. For any mode of terrorist attack, expenditures include the per-unit price times the number of units of the activity. The price of the attack reflects the additional costs, in terms of resources and risks, of performing each kind of event. The risks associated with one type of terrorist event would increase when a government takes actions, such as installing metal detectors or increasing security at embassies, to harden one type of target. Such actions would increase the relative costs of one attack mode *vis-à-vis* the costs of another attack mode that had not been influenced by the government's policy.

The choice-theoretic model leads to some testable hypotheses with respect to terrorism. If a government policy increases the relative cost or price of one kind of terrorist mode of attack, then terrorists are anticipated to substitute those modes whose prices are unchanged. The greatest substitution will occur between modes that achieve similar purposes – for example, between hostage-taking events, or between different operations directed at diplomatic personnel. The overall level of terrorism need not decline. To achieve a general decline in terrorism, the government must either reduce terrorist resources in general, or else raise the costs of all terrorist operations relative to nonterrorist activities. Piecemeal policies, aimed at one or two modes of attack, will not necessarily curb terrorism.

Like the terrorists, the government also faces a choice-theoretic problem as it allocates its scarce resources, generated from taxes and debt, to meet social goals and curb terrorism. Just as the terrorists must make optimizing decisions based on government actions and their beliefs about future government actions, the government must make its own optimizing decisions based on past terrorist acts and its belief about future acts. In particular, the government attempts to minimize the costs or impact associated with a terrorist campaign when it decides upon

[8]   This section draws from the work of Enders and Sandler (1993), Islam and Shahin (1989), Kirk (1983), Landes (1978), Lapan and Sandler (1988), Sandler and Lapan (1988), Sandler *et al.* (1987), Sandler, Tschirhart, and Cauley (1983), and Shahin and Islam (1990, 1992).

deterrence, intelligence gathering, and responses to terrorist demands. Both the terrorist group and the government must choose strategies based on how they *anticipate* the other side will react to its optimizing choices.

13.5.1 A specific example

As a specific example of the choice-theoretic approach, we briefly present Landes' (1978) model of skyjacking choice, which derived from the work of Becker (1968) and Ehrlich (1973). A hijacker is contemplating forcing an aircraft from country i to country j. Three outcomes are allowed in the model: success, apprehension and no conviction, and apprehension and conviction. Landes' (1978) notation is as follows:

P_a = offender's subjective estimate of the probability of apprehension;

P_c = offender's estimate of the conditional probability of imprisonment, given apprehension;

W_j = the offender's wealth from a successful mission to country j;

W_i = the offender's wealth in country i;

S = the monetary value of imprisonment; and

C = the monetary value of capture without imprisonment.

The potential offender decides to hijack when the expected utility,

$$EU = (1 - P_a)U(W_j) + P_a P_c U(W_i - S) + P_a(1 - P_c)U(W_j - C)$$
(13.20)

is greater than the utility associated with no hijacking – i.e., $U(W_i)$. An offensive function is derived that relates the number of hijackings to the average value of P_a, P_c, S, C, the wealth differential between country i and j, and other environmental factors (e.g., relative political freedom between the two countries). Landes (1978) is primarily interested in evaluating the deterrence effects of government policies toward hijackings.

13.5.2 Other choice-theoretic analyses

Many such analyses exist and, hence, our review is necessarily brief and selective. Kirk (1983) puts forth a rent-seeking model of terrorism, in which terrorists use violence as a means of extorting rents from the government. According to Kirk (1983), individuals will resort to violence if terrorism represents a cost-effective means of rent seeking. Terrorists were depicted as choosing a level of attacks and nonviolent political activities to maximize their net gain from rent seeking. On the other hand, the government attempts to deter, to set rents, and to allow nonviolent political activities to minimize the costs of terrorism. Kirk demonstrated that an expansion of government size augments potential rents and may promote terrorism.

Islam and Shahin (1989) adopt a state-preference approach to examine the implications of government policy on hostage taking. In particular, these authors examined the effectiveness of three alternative government policies: a no-negotiation strategy, negotiation, and punitive attack. The terrorist is depicted as choosing the number of hostages and as manipulating of the media so as to maximize his or her expected utility, where each outcome's payoff is weighted by terrorist's subjective estimate of the probability of the three states or policies. This study differs significantly from that of Lapan and Sandler (1988), where payoffs are uncertain and the strategic interactions of the adversaries are crucial. In Lapan and Sandler (1988), a policy of never negotiating with terrorists may be time inconsistent if attacks are not *fully* deterred and the government finds itself in a situation in which the costs of capitulation are less than those of standing firm. Reputation effects become an important consideration, because a capitulation may stimulate future attacks whose costs must be included when deciding on a response. Hostage-taking models were also presented in Sandler and Scott (1987), Sandler, Tschirhart, and Cauley (1983), Scott (1989, 1991), Selten (1988), and Shahin and Islam (1990, 1992).

A final example is associated with Lee (1988) and Lee and Sandler (1988) who examined whether nations, faced with the threat of terrorism, will be motivated to engage in the efficient amount of retaliation against terrorists. These authors showed that the problem confronting the efforts of nations to achieve an optimal retaliation against terrorists is *understated by the traditional free-rider analysis*. Free riding is relevant, since a retaliatory attack that weakens terrorists, who threaten a set of countries, provides nonexcludable benefits to all potential targets. Lee (1988) demonstrated that nations have the option of actually selling or reducing the public good of retaliation, provided through the efforts of others, by offering safe havens to terrorists in return for the terrorists' pledge to attack elsewhere. When an agent sells or undoes the public good of deterrence provided by others, the agent is termed a *paid rider*. Such behavior will lead to a position worse than the standard independent-adjustment equilibrium and may eliminate the incentives of others to contribute anything to the public good of retaliation and deterrence. This follows because the deterrence provided by some nations, which is costly to achieve, may be undone by opportunistic behavior on the part of the paid rider. The paid-rider option has a payoff structure that dominates that of free riding (Lee, 1988); hence, international cooperation in deterring terrorism is more difficult to achieve than first supposed.

13.6   A review of some empirical analyses

One empirical line of analysis examines whether terrorist incidents encourage (discourage) further acts through a demonstration effect that gives rise to imitation or diffusion. Studies may hypothesize at least three types of intertemporal, interspatial relationships among incidents: (1) the absence of any dependency; (2) the presence of a contagion process; and (3) the presence of a reversible contagion process. Let λ, which denotes the probability that the $i + 1$st event will take place in interval $(t, t + 1)$, equal

$$\lambda(i, t) = a + bi, \qquad (13.21)$$

where a and b are nonnegative constants. If there is no dependence between events, then $b = 0$ and λ is a constant.[9] In this case, a (random) Poisson distribution would underlie the occurrence of events. If, however, $b > 0$, then a contagious Poisson process applies. Hamilton and Hamilton (1983) used a more general representation

$$\lambda(i, t) = A\exp(\alpha + \beta i + \gamma i^2), \qquad (13.22)$$

that also permits a reversible contagion for $\beta > 0$ and $\gamma < 0$.

A probability distribution is first fitted to the time series of terrorist events. Next, the fitted distribution is tested against those that denote (random) Poisson, contagious Poisson, and reversible Poisson by using chi-square goodness-of-fit test statistics. Based on the chi-square test, a study concludes whether a contagion process applies or not. To date, the results have been mixed. For instance, Midlarsky (1980) uncovered a contagious Poisson, while Hamilton and Hamilton (1983) found a contagious Poisson in only three of sixteen countries. Holden (1987) extended the procedure by allowing the contagion to possess a memory that fades. Specifically, Holden investigated the effect that successful (failed) hijackings have on generating additional hijackings. He found that each successful hijacking generated approximately 0.5 new incidents within the next thirty-three days. Failed events had no effect – good or bad – on generating additional incidents.

[9]   The analysis of this paragraph derives from Hamilton and Hamilton (1983), Holden (1987), Midlarsky (1970, 1978), and Midlarsky, Crenshaw, and Yoshida (1980).

In economics, most of the empirical literature on terrorism has been preoccupied with ascertaining the effectiveness of passive and active antiterrorist policies including the following: the installation of metal detectors in airports (instituted on January 5, 1973 in the US and shortly thereafter elsewhere), the fortification of US embassies (October 1976 and thereafter), the US retaliatory raid on Libya (April 15, 1986), the enacting of UN conventions and resolutions forbidding skyjackings and hostage taking, the 1984 Reagan get-tough on terrorism laws, and Israeli retaliatory raids. This literature examined two issues: (1) the effectiveness of the policy in decreasing the time series of the targeted event (e.g., did metal detectors decrease skyjackings?); and (2) the impact of the policy on related time series (Sandler, Enders, and Lapan, 1991).

To examine the effectiveness of specific terrorist-thwarting policies, Cauley and Im (1988), Enders, Sandler, and Cauley (1990a, 1990b) and Brophy-Baermann and Conybeare (1994) applied an econometric forecasting technique known as interrupted time-series analysis. Enders, Sandler, and Cauley (1990b) showed that the installation of metal detectors reduced the number of transnational skyjackings by nearly 1.3 per quarter. Moreover, US domestic skyjackings were reduced by 5.6 incidents per quarter after January 1973 from a preintervention mean of 6.7 per quarter. These authors also demonstrated that terrorists switched their hostage mission to kidnappings and barricade attacks, which were not protected by metal detectors. Clearly, terrorists responded to the increased risks posed by screening devices by changing the type of hostage mission. A clear substitution effect has resulted from the change in relative costs.

These researchers calculated that the UN conventions had no significant deterring effects. Also the 1984 Reagan get-tough laws were ineffective. Perhaps surprising, the Libyan raid appeared to provoke attacks against US and UK interests. This peak in attacks disappeared within three months.

In a recent article, Brophy-Baermann and Conybeare (1994) used interrupted time-series techniques to evaluate the effectiveness of Israeli retaliatory raids on the suppression of terrorist attacks directed at Israeli interests. Their study represents a novel and important application of the notion of rational expectations theory, developed by Robert Lucas and others. According to Brophy-Baermann and Conybeare (1994, p. 17),

If terrorists have rational expectations, it will be difficult to alter the incidence of attacks from the natural process, unless terrorists can be surprised by an unexpected rate of retaliation that will cause a temporary deviation in attacks from the natural rate. Rational expectations also implies that governments may be better off if they are subject to a nondiscretionary retaliatory rule than if they have full latitude in setting the rate of response.

These authors used interrupted time-series techniques to test their hypothesis concerning raid-induced deviations of terrorist attacks from a natural rate. In particular, they investigated the impact of Israeli retaliations on Palestine Liberation Organization (PLO) bases in Syria during September 1972 following the Black September group's killing of Israeli athletes at the Olympic Games in Munich; on Palestinian guerrilla bases in Lebanon during March 1978 (Operation Litani) following a Haifa bus hijacking; on Palestinian bases in Lebanon during June 1982 following an attempted assassination of the Israeli ambassador in London; and on other targets during May 1974, October 1985, and April 1988 following terrorist attacks on Israeli interests. The authors first identified the natural rate of attack on Israeli interests to be 2.13 per quarter. Only for the September 1972 raid, which represented an unexpectedly large retaliation, was there a deviation from the natural rate after the raid. But consistent with the theory, this deviation dissipated within three quarters. None of the other raids caused a significant deviation, thus supporting the theory and leading one to question the efficacy of such retaliatory raids.

To ascertain the interrelationships among time series, Enders and Sandler (1993) combined interrupted time-series analysis with the vector autoregression (VAR) technique to examine the policy impacts on a host of terrorist attack modes. This study drew the following conclusions:

1   The Libyan raid caused a number of different terrorist attacks to increase. A small portion of this increase spilled over to nations not involved in the retaliatory strike.
2   Fortification of US embassies and missions in 1976 reduced attacks against US interests, but resulted in a substitution into assassinations.
3   Metal detectors decreased skyjackings and threats, but increased assassinations and hostage events not protected by the detectors.
4   The benefits from metal detectors cannot be adequately measured by the value placed on a reduced number of skyjackings since other events were affected indirectly.
5   The identification of substitutes and complements was sensitive to VAR interactions.
6   All time series showed some interrelationship: the finer is the disaggregation, the greater the interaction.

In another study, Enders and Sandler (1991) used VAR techniques to ascertain the causality between transnational terrorist attacks and tourism in Spain during 1970–88.[10] They found that terrorist events had a significant negative impact on the number of tourists visiting Spain. A typical incident was estimated as scaring away just over 140,000 tourists when all monthly impacts were combined. The causality was unidirectional: terrorism affected tourism, but not the reverse. In a follow-up study, Enders, Sandler, and Parise (1992) attempted to calculate the impact of terrorism on European tourism. Their results showed that terrorists had been successful in deterring tourism and that there was a generalization effect: an incident in one nation acted to deter tourism in neighboring nations. The negative externality has important consequences for the proper amount of expenditures used to thwart terrorism, since countries are unlikely to account for these spillovers when allocating resources to terrorism prevention. In absolute amounts, the revenue losses appeared sizable; using a 5 percent real interest rate, these authors found that continental Europe lost over 16 billion Special Drawing Rights (SDRs) in revenues since 1974. Austria and Greece showed pronounced losses in tourist revenues in the latter 1980s following significant attacks, and there was a strong upward drift in the losses for continental Europe.

13.7   Game-theoretic analysis of terrorism

In recent years, game theory has been applied to the study of terrorism.[11] Because strategic interactions often characterize the interface between terrorists and government, game theory is an appropriate tool for analysis. Strategic interactions may also occur among governments confronted with the threat of terrorism, or among terrorist groups, faced with the threat of government reprisals.[12]

We first turn to a simple game representation that may underlie a choice of four nations to form and abide by an international agreement pledging to punish a state sponsor of terrorism. This hypothetical example could also apply to agreements not to negotiate with hostage takers. Suppose that each signatory would confer a benefit of 5 from deterrence to itself and to the other three nations in the agreement. If all four abide by the agreement, each nation receives total benefits (before

[10] Nelson and Scott (1992) use the techniques developed in Enders and Sandler (1991) to investigate the causality between terrorism and media attention.

[11] Articles include Cauley and Sandler (1988), Lapan and Sandler (1988, 1993), Lee (1988), Sandler and Lapan (1988), Sandler, Tschirhart, and Cauley (1983), Scott (1989) and Selten (1988).

[12] On this issue, Lee (1988) and Cauley and Sandler (1988) rely on the Prisoner's Dilemma to analyze intercountry strategic relationships.

Strategies of the other three nations

	No other nation abides	One other nation abides	Two other nations abide	Three other nations abide
Abides	−5	0	5	10
Does not abide	0	5	10	15

Nation *i*'s strategies

Figure 13.4 Game matrix: Prisoner's Dilemma and retaliation

costs) equal to 20 (= 5 × 4). Each signatory, however, faces a private cost of 10 to make good on its commitment. These costs would arise, in part, from resources assigned to retaliation. Additional private costs may be associated with retribution by the targeted sponsor.

In figure 13.4, the payoffs to nation *i*, based on its own strategy and those of the other nations, are listed. Each nation has two strategies: abide or not abide. In total, there are eight possible strategic outcomes that can occur. If all nations abide, then nation *i* receives a *net* payoff of 10 – the difference between benefits of 20 and private costs of 10. If however, nation *i* does not abide while the other three nations abide, then nation *i* receives 15 (5 times the number of abiders), because it has no private costs to pay. When nation *i* and two other nations abide, nation *i* receives 5 – the difference between private benefits of 15 and private costs of 10. When nation *i* does not abide but two other nations abide, then nation *i* receives 10, since it has no private costs. The other four payoffs are computed similarly and are listed in the table. For nation *i*, the dominant strategy that is best regardless of the strategy of the others is to *not abide*, since the payoffs in the bottom row exceed those in the top regardless of the other nations' strategies. Because all nations view the game as does *i*, none abides when called upon and the payoff to each nation is zero. Each nation hopes in vain, given the payoff matrix hypothesized, that it can get away with reneging, while the others support the agreement. Collective failure results because each nation could receive 10 in net benefits if all were to cooperate. The payoff scheme depicted is characteristic of an *n*-player Prisoner's Dilemma and is behind the failure to achieve many international actions, including ending arms races between belligerent nations (see chapter 4).

Potential escapes to the Prisoner's Dilemma exist. If the participants interact repeatedly and take a sufficiently far-sighted view to weigh the short-run gains from reneging against the long-run gains from cooperating, then a cooperative agreement might be achieved (Sandler, 1992, pp. 79–89). Another potential escape involves the provision of an enforcement mechanism that punishes defecting nations with sanctions that exceed the gains from defecting. In figure 13.4, sanctions greater than 5 would make the resulting payoffs from abiding larger than those from reneging. As a consequence, nations would abide by the agreement. Unfortunately, enforcement poses its own collective action problem, because nations are reluctant to establish a sanction mechanism that may, one day, be directed against them.

Agreements may be possible when payoffs favor cooperation. That is, the underlying game structure may be something other than the Prisoner's Dilemma, which is only one of many different game structures. To date, these other game structures have not been utilized by the terrorism literature concerned with international agreements.

Game theory is also applicable to the deterrence decision between countries when two or more nations are targeted by the same terrorist group (Sandler and Lapan, 1988). If each nation decides its deterrence independently, then each may allocate too many resources to inducing the terrorists to switch their venue. This follows because the nations do not take into account the negative influence (by inducing terrorists to operate on another nation's soil) that their deterrence choices create for others. In consequence, too much may be spent on controlling terrorism as each nation tries to force the terrorists to stage their events elsewhere. If these nations were to share intelligence concerning the group's true preferences for attacking alternative targets, then the overdeterrence problem would be aggravated as nations are better able to calculate what it takes to make terrorists go elsewhere. Piecemeal policy, in which intelligence but not deterrence decisions are shared, may make everyone worse off. A grand strategy for coordinating policy on all fronts is required to handle transnational terrorism.

If, however, a nation's citizens or property are targeted on foreign soil, then underdeterrence may be a relevant consideration when assessing deterrence abroad. This follows because the host country to the attack may not account for the positive externalities (by safeguarding other countries' people and property) that its deterrence confers on others. The host country may consequently allocate too few resources to deterring attacks. This problem may be especially acute if the terrorists do not ever target the host nation's people. Thus, both positive and negative externalities may be germane to the deterrence decision.

Selten (1988) applied advanced game-theoretic methods to examine kidnappings. Two sets of players are identified: the kidnapper and the target of the ransom demand. The hostage is a pawn. In this game, the kidnapper must first decide whether to kidnap and, if a kidnapping takes place, how much ransom to demand. The target of the ransom must then decide how much ransom, if any, to pay. Finally, the kidnapper must decide whether to release or harm the hostage. For the case of complete information, Selten displayed the subgame perfect equilibrium of the game in which neither player can improve his or her payoff at any stage of the game. In a subsequent analysis, Lapan and Sandler (1993) studied the interface between terrorists and government when the terrorists are well-informed but the government is ignorant about the terrorists' resources and must use first-period attacks to update its beliefs. These authors showed that a government may be better off if it concedes provided that the terrorists' initial attack equals or exceeds a threshold level. This so-called signaling equilibrium allows the government to minimize costs even though its inference about terrorist group strength may be wrong, since it might concede to a weak group. Many other game applications are possible in this developing area. For example, terrorist campaigns can be analyzed in a multi-period game model. Also two-sided incomplete information, where both the government and the terrorists are ill-informed, can be studied.

13.8   Concluding remarks

In the course of this chapter, we demonstrate that rational-actor models have been employed to investigate a wide range of issues concerning nonconventional conflict. Both theoretical and empirical tools have been applied to the study of revolutions, insurrections, guerrilla wars, and terrorism. In choosing articles to discuss, we focus on pieces representative of other studies not mentioned. Despite the simple empirical and theoretical tools used, the literature has generated numerous insights on nonconventional conflict. For example, strategic interactions among nations must be accounted for when analyzing the proper response to the threat of terrorism. The true effectiveness of antiterrorism policies is best evaluated with VAR techniques that acknowledge the interrelationships among diverse terrorist modes of attacks. Moreover, retaliatory raids appear to have no lasting effect on curbing terrorist attacks. In the case of revolutions, the personal gains of the revolution's leaders must be sufficient for them to motivate others. That is, selective incentives must exist to provide incentives to revolutionary organizers. Revolutions may come as a surprise, owing to the suppression of one's true preferences and the eventual appearance of bandwagon effects. Strategic interactions between the government and guerrilla forces are best studied in a dynamic framework. For such a framework, government policies may lead to unstable equilibria when guerrilla warfare is involved. Further application of game theory, backed by empirical testing, should lead to further insights. Much remains to be done.

14   Conclusions and research agenda for the future

By this point, the reader should be convinced that defense economics has a sufficiently wide scope that it draws from, and contributes to, numerous subfields of economics. In addition, defense economics has an interdisciplinary orientation that ties it to political science, history, sociology, and policy science. As such, the modern study of defense economics draws its methodologies from the latest theoretical advances and empirical tools. Defense economics is an applied field interested in policy recommendations that account for relevant institutional aspects (e.g., the relationship between the US Congress and the Department of Defense in the US procurement process). It is these aspects that differentiate the study of defense issues from analogous investigations in other areas of economics.

Contributions to defense economics have been prevalent in the economic journals since the mid 1960s, and have appeared in general and field journals. Contributors have included many of the best minds in economics. Important advances in some topics, such as procurement (e.g., Tirole, 1986; Cummins, 1972; Rogerson, 1990) have been developed as a policy concern in defense economics, but had wider application to nondefense issues. Methodologies developed for a defense issue (e.g., the estimation of the demand for defense among allies) have been applied to other areas of economics (e.g., the estimation of the demand for agricultural research by Khanna, Huffman, and Sandler, 1994). There are many new issues to investigate. The momentous events of the last five years, leading to the collapse of the Soviet Union and Eastern European governments, have raised new concerns for defense economics. These include questions about alliance structure, conversion, nonconventional security threats, the role of United Nations peacekeeping forces, and the allocation of resources to defense needs.

The current chapter has three primary purposes: (1) to summarize some of the major findings (section 14.1), (2) to indicate some of the main methodological advances in the field (section 14.2), and (3) to present an agenda for future research (section 14.3). Given the vast amount of material covered, we have to be understandably selective in fulfilling these three purposes.

14.1 Some primary findings

A primary finding involves the characterization of defense as a public good shared by allies. If defense is purely public among allies, then free-riding incentives exist, and this, in turn, implies that the large well-endowed allies may shoulder the burden of the smaller allies. This gives rise to an "exploitation of the large by the small" (Olson and Zeckhauser, 1966). Free riding among allies also implies a Pareto-inefficient allocation of resources as allies fail to account for the spillover benefits that their defense provision confers on others. In the past twenty-five years, the free-rider notion for allies has been refined in a number of important ways. First, researchers have included ally-specific or private benefits derived from defense expenditures. Second, the analysis has been expanded to include a host of jointly produced defense benefits that vary in their degree of publicness (e.g., the extent of excludability). Third, the strategic interaction with the allies' opponents has been included. Fourth, trade considerations have been introduced. These refinements have had a profound effect on suboptimality and exploitation considerations. For example, the mix of excludable to total benefits is related to the degree of suboptimality: the closer is this ratio to one, the smaller the suboptimality. Moreover, exploitation is less likely when excludable benefits comprise the bulk of the benefits. Trade influences and adversarial reactions can also lessen the problem of suboptimality (see chapter 2). In short, modern refinements have put burden sharing and suboptimality concerns in better perspective.

Since the early test of the exploitation hypothesis by Olson and Zeckhauser (1966), empirical analysis of alliance burden sharing has come a long way. Empirical results have demonstrated that free-riding behavior has varied among alliances and over time. The use of simultaneous equations to estimate the demand for military expenditures has been a significant empirical development. If strategic interactions among allies and adversaries are present, as are expected, then the countries' demand equations do not have independent errors. In recent years, statistical tests have been developed to distinguish the allocative process, technology of public good aggregation, and the identity of the decision maker (see chapter 3).

In terms of arms race analysis, the most influential advance has been the incorporation of strategic considerations in the Richardsonian arms race model by Brito (1972) and Intriligator (1975). This analysis has focused on the "cone of deterrence" and its implications for stability. A host of topics have been illuminated with this device including the possibility of accidental nuclear warfare, the instability of arms control, and the influence of weapon properties on stability and war initiation. Another significant development has been the introduction of supply-side considerations, so that resource constraints are included in the so-called economic warfare model of arms races. Differential game models have emphasized the decision makers' objectives and the intertemporal constraints that they face.

For procurement, the major theoretical advance has come from applying the modern theory of incentive contracts and asymmetric information. Thus, in recent years, there is a more informed understanding of the effects and desirability of alternative contractual arrangements such as fixed-price, cost-plus, and incentive contracts. Simple rules of thumb that once rejected cost-plus contracting as inherently inefficient may not hold when information structures and other aspects are considered.

Since the mid 1970s, military manpower studies have moved their focus away from contrasting volunteer and conscripted forces. Recent studies have investigated labor supply issues involving the military. In particular, occupational choice and retention rates have been related to a host of factors that include gender and race. Other studies have examined labor supply characteristics of reserve forces and the role of reserves in the post cold war era.

Studies of defense industries have examined scale economies, profitability, regional impacts, competitive forces, and a host of other issues. Much of this literature has been concerned with similarity and differences between defense industries and nondefense industries. For example, Trevino and Higgs (1992) have found that the defense industries are more profitable than their nondefense counterparts. In addition, significant scale economies exist in the manufacture of most defense weapons owing to high development costs (Hartley, 1991b, chapter 8). Military R & D is heavily subsidized in most countries and this practice could crowd out private R & D. Defense industries are, in general, noncompetitive and characterized by one or two firms. In recent years, concentration ratios appear to be increasing.

Following the provocative studies by Benoit (1973, 1978) that suggested that defense is growth enhancing in some developing countries, subsequent papers have reexamined the relationship between growth and defense. Although the evidence has been mixed, some consensus has emerged. Defense does not stimulate growth in developed economies especially when it crowds out private investment. In addition, defense does not enhance growth in developing countries during full-employment years when all direct and indirect influences are taken into account. Nevertheless, some positive externalities from the defense sector are derived, but these appear to be overwhelmed by crowding out of investment. Both demand and supply elements must be included if the relationship of defense and growth is to be understood.

For industrial and alliance policies, countries must consider foreign and domestic sources of weapons if efficiency is to be promoted. Surprisingly, international collaboration in arms development and procurement has not always proved to be successful. Such arrangements often increase the number of missions that a weapon is intended to accomplish, so as to please the constituent nations' mission requirements. There are also the inevitable demands for work sharing. The end result may be a complex, expensive weapon that does not fully fulfill any mission and that takes a longer time to develop. In short, scale economies from larger production runs may not compensate for other transactions-cost considerations that raise costs for joint ventures (Hartley, 1991b, chapter 9). In terms of alliance policies, tighter alliance structures offer the possibility of cost savings from standardization and interoperability of weapons, shared infrastructure, common R & D, and mission specialization among allies. To date, modern-day alliances have been rather loose with most weapon acquisition and defense budget decisions made independently at the national level with little or no collaboration with one's allies. These cost-saving opportunities are especially important if nations continue to downsize their military.

Arms trade offers nations an opportunity to exploit scale economies while limiting domestic acquisition of new weapons. The export of weapons presents real risks if these weapons get into the hands of the supplier's enemies. Thus, arms trade puts a nation at somewhat greater risk, and this risk must be balanced by larger domestic forces. Inasmuch as arms-exporting nations are unlikely to account for the negative externalities that their weapons trade imposes on the world at large, supra-optimal trade is likely to result. Some studies (e.g., Kinsella, 1994) have shown that arms trade has led to regional instability. In the last two decades, arms trade has been an important component of world trade. Moreover, arms exports have been concentrated with five nations (i.e., the US, the ex-Soviet Union, France, the UK, and China).

Disarmament comes at a cost in terms of verification, new weapon development, the destruction of weapon stockpiles, the displacement of workers, and the formulation of new defense doctrines. As such, arms control must be viewed as an investment process with a stream of expected costs and expected benefits that must be properly discounted over a time horizon. Peace dividends, while positive, are unlikely to be as large as thought at the end of the cold war, because of the need to protect against new threats and the requisite costs of downsizing. In the latter case, resources are required to facilitate conversion of portions of the defense sector to nondefense activities. As compared to past conversions following World Wars I and II, the Korean War, and the Vietnam War, the conversion following the cold war is on a more modest scale.

Rational-actor models have much to say for the study of nonconventional conflict. For example, leaders of revolutions may overcome potential free-rider problems through the use of selective incentives to motivate their followers. Once a revolution has attained a certain level of success, a bandwagon effect may ensue. Since this level may be difficult to predict beforehand, successful revolutions may come as a surprise after the fact, even to the experts. Throughout our analysis of nonconventional conflict, terrorists and insurgents have been shown to behave in a rational and predictable fashion. Thus, when formulating antiterrorism policies, the authorities must anticipate that terrorists may substitute among attack modes and targets. To evaluate antiterrorism policies, researchers must consider the interrelationship among different time series for attack modes. Hence, vector autoregressive (VAR) techniques are particularly well-suited for this study. Game theory, which accounts for strategic interactions among agents, is also a useful tool for investigating nonconventional forms of conflict. With this tool, we have seen why governments do not form cooperative agreements to thwart terrorism, or else renege on their obligations after signing an agreement. Strategic actions may yield results that seem surprising at first.

14.2   Primary methodological advances

The study of defense economics has blossomed in the last three decades and has embraced many of the advances and new techniques in both theoretical and empirical economics. On the theoretical side, game theory has been applied to a wide range of topics including the study of alliances, arms races, procurement, and nonconventional conflict. Most applications have involved noncooperative games; however, cooperative games are relevant for the study of club structures such as alliances. Researchers have used differential game analysis to examine arms races (chapter 4) and guerrilla warfare (chapter 13) within a dynamic framework. Games of incomplete and imperfect information have been formulated to investigate terrorism (Lapan and Sandler, 1993) and procurement. When information is incomplete, Bayesian learning becomes a consideration in which agents update their priors based on observations in preceding periods. Moreover, the credibility of threats must be assessed in a framework that accounts for the entire game tree and the sequence of moves. By examining credibility, one may be able to eliminate uninteresting Nash equilibria based on noncredible threats from the set of possible outcomes.

Advances in the analysis of uncertainty have been applied to the study of defense economics. Most notably, the notion of asymmetric information, where one party is informed and the other is not, has been used. In particular, principal–agent analysis has been employed in the study of procurement. In a principal–agent problem, there is a random variable that severs the link between an agent's effort and the resulting outcome or output, so that the principal cannot necessarily intuit the agent's effort from observing the outcome. That is, high (low) effort may be associated with low (high) output. In light of this informational asymmetry, the principal must devise a fee-to-output incentive scheme that motivates high effort. As such, issues involving moral hazard and risk attitudes have figured prominently.

Perhaps, no single field of economics has contributed so many new theoretical paradigms to defense economics as has public economics. Specifically, developments in the theory of public goods, clubs, and externalities have been useful, inasmuch as defense provision often involves market failures both within and among nations. Public choice analysis offers an alternative perspective on curing market failures through state intervention by emphasizing the motivation of public officials to pursue goals at odds with those of the public. Principles of collective action have been applied.

On the empirical side, the latest developments in econometrics have been carried over to defense economics. For example, time-series tools have been applied to study the demand for military expenditures, arms races, terrorism, and growth and defense. These tools include seemingly unrelated regressions (SUR), interrupted time series, spectral analysis, Granger causality, cointegration tests, and vector autoregressions (VARs). Thus, for example, Joerding (1986) and Chowdhury (1991) have determined whether defense expenditures Granger cause economic growth, or the reverse. Enders and Sandler (1993) attempted to evaluate the effectiveness of passive and active means to thwart terrorism by combining interrupted time-series techniques and VAR modeling. Simultaneous-equations estimation has been applied frequently in the last decade to the study of defense economics. For instance, Sandler and Murdoch (1990) employed simultaneous equations to estimate a system of demands for military expenditures for the NATO allies. Procedures for testing between alternative models have appeared and have been based on both nested and non-nested tests. Other simultaneous-equations estimations have been performed by McGuire (1982) and Okamura (1991).

14.3   An agenda for research

Although defense economics has accomplished much in its theoretical, empirical, and institutional analysis to date, there remains a rich agenda for future research. Some key areas for further research are indicated. There is a need to marry the static resource allocation model of alliances with the dynamic model of arms races. In the alliance model, the focus is on the public good characteristics and their implications for burden sharing, free riding, and exploitation; in the arms race model, the emphasis is on investigating regions of stability and the interalliance interaction. The alliance model treats threat as static and exogenous, whereas the arms race model views the adversaries as unitary actors. Neither approach gives a satisfactory or complete depiction.

The theory of alliances can be extended in a number of additional directions:

(i)   Trade aspects among allies need further study, with Wong (1991) and Jones (1988) providing an informed first step.

(ii)   The number of alliances and their optimal degree of overlap should be examined with cooperative game theory.

(iii)   A multi-product investigation needs to be formulated based on notions of economies of scope.

(iv)   Informational asymmetries should be introduced in which dominant allies are better informed than others.

(v)   A repeated game framework should be developed. In the first stage, the alliance size is determined, while in the second stage, allies' defense contributions are chosen. Additional stages to the game can be added with different choice variables at each stage.

(vi)   There is a need to study the joint product mix decision, which, to date, has been exogenous.

(vii)   The supply side needs to be developed to a greater extent, because the theory of alliances remains primarily a demand-based theory. This problem can be rectified, in part, by focusing on defense costs differences among allies, as initiated by McGuire (1990b). Supply-side considerations also involve the study of joint weapon development, trade in weaponry, and the net benefits from joint R & D projects.

The empirical analysis of the demand for military expenditures for alliances and individual countries should be refined. More reliable data are needed that apply consistent definitions for defense across countries. Time series for relative prices of defense to nondefense goods must also be developed and included in the estimations. Additionally, there is a need to develop further tests for distinguishing the allocative process within alliances along the lines of McGuire and Groth (1985). Another advancement involves testing the impure public good model of McGuire (1990b) with autospatial regression techniques that account for the spatial spread of spillovers. Political factors (e.g., the party in power, rent-seeking) should be incorporated in the demand models. Finally, defense demand should be estimated in which defense is disaggregated into finer components – operations and maintenance, procurement, personnel, and R & D.

In the case of arms race modeling and testing, a few suggested chores follow:

(i)   Arms race models, especially those with strategic interactions, should be tailored to regional arms races and to nonconventional forms of conflict, such as terrorism.

(ii)   Further development of multi-polar deterrence models, along the lines of Wolfson (1992), should be attempted.

(iii)   As regional and conventional conflicts are studied, arms race models must include supply-side considerations. A truly dynamic analysis of economic warfare that accounts for these supply-side factors is required.

(iv)   Advanced time series methods should be used to estimate arms race equations. Simultaneous-equations methods also need to be applied.

(v)   Researchers must devise empirical means for distinguishing among alternative models (e.g., between arms-using and arms-building models).

(vi)   A general equilibrium analysis should be developed that incorporates arms races, alliance considerations, and arms trade.

In recent years, economists have made great strides in studying procurement. This has followed, in part, the application of game theory and incentive contracting theory to the study of procurement. The frontier of this analysis can be pushed out further if three-player game models are used to include the defense contractor, the Congress, and the Department of Defense, or their equivalent. To date, two-player games have been formulated, so that one player is exogenous and, hence, ignored. Multi-level principal–agent problems with the possibility of collusion between adjacent levels should be investigated. Studies need to analyze the trade-offs between force size and technological sophistication as done in Rogerson (1990). There is also the need to examine public choice aspects of the procurement process, including the role and impact of special interest groups and rent seeking. Additional studies should focus on the time profile from development to production of diverse defense systems (Cavin, 1991). More work is required on the learning curves where parameters are endogenous.

Given the paucity of data, empirical studies on procurement have been few. Empirical investigations are needed in terms of comparative country studies, comparative industry studies, and comparative contract studies. Further empirical analyses must examine economies of scale, economies of scope, production runs, and the export sector for defense industries. In an era of downsizing of military investment, there is a need for analytical and empirical investigations of successful and failed conversion.

There is also scope for further study of defense and its industrial base. Issues worthy of additional attention include:

(i)   an investigation of the optimal mix of home-produced weapons and imports;
(ii)   an investigation of the optimal mix of civil and defense products within firms to curb the impacts of conversion;
(iii)   additional study of the desirability to trade and specialize in weapons within an alliance;
(iv)   an analysis of the costs and benefits of the defense industrial base;
(v)   a presentation of the gains and losses associated with the use of foreign suppliers and the practice of work-sharing arrangements; and
(vi)   additional studies of the efficiency of joint ventures among allies.

The end to the cold war poses new challenges to military manpower studies. As military forces are downsized, the optimal mix between reserve and active forces grows in importance. Additionally, the makeup of these reserve forces requires further study – e.g., should these forces be used in combat or should they be used in support roles? Also, the ability to call up reserve forces and project them to trouble spots are important issues. Competition among the branches of the military for personnel requires further study. There is a need for additional examination of occupational choices and related issues, including an analysis of retention rates and the effects of gender and race. Advanced microeconomic techniques dealing with the analysis of tournaments and principal–agent can be applied to the study of recruitment strategies. Further studies are required on the mobility of labor between civil and defense sectors (Lerner, 1992) if conversion is to be better understood. Military training also poses a host of issues that deserve further attention. In particular, what are the net benefits from training and who should shoulder the costs – the volunteer or the government? What is the optimal length of service given training costs? To answer these questions, we must acquire a fuller understanding about the transferability of skills between the defense and civil sectors. Also, employment contracts in the military should be designed to account for quit rates and the specificity of training.

For studies of growth and defense, the primary chore is to integrate demand-side and supply-side elements in order to include direct and indirect effects on growth. Studies of endogenous growth can provide a host of techniques and insights applicable to the growth and defense issue. Time-series cross-section estimates should be presented for countries that are sufficiently similar to warrant grouping them in the same cohort. New Feder-Ram studies should involve simultaneous equations, ally spillovers, and investment demand.

For industrial policies, additional studies are needed to evaluate the role of government subsidization of R & D (Lichtenberg, 1990). Alternative subsidy arrangements should be compared on efficiency and equity grounds. A better understanding of technical spillovers to nondefense industries from defense industries is required. The desirability of allies to pool resources when developing new weapons must be addressed further. Surely, the study of competitive structures of the defense industry deserves further analysis. For alliance policy, the primary issue for future research concerns the optimal design of alliance structure based on transaction costs considerations. Should alliances be loose or tight? How should weapons be funded in alliances – commonly or independently? Should allies specialize efforts on different missions? The optimal partition of nations among alliances also require more study.

Future studies in arms trade need to assess more accurately the risks associated with arms exportation. In particular, the proper force structure must be ascertained with and without arms exports. As a related topic, there needs to be analysis of the net economic benefits, if any, from arms trade. In the case of arms restrictions, who gains and who loses? Also additional studies are required to investigate the influence of past arms sales on regional stability. Studies are also needed to ascertain the effectiveness of sanctions to punish nations that promote arms proliferation and that violate arms embargoes. Finally, there should be additional studies on arms trade and technology transfers.

For arms control and conversion, the following agenda is suggested:

(i) Further investigations of conversion as an investment strategy and process should be undertaken.

(ii) Better calculations of the peace dividend is needed that adjust for the short-run disruptions and costs associated with downsizing.

(iii) An application of advances in game theory, especially those concerned with bilateral and multilateral bargaining, to the arms control issue is needed.

(iv)   More research should be done on the role of the government policy in minimizing the cost of adjustment during conversion.

(v)   There needs to be further study of the stability (instability) of arms reduction. How far should arms reductions be carried? How should these reductions be allocated among weapon classes?

(vi)   Future studies of disarmament should account for the economic structure of the economy (i.e., planned, market or transitional; developed or developing).

(vii) The economics of regulation should be applied to the arms control issue.

(viii) There is a need to study the role of the UN peacekeeping effort in the post cold war era. How should burdens be shared for peace-keeping? Should the UN have an integrated general command for its peacekeeping operations, modeled after NATO? When should the UN intervene in a conflict? How many interventions can the UN consider at a time? The whole mission and operation of UN peacekeeping are in need of careful analysis.

(ix)   Arms control should be studied in a framework that accounts for positive and negative externalities.

Despite the recent interest and analyses of nonconventional conflict, much remains to be done. To date, a limited number of technologies of conflict have been integrated into the analysis (Grossman, 1991; Hirshleifer, 1991, 1994), but this needs to be rectified. More sophisticated models are required for predicting political revolutions and their likely outcomes. Dynamic elements must be introduced into the existing general equilibrium studies. Moreover, alternative strategic assumptions should be investigated. Uncertainty should be included in the investigations of guerrilla warfare and insurrections. In the case of terrorism, empirical studies are required to examine terrorist substitution among targets (e.g., business, military, official, and others). A multi-period model of terrorist campaigns should be developed. Also two-sided incomplete information should be included in a game analysis of terrorist/government interactions.

14.4   Concluding remarks

Defense economics includes a wide range of contributions that have applied economic methods and reasoning to a host of defense and peace related issues. Much remains for future research for this policy-oriented field. The next three decades should rival the field's first three decades in terms of contributions and new insights.

References

Abelson, R.P., 1963. "A Derivation of Richardson's Equations," *Journal of Conflict Resolution*, 7(1), 13–15.

ACDA, 1993. *World Military Expenditures and Arms Transfers, 1991/2*. Washington DC: US Arms Control and Disarmament Agency.

ACOST, 1989. *Defence R&D: A National Resource*. London: HMSO.

Adams, F. Gerald, Behrman, Jere, R., and Boldin, Michael, 1991. "Government Expenditures, Defense, and Economic Growth in LDCs: A Revised Perspective," *Conflict Management and Peace Science*, 11(2), 19–35.

Adams, K. and Adams, W.J., 1972. "The Military–Industrial Complex: A Market Structure Analysis," *American Economic Review*, 62(2), 279–87.

Agapos, A.M., 1975. *Government–Industry and Defense: Economics and Administration*. Alabama: University of Alabama Press.

Alexander, W. Robert J., 1990. "The Impact of Defence Spending on Economic Growth: A Multi-Sectoral Approach to Defence Spending and Economic Growth with Evidence from Developed Economies," *Defence Economics*, 2(1), 39–55.

Altman, H., 1969. "Earnings, Unemployment and the Supply of Enlisted Volunteers," *Journal of Human Resources*, 4(1), 38–59.

Altman, S.H. and Barro, R.J., 1971. "Officer Supply – The Impact of Pay, the Draft and the Vietnam War," *American Economic Review*, 61(4), 649–64.

Altman, S.H. and Fechter, A.E., 1967. "The Supply of Military Personnel in the Absence of the Draft'," *American Economic Review, Papers and Proceedings*, 57(2), 19–31.

Anderton, Charles H., 1986. "Optimality and the Ineffectiveness of the Strategic Defense Initiative," *Conflict Management and Peace Science*, 9(2), 31–43.

1989. "Arms Race Modeling: Problems and Prospects," *Journal of Conflict Resolution*, 33(2), 346–67.

1990a. "The Inherent Propensity Toward Peace or War Embodied in Weaponry," *Defence Economics*, 1(3), 197–219.

1990b. "Teaching Arms–Race Concepts in Intermediate Microeconomics," *Journal of Economic Education*, 21(2), 148–67.

1992. "A New Look at the Relationship among Arms Races, Disarmament, and the Probability of War," in Chatterji, Manas and Forcey, Linda Rennie (eds.), *Disarmament, Economic Conversion, and Management of Peace*. New York: Praeger, pp. 75–87.

1993. "Arms Race Modelling and Economic Growth," in Payne, James E., and

Sahu, Arandi P. (eds.), *Defense Spending and Economic Growth*. Boulder, CO: Westview Press.

Anderton, Charles H. and Fogarty, Thomas, 1990. "Consequential Damage and Nuclear Deterrence," *Conflict Management and Peace Science*, 11(1), 1–15.

Andreoni, James, 1989. "Giving with Impure Altruism: Applications to Charity and Ricardian Equivalence," *Journal of Political Economy*, 97(6), 1447–58.

1990. "Impure Altruism and Donations to Public Goods: A Theory of Warm-Glow Giving," *Economic Journal*, 100(3), 464–77.

Anthony, Ian, 1993. "The United States: Arms Exports and Implications for Arms Production," in Wulf, H. (ed.), *Arms Industry Limited*. Oxford: Oxford University Press and SIPRI.

Anton, James J. and Yao, Dennis A., 1987. "Second Sourcing and the Experience Curve: Price Competition in Defense Procurement," *Rand Journal of Economics*, 18(1) (Spring), 57–76.

1990. "Measuring the Effectiveness of Competition in Defence Procurement: A Survey of the Empirical Literature," *Journal of Policy Analysis and Management*, 9(1), 60–79.

Arditti, F. and Peck, M.J., 1964. *Defense Contractors and Labor Adjustment*. Santa Monica: Rand.

Ash, Colin, Udis, Bernard, and McNown, Robert F., 1983. "Enlistments in the All–Volunteer Forces: A Military Personnel Supply Model and Its Forecasts," *American Economic Review*, 73(1), 145–55.

Asher, Harold, 1956. *Cost–Quantity Relationship in the Airframe Industry*. Santa Monica: Rand.

Atesoglu, H. Sonmez and Mueller, Michael, J., 1990. "Defence Spending and Economic Growth," *Defence Economics*, 2(1), 19–27.

Atkinson, Scott E., Sandler, Todd, and Tschirhart, John, 1987. "Terrorism in a Bargaining Framework," *Journal of Law and Economics*, 30(1), 1–21.

Austin, R. and Larkey, P., 1992. "The Unintended Consequences of Micromanagement: The Case Study of Procuring Mission Critical Computer Resources," *Policy Sciences*, 25(1), 3–28.

Ayanian, Robert, 1992. "Force Deployment and the Production of Security: Why is the United States in NATO?" *Defence Economics*, 3(2), 99–112.

Baek, Ehung Gi, 1991. "Defence Spending and Economic Performance in the United States: Some Structural VAR Evidence," *Defence Economics*, 2(3), 251–64.

Bailey, Martin J., 1967. "Defence Decentralization Through Internal Prices," in Enke, S. (ed.), *Defense Management*. New Jersey: Prentice-Hall.

Ball, Nicole, 1986. "Converting the Workforce: Defence Industry Conversion in the Industrialised Countries," *International Labour Review*, 125(4), 401–22.

Baran, Paul A. and Sweezy, Paul M., 1966. *Monopoly Capital*. New York: Monthly Review Press.

Baron, David P., 1988. "Procurement Contracting: Efficiency, Renegotiation and Performance Evaluation," *Information Economics and Policy*, 3(2), 109–42.

Baron, David P. and Besanko, David, 1987. "Monitoring, Moral Hazard, Asymmetric Information, and Risk Sharing in Procurement Contracting," *Rand Journal of Economics*, 18(4) 509–32.

Barro, Robert J., 1991. "Economic Growth in a Cross Section of Countries," *Quarterly Journal of Economics*, 106(2), 407–43.

Baumol, William, 1982. "Contestable Markets: An Uprising in the Theory of Industrial Structure," *American Economic Review*, 72, 1–15.

Baumol, William, Panzar, John, and Willig, Robert, 1982. *Contestable Markets and the Theory of Industry Structure*. New York: Harcourt Brace Jovanovich.

Becker, G.S., 1964. *Human Capital: A Theoretical and Empirical Analysis with Special Reference to Education*. New York: Columbia University Press.

1968. "Crime and Punishment: An Economic Approach," *Journal of Political Economy*, 78(2), 169–217.

Beer, Francis A., 1972. *The Political Economy of Alliances*. Beverly Hills, CA: Sage.

Bellany, Ian, 1978. *A Statistical Analysis of Factors Affecting Voluntary Enlistment into the UK Armed Forces: 1960–1976*. Centre for the Study of Arms Control and International Security, University of Lancaster.

1983. *Why Men Enlist: The Royal Navy and the Royal Air Force, 1970–80*. Lancaster: Bailrigg Paper on International Security, No.6, University of Lancaster.

Benoit, Emile, 1973. *Defense and Economic Growth in Developing Countries*. Boston: D.C. Heath.

1978. "Growth and Defense in Developing Countries," *Economic Development and Cultural Change*, 26(2), 271–87.

Benoit, Emile and Boulding, Kenneth (eds.), 1963. *Disarmament and the Economy*. New York: Harper and Row.

Berejikian, Jeffrey, 1992. "Revolutionary Collective Action and the Agent–Structure Problem," *American Political Science Review*, 86(3), 647–57.

Berger, M.C. and Hirsch, B.T., 1983. "The Civilian Earnings Experience of Vietnam-Era Veterans," *Journal of Human Resources*, 18(4) (Fall), 453–79.

Bergstrom, Theodore C., Blume, Lawrence, and Varian, Hal, 1986. "On the Private Provision of Public Goods," *Journal of Public Economics*, 29(1), 25–49.

Bergstrom, Theodore C. and Goodman, Robert P., 1973. "Private Demands for Public Goods," *American Economic Review*, 63(3), 280–96.

Berner, J. Kevin and Daula, Thomas V., 1993. "Recruiting Goals, Regime Shifts and the Supply of Labor to the Army," *Defence Economics* 4(4), 315–28.

Binkin, Martin, 1984. *America's Volunteer Military: Progress and Prospects*. Washington DC: The Brookings Institution.

Binkin, Martin and Kyriakopoulos, Irene, 1979. *Youth or Experience? Manning the Modern Military*. Washington DC: The Brookings Institution.

1981. *Paying the Modern Military*. Washington DC: The Brookings Institution.

Biswas, Basudeb and Ram, Rati, 1986. "Military Expenditures and Economic Growth in Less Developed Countries: An Augmented Model and Further Evidence," *Economic Development and Cultural Change*, 34(2), 361–72.

Bittleston, Michael, 1990. *Co-operation or Competition? Defence Procurement Options for the 1990s*. London: Adelphi Paper 250, IISS.

Blackaby, Frank and Ohlson, Thomas, 1987. "Military Expenditure and the Arms Trade: Problems of the Data," in Schmidt, C. (ed.)., *The Economics of Military Expenditures*. London: Macmillan.

Bolton, Roger E., 1966. *Defense Purchases and Regional Growth*. Washington DC: The Brookings Institution.

Boot, Ray, 1990. *From Spitfire to Eurofighter*. Shrewsbury: Airlife.

Booth, Mark C., Hartley, Keith. and Powell, Melanie, 1990. "Industry: Structure, Performance and Policy," in Maynard, A. and Tether, P. (eds.), *Preventing Alcohol and Tobacco Problems*, vol. I. Aldershot: Avebury.

Borcherding, Thomas E., 1971. "A Neglected Cost of a Voluntary Military," *American Economic Review*, 61 (1), 195–6.

Borcherding, Thomas E. and Deacon, Robert T., 1972. "The Demand for the Services of Non–Federal Governments," *American Economic Review*, 62(5), 891–901.

Bougrov, Evguene, 1994. "Conversion in Transitional Economies: The Case of the Former USSR and Russia," *Defence and Peace Economics*, 5(2), 153–66.

Boulding, Kenneth E., 1960. "The Domestic Implications of Arms Control," *Daedalus* (Fall), 848.

1962. *Conflict and Defense: A General Theory*. New York: Harper and Row.

Bower, Anthony G, and Osband, Kent, 1991. "When More is Less: Defense Profit Policy in a Competitive Environment," *Rand Journal of Economics*, 22(1), 107–19.

Bowman, W., Little, R. and Sicilia, G.T. (eds.), 1986. *The All-Volunteer Force After A Decade*. Washington DC: Pergamon–Brassey's.

Boyer, Mark A., 1989. "Trading Public Goods in the Western Alliance System," *Journal of Conflict Resolution*, 33(4), 700–27.

1990. "A Simple and Untraditional Analysis of Western Alliance Burden-Sharing," *Defence Economics*, 1(3), 243–59.

Brada, Josef C. and Graves, Ronald L., 1988. "The Slowdown in Soviet Defense Expenditures," *Southern Economic Journal*, 54(4), 969–84.

Braddon, Derek, Dowdall, P., Kendry, A., and Reay, S., 1992. *Defence Procurement and the Defence Industry Supply Chain*. Bristol: University of West of England, Research Unit in Defence Economics.

Brams, Steven J., 1985. *Superpower Games*. New Haven, CT: Yale University Press.

Brams, Steven J., Davis, Morton D. and Straffin, Philip D. Jr., 1979. "The Geometry of the Arms Race," *International Studies Quarterly*, 23(4), 567–88.

Brams, Steven J. and Kilgour, Marc, 1988. "National Security Games," *Synthese*, 76(2), 185–200.

Bramson, A., 1990. *Pure Luck: Authorised Biography of Sir Thomas Sopwith*. Northampton: Patric Stephens.

Brauer, Jurgen, 1991. "Arms Production in Developing Nations: The Relation to Industrial Structure, Industrial Diversification and Human Capital Formation," *Defence Economics*, 2(2), 165–74.

Brennan, T., 1990. "Cross-Subsidization and Cost Mis-Allocation by Regulated Monopolists," *Journal of Regulatory Economics*, 2(1), 37–52.

Brito, Dagobert L., 1972. "A Dynamic Model of an Armament Race," *International Economic Review*, 13(2), 359–75.

Brito, Dagobert L. and Intriligator, Michael D., 1974. "Uncertainty and the Stability of the Armament Race," *Annals of Economic and Social Measurement*, 3(1), 279–92.

1977. "Nuclear Proliferation and the Armaments Race," *Journal of Peace Science*, 2(1), 231–8.

1981. "Strategic Arms Limitation Treaties and Innovations in Weapons Technology," *Public Choice*, 37(1), 41–59.

1989. "An Economic Model of Guerrilla Warfare," *International Interactions*, 15(3), 319–29.

1992. "Narco-Traffic and Guerrilla Warfare: A New Symbiosis," *Defence Economics*, 3(4), 263–74.

Brophy-Baermann, Bryan and Conybeare, John, 1994. "Retaliating Against Terrorism: Rational Expectations and the Optimality of Rules Versus Discretion," *American Journal of Political Science*, 38(1), 196–210.

Brown, C., 1985. "Military Enlistments: What Can We Learn from Geographic Variation?" *American Economic Review*, 75(1), 228–34.

Browning, H.L., Lopreato, S.C. and Poston, D.L., 1973. "Income and Veteran Status: Variations among Mexican Americans, Blacks and Anglos," *American Sociological Review*, 38(1), 74–85.

Bruce, Neil, 1990. "Defense Expenditures by Countries in Allied and Adversarial Relationships," *Defence Economics*, 1(3), 179–95.

Brunette, R., 1989. "US Congress Requires Limitations on Competition for Innovative Defense Contractors and Sub-contractors," *National Contract Management Journal*, 23(1), 85–9.

Bryant, R. and Wilhite, Al, 1990. "Military Experience and Training Effects on Civilian Wages," *Applied Economics*, 22(1), 69–82.

Brzoska, Michael, 1987a. "Current Trends in Arms Transfers," in Deger, S. and West, R. (eds.), *Defence, Security and Development*. London: Frances Pinter.

1987b. "The Arms Trade: Can it be Controlled," *Journal of Peace Research*, 24(4), 327–33.

1994. "The Financing Factor in Military Trade," *Defence Economics*, 5(1).

Buchanan, James M., 1986. *Liberty, Market and the State*. Brighton: Wheat-sheaf.

Buck, David, Hartley, Keith, and Hooper, Nicholas, 1993. "Defence Research and Development, Crowding-Out and the Peace Dividend," *Defence Economics*, 4(2), 161–78.

Buddin, Richard, 1993. "Recruiting for Joint Active/Reserve Tours," *Defence Economics*, 4(1), 15–32.

Bueno de Mesquita, Bruce and Lalman, David, 1988. "Arms Races and the Opportunity for Peace," *Synthese*, 76(2), 263–83.

Burnett, William B., 1987. "Competition in the Weapons Acquisition Process: The Case of US Warplanes," *Journal of Policy Analysis and Management*, 7(1), 17–39.

Byers, J.D. and Peel, D.A., 1989. "The Determinants of Arms Race Expenditures of NATO and the Warsaw Pact: Some Further Evidence," *Journal of Peace Research*, 26(1), 69–77.

Callaghan, Thomas A. Jr., 1975. *US–European Economic Co-operation in Military and Civil Technology*. Washington DC: Georgetown University.

Cannes, M.E., 1975. "The Simple Economics of Incentive Contracting: A Note," *American Economic Review*, 65, 478–83.

Carr, Jack L., 1989. "Government Size and Economic Growth: A New

Framework and Some Evidence from Cross-Section and Time-Series Data," *American Economic Review*, 79(1), 267–71.

Caspary, W.R., 1967. "Richardson's Models of Arms Race: Description, Critique, and an Alternative Model," *International Studies Quarterly*, 11(1), 63–90.

Catrina, C., 1988. *Arms Transfers and Dependence*. London: Taylor and Frances.

Cauley, Jon and Im, Eric I., 1988. "Intervention Policy Analysis of Skyjackings and Other Terrorist Incidents," *American Economic Review*, 78(2), 27–31.

Cauley, Jon and Sandler, Todd, 1988. "Fighting World War III: A Suggested Strategy," *Terrorism*, 11(3), 181–95.

Cauley, Jon, Sandler, Todd, and Cornes, Richard, 1986. "Nonmarket Institutional Structures: Conjectures, Distribution, and Efficiency," *Public Finance*, 41(2), 153–72.

Caves, Richard E. and Marin, Dalia, 1992. "Countertrade Transactions: Theory and Evidence," *Economic Journal*, 102(414), 1171–83.

Cavin, Edward S., 1991. "An Optimal Control Model of New Weapon System Development," *Defence Economics*, 3(1), 19–33.

CBO, 1987. *Effects of Weapons Procurement Stretch-Outs on Costs and Schedules*. Washington DC: Congressional Budget Office, November.

1990. *US Costs of Verification and Compliance Under Pending Arms Treaties*. Washington DC: Congressional Budget Office, September.

1991. *The START Treaty and Beyond*. Washington DC: Congressional Budget Office, October.

1992a. *Environmental Clean up Issues Associated with Closing Military Bases*. Washington DC: Congressional Budget Office, August.

1992b. *Limiting Conventional Arms Exports to the Middle East*. Washington DC: Congressional Budget Office.

1993. *Options for Fighter and Attack Aircraft: Costs and Capabilities*. Washington DC: Congressional Budget Office, May.

Celmer, Marc, 1987. *Terrorism, US Strategy and Reagan*. Westport, CT: Greenwood Press.

Chadwick, R.C., 1986. "Richardson Processes and Arms Transfers, 1971–80: A Preliminary Analysis," *Journal of Peace Research*, 23(4), 309–28.

Chakrabarti, Alok K., Glismann, Haas H., and Horn, Ernst-Jurgen, 1992. "Defence and Space Expenditures in the US: An Inter-firm Analysis," *Defence Economics*, 3(2), 169–90.

Chalmers, James A. and Shelton, Robert B., 1975. "An Economic Analysis of Riot Participation," *Economic Inquiry*, 13(3), 322–36.

Chalmers, Malcolm and Greene, Owen, 1994. *Background Information: An Analysis of Information Provided to the UN on Military Holdings and Procurement through National Production in the First Year of the Register of Conventional Arms*. Bradford: Department of Peace Studies.

Chan, Steve, 1985. "The Impact of Defense Spending on Economic Performance: A Survey of Evidence and Problems," *Orbis* 29(2), 403–34.

Chan, Steve and Mintz, Alex (eds.), 1992. *Defense, Welfare and Growth*. London: Routledge.

Chinworth, Michael W., 1992. *Inside Japan's Defense*. Washington DC: Brassey's (US).

Chowdhury, Abdur R., 1991. "Defense Spending and Economic Growth," *Journal of Conflict Resolution*, 35(1), 80–97.

Cmnd, 4079, 1969. *Standing Reference on the Pay of the Armed Forces*. London: National Board for Prices and Incomes Report No.116, HMSO.

Conybeare, John A.C., 1992. "A Portfolio Diversification Model of Alliances: The Triple Alliance and Triple Entente, 1879–1914," *Journal of Conflict Resolution*, 36(1), 53–85.

Conybeare, John A.C., Murdoch, James, and Sandler, Todd, 1994. "Alternative Collective-Goods Models of Military Alliances: Theory and Empirics," *Economic Inquiry*, 32(4).

Conybeare, John A.C. and Sandler, Todd, 1990. "The Triple Entente and the Triple Alliance 1880–1914: A Collective Goods Approach," *American Political Science Review*, 84(4), 1197–206.

Cooper, Sir Frank, 1985. *Preconditions for the Emergence of a European Common Market in Armaments*. Brussels: Centre for European Policy Studies.

Cooper, Julian, 1991. "The Soviet Defence Industry and Conversion," in Paukert, L. and Richards, P. (eds.), *Defence Expenditure, Industrial Conversion and Local Employment*. Geneva: ILO.

1993. "The Soviet Union and the Successor Republics: Defence Industries Coming to Terms with Disunion," in Wulf, H. (ed.), *Arms Industry Limited*. Stockholm: SIPRI.

Cooper, Ron A., Hartley, Keith, and Harvey, Charles, 1970. *Export Performance and the Pressure of Demand*. London: Allen and Unwin.

Cornes, Richard, 1992. *Duality and Modern Economics*. Cambridge: Cambridge University Press.

Cornes, Richard and Sandler, Todd, 1984. "Easy Riders, Joint Production, and Public Goods," *Economic Journal*, 94(3), 580–98.

1986. *The Theory of Externalities, Public Goods, and Club Goods*. New York: Cambridge University Press.

Cowen, Tyler and Lee, Dwight, 1992. "The Usefulness of Inefficient Procurement," *Defence Economics*, 3(3), 219–28.

Creasey, Pauline and May, Simon (eds.), 1988. *The European Armaments Market and Procurement Co-operation*. London: Macmillan.

Crenshaw, Martha, 1992. "Current Research on Terrorism: The Academic Perspective," *Studies in Conflict and Terrorism*, 15(1), 1–11.

Crothier, P. and Moravcsik, A., 1991. "Defense and the Single Market: The Outlook for Collaborative Ventures," *International Defense Review*, 9, 949–63.

CRS, 1994. *F-22 Aircraft Program*. Washington DC: Congressional Research Service.

Cummins, J. Michael, 1977. "Incentive Contracting for National Defense: A Problem of Optimal Risk Sharing," *Bell Journal of Economics*, 8(1), 168–85.

Cusack, Thomas R. and Ward, Michael D., 1981. "Military Spending in the United States, Soviet Union, and the People's Republic of China," *Journal of Conflict Resolution*, 25(3), 429–69.

Dale, C. and Gilroy, C., 1985. "The Outlook for Army Recruiting," *Eastern Economic Review*, 11(2), 107–22.

Dasgupta, Dipankar and Itaya, Jun-ichi, 1992. "Comparative Statics for the

Private Provision of Public Goods in a Conjectural Variations Model with Heterogeneous Agents," *Public Finance*, 47(1), 17–31.

De Long, J. Bradford and Summers, Lawrence H., 1991. "Equipment Investment and Economic Growth," *Quarterly Journal of Economics*, 106(2), 445–502.

De Mayo, P., 1983. "Bidding on New Ship Construction," in Englebrecht-Wiggans, R., *et al.* (eds.), *Auction, Bidding and Contracting*. New York: New York University Press.

DeBoer, L. and Brorsen, B.W., 1989. "The Demand for and Supply of Military Labor," *Southern Economic Journal*, 55(4), 853–69.

Deger, Saadet, 1986a. "Economic Development and Defense Expenditure," *Economic Development and Cultural Change*, 35(1), 179–96.

1986b. *Military Expenditure in Third World Countries: The Economic Effects*. London: Routledge & Kegan Paul.

1989. "Recent Patterns of Arms Trade and Regional Conflict," in Rotblat, J. and Holdren, J.P. (eds.), *Building Global Security Through Cooperation: Annals of Pugwash*. Berlin: Springer-Verlag.

Deger, Saadet and Sen, Somnath, 1990a. *Military Expenditure: The Political Economy of International Security*. Oxford: Oxford University Press and SIPRI.

1990b. "Military Security and the Economy: Defence Expenditure in India and Pakistan," in Hartley, Keith and Sandler, Todd (eds.), *The Economics of Defence Spending: An International Survey*. London: Routledge, pp. 189–227.

1991. "Military Expenditure, Aid and Economic Development," *Annual Conference on Development Economics*. Washington DC: World Bank.

Deger, Saadet and Smith, Ron P., 1983. "Military Expenditures and Growth in Less Developed Countries," *Journal of Conflict Resolution*, 27(2), 335–53.

Demong, Richard F. and Strayer, David E., 1981. "The Underlying Theory of Incentive Contracting," *Defense Management Journal* (First Quarter), 42–51.

Demski, Joel S., Sappington, David E.M., and Spiller, Pablo T., 1987. "Managing Supplier Switching," *Rand Journal of Economics*, 18(1) (Spring), 77–97.

Denoon, David B.H. (ed.), 1986. *Constraints on Strategy*. Washington DC: Pergamon–Brassey's.

Dertouzos, J., 1985. *Recruiter Incentives and Enlistment Supply*. Santa Monica: Rand.

Dews, E. *et al.*, 1979. *Acquisition Policy Effectiveness: Department of Defense Experience in the 1970s*. Santa Monica: Rand.

Dixit, Avinash and Nalebuff, Barry, 1991. *Thinking Strategically*. New York: W.W. Norton & Co.

Dorfer, I., 1983. *Arms Deal: The Selling of the F-16*. New York: Praeger.

Downes, Cathy, 1991. "Military Manpower: Strategic Asset, Liability or Non-entity?" *Defence Economics*, 2(4), 353–64.

Draper, Alan G., 1990. *European Defence Equipment Collaboration*. London: Macmillan.

Drown, Jane Davis, Drown, Clifford, and Campbell, Kelly (eds.), 1990. *A Single European Arms Industry?* London: Brassey's.

Dudley, Leonard, 1979. "Foreign Aid and the Theory of Alliances," *Review of Economics and Statistics*, 61(4), 564–71.

Dudley, Leonard and Montmarquette, Claude, 1981. "The Demand for Military Expenditures: An International Comparison," *Public Choice*, 37(1), 5–31.

Dumas, Lloyd J., 1977. "Economic Conversion, Productive Efficiency and Social Welfare," *Journal of Sociology and Social Welfare*, 4(3–4), 567–96.

Dunleavy, Patrick, 1991. *Democracy, Bureaucracy and Public Choice*. London: Harvester Wheatsheaf.

Dunne, Paul, 1993. "The Changing Military Industrial Complex in the UK," *Defence Economics*, 4(2), 113–22.

Dunne, Paul and Smith, Ron P., 1990. "Military Expenditures and Unemployment in the OECD," *Defence Economics*, 1(1), 57–73.

Dunsire, Andrew, Hartley, Keith, and Parker, David, 1991. "Organisational Status and Performance: Summary of the Findings," *Public Administration*, 69(1), 21–40.

Dussauge, Pierre, 1987. "The Conversion of Military Activities," in Blackaby, F. and Schmidt, C. (eds.), *Peace, Defence and Economic Analysis*. London: Macmillan.

Dussauge, Pierre and Garrette, Bernard, 1993. "Industrial Alliances in Aerospace and Defence: An Empirical Study of Strategic and Organizational Patterns," *Defence Economics*, 4(1), 45–62.

EC, 1989. *Public Procurement in the Excluded Sectors, Bulletin of the European Communities*. Luxembourg: EC.

  1992. *The Economic and Social Impact of Reductions in Defence Spending and Military Forces on the Regions of the Community*. Brussels: EC, DGXVI.

Eden, P., 1972. "US Human Capital Loss in Southeast Asia," *Journal of Human Resources*, 7(3), 384–94.

Edgar, Alistair D. and Haglund, David G., 1993. "Japanese Defence Industrialisation," in Matthews, R. and Matsuyama, K. (eds.), *Japan's Military Renaissance?* London: Macmillan.

Ehrlich, Isaac, 1973. "Participation in Illegitimate Activities: A Theoretical and Empirical Investigation," *Journal of Political Economy*, 81(3), 521–65.

EIU, 1963. *The Economic Effects of Disarmament*. London: Economists Intelligence Unit.

Elstub, St. J., 1969. *Productivity of the National Aircraft Effort*. London: HMSO.

Enders, Walter, Parise, Gerald F., and Sandler, Todd, 1992. "A Time-Series Analysis of Transnational Terrorism: Trends and Cycles," *Defence Economics*, 3(4), 305–20.

Enders, Walter and Sandler, Todd, 1991. "Causality Between Transnational Terrorism and Tourism: The Case of Spain," *Terrorism*, 14(1), 49–58.

  1993. "The Effectiveness of Anti-Terrorism Policies: Vector-Autoregression-Intervention Analysis," *American Political Science Review*, 87(4), 829–44.

Enders, Walter, Sandler, Todd, and Cauley, Jon, 1990a. "U.N. Conventions, Technology and Retaliation in the Fight Against Terrorism: An Econometric Evaluation," *Terrorism and Political Violence*, 2(1), 83–105.

  1990b. "Assessing the Impact of Terrorist-Thwarting Policies: An Intervention Time Series Approach," *Defence Economics*, 2(1), 1–18.

Enders, Walter, Sandler, Todd, and Parise, Gerald F., 1992. "An Econometric Analysis of the Impact of Terrorism on Tourism," *Kyklos*, 45(4), 531–54.

Enke, Stephen (ed.), 1967. *Defense Management*. Englewood Cliffs: Prentice-Hall.

Epps, T.W., 1973. "An Econometric Analysis of the Effectiveness of the US Army's 1971 Paid Advertising Campaign," *Applied Economics*, 5(4), 261–9.

Failing, M., 1989. "A Layman's Guide to the Federal Fraud Laws," *National Contract Management Journal*, 23(1) (Summer), 37–54.

Faini, Riccardo, Annez, Patricia, and Taylor, Lance, 1984. "Defence Spending, Economic Structure, and Growth Evidence among Countries and Over Time," *Economic Development and Cultural Change*, 32(3), 487–98.

Faltas, S., 1986. *Arms Markets and Armament Policy: The Changing Structure of Naval Industries in Western Europe*. Netherlands: Nijhoff.

Feder, Gershon, 1983. "On Exports and Economic Growth," *Journal of Development Economics*, 12(1/2), 59–73.

Fischer, D., 1984. "Weapons Technology and the Intensity of Arms Races," *Conflict Management and Peace Science*, 8(1), 49–70.

Fisher, Anthony C., 1969. "The Cost of the Draft and the Cost of Ending the Draft," *American Economic Review*, 59(3), 239–54.

Fisher, F.M. and Morton, A.S., 1967. "Re-enlistment in the US Navy: A Cost-Effectiveness Study," *American Economic Review, Papers and Proceedings*, 57(2), 32–8.

Fontanel, Jacques, 1989. *French Arms Industry*. France: Cahiers du CEDSI, 10, Grenoble.
  1994. "The Economics of Disarmament: A Survey," *Defence and Peace Economics*, 5(2).

Fontanel, Jacques, and Ward, Michael D., 1993. "Military Expenditures, Armament and Disarmament," *Defence Economics*, 4(1), 63–78.

Foss, C.F. and McKenzie, P., 1988. *The Vickers Tank*. Wellingborough: Patrick Stephens.

Fox, Ronald J., 1974. *Arming America: How the US Buys Weapons*. Boston: Harvard University Press.

Frankenstein, J., 1993. "The People's Republic of China: Arms Production, Industrial Strategy and Problems of History," in Wulf, H. (ed.), *Arms Industry Limited*. Oxford: Oxford University Press and SIPRI.

Fritz–Aβmus, Dieter and Zimmermann, Klaus, 1990. "West German Demand for Defence Spending," in Hartley, Keith and Sandler, Todd (eds.), *The Economics of Defence Spending*. London: Routledge, pp. 118–47.

Galbraith, John Kenneth, 1972. *The New Industrial State*. London: André Deutsch, second edition.

Gansler, Jacques S., 1980. *The Defense Industry*. Cambridge, MA: MIT Press.
  1989a. *Affording Defense*. Cambridge, MA: MIT Press.
  1989b. "Affording Defense: The Changes That are Needed," *National Contract Management Journal*, 23(1), 1–22.

Gates, Thomas F., 1970. *President's Commission on an All-Volunteer Force: Report*. Washington DC: US Government Printing Office.

Gillespie, J.V., Zinnes, Dina A., and Rubison, R.M., 1978. "Accumulation in Arms Race Models: A Geometric Lag Perspective," *Comparative Political Studies*, 10(4), 475–96.

Gillespie, J.V., Zinnes, Dina A., Tahim, G.S., Schrodt, P.A., and Rubison, R. M., 1977. "An Optimal Control Model of Arms Races," *American Political Science Review*, 7(1), 226–44.

Goff, Brian L. and Tollison, Robert D., 1990. "Is National Defense a Pure Public Good?," *Defence Economics*, 1(2), 141–7.

Goldberg, Matthew S. and Warner, J. T., 1987. "Military Experience, Civilian Experience and the Earnings of Veterans," *Journal of Human Resources*, 22(1), 62–81.

Gonzales, Rodolfo A. and Mehay, Stephen L., 1990. "Publicness, Scale, and Spillover Effects in Defense Spending," *Public Finance Quarterly*, 18(1–3), 273–90.

1991. "Burden Sharing in the NATO Alliance: An Empirical Test of Alternative Views," *Public Choice*, 68(3), 107–16.

Greene, Kenneth V. and Newlon, Daniel H., 1973. "The Pareto Optimality of Eliminating a Lottery Draft," *Quarterly Review of Economics and Business*, 13(4), 61–70.

Greenwood, David, 1979. *European Technological Co-operation and Defence Procurement*. Brussels: EC.

Greer, Willis R. and Liao, Shu S., 1984. "A New Look at Risk and Profitability in Defense Contracting," *National Contract Management Journal* (Summer), 23–30.

1986. "An Analysis of Risk and Return in the Defense Market: Its Impact on Weapon System Competition," *Management Science*, 32(10) (October), 1259–73.

Grobar, Lisa M., 1992. "Country Survey II: Sri Lanka," *Defence Economics*, 3(2), 135–46.

Grobar, Lisa M. and Porter, Richard C., 1989. "Benoit Revisited: Defense Spending and Economic Growth in LDCs," *Journal of Conflict Resolution*, 33(2), 318–45.

Grobar, Lisa M., Stern, Robert M. and Deardorff, Alan V., 1990. "The Economic Effects of International Trade in Armaments in the Major Western Industrialized and Developing Countries," *Defence Economics*, 1(2), 97–120.

Grossman, Herschel I., 1991. "A General Equilibrium Model of Insurrections," *American Economic Review*, 81(4), 912–21.

1992. "Foreign Aid and Insurrections," *Defence Economics*, 3(4), 275–88.

Gruneberg, D.S., 1994. "The Defence Firm and Trends in Civil and Military Technologies: Integration Versus Differentiation," in Latham, A. and Hooper, N. (eds.), *The Future of the Defence Firm in Europe, North America and East Asia*. Holland: Kluwer.

Haglund, David (ed.), 1989. *The Defence Industrial Base and the West*. London: Routledge.

Hall, G.R. and Johnson, R.E., 1967. *Aircraft Co-Production and Procurement Strategy*. Santa Monica: Rand, R–450–PR, May.

Hall, P. and Markowski, S., 1994. "On The Normality and Abnormality of Offset Obligations," *Defence Economics*, 5(3), 173–88.

Hamilton, Lawrence C. and Hamilton, James D., 1983. "Dynamics of Terrorism," *International Studies Quarterly*, 27(1), 39–54.

Hammond, C.P. and Graham, D.R., 1983. "A Model for Estimating the Costs of

Changes for Navy Shipbuilding Programmes," in Engelbrecht-Wiggans, R., et al. (eds.), *Auctions, Bidding and Contracting*. New York: New York University Press.

Hansen, Laurna, Murdoch, James C., and Sandler, Todd, 1990. "On Distinguishing the Behavior of Nuclear and Non-Nuclear Allies in NATO," *Defence Economics*, 1(1), 37–55.

Hansen, W. Lee and Weisbrod, Burton A., 1967. "The Economics of the Military Draft," *Quarterly Journal of Economics*, 81(3), 395–421.

Harkavy, R.E., 1987. "Arms Resupply During Conflict: A Framework for Analysis," in Schmidt, C. (ed.), *The Economics of Military Expenditures*. London: Macmillan.

Hartley, Keith, 1969. "Estimating Military Aircraft Production Outlays: The British Experience," *Economics Journal*, 79 (4), pp. 861–81.

1972. "The Export Performance of the British Aircraft Industry," *Bulletin of Economic Research*, 24(2), 81–6.

1975. "Short–run Employment Functions and Defence Contracts in the UK Aircraft Industry," *Applied Economics*, 7, 223–33.

1983. *NATO Arms Co-operation*. London: Allen and Unwin.

1985. "Defence Procurement and Industrial Policy," in Roper J. (ed.), *The Future of British Defence Policy*. London: Gower.

1986. "Defence, Industry and Technology: Problems and Possibilities for European Collaboration," in Hall, G. (ed.), *European Industrial Policy*. London: Croom Helm.

1987. "Public Procurement and Competitiveness: A Community Market for Military Hardware and Technology?" *Journal of Common Market Studies*, 25 (3), 237–47.

1991a. "Public Purchasing," *Public Money and Management*, 11(1) (Spring), 45–9.

1991b. *The Economics of Defence Policy*. London: Brasseys.

1992. "Competition in Defence Contracting in the UK," *Public Procurement Law Review*, 6, 440–54.

1993a. "Aerospace: the Political Economy of an Industry," in de Jong, H.W. (ed.), *The Structure of European Industry*. London: Kluwer, third revised edition.

1993b. "Defence," in Harrison, A. (ed.), *From Hierarchy to Contract*. Oxford: Policy Journals.

Hartley, Keith, (ed.), 1994. "The Economics of Disarmament: Special Issue," *Defence and Peace Economics*, 5(2).

Hartley, Keith and Corcoran, William J., 1975. "Short–Run Employment Functions and Defence Contracts in the UK Aircraft Industry," *Applied Economics*, 7, 223–33.

Hartley, Keith and Cox, Andrew, 1992. "The Costs of Non-Europe in Defence Procurement, Executive Summary," Brussels: EC (unpublished).

Hartley, Keith and Hooper, Nicholas, 1990. "The Economics of Defence," *Disarmament, and Peace: An Annotated Bibliography*. Aldershot: Elgar.

1991a. "UK Defence and Dependence: Economic Burden or Benefit?" in Hutton, J, Hutton, S, Pinch, T., and Sheill, A. (eds.), *Dependency to Enterprise*. London: Routledge.

1991b. "Economic Adjustment," in Kirby, S. and Hooper, N. (eds.), *The Cost of Peace*. Reading: Harwood.

1993. *The Economic Consequences of the UK Government's Decision on the Hercules Replacement*. University of York, UK: Research Monograph 2, Centre for Defence Economics.

Hartley, Keith, Hussain, Farooq, and Smith, Ron, 1987. "The UK Defence Industrial Base." *Political Quarterly*, 58(1), 62–72.

Hartley, Keith and Lynk, Edward, 1983a. "Budget Cuts and Public Sector Employment: The Case of Defence," *Applied Economics*, 15(4), 531–40.

1983b. "Labour Demand and Allocation in the UK Engineering Industry," *Scottish Journal of Political Economy*, 3(1), 42–53.

Hartley, Keith and Martin, Stephen, 1993. "Evaluating Collaborative Programmes," *Defence Economics*, 4(2), 195–211.

Hartley, Keith and Peacock, Alan, 1978. "Combined Defence and International Economic Co-operation," *World Economy*, 1(3), 327–39.

Hartley, Keith and Sandler, Todd (eds.), 1990. *The Economics of Defence Spending: An International Survey*. London: Routledge.

Hartley, Keith and Tisdell, Clem, 1981. *Micro-Economic Policy*. London: Wiley, chapter 14.

Hartley, Keith and Watt, Peter, 1981. "Profits, Regulation and the UK Aerospace Industry," *Journal of Industrial Economics*, 29(4) (June), 413–28.

Hartley, Keith *et al.*, 1993. *Economic Aspects of Disarmament: Disarmament as an Investment Process*. New York: United Nations Institute for Disarmament Research (UNIDIR).

Hartley, Thomas and Russett, Bruce, 1992. "Public Opinion and the Common Defense: Who Governs Military Spending in the United States?" *American Political Science Review*, 86(4), 905–15.

Harvey, R.A., 1980. *International Aerospace Collaboration*. London: British Aerospace.

Hawes, M.K., 1989. "The Swedish Defence Industrial Base," in Haglund D.G. (ed.), *The Defence Industrial Base and the West*. London: Routledge.

Hayward, Keith, 1989. *The British Aircraft Industry*. Manchester: Manchester University Press.

HCP 22–I, 1982. *Ministry of Defence Organisation and Procurement*. London: Defence Committee, House of Commons, HMSO.

HCP 53, 1981. *RAF Pilot Training*. London: House of Commons, Defence Committee, HMSO.

HCP 189, 1991. *Ministry of Defence: Initiatives on Defence Procurement*. National Audit Office. London: HMSO, February.

HCP 247, 1991. *Ministry of Defence: Collaborative Projects*. London: National Audit Office, HMSO.

HCP 518, 1986. *The Defence Implications of the Future of Westland plc*. London: Defence Committee, HMSO.

Hess, R.W. and Romanoff, H.P., 1987. *Aircraft Airframe Cost Estimating Relationships*. Santa Monica: Rand, December.

Hewitt, Daniel, 1992. "Military Expenditures Worldwide: Determinants and Trends, 1972–1988," *Journal of Public Policy*, 12(2), 105–52.

360   References

Hildebrandt, Gregory G., 1990. "Services and Wealth Measures of Military Capital," *Defence Economics*, 1(2), 159–76.

Hilton, Brian and Vu, Anh, 1991. "The McGuire Model and the Economics of the NATO Alliance," *Defence Economics*, 2(2), 105–21.

Hirshleifer, Jack, 1983. "From Weakest-Link to Best Shot: The Voluntary Provision of Public Goods," *Public Choice*, 41(3), 371–86.

1991. "The Paradox of Power," *Economics and Politics*, 3(3), 177–200.

1994. "The Dark Side of the Force," *Economic Inquiry*, 32(1), 1–10.

Hitch, C.J., 1965. *Decision-Making for Defense*. Los Angeles: University of California Press.

Hitch, C.J. and McKean, Roland N., 1960. *The Economics of Defense in the Nuclear Age*. Cambridge, MA: Harvard University Press.

Holden, Robert T., 1987. "Time Series Analysis of a Contagious Process," *Journal of the American Statistical Association*, 82(4), 1019–26.

Hooper, Nicholas and Buck, David, 1991. "Defence Industries and Equipment Procurement Options," in Kirby, S. and Hooper, N. (eds.), *The Cost of Peace*. Reading: Harwood.

Hooper, Nicholas and Hartley, Keith, 1993. *Defence Companies Adjusting to Change*. University of York: Research Monograph 3, Centre for Defence Economics.

Horne, D.K., 1985. "Modelling Army Enlistment Supply for the All-Volunteer Force," *Monthly Labor Review*, 108(8), 35–9.

Huang, Chi and Mintz, Alex, 1990. "Ridge Regression Analysis of the Defence–Growth Tradeoff in the United States," *Defence Economics*, 2(1), 19–37.

1991. "Defence Expenditures and Economic Growth: The Externality Effect," *Defence Economics*, 3(2), 35–40.

IEPG, 1986. *Towards A Stronger Europe*. Brussels: NATO.

1988. *Luxembourg Communique and Action Plan on a Stepwise Development of a European Armaments Market*, November. Brussels: IEPG.

Im, Eric I., Cauley, Jon, and Sandler, Todd, 1987. "Cycles and Substitutions in Terrorist Activities: A Spectral Approach," *Kyklos*, 40(2), 238–55.

IMPS, 1990. *The New Industrial Challenge: the Need for Defence Diversification*. London: IMPS, MS, TGWU.

Intriligator, Michael D., 1975. "Strategic Considerations in the Richardson Model of Arms Races," *Journal of Political Economy*, 83(2), 339–53.

1982. "Research on Conflict Theory," *Journal of Conflict Resolution*, 26(2), 307–27.

1990. "On the Nature and Scope of Defence Economics," *Defence Economics*, 1(1), 3–11.

1991. "On the Nature and Scope of Defence Economics: A Reply to Judith Reppy's Comment," *Defence Economics*, 2(3), 273–4.

1992. "The Economics of Disarmament as an Investment Process," *UNIDIR Newsletter*. Geneva: UNIDIR, September, 7–9.

1994. "Economic Aspects of Disarmament: Arms Race and Arms Control Issues," *Defence and Peace Economics*, 5(2), 121–9.

Intriligator, Michael D. and Brito, Dagobert L., 1976. "Formal Models of Arms Races," *Journal of Peace Sciences*, 2(1), 77–88.

1978. "Nuclear Proliferation and Stability," *Journal of Peace Science*, 3(1), 173–83.

1984. "Can Arms Races Lead to the Outbreak of War?" *Journal of Conflict Resolution*, 28(1), 63–84.

1985. "Wolfson on Economic Warfare," *Conflict Management and Peace Science*, 8(2), 21–6.

1987. "The Stability of Mutual Deterrence," in Kugler, Jacek, and Zagare, Frank (eds.), *Exploring the Stability of Mutual Deterrence*. Boulder: Lynne Rienner, pp. 13–19.

1988. "A Predator–Prey Model of Guerrilla Warfare," *Synthese*, 76(2), 235–44.

1989a. "Arms Race Modeling: A Reconsideration," in Gleditsch, Nils Peter and Njolstad, Olav (eds.), *Arms Races: Technological and Political Dynamics*. London: Sage, pp. 58–77.

1989b. "A Possible Future for the Arms Race," in Gleditsch, Nils Peter and Njolstad, Olav (eds.), *Arms Races: Technological and Political Dynamics*. London: Sage, pp. 376–83.

Isard, Walter, 1988. *Arms Races, Arms Control and Conflict Analysis: Contributions from Peace Science and Peace Economics*. New York: Cambridge University Press.

Isard, Walter and Anderton, Charles H., 1985. "Arms Race Models: A Survey and Synthesis," *Conflict Management and Peace Science*, 8(2), 27–98.

1988. "A Survey of Arms Race Models," in Isard, Walter (ed.), *Arms Races, Arms Control and Conflict Analysis*. New York: Cambridge University Press, pp. 17–85.

Islam, Muhammad Q. and Shahin, Wassim N., 1989. "Economic Methodology Applied to Political Hostage-Taking in Light of the Iran–Contra Affair," *Southern Economic Journal*, 55(4), 1019–24.

Jack, Bryan, 1991. "International Public Goods: The Economics of Their Provision and Cost-Control Incentives under the Cournot–Nash Hypothesis," Unpublished Ph.D. dissertation, College Park, MD: University of Maryland.

Joerding, Wayne, 1986. "Economic Growth and Defense Spending: Granger Causality," *Journal of Economic Development*, 21(2), 35–40.

Johns, A. Andrew, Pecchenino, Rowena A., and Schreft, Stacey L., 1993. "The Macroeconomics of Dr. Strangelove," *American Economic Review*, 83(1), 43–62.

Jones, Philip R., 1988. "Defense Alliances and International Trade," *Journal of Conflict Resolution*, 32(1), 123–40.

1992. "Inefficiency in International Defence Alliances and the Economics of Bureaucracy," *Defence Economics*, 3(2), 127–33.

Jones-Lee, Michael W., 1990a. "Defense Expenditure and the Economics of Safety," *Defence Economics*, 1(1), 13–16.

1990b. "Defence Expenditure and the Economics of Safety: A Reply," *Defence Economics*, 2(1), 73.

Kahn, S., 1993. "Advanced Technology Projects and International Procurement: the Case of the European Space Agency," *Public Procurement Law Review*, No.1, 13–39.

Kapstein, E.B., 1989. *Corporate Alliances and Military Alliances: The Political Economy of NATO Arms Collaboration*. Cambridge, MA: John M. Olin Institute for Strategic Studies.

Kaufman, Richard F., 1983. "Soviet Defense Trends," Staff Study, Subcommittee on International Trade, Finance, and Security Economics, Joint Economic Committee, US Congress, Washington DC.

Kaun, D.E., 1988. "Where Have All the Profits Gone? An Analysis of the Major US Defense Contractors 1950–1985," Research Paper No. 4. University of California Institute on Global Conflict and Co-operation.

Keegan, John, 1989. *The Second World War*. London: Hutchinson.

Kennedy, Gavin, 1983. *Defense Economics*. London: Duckworth.

Kennedy, Paul, 1988. *The Rise and Fall of the Great Powers*. London: Fontana.

Kerstens, K. and Meyermans, E., 1993. "The Draft Versus An All-Volunteer Force: Issues of Efficiency and Equity in the Belgian Draft," *Defence Economics*, 4(3), 271–84.

Khanna, Jyoti, Huffman, Wallace E., and Sandler, Todd, 1994. "Agricultural Research Expenditures in the US: A Public Goods Perspective," *Review of Economics and Statistics*, 76(2), 267–77.

Kiker, B.F. and Birkeli, J., 1972. "Human Capital Losses Resulting from US Casualties of War in Vietnam," *Journal of Political Economy*, 80(5), 1023–30.

Kinsella, David, 1990. "Defence Spending and Economic Performance in the United States: A Causal Analysis," *Defence Economics*, 1(4), 295–309.

1994. "The Impact of Superpower Arms Transfers on Conflict in the Middle East," *Defence and Peace Economics*, 5(1), 19–36.

Kirby, Stephen and Hooper, Nicholas (eds.), 1991. *The Cost of Peace*. Reading: Harwood.

Kirk, R.M., 1983. "Political Terrorism and the Size of Government: A Positive Institutional Analysis of Violent Political Activity," *Public Choice*, 40(1), 41–52.

Klepsch, E., 1978. *European Armaments Procurement Co-operation*. Luxembourg: European Parliament.

Knorr, Klaus, 1985. "Burden-Sharing in NATO: Aspects of US Policy," *Orbis*, 29(3), 517–36.

Kolodziej, Edward A., 1987. *Making and Marketing Arms: The French Experience and Its Implications for the International System*. New Jersey: Princeton University Press.

Kovacic, William E., 1991. "Commitment in Regulation: Defense Contracting and Extensions to Price Caps," *Journal of Regulatory Economics*, 3(3), 219–40.

1992. "Regulatory Controls as Barriers to Entry in Government Procurement," *Policy Sciences*, 25, 29–42.

Kuenne, Robert E., 1989. "Conflict in Mature Rivalry," *Journal of Conflict Resolution*, 33(3), 554–6.

Kuran, Timur, 1989. "Sparks and Prairie Fires: A Theory of Unanticipated Political Revolution," *Public Choice*, 61(1), 41–74.

1991a. "The East European Revolution of 1989: Is It Surprising That We Were Surprised?" *American Economic Review*, 81(2), 121–5.

1991b. "Now Out of Never: The Element of Surprise in the East European Revolution of 1989," *World Politics*, 44(1), 7–48.

Laffont, Jean-Jacques, 1986. "Towards a Normative Theory of Incentive Contracts between Government and Private Firms," *Economic Journal*, Supplement, 97, 17–31.

Laffont, Jean-Jacques and Tirole, Jean, 1986. "Using Cost Observation to Regulate Firms," *Journal of Political Economy*, 94(3), 614–41.

1993. *A Theory of Incentives in Procurement and Regulation.* Cambridge, MA: MIT.

Lambelet, J.C., 1973. "Towards a Dynamic Two-Theater Model of the East–West Arms Race," *Journal of Peace Science*, 1(1), 1–38.

Lanchester, F., 1916. *Aircraft in Warfare, the Dawn of the Fourth Arm.* London: Constable.

Landau, Daniel, 1986. "Government and Economic Growth in Less Developed Countries: An Empirical Study for 1960–1980," *Economic Development and Cultural Change*, 35(1), 35–75.

Landes, William M., 1978. "An Economic Study of US Aircraft Hijackings, 1961–1976," *Journal of Law and Economics*, 21(1), 1–31.

Lapan, Harvey E. and Sandler, Todd, 1988. "To Bargain or Not to Bargain: That Is the Question," *American Economic Review*, 78(2), 16–20.

1993. "Terrorism and Signalling," *European Journal of Political Economy*, 9(3), 383–97.

Large, Joseph P., 1974. *Bias in Initial Cost Estimates: How Low Estimates Can Increase the Cost of Acquiring Weapon Systems.* Santa Monica: Rand, July.

Large, Joseph P., Hoffmayer, K., and Kontrovich, F., 1974. *Production Rate and Production Cost.* Santa Monica: Rand, R–1609, December.

Lasso, H.L., 1987. "Economic Growth, Military Expenditure, the Arms Industry and Arms Transfer in Latin America," in Schmidt, C. (ed.), *The Economics of Military Expenditures.* London: Macmillan.

Latham, A. and Slack, M., 1990. *The Evolving European Defence Sector: Implications for Europe and North America.* Kingston, Canada: National Defence College.

Lebovic, James H. and Ishaq, Ashfaq, 1987. "Military Burden, Security Needs, and Economic Growth in the Middle East," *Journal of Conflict Resolution*, 31(1), 106–38.

Lee, Dwight R., 1988. "Free Riding and Paid Riding in the Fight Against Terrorism," *American Economic Review*, 78(2), 22–6.

1990. "The Politics and Pitfalls of Reducing Waste in the Military," *Defence Economics*, 1(2), 129–39.

Lee, Dwight R. and Sandler, Todd, 1989. "On the Optimal Retaliation Against Terrorists: The Paid-Rider Option," *Public Choice*, 61(2), 141–52.

Leigh, D.E. and Berney, R.E., 1971. "The Distribution of Hostile Casualties on Draft-Eligible Males with Differing Socio-Economic Characteristics," *Social Science Quarterly* 51(4), 932–40.

Leitzel, Jim, 1992. "Competition in Procurement," *Policy Sciences*, 25(1), (February), 43–56.

Leontief, Wassily and Duchin, Faye, 1983. *Military Spending.* Oxford: Oxford University Press.

Lerner, Joshua, 1992. "The Mobility of Corporate Scientists and Engineers between Civil and Defense Activities: Implications for Economic Competitiveness in the Post-Cold War Era," *Defence Economics*, 3(3), 229–42.

Levine, Paul, Sen, Somnath and Smith, Ron, 1994. "A Model of the International Arms Market," *Defence and Peace Economics*, 5(1), 1–18.

Lichbach, Mark I., 1992. "Nobody Cites Nobody Else: Mathematical Models of Domestic Political Conflict," *Defence Economics* 3(4), 341–57.

Lichtenberg, Frank R., 1989. "Contributions to Federal Election Campaigns by Government Contractors," *Journal of Industrial Economics*, 38(1), 31–48.

1990. "US Subsidies to Private Military R & D Investment: The Defense Department's Independent R & D Policy," *Defence Economics*, 1(2), 149–58.

1992. "A Perspective on Accounting for Defence Contracts," *Accounting Review*, 67(4) (October), 741–52.

Lightman, E.S., 1975. "Economics of Supply of Canada's Military Manpower," *Industrial Relations*, 14(2), 209–19.

Lim, David, 1983. "Another Look at Growth and Defense in Less Developed Countries," *Economic Development and Cultural Change*, 31(2), 377–84.

Linden, Mikael, 1991. "The Dynamics and the Instability of the Middle East Military Expenditures in Years 1955–1984," *Defence Economics*, 2(3), 199–208.

Looney, Robert E. and Mehay, Stephen L., 1990. "United States Defence Expenditures: Trends and Analysis," in Hartley, Keith and Sandler, Todd (eds.), *The Economics of Defence Spending*. London: Routledge, pp. 13–40.

Lorrell, M.A., 1980. *Multinational Development of Large Aircraft*. Santa Monica: Rand.

Lovell, C.A., Knox, Morey, Richard, C., and Wood, Lisa, 1991. "Cost-Efficient Military Recruiting: An Econometric Approach," *Defence Economics*, 2(4), 339–52.

Lovering, John, 1993. "Restructuring the British Defence Industrial Base After the Cold War," *Defence Economics*, 4(2), 91–112.

Lucas, 1976. "Lucas Aerospace," Combined Shop Stewards Committee, Corporate Plan, mimeo.

Lucier, C.E., 1979. "Changes in the Values of Arms Race Parameters," *Journal of Conflict Resolution*, 23(1), 17–39.

Luterbacher, Urs, 1975. "Arms Race Models: Where Do We Stand?" *European Journal of Political Research*, 3(2), 199–217.

Lynch, J. (ed.), 1987. *Economic Adjustment and Conversion of Defence Industries*. London: Westview Press.

Lynk, Edward and Hartley, Keith, 1985. "Input Demands and Elasticities in UK Defence Industries," *International Journal of Industrial Organization*, 3(1), 71–84.

Majeski, Stephen J., 1984. "Arms Races as Iterated Prisoner's Dilemma Games," *Mathematical Social Sciences*, 7(3), 253–66.

1985. "Expectations and Arms Races," *American Journal of Political Science*, 29(2), 217–45.

Majeski, Stephen J. and Jones, David L., 1981. "Arms Race Modelling: Causality Analysis and Model Specification," *Journal of Conflict Resolution*, 25(2), 259–88.

Martin, C.E. *et al.*, 1992. "Team–based Incremental Acquisition of Large-scale Unprecedented Systems," *Policy Sciences*, 25(1), 57–76.

Martin, Stephen, 1991. "Economic Collaboration and European Security," in Kirby, S. and Hooper, N. (eds.), *The Cost of Peace*. Reading: Harwood.

Matthews, Ron, 1992. *European Armaments Collaboration*. Reading: Harwood.

Mayer, Kenneth R., 1991. *The Political Economy of Defence Contracting*. London: Yale University Press.

Mayer, T.F., 1986. "Arms Races and War Initiation: Some Alternatives to the Intriligator–Brito Model," *Journal of Conflict Resolution*, 30(1), 3–28.

McAfee, R. Preston and McMillan, John, 1986a. "Bidding for Contracts: A Principal–Agent Analysis," *Rand Journal of Economics*, 17(3), 326–38.

1986b. *Incentives in Government Contracting*. Toronto: University of Toronto Press.

McCall, John J., 1970. "The Simple Economics of Incentive Contracting," *American Economic Review*, 60, December, 837–46.

McClelland, Grigor W., 1990. "Defence Expenditure and the Economics of Safety: A Comment," *Defence Economics*, 2(1), 69–72.

McFadden, Gordon S. (ed.), 1984. *Economic Conversion: Revitalising America's Economy*. Cambridge, MA: Ballinger.

McGuire, Martin C., 1965. *Secrecy and the Arms Race*. Cambridge, MA: Harvard University Press.

1974. "Group Size, Group Homogeneity, and the Aggregate Provision of a Pure Public Good Under Cournot Behavior," *Public Choice*, 18(2), 107–26.

1977. "A Quantitative Study of the Strategic Arms Race in the Missile Age," *Review of Economics and Statistics*, 59(3), 328–39.

1982. "US Assistance, Israeli Allocation, and the Arms Race in the Middle East," *Journal of Conflict Resolution*, 26(2), 199–235.

1987. "US Foreign Assistance, Israeli Resource Allocation and the Arms Race in the Middle East: An Analysis of Three Interdependent Resource Allocation Processes," in Schmidt, C. (ed.), *The Economics of Military Expenditures*. London: Macmillan.

1990a. *Coping with Foreign Dependence: The Simple Analytics of Stockpiling Versus Competition*. Singapore: Institute of South East Asian Studies.

1990b. "Mixed Public-Private Benefit and Public-Good Supply with Application to the NATO Alliance," *Defence Economics*, 1(1), 17–35.

1991. "Factor Migration, Trade and Welfare under Threat of Commercial Disruption," *Osaka Economic Papers*, 40(3), 165–80.

McGuire, Martin C. and Groth, Carl H., 1985. "A Method for Identifying the Public Good Allocation Process within a Group," *Quarterly Journal of Economics*, 100 (Supplement), 915–34.

McKean, Ronald N., 1967. "Remaining Difficulties in Program Budgeting," in Enke, S. (ed.), *Defense Management*. Englewood Cliffs: Prentice-Hall.

McKinlay, Robert, 1989. *Third World Military Expenditure: Determinants and Implications*. London: Pinter.

McNamara, Robert S., 1991. "The Post Cold–War World: Implications for Military Expenditure in the Developing Countries," *Annual Conference on Development Economics*. Washington DC: World Bank, pp. 95–140.

McNaugher, Thomas L., 1990. *Defense Management Reform: For Better or for Worse?* Washington DC: Brookings Institution, reprint.

McWilliams-Tullberg, Rita, 1987. "Military-related Debt in Non-oil Developing Countries, 1972–1982," in Schmidt, C. and Blackaby, F. (eds.), *Peace, Defence and Economic Analysis.* London: Macmillan.

Mehay, Stephen L., 1991. "Reserve Participation Versus Moonlighting: Are they the Same?" *Defence Economics*, 2(4), 325–37.

Melese, Francois, Blandin, James, and Fanchon, Phillip, 1992. "Benefits and Pay: The Economics of Military Compensation," *Defence Economics*, 3(3), 243–54.

Melman, Seymour, 1974. *The Permanent War Economy.* New York: Simon and Schuster.

1983. *Profits Without Production.* New York: Knopf.

Melman, Seymour (ed.), 1971. *The War Economy of the United States: Readings on Military Industry and Economy.* New York: St Martin's Press.

Mickolus, Edward F., 1980. *Transnational Terrorism: A Chronology of Events 1968–1979.* Westport, CT: Greenwood Press.

1982. *International Terrorism: Attributes of Terrorist Events, 1968–1977* (ITERATE 2). Ann Arbor, MI: Inter-University Consortium for Political and Social Research.

1989. "What Constitutes State Support to Terrorists?" *Terrorism and Political Violence*, 1(3), 287–93.

Mickolus, Edward F., Sandler, Todd, and Murdock, Jean, 1989. *International Terrorism in the 1980s: A Chronology of Events*, vol. I (1980–1983) and vol. II (1984–1987). Ames, IA: Iowa State University Press.

Mickolus, Edward F., Sandler, Todd, Murdock, Jean, and Fleming, Peter, 1989. *International Terrorism: Attributes of Terrorist Events 1978–1987* (ITERATE 3). Falls Church, VA: Vinyard Software Inc.

Midlarsky, Manus I., 1970. "Mathematical Models of Instability and a Theory of Diffusion," *International Studies Quarterly*, 14(1), 60–84.

1978. "Analyzing Diffusion and Contagion Effects: The Urban Disorders of 1960s," *American Political Science Review*, 72(3), 996–1008.

Midlarsky, Manus I., Crenshaw, Martha, and Yoshida, Fumihiko, 1980. "Why Violence Spreads: The Contagion of International Terrorism," *International Studies Quarterly*, 24(2), 262–98.

Mintz, Alex and Huang, Chi, 1990. "Defense Expenditures, Economic Growth and the 'Peace' Dividend," *American Political Science Review*, 84(4), 1283–93.

Mintz, Alex and Stevenson, Randolph T., 1993. "Defense Expenditures, Economic Growth and the 'Peace Dividend': A Longitudinal Analysis of 103 Countries," unpublished manuscript, College Station, TX: Texas A & M University.

MoD, 1988. *Learning from Experience.* London: Ministry of Defence.

Molas-Gallart, Jordi, 1992. *Military Production and Innovation in Spain.* London: Harwood.

Moll, Kendall D. and Luebbert, Gregory M., 1980. "Arms Race and Military Expenditure Model: A Review," *Journal of Conflict Resolution*, 24(1), 153–85.

Moore, Frederick T., 1967. "Incentive Contracts," in Enke, S. (ed.), *Defense Management.* New Jersey: Prentice-Hall.

Moravcsik, A., 1989. *1992 and the Future of the European Armaments Industry.* Cambridge, MA: John M. Olin Institute for Strategic Studies.

Mueller, Dennis C., 1989. *Public Choice II.* Cambridge: Cambridge University Press.

Mueller, Michael J. and Atesoglu, H. Sonmez, 1993. "Defense Spending, Technological Change, and Economic Growth in the United States," *Defence Economics*, 4(3), 259–69.

Murdoch, James C. and Sandler, Todd, 1982. "A Theoretical and Empirical Analysis of NATO," *Journal of Conflict Resolution*, 26(2), 237–63.

1984. "Complementarity, Free Riding, and the Military Expenditures of NATO Allies," *Journal of Public Economics*, 25(1–2), 83–101.

1985. "Australian Demand for Military Expenditures: 1961–1979," *Australian Economic Papers*, 44(1), 142–53.

1986. "The Political Economy of Scandinavian Neutrality," *Scandinavian Journal of Economics*, 88(4), 583–603.

1990. "Swedish Military Expenditures and Armed Neutrality," in Hartley, Keith and Sandler, Todd, (eds.), *The Economics of Defence Spending.* London: Routledge, 148–76.

1991. "NATO Burden Sharing and the Forces of Change: Further Observations," *International Studies Quarterly*, 35(1), 109–14.

Murdoch, James C., Sandler, Todd, and Hansen, Laurna, 1991. "An Econometric Technique for Comparing Median Voter and Oligarchy Choice Models of Collective Action: The Case of the NATO Alliance," *Review of Economics and Statistics*, 73(4), 624–31.

Nadal, Alejandro E., 1994. "Military R&D: The Economic Implications of Disarmament and Conversion," *Defence and Peace Economics*, 5(2), 131–51.

NATO, 1993. "Defense Expenditures of NATO Countries," *NATO Review*, 1, Brussels, February, p. 35.

Nelson, Paul S. and Scott, John L., 1992. "Terrorism and the Media: An Empirical Analysis," *Defence Economics*, 3(4), 329–39.

Nolan, J.E., 1986. *Military Industry in Taiwan and South Korea.* London: Macmillan.

Oi, Walter Y., 1967. "The Economic Cost of the Draft," *American Economic Review*, 57(2), 59–62.

Okamura, Minuro, 1991. "Estimating the Impact of the Soviet Union's Threat on the United States–Japan Alliance: A Demand System Approach," *Review of Economics and Statistics*, 73(2), 200–7.

Olson, Mancur, 1965. *The Logic of Collective Action.* Cambridge, MA: Harvard University Press.

1993. "Dictatorship, Democracy, and Development," *American Political Science Review*, 87(3), 567–76.

Olson, Mancur and Zeckhauser, Richard, 1966. "An Economic Theory of Alliances," *Review of Economics and Statistics*, 48(3), 266–79.

1967. "Collective Goods, Comparative Advantage, and Alliance Efficiency," in McKean, Roland (ed.), *Issues of Defense Economics.* New York: National Bureau of Economics Research, pp. 25–48.

OMB, 1987. *Impact of Offsets in Defense-Related Exports.* Washington DC: Office of Management and Budget, Executive Office of the President of the USA.

Oneal, John R., 1990a. "Testing the Theory of Collective Action: NATO Defense Burdens, 1950–1984," *Journal of Conflict Resolution*, 34(3), 426–48.

1990b. "The Theory of Collective Action and Burden Sharing in NATO," *International Organization*, 44(3), 379–402.

1991. "Rejoinder to Murdoch and Sandler," *International Studies Quarterly*, 35(1), 115–17.

1992. "Budgetary Savings from Conscription and Burden Sharing in NATO," *Defence Economics*, 3(2), 113–25.

Oneal, John R. and Elrod, Mark A., 1989. "NATO Burden Sharing and the Forces of Change," *International Studies Quarterly*, 33(4), 435–56.

Oneal, John R. and Diehl, Paul F., 1992. "The Theory of Collective Action and NATO Defense Burdens: New Empirical Tests," unpublished manuscript, Tuscaloosa, AL: University of Alabama.

Oppenheimer, Joe, 1979. "Collective Goods and Alliances: A Reassessment," *Journal of Conflict Resolution*, 23(3), 387–407.

Ordeshook, Peter C., 1986. *Game Theory and Political Theory*. New York: Cambridge University Press.

Ostrom, Charles W., 1977. "Evaluating Alternative Foreign Policy Decision-Making Models: An Empirical Test Between an Arms Race Model and an Organizational Politics Model," *Journal of Conflict Resolution*, 21(2), 235–66.

OTA, 1989. *Holding the Edge: Maintaining the Defense Technology Base*. Washington DC: Office of Technology Assessment.

1990. *Arming Our Allies*. Washington DC: Office of Technology Assessment.

Palmer, Glenn, 1990a. "Alliance Politics and Issue Areas: Determinants of Defense Spending," *American Journal of Political Science*, 34(1), 190–211.

1990b. "Corralling the Free Rider: Deterrence and the Western Alliance," *International Studies Quarterly*, 34(2), 147–64.

1991. "Deterrence, Defense Spending, and Elasticity: Alliance Contributions to the Public Good," *International Interactions*, 7(2), 157–69.

Paukert, Liba and Richards, Peter (eds.), 1991. *Defence Expenditure, Industrial Conversion and Local Employment*. Geneva: ILO.

Payne, James E. and Ross, Kevin L., 1992. "Defence Spending and the Macro-Economy," *Defence Economics*, 3(2), 161–8.

Pearson, F.S., 1989. "The Correlates of Arms Importation," *Journal of Peace Research*, 26(2), 153–64.

Peck, M. and Scherer, F., 1962. *The Weapons Acquisition Process*. Boston: Harvard University Press.

Peeters, W.A., 1993. "Incentives in Government Procurement Contracts," *Public Procurement Law Review*, 4, 197–209.

Peeters, W. and Veld, J., 1989. "The Use of Alternative Contract Types in Europe as Protection Against Overruns," *National Contract Management Journal*, 23 (1) (Summer), 23–5.

Perry, Robert, Smith, G.K., Harman, A., and Henrichsen, S., 1971. *System Acquisition Strategies*. Santa Monica: Rand, R733, June.

Phlips, Louis, 1974. *Applied Consumption Analysis*. Amsterdam: North-Holland Publishing Co.

Poussard, J.P., 1983. "Military Procurement in France: Regulations and

Incentive Contracts," in Englebrecht-Wiggans, R. *et al.* (eds.), *Auctions Bidding and Contracting*. New York: New York University Press.

Pownall, Grace, 1986. "An Empirical Analysis of the Defense Contracting Industry: The Cost Accounting Standards Board," *Journal of Accounting Research*, 24(2) (Autumn), 291–315.

Pratten, C., 1988. "A Survey of Economies of Scale," *Research on the Costs of Non-Europe. Basic Findings*, vol.II. Luxembourg: EC.

Pryor, Frederic L., 1968. *Public Expenditures in Communist and Capitalist Nations*. Homewood, IL: Irwin.

Pugh, Philip, 1986. *The Cost of Sea Power*. London: Conway.

1993. "The Procurement Nexus," *Defence Economics*, 4(2), 179–94.

Quester, A. and Nakada, M., 1983. "The Military's Monopsony Power." *Eastern Economic Journal*, 9(4), 295–308.

Ram, Rati, 1986. "Government Size and Economic Growth: A New Framework and Some Evidence from Cross-Section and Time-Series Data," *American Economic Review*, 76(1), 191–203.

1987. "Exports and Economic Growth in Developing Countries: Evidence from Time Series and Cross Section Data," *Economic Development and Cultural Change*, 36(1), 51–72.

1989. "Government Size and Economic Growth: A New Framework and Some Evidence from Cross-Section and Time-Series Data: Reply," *American Economic Review*, 79(1), 281–4.

Rao, V.V. Bhanoji, 1989. "Impact of Government Size on Economic Growth: A Re-examination," *American Economic Review*, 79(1), 183–204.

Rapoport, Anatol, 1957. "Lewis F. Richardson's Mathematical Theory of War," *Journal of Conflict Resolution*, 1(3), 249–304.

Rasler, Karen and Thompson, William R., 1988. "Defense Burdens, Capital Formation, and Economic Growth," *Journal of Conflict Resolution*, 32(1), 61–86.

Ratner, Jonathan and Thomas, Celia, 1990. "The Defense Industrial Base and Foreign Supply of Defence Goods," *Defence Economics*, 2(1), 57–68.

Rattinger, Hans, 1975. "Armaments, Detente, and Bureaucracy: The Case of the Arms Race in Europe," *Journal of Conflict Resolution*, 19(4), 571–95.

Reichelstein, Stefan, 1992. "Constructing Incentive Schemes for Government Contracts: An Application of Agency Theory," *Accounting Review*, 67(4) (October), 712–31.

Reisinger, W., 1983. "East European Military Expenditures in 1970s: Collective Good or Bargaining Offer?" *International Organization*, 37(1), 143–55.

Renner, Michael, 1992. *Economic Adjustment After the Cold War*. Aldershot: UNIDIR, Dartmouth.

Reppy, Judith, 1991. "On the Nature and Scope of Defence Economics: A Comment," *Defence Economics*, 2(3), 269–71.

Riardon, Michael and Sappington, David E.M., 1989. "Second Sourcing," *Rand Journal of Economics*, 20(1), 41–58.

Rich, M., Stanley, W., Birkler, J., and Hesse, M., 1981. *Multi-national Co-production of Military Aerospace Systems*. Santa Monica: Rand.

Richards Peter J., 1991. "Disarmament and Employment," *Defence Economics*, 2(4), 295–312.

Richardson, Lewis F., 1960. *Arms and Insecurity: A Mathematical Study of the Causes and Origins of War*. Pittsburgh, PA: Homewood.

Ridge, Michael and Smith, Ron, 1991. "UK Military Manpower and Substitutability," *Defence Economics*, 2(4), 283–94.

Rob, Rafael, 1986. "The Design of Procurement Contracts," *American Economic Review*, 76(3), 378–89.

Roemer, John E., 1985. "Rationalizing Revolutionary Ideology," *Econometrica*, 53(1), 85–108.

Rogerson, William P., 1989. "Profit Regulation of Defence Contractors and Prizes for Innovation," *Journal of Political Economy*, 97(6), 1284–305.

   1990. "Quality and Quantity in Military Procurement," *American Economic Review*, 80(1), 83–92.

   1991a. "Incentives, the Budgetary Process, and Inefficiently Low Production Rates in Defense Procurement," *Defence Economics*, 3(1), 1–18.

   1991b. "Excess Capacity in Weapons Production: An Empirical Analysis," *Defence Economics*, 2(3), 235–50.

   1992a. *An Economic Framework for Analysing DoD Profit Policy*. Santa Monica: Rand.

   1992b. "Overhead Allocation and Incentives for Cost Minimisation in Defense Procurement," *Accounting Review*, 67(4), 671–90.

Ross, Jeffrey Ian and Gurr, Ted Robert, 1989. "Why Terrorism Subsides: A Comparative Study of Canada and the United States," *Comparative Politics*, 21(4), 405–26.

Rothschild, Kurt W., 1973. "Military Expenditure, Exports and Growth," *Kyklos*, 26(4), 804–14.

Russett, Bruce M., 1970. *What Price Vigilance?* New Haven: Yale University Press.

Russett, Bruce M. and Slemrod, J., 1993. "Diminished Expectations of Nuclear War and Increased Personal Savings: Evidence from Individual Survey Data," *American Economic Review*, 83(4), 1022–33.

Russett, Bruce M. and Sullivan, John D., 1971. "Collective Goods and International Organization," *International Organization* 25(3), 845–65.

Sabrosky, Alan Ned, 1982. "Defence with Fewer Men? The American Experience," in Harries-Jenkins, G. (ed.), *Armed Forces and the Welfare Societies: Challenges in the 1980s*. London: Macmillan.

Sampson, Anthony, 1977. *The Arms Bazaar: The Companies, the Dealers, the Bribes: From Vickers to Lockheed*. London: Hodder and Stoughton.

Samuelson, W., 1983. "Competitive Bidding for Defence Contracts," in Engelbrecht-Wiggans, R. *et al.* (eds.), *Auctions, Bidding and Contracting*. New York: New York University Press.

Sandler, Todd, 1977. "Impurity of Defense: An Application to the Economics of Alliances," *Kyklos*, 30(3), 443–60.

   1988. "Sharing Burdens in NATO," *Challenge*, 31(2), 29–35.

   1992. *Collective Action: Theory and Applications*. Ann Arbor, MI: University of Michigan Press.

Sandler, Todd and Cauley, Jon, 1975. "On the Economic Theory of Alliances," *Journal of Conflict Resolution*, 19(2), 330–48.

Sandler, Todd and Forbes, John F., 1980. "Burden Sharing, Strategy, and the Design of NATO," *Economic Inquiry*, 18(3), 425–44.

Sandler, Todd and Lapan, Harvey E., 1988. "The Calculus of Dissent: An Analysis of Terrorists' Choice of Targets," *Synthese*, 76(2), 245–61.

Sandler, Todd and Murdoch, James C., 1986. "Defense Burdens and Prospects for the Northern European Allies," in Denoon, David B.H. (ed.), *Constraints on Strategy: The Economics of Western Security*. Washington DC: Pergamon–Brassey's, pp. 59–113.

1990. "Nash–Cournot or Lindahl Behavior?: An Empirical Test for the NATO Allies," *Quarterly Journal of Economics*, 105(4), 875–94.

Sandler, Todd and Posnett, John, 1991. "The Private Provision of Public Goods: A Perspective on Neutrality," *Public Finance Quarterly*, 19(1), 22–42.

Sandler, Todd and Scott, John L., 1987. "Terrorist Success in Hostage-Taking Incidents," *Journal of Conflict Resolution*, 31(1), 35–53

Sandler, Todd, Enders, Walter, and Lapan, Harvey E, 1991. "Economic Analysis Can Help Fight International Terrorism," *Challenge*, 34(1), 10–17..

Sandler, Todd, Tschirhart, John, and Cauley, Jon, 1983. "A Theoretical Analysis of Transnational Terrorism," *American Political Science Review*, 77(1), 36–54.

Sandler, Todd, Atkinson, Scott E., Cauley, Jon, Im, Eric I., Scott, John, and Tschirhart, John, 1987. "Economic Methods and the Study of Terrorism," in Wilkinson, Paul and Stewart, Alastair M. (eds.), *Contemporary Research on Terrorism*. Aberdeen: Aberdeen University Press, pp. 376–89.

Scheetz, Thomas, 1991. "The Macroeconomic Impact of Defence Expenditures: Some Econometric Evidence for Argentina, Chile, Paraguay, and Peru," *Defence Economics*, 3(1), 65–81.

Schelling, Thomas C., 1966. *Arms and Influence*. New Haven, CT: Yale University Press.

1980. *The Strategy of Conflict*. Cambridge, MA: Harvard University Press.

Schelling, Thomas C. and Halperin, Morton H., 1985. *Strategy and Arms Control*. London: Brassey's.

Scherer, F., 1964. *The Weapons Acquisition Process: The Economic Incentives*. Boston: Harvard University Press.

Schmidt, Christian, 1993. "La Dimension Économiqué des Nouvelles Données de la Sécurité Internationale," *Economie Appliquée*, 46(3), 1–179.

Schmidt, Christian (ed.), 1987. *The Economics of Military Expenditures: Military Expenditures, Economic Growth and Fluctuations*. London: Macmillan.

Schmidt, Christian and Blackaby, Frank (eds.), 1987. *Peace, Defence and Economic Analyses*. London: Macmillan.

Schrodt, Philip A., 1978. "Richardson's N-Nation Model and the Balance of Power," *American Journal of Political Science*, 22(2), 364–90.

Scott, J.D., 1962. *Vickers: A History*. London: Weidenfeld and Nicolson.

Scott, John L., 1989. "The Role of Information in the War on Terrorism," unpublished dissertation, Columbia, SC: University of South Carolina.

1991. "Reputation Building in Hostage Taking Incidents," *Defence Economics*, 2(3), 209–18.

Selten, Reinhard, 1988. "A Simple Game Model of Kidnappings," in Selten, Reinhard (ed.), *Models of Strategic Rationality*. Boston, MA: Kluwer Academic Publishing Co., pp. 77–83.

Shahin, Wassim N. and Islam, Muhammad Q., 1990. "The Contribution of

Economic Methodology to Our Understanding of Terrorism," *Journal of Interdisciplinary Economics*, 3(3), 197–207.

1992. "Combating Political Hostage-taking: An Alternative Approach," *Defence Economics*, 3(4), 321–7.

Shubik, Martin, 1983. "On Auctions, Bidding and Contracting," in Engelbrecht-Wiggans, R. *et al.* (eds.), *Auctions, Bidding and Contracting*. New York: New York University Press.

1987. "The Uses, Value and Limitations of Game Theoretic Methods in Defence Analysis," in Schmidt, Christian and Blackaby, Frank (eds.), *Peace, Defence and Economic Analysis*. London: Macmillan, 53–84.

Simaan, M. and Cruz, J.B., Jr., 1973. "A Multistage Game Formulation of Arms Race and Control and Its Relationship to Richardson's Model," *Modeling and Simulation*, 4, 149–53.

1975. "Formulation of Richardson's Model of Arms Race from a Differential Game Viewpoint," *Review of Economic Studies*, 42(1), 67–77.

SIPRI, 1991. *Yearbook 1991: World Armaments and Disarmament*. Oxford: Stockholm International Peace Research Institute, Oxford University Press.

1993. *Yearbook: World Armaments and Disarmament*. Stockholm: Stockholm International Peace Research Institute.

Sissons, L.G., 1986. *Cost Estimating for Defence Contracts*. London: Crown Eagle, Government Contracting Series, Longman.

Skocpol, Theda, 1979. *States and Social Revolutions: A Comparative Analysis of France, Russia, and China*. New York: Cambridge University Press.

Smith, C.H., 1983. "Evaluation of Competitive Alternatives for Weapon System Production," in Engelbrecht-Wiggans, R. *et al.* (eds.), *Auctions, Bidding and Contracting*. New York: New York University Press.

Smith, Dan and Smith, Ron, 1983. *The Economics of Militarism*. London: Pluto Press.

Smith, G. *et al.*, 1988. *A Preliminary Perspective on Regulatory Activities and Effects in Weapons Acquisition*. Santa Monica: Rand, R–3578, March.

Smith, Marvin M., 1991. "Officer Commissioning Programs," *Defence Economics*, 2(4), 313–24.

Smith, Ron, 1980a. "The Demand for Military Expenditures," *Economic Journal*, 90(4), 811–20.

1980b. "Military Expenditure and Investment in OECD Countries, 1954–1973," *Journal of Comparative Economics*, 4(1), 19–32.

1987. "The Demand for Military Expenditures: A Correction," *Economic Journal*, 97(4), 989–90.

1989. "Models of Military Expenditures," *Journal of Applied Econometrics*, 4(4), 345–59.

1990a. "Defence Procurement and Industrial Structure in the UK," *International Journal of Industrial Organisation*, 8(2), 185–206.

1990b. "Defence Spending in the United Kingdom," in Hartley, Keith and Sandler, Todd (eds.), *The Economics of Defence Spending*. London: Routledge, pp. 76–92.

Smith, Ron and Fontanel, Jacques, 1987. "Weapons Procurement: Domestic Production versus Imports," in Bellany, I. and Huxley, T. (eds.), *New Conventional Weapons and Western Defence*. London: Frank Cass.

Smith, Ron, Humm, Anthony and Fontanel, Jacques, 1985. "The Economics of Exporting Arms," *Journal of Peace Research*, 22(3), 239–47.

Smoker, P., 1965. "On Mathematical Models in Arms Races," *Journal of Peace Research*, 2(1), 94–5.

Solnick, Loren M., Henderson, David R., and Kroeschel, Capt. Joseph W., 1991. "Using Quit Rates to Estimate Compensating Wage Differentials in the Military," *Defence Economics*, 2(2), 123–34.

Southwood, Peter, 1991. *Disarming Military Industries*. London: Macmillan.

SPSG, 1991. *Future Relations Between Defence and Civil Science and Technology*. London: Science Policy Support Group.

Starr, Harvey, 1974. "A Collective Goods Analysis of the Warsaw Pact after Czechoslovakia," *International Organization*, 28(2), 521–32.

Stewart, Douglas B., 1991. "Economic Growth and the Defense Burden in Africa and Latin America: Simulations from a Dynamic Model," *Economic Development and Cultural Change*, 40(1), 189–207.

Stigler, George J. and Friedland, C., 1971. "Profits of Defense Contractors," *American Economic Review*, 61(4), 692–94.

Stoll, Richard J., 1982. "Let the Researcher Beware: The Use of the Richardson Equations to Estimate the Parameters of a Dyadic Arms Acquisition Process," *American Journal of Political Science*, 26(1), 77–89.

Sur, Serge (ed.), 1991a. *Verification of Current Disarmament and Arms Limitation Agreements: Ways, Means and Practices*. Aldershot: Dartmouth and UNIDIR.

    1991b. *Disarmament Agreements and Negotiations: The Economic Dimension*. Aldershot: Dartmouth and UNIDIR.

    1992. *Disarmament and Limitations of Armaments: Unilateral Measures and Policies*. New York: UNIDIR, United Nations.

Taylor, J.G., 1974. "Solving Lanchester-Type Equations for Modern Warfare with Variable Coefficients," *Operations Research*, 26(4), 756–70.

Taylor, Michael, 1988. "Rationality and Revolutionary Collective Action," in Taylor, Michael (ed.), *Rationality and Revolution*. New York: Cambridge University Press, pp. 63–97.

Taylor, Trevor, 1993a. "Japan's Policy on Arms Exports," in Matthews, R. and Matsuyama, K. (eds.), *Japan's Military Renaissance?* London: Macmillan.

    1993b. "West European Defence Industrial Issues for the 1990s," *Defence Economics*, 4(2), 113–22.

Taylor, Trevor and Hayward, Keith, 1989. *The UK Defence Industrial Base*. London: Brassey's.

Thies, Wallace J., 1987. "Alliances and Collective Goods: A Reappraisal," *Journal of Conflict Resolution*, 3(3), 298–332.

Thomas, George W. and Kocher, Kathryn M., 1993. "Gender Differences in Turnover Amongst US Army Reservists," *Defence Economics*, 4(4), 339–52.

Thomas, Jacob K. and Tung, Samuel, 1992. "Cost Manipulation Incentives under Cost Reimbursement: Pension Costs for Defense Contracts," *Accounting Review*, 67(4), 691–711.

Thomas, R. William, Stekler, H.O., and Glass, Wayne G., 1991. "The Economic Effects of Reducing US Defence Spending," *Defence Economics*, 2(3), 183–98.

Thompson, S. and Wright, M. (eds.), 1988. *Internal Organisation, Efficiency and Profit*. Oxford: Philip Allan.

Tirole, Jean, 1986. "Procurement and Renegotiation," *Journal of Political Economy*, 94(2), 235–59.

1988, *The Theory of Industrial Organization*. Cambridge, MA: MIT Press.

Todd, Daniel, 1988. *Defence Industries: A Global Prospective*. London: Routledge.

Treddenick, J., 1987. *The Economic Consequences of the Arms Trade*. Kingston, Canada: Royal Military College of Canada.

Trevino, Ruben and Higgs, Robert, 1992. "Profits of US Defence Contractors," *Defence Economics*, 3(3), 211–18.

Trice, R.H., 1989. *International Co-operation in Military Aircraft Programs*. Cambridge, MA: John M. Olin Institute for Strategic Studies.

Tullock, Gordon, 1974. *The Social Dilemma: The Economics of War and Revolution*. Blacksburg, VA: University Publications.

Turpin, Colin, 1989. *Government Procurement and Contracts*. London: Longman.

Udis, Bernard, 1992. "Weapons Procurement in the United States," *Public Procurement Law Review*, 6 pp. 455–70.

Udis, Bernard and Maskus, Keith E., 1991. "Offsets As Industrial Policy: Lessons From Aerospace," *Defence Economics*, 2(2), 151–64.

Ullman, J.E. (ed.), 1970. *Potential Civilian Markets for the Military Electronics Industry*. New York: Praeger.

UN, 1989. *Study on the Economic and Social Consequences of the Arms Race and Military Expenditures*. New York: A/43/368 DDA Study Series No 19, United Nations.

1993. *Economic Aspects of Disarmament: Disarmament as an Investment Process*. New York: United Nations.

UNDP, 1992. *Human Development Report 1992*, United Nations Development Programme. Oxford: Oxford University Press.

US Arms Control and Disarmament Agency, 1991. *World Military Expenditures and Arms Transfers: 1990*. Washington DC: US Government Printing Office.

US Congressional Budget Office, 1993. *Assessing Future Trends in the Defense Burdens of Western Nations*. Washington DC: US Congressional Budget Office.

US Department of State, 1986. *Patterns of Global Terrorism*. Washington DC: US Department of State.

1993. *Patterns of Global Terrorism*. Washington DC: US Department of State.

van Ypersele de Strihou, Jacques, 1967. "Sharing the Defence Burden Among Western Allies," *Review of Economics and Statistics*, 49(4), 527–36.

Voss, Anthony, 1992. *Converting the Defence Industry*. Oxford: Oxford Research Group, Current Decisions Report No.9.

Wagner, R. Harrison, 1983. "The Theory of Games and the Problem of International Cooperation," *American Political Science Review*, 77(2), 330–46.

Wainwright, H. and Elliott, D., 1982. *The Lucas Plan*. London: Allison and Basby.

Walker, William and Gummett, Philip, 1993. *Nationalism, Internationalism and the European Defence Market*. Paris: Institute for Security Studies.

Walker, William and Willett, Susan, 1993. "Restructuring the European Defence Industrial Base," *Defence Economics*, 4(2), 141–60.

Wallace, Michael D., 1974. "Armaments and Escalation: Two Competing Hypotheses," *International Studies Quarterly*, 26(1), 37–56.

1979. "Arms Races and Escalation," *Journal of Conflict Resolution*, 23(1), 3–16.

Wallace, Michael D. and Wilson, J.M., 1978. "Non-Linear Arms Race Models," *Journal of Peace Research*, 15(2), 175–92.

Ward, Michael D., 1984. "Differential Paths to Parity: A Study of the Contemporary Arms Race," *American Political Science Review*, 78(2), 297–317.

Ward, Michael D. and Davis, David, 1992. "Sizing Up the Peace Dividend: Economic Growth and Military Spending in the United States, 1948–1996," *American Political Science Review*, 86(3), 748–55.

Ward, Michael D., Davis, David, Penubarti, Mohan, Rajmaira, Sheen, and Cochran, Mali, 1991. "Military Spending in India – Country survey I," *Defence Economics*, 3(1), 41–63.

Ward, Michael D. and Mintz, Alex, 1987. "Dynamics of Military Spending in Israel," *Journal of Conflict Resolution*, 31(1), 86–105.

Warr, Peter G., 1983. "The Private Provision of a Public Good is Independent of the Distribution of Income," *Economics Letters*, 13, 207–11.

Weber, Shlomo and Wiesmeth, Hans, 1991. "Economic Models of NATO," *Journal of Public Economics*, 46(2), 181–97.

Weisman, Adam R., 1987. "The Prevention of Fraud, Waste and Mismanagement in Defense Contracting," *CPA Journal*, June, 26–33.

Whiting, Alan (ed.), 1976. *The Economics of Industrial Subsidies*. London: HMSO.

Whynes, David K., 1979. *The Economics of Third World Military Expenditure*. London: Macmillan.

Wilkinson, Paul, 1986. "Trends in International Terrorism and the American Response," in Freedman, Lawrence ,*et al.* (eds.), *Terrorism and International Order*. London: Routledge & Kegan Paul, pp. 37–55.

1992. "The European Response to Terrorism: Retrospect and Prospect," *Defence Economics*, 3(4), 289–304.

Willett, Susan, 1990. "Conversion Policy in the UK," *Cambridge Journal of Economics*, 14, 469–82.

1991. *Controlling the Arms Trade*. London: Council for Arms Control, Faraday Discussion Paper 18, University of London.

Willett, Susan (ed.), 1993. "The Restructuring of the UK and European Defence Industrial Base," *Defence Economics*, 4(2), 83–211.

Williamson, Oliver E., 1965. *Defense Contracts: An Analysis of Adaptive Response*. Santa Monica: Rand, RM–4363.

1986, *Economic Organization*. Brighton: Wheatsheaf.

Wing, Martin M., 1991. "Defence Spending and Employment in Indonesia," *Defence Economics*, 3(1), 83–92.

Wiseman, Jack, 1991. "Privatization in the Command Economy," in Ott, A. and Hartley, K. (eds.), *Privatization and Economic Efficiency*. Aldershot: Elgar.

Withers, Glenn A., 1972. "The Wage Cost of an All-Volunteer Army," *Economic Record*, 48(123), 321–39.

1977. "Armed Forces Recruitment in Great Britain," *Applied Economics*, 9(4), 289–306.

1991. "The Human Resource Dimension of Defence Economics: An Introduction," *Defence Economics*, 2(4), 279–82.

Wolfson, Murray, 1968. "A Mathematical Model of the Cold War," *Peace Research Society: Conference*, 9, 107–23.

1985. "Notes on Economic Warfare," *Conflict Management and Peace Science*, 8(1), 1–20.

1990. "Perestroika and the Quest for Peace," *Defence Economics*, 1(3), 221–32.

1992. "Do Zones of Deterrence Exist?" in Wolfson, Murray (ed.), *Essays on the Cold War*. London: Macmillan, pp. 99–104.

Wolfson, Murray and Farrell, John P., 1989. "Foundations of a Theory of Economic Warfare and Arms Control," *Conflict Management and Peace Science*, 10(2), 47–75.

Wolfson, Murray, Puri, Anil, and Martelli, Mario, 1992. "The Nonlinear Dynamics of International Conflict," *Journal of Conflict Resolution*, 36(1), 119–49.

Wong, Kar-yiu, 1991. "Foreign Trade, Military Alliance, and Defence-Burden Sharing," *Defence Economics*, 2(2), 83–103.

Wulf, Herbert, 1987. "Arms Transfer Control: The Feasibility and the Obstacles," in Deger, S. and West, R. (eds.), *Defence, Security and Development*. London: Pinter.

1993a. "The Soviet Union and the Successor Republics: Arms Exports and the Struggle with the Heritage of the Military–Industrial Complex," in Wulf, H. (ed.), *The Arms Industry Limited*. Oxford: Oxford University Press and SIPRI.

Wulf, Herbert (ed.) 1993b. *The Arms Industry Limited*. Oxford: Oxford University Press and SIPRI.

Zellner, A., 1962. "An Efficient Method of Estimating Seemingly Unrelated Regressions and Tests of Aggregation Bias," *Journal of the American Statistical Association*, 57(2), 348–68.

Zinnes, Dina A., and Gillespie, J.V., 1973. "Analysis of Arms Race Models," *Modeling and Simulation*, 4, 145–8.

Author index

Subject index